Exporting Africa

The economic crisis which has hit Africa in the past decade is raising questions about Africa's future position in world trade and whether it has any chance of developing a competitive industrial structure.

Professor Wangwe addresses these questions on the basis of commissioned studies of fifty-five exporting manufacturers in six African countries carried out by local experts of considerable standing in the field. He examines the question of why some firms in the Sub-Saharan economies have been able to maintain their positions in the world market despite generally unfavourable circumstances. In particular the papers seek to understand how these firms have been able to sustain their competitiveness in the face of rapid technological change in the international economy in the context of the threats and promises such change presents to Africa. A case is made for selective complementary investments by governments to build the technological capabilities which are necessary for attaining and maintaining competitiveness.

The country studies present new empirical research and an innovative conceptual framework which will be of interest to academics in the development field and to government and international policy makers.

Samuel M. Wangwe is Director of the Economic and Research Foundation, Dar es Salaam. He was Senior Research Fellow at UNU/INTECH between 1991 and 1994.

UNU/INTECH Studies in New Technology and Development

Series editors: Charles Cooper and Swasti Mitter

The books in this series reflect the research initiatives at the United Nations University Institute for New Technologies (UNU/INTECH) based in Maastricht, the Netherlands. This institute is primarily a research centre within the UN system and evaluates the social, political and economic environment in which new technologies are adopted and adapted in the developing world. The books in the series explore the role that technology policies can play in bridging the economic gap between nations, as well as between groups within nations. The authors and contributors are leading scholars in the field of technology and development; their work focuses on:

- the social and economic implications of new technologies;
- processes of diffusion of such technologies to the developing world;
- the impact of such technologies on income, employment and environment;
- the political dynamics of technological transfer.

The series is a pioneering attempt at placing technology policies at the heart of national and international strategies for development. This is likely to prove crucial in the globalized market, for the competitiveness and sustainable growth of poorer nations.

1 Women Encounter Technology
Changing Patterns of Employment in the Third World
Edited by Swasti Mitter and Sheila Rowbotham

2 In Pursuit of Science and Technology in Sub-Saharan Africa
J.L. Enos

3 Politics of Technology in Latin America
Edited by Maria Inês Bastos and Charles M. Cooper

4 Exporting Africa
Technology and Industrialization in Sub-Saharan Africa
Edited by Samuel M. Wangwe

Exporting Africa

Technology, Trade and Industrialization in Sub-Saharan Africa

Edited by Samuel M. Wangwe

London and New York

  The United Nations University **INTECH** Institute for New Technologies

Published in association with the UNU Press

First published 1995
by Routledge
11 New Fetter Lane, London EC4P 4EE

Simultaneously published in the USA and Canada
by Routledge
29 West 35th Street, New York, NY 10001

© UNU/INTECH

Typeset in Times by Florencetype Ltd, Stoodleigh, Devon
Printed and bound in Great Britain by T.J. Press (Padstow) Ltd,
Padstow, Cornwall

British Library Cataloguing in Publication Data
A catalogue record for this book is available from
the British Library

Library of Congress Cataloging in Publication Data
A catalogue record for this book has been requested

ISBN 0-415-12691-6
ISSN 1359-7922

Contents

vi *Contents*

Tables

Contributors

M.S.D. Bagachwa is Associate Research Professor, Economic Research Bureau at the University of Dar es Salaam.

Bouabre Bohoun is Assistant Professor, GERIDA Faculté des Sciences Economiques at the Université Nationale de Côte d'Ivoire in Abidjan.

Gerrishon K. Ikiara is Senior Lecturer, Economics Department of the University of Nairobi.

Oussou Kouassy is Lecturer, GERIDA Faculty des Sciences Economique at the Université Nationale de Côte d'Ivoire in Abidjan.

Roland Lamusse is Professor of Economics in the Faculty of Social Studies and Humanities at the University of Mauritius.

A.V.Y. Mbelle is Senior Lecturer, Economics Department at the University of Dar es Salaam.

Dan Ndlela is an Economist with Zimconsult in Harare.

Oluremi Ogun is Lecturer, Economics Department at the University of Ibadan.

Peter Robinson is an Economist with Zimconsult in Harare.

Samuel M. Wangwe is Director of the Economic and Research Foundation, Dar es Salaam. He was Senior Research Fellow at the United Nations University Institute for New Technologies between 1991 and 1994.

Acknowledgements

Many people and institutions have contributed to this book. Prof. Charles Cooper, Director of UNU/INTECH, has provided insightful intellectual guidance in several stages of this study. Martin Bell of Sussex University gave very helpful comments especially at the project design stage. The academic staff at UNU/INTECH offered useful comments in INTECH seminars at several stages of project design and implementation. I would also like to mention Prof. Jeffrey James of Tilburg University, with whom I held helpful discussions at the early stages of this project.

Many individuals and institutions in the six African countries gave us good cooperation at the data collection stage and many individuals in companies in Europe offered their valuable time for interviews. I would also like to thank all the participants (academic, policy-makers and industrialists) at the workshop which was held in Arusha (Tanzania) in May 1993, at which preliminary findings were discussed. Prof. Manfred Bienefeld of Carleton University read all the papers presented at the workshop, provided excellent comments and useful insights on the various drafts.

I thank IDRC for funding the Arusha workshop, without which the many useful interactions and comments would not have been possible. Sen McGlinn went through several drafts and improved the text considerably and with impressive tolerance and commitment to this work. This book would not have been completed without consistent cooperation from the staff at INTECH. If there are errors remaining, they are mine.

Part I

Exporting Africa: an analysis

1 Introduction

BACKGROUND

The economic crisis which has hit Africa in the past decade is raising questions about future prospects for the continent. Questions have been raised about the future position of Africa in world trade and whether Africa has any chance of developing a competitive industrial structure. This book is a modest attempt to address these questions. The stance taken is that there are lessons to be drawn from firms which have been exporting and are continuing to export manufactured products from Africa. A study of such firms can provide useful insights into the process by which they have been maintaining their position in the world market in spite of the general crisis conditions. Some exporting firms have been losing or changing their positions in world trade. Useful lessons can also be derived from the experience of these firms. This book brings insights from the experience of 55 exporting firms from six countries in Africa and draws out some policy implications regarding the prospects of restructuring for export orientation.

In the 1970s, and especially in the 1980s, many countries in Africa experienced economic crises of varying severity. Their economies have been characterized by weak growth in the productive sectors, with the initial spurt of industrial growth faltering, by poor export performance, reflected in the falling share of African exports in world trade and the unchanged export structure, and by increasing debt, a deteriorating economic and social infrastructure and increasing environmental degradation. This crisis has important implications for the prospects of transforming African economies, as envisaged by African governments (e.g. in the Lagos Plan of Action of 1980). The crisis has implications in two policy areas of particular relevance to the theme of this book: the previous import-substitution approach to industrialization as a means of economic transformation, and the position of Africa in world trade.

Debates on the causes of the crisis have centred on two categories of factors. The first category comprises exogenous factors such as bad weather, deteriorating terms of trade, fluctuating international interest rates and reduced inflows of foreign aid. The second category of explanations emphasizes endogenous factors such as inappropriate domestic policies, including incentive structures, and the mismanagement of public resources. The first line of argument, emphasizing exogenous factors, has largely been heard from governments in Africa and the UN Economic Commission for Africa (UNECA). Particular emphasis has been placed on the vulnerability of the performance of African economies to the vagaries of weather and to the unfavourable international environment, in particular to primary commodity prices, resource flows and debt conditions (UNECA, 1988).[1] The second category of explanation, emphasizing the domestic policy inadequacies, has been argued by the Bretton Woods Institutions, as formulated in the Berg report (World Bank, 1981).[2]

One response to these crises has been the adoption of economic reforms. Most economic reforms have been implemented under the influence of multilateral financial institutions, notably the International Monetary Fund and the World Bank (IMF).[3] According to these institutions, the rationale of these reforms is that Africa's slowness to respond to changing circumstances basically reflects domestic policy inadequacies, and it is these policy inadequacies that need to be addressed. In order to realize economic recovery, stabilization of the macro balance has been accorded high priority in policy-making. The conditions attached to external support have primarily been concerned with macroeconomic policy variables.

The nature and content of economic reforms carried out in various countries in Africa have varied in terms of coverage and emphasis. However, the main elements of economic reform have been liberalization of internal and external trade, greater reliance on market forces (i.e. price liberalization, devaluations and interest rate adjustments), tight monetary policies, mainly in the form of credit squeezes, and tight fiscal policy in the form of budget cuts and public sector reforms. These policies have primarily been designed to restore equilibrium, especially in the balance of payments and the fiscal and monetary variables. The policies followed in the structural adjustment programmes (SAPs) have succeeded in addressing the two policy areas which are relevant to the main theme of this book:

improving the position of Africa in world trade and enhancing the role of industrialization in economic transformation.

THE POSITION OF AFRICA IN WORLD TRADE

The current position of Africa in world trade is characterized by two main features: first, it has a small and declining share in world trade and second, its presence in world trade is largely confined to primary exports and the importation of non-primary products.

Africa's share in world trade is not only small, it has been declining. It varied from 4.1 to 4.9 per cent of world trade during 1960–65, fluctuated around 4.4 per cent during the 1970s and declined consistently to 2.3 per cent in 1987 (UNCTAD, 1993a).[4] The share of Africa in world exports declined from 4.7 per cent in 1975 to 2.0 per cent in 1990. The share of Africa's least developed countries declined more drastically, from 0.6 per cent to 0.2 per cent over the same period (UNIDO, 1993).[5] During 1980–87, while world exports were growing at 2.5 per cent per year, Africa's exports were declining at an annual rate of 7.4 per cent. The share of non-oil primary exports declined even more dramatically, from 7 per cent to 4 per cent, over the same period (Sharma, 1993).[6] Manufactured exports, though small, have exhibited a similar trend. The share of manufactured exports from Sub-Saharan Africa (SSA) in world trade declined from 0.38 per cent in 1965 to 0.23 per cent in 1986 (Riddell, 1990).[7] In relation to other developing countries, the share of Africa's manufactured exports declined from 5.2 per cent in 1975 to 2.6 per cent in 1985 and further to 2.5 per cent in 1990 (UNIDO, 1993). A preliminary study of the impact of the Single European Market has indicated that SSA countries lost their share mainly to other developing countries during 1987–91, in spite of preferential market access accorded to Africa through the Lomé Convention (UNCTAD, 1993b).[8] These trends suggest that Africa has lagged in competitiveness relative to the rest of the world economy, indicating that productivity growth and technological learning and innovations in the export sector in Africa have been low relative to other regions. This problem of lack of competitiveness, in traditional and non-traditional exports, will need to be faced if Africa is to improve its position in world trade.

A major concern of structural adjustment programmes has been to shift the incentive structure in favour of tradables, with a view to improving the position of Africa in world trade. However, the response of African exports to the incentive structure built into the structural adjustment programmes has been disappointing in terms of the values of export earnings which have been attained and the lack of change in the export structure. Recent efforts to revive exports within the traditional setting have provided further evidence that exports cannot be an engine of growth if the export structure remains unchanged, because of the poor prospects of making break-throughs in foreign exchange earning. Evaluating the impact of structural adjustment programmes in Sub-Saharan Africa, Husain (1994)[9] has indicated that for 1985–90 the export volumes of nine major export commodities in countries which had undertaken adjust-ment programmes increased by 75 per cent as compared with the 1977–79 averages. Yet export earnings from these exports had fallen by 40 per cent over the same period, because of deteriorating barter terms of trade (Husain, 1994).

Africa's major exports have been primary agricultural and mineral products. The structure of exports has hardly changed in much of Sub-Saharan Africa in the past two or three decades. The share of primary commodities in total exports from Sub-Saharan Africa has declined marginally, from 92 per cent in 1965 to 86 per cent in 1987 (World Bank, 1989).[10] For the low-income countries of Sub-Saharan Africa this share has even increased marginally, from 92 per cent in 1965 to 94 per cent in 1987 (World Bank, 1989). The export structure dominated by primary products is thus not changing to any significant extent.

The unchanging structure of exports may suggest that the export pessimism associated with traditional primary commodities has not been taken seriously in the design and implementation of develop-ment policies (before and after structural adjustment programmes). The first period of export pessimism was based either on declining terms of trade for primary products (Prebisch, 1954)[11] or on the notion that the absorptive capacity of foreign markets was low (i.e. elasticity pessimism) as argued by Nurkse (1959).[12] The future of most of these traditional commodity exports is rather bleak, considering the low income elasticities of demand associated with these products. Markets for many of these commodities are showing signs of saturation. A recent study has examined Africa's main primary exports[13] and concluded that the path followed in Africa, of exporting mineral and agricultural resources, is a dead end because of their poor prospects in the world market (Brown and Tiffen, 1992).[14] For instance, studies of the world cocoa market, in which exports from Africa comprise 55 per cent of traded volume, have shown that over a 20-year period (1960/65 to 1980/85), cocoa consumption increased by only 40 per cent, with negligible increases in the major consumer markets such as the EU (12 per cent) and US (19 per cent) over the same period (ITC, 1987).[15] Consumption of *robusta* coffee (dominant in Africa) has stagnated at 12.5 million bags since the mid-1970s, while world exports of *arabica* coffee doubled between the 1960s and 1980s (Brown and Tiffen, 1992). For coffee from Africa, these trends are aggravated by problems of product quality, delays and unreliability.

The empirical evidence that is available on terms of trade in Sub-Saharan Africa seems to suggest that the export pessimism thesis continues to hold. A World Bank study, taking the year 1980 as the base, has indicated that the terms of trade index declined to 91 in 1985 and 84 in 1987 (World Bank, 1989). In a recent, more general survey of empirical studies on this subject, Killick (1992) has concluded that 'there is now wider acceptance than was formerly the case of the declining real commodity price thesis' (p. 3).[16] If the importance of technological change is taken into consideration, this problem of export structures is even more serious, since the production of most traditional exports is associated with relatively limited technological dynamism.

Institutional/cognitive analysis can contribute towards understanding uneven patterns of economic performance and towards explaining path dependence (e.g. why some economics continue to stagnate). While learning is an incremental process filtered by the culture of a society, there is no guarantee that the stock of knowledge a society has accumulated will always enable it to confront new problems successfully. Societies that get stuck embody belief systems and institutions that fail to confront and solve new problems of societal complexity (North, 1994).[17] The rationality assumption of neoclassical theory would suggest that 'political entrepreneurs' (as per the new political economy) in stagnating economies could turn around the bad performance of their economies by simply altering the rules of the game. In fact, the difficulty is in the nature of the political market and the underlying belief systems of the actors (North, 1994).

The institutional/cognitive approach to contemporary development problems implies that:

- an admixture of formal rules, informal norms and enforcement characteristics shape economic performance. While the rules may be changed overnight, informal norms take time to change. Even if a poor performer adopts the formal rules of a good performer, differences in performance may persist because of differences in informal norms and enforcement.

- the essence of development policy is the creation of policies that will create and enforce appropriate rules and norms. Both institutions and belief systems must change for successful reform to be realized.
- the key to long-run growth is adaptive rather than allocative efficiency. Adaptive efficiency results from the evolution of flexible institutional structures that can survive shocks and changes.

Africa's position in the new global trade relations will largely be determined by what action is taken in Africa in two directions: first, increasing the regional and international competitiveness of its production activities, and second, changing the structure of exports towards more dynamic, non-traditional products (in terms of their demand prospects and their potential to effect technological change). The need to effect change in the export structure will inevitably bring discussions of policy issues relating to export diversification, the transformation of production structures and industrialization back on the agenda.

INDUSTRIALIZATION AND ECONOMIC TRANSFORMATION

The performance of Africa's industrial sector, in terms of growth and structural change, has been poor relative to other regions. Between 1980 and 1986, manufacturing value added (MVA) growth in SSA averaged 0.3 per cent, compared to 5.9 per cent in all developing countries and 7.7 per cent per annum in Southeast Asia (Riddell, 1990, pp. 10–15). The rate of growth of manufacturing value added in Africa has decelerated, from 5.1 per cent during 1975–85 to 3.5 per cent during 1985–90, while Southeast Asia enjoyed growth rates of 7.7 per cent and 8.8 per cent in the same periods (UNIDO, 1993). In terms of structural change, industry in SSA has remained more dominated by traditional and technologically simple consumer goods industries than industry in other regions.

In spite of the dismal performance of much of industry in Africa, debates during the 1980s on Africa's economic development in general and on economic recovery in particular have not given adequate attention to the role of industry (Riddell, 1990, p. 3). In some cases, industry has been identified as having been responsible for much of the waste of resources and a cure has been sought in diverting resources from industry to other sectors such as agriculture. The tendency to give less attention to industry is rather paradoxical for at least two reasons. First, the literature on economic development ascribes a high degree of dynamism to industry, a perception which has not been proved wrong. Second, industry has been instrumental to the generation and diffusion of technology, which is an important source of dynamism and competitiveness in any economy. The neglect of the role of industry amounts to the omission of a major source of technological dynamism in the development of SSA. What is needed now is to address the industrialization problem in the context of changed circumstances.

The approach taken in the economic reforms has influenced recent debates on industrialization in Africa. It is notable that in recent years discussions of industrial strategy in Africa have emphasized the importance of restructuring the supply side of the economy towards export orientation and to make it more competitive internationally. Such discussions have stressed the need to change the price structures which were associated with import substitution strategies by a return to the market.

Industrial restructuring is one component of the wider economic reforms adopted in many African countries. One implicit assumption of economic reforms and industrial restructuring is that enterprise-level inefficiencies are a reflection of distorted or inappropriate macroeconomic policies. It is suggested that if appropriate adjustments could be put in place at the macro level, enterprises would receive the right signals through the market. In response to these signals, enterprises would restructure appropriately. According to this approach, appropriate changes in policies (e.g. market prices, a realistic exchange rate, interest rates and competition) are expected to induce restructuring by favouring the expansion of efficient enterprises and the contraction of inefficient ones. This approach has been associated with the World Bank, especially in its earlier publications (World Bank, 1981). According to this approach, the reform and restructuring of industry is essentially a macroeconomic issue amounting to restructuring the supply side by putting in place appropriate macroeconomic and sectoral policies.[18]

One implication of the current shift towards export orientation in the industrialization debates has been to tilt the balance from import substitution strategies towards export-oriented industrialization. The debate between import substitution industrialization (ISI) and export-oriented industrialization (EOI) strategies is in many respects a debate between the structuralist and the neoclassical schools (Weiss, 1988).[19] The structuralists have criticized the neoclassical school for failure to recognize the untenability of the static equilibrium and the pervasive market failures arising from various structural rigidities. In the structuralist tradition, the importance of various externalities and dynamic considerations is stressed. In their critique the neoclassical school has stressed the structural school's neglect of the role of prices and markets in resource allocation, while the radical perspective stresses the structuralists' inability to analyse the role of class formation in these countries and the constraints posed by the external economic environment. This debate between the contending schools has tended to be polarized.

One reflection of the polarity between these competing schools of thought on development is manifest in the way that the underlying assumption, that ISI and EOI are necessarily competitive alternatives, has often been carried too far. In recent years it has become increasingly evident that the rather strict separability between ISI and EOI which was assumed is questionable on both methodological and empirical grounds. In many respects, some of the propositions which were thought to apply exclusively to ISI or to EOI are increasingly appearing either to be applicable to both approaches or at least not to be confined exclusively to either one of them.

The propositions that export orientation is inevitably inimical to the establishment of domestic linkages and that a successful capitalist industrialization is not a viable option for developing countries have been put in question by the realities of industrialization in several developing countries of Southeast Asia. On the other hand, the rather common claim that EOI promotes faster growth in total factor productivity (TFP) has been questioned on methodological grounds, related to the problems of estimating TFP under conditions of restrictive trade environments, and on empirical grounds, since some country studies have suggested that the differences between EOI and ISI are probably more likely to be reflected in the direction of research and development (R&D) than in its level (Bhagwati and Srinivasan, 1975).[20]

The efficacy of market forces associated with these approaches is being subjected to serious reconsideration. It has now become evident that EOI can be preceded by and can even build on the achievements of ISI. Arguing that the success story of Korea is much more complex than the neoclassical paradigm would suggest, it has been revealed that Korea promoted labour-intensive import substitution as well as exports, and that most of the later exports resulted from early import substitution (World Bank, 1985).[21] Selecting potential infant industries and giving them early encouragement to export can contribute to successful EOI and may became instrumental to technologically dynamic industrialization, as the experience of countries such as South Korea has shown (Westphal, 1981; Pack and Westphal, 1986; Jacobsson and Alam, 1994).[22] In addition, some recent experiences in attempting to make the shift from ISI to EOI by relying mainly on market forces have not been very successful.

Taking into consideration these objections to the strict separability between import substitution and export orientation, this study proceeds on the premise that import substitution and export orientation are not necessarily competing alternatives but rather could converge and reinforce each other. If ISI is efficient it can form the basis of EOI, and EOI can be consistent with further development of efficient linkages and the acquisition of technological capabilities among domestic industries. The challenge is to blend ISI and EOI through a mix of policies which aim at maximizing the benefits from increased domestic demand and stimulating both substantial (and efficient) import substitution and increased export orientation on the basis of growing technological capabilities.

Export orientation and competition provide incentives for improving efficiency but this presupposes the ability to respond, i.e. it supposes capabilities in terms of skills and technological endowments. In fact the supply response of African industry to the kinds of incentives the structural adjustment programmes have provided has been disappointing.

In this context, Lall *et al.* (1993)[23] have rightly pointed out that the role of capability factors continues to be neglected in studies of African industrialization, while SAPs continue to be designed with an almost exclusive focus on incentive factors. The authors cited one study by the World Bank (1989) as an exception, for having observed that most industries in Africa remain isolated from world markets and new technologies and continue to operate at costs higher than world prices. The study suggests that acceleration of industrial capacity growth would be wasted unless the capacity to design, manage and use it was also improved (World Bank, 1989). In addition, the study calls for a shift from central planning to a market approach, from regulation to competition and from failed attempts to transplant technology to the systematic building up of capabilities (World Bank, 1989). The study by Lall *et al.* (1993) noted that although external shocks and inappropriate policies have influenced the performance of African industry, the widespread absence of competitiveness and technological dynamism is also explained by other constraints related to the lack of the capabilities needed to set up modern industry and operate it efficiently. Overall, little attention is given to the need for supportive policies which could complement market forces in ensuring technological dynamism. This suggests that the process of restructuring for export orientation has been only partially understood.

In the context of new technologies and rapidly changing world market conditions, the process of restructuring for export orientation is going to pose a challenge to developing countries, especially the less developed among them, most of which are found in Africa. The question which needs to be addressed is what constraints are likely to be encountered and what opportunities could emerge for these economies in this restructuring process.

One major consideration which will influence the way the industrialization problem is conceptualized relates to the changing character of innovations and technological change, and their role in international trade and competitiveness. The stance which this book takes recognizes that the Schumpeterian conceptualization of technological change, with its emphasis on learning and the accumulation of technological capabilities, can have considerable implications for the conceptualization of the industrialization problem in Africa. Industrialization, for the less industrialized countries in Africa, will have to take place under conditions of accelerating technical change and the pervasive application of new technologies. The main theme of this book is to demonstrate how some firms in Africa are coping with challenges from changing technological and world market conditions.

Some country studies have suggested that the problem of lack of competitiveness could be partly explained by more deep-seated structural and institutional problems in these countries and partly by the fact that, for geographical and infrastructural reasons, SSA firms were increasingly isolated from the dynamics of efficient change occurring elsewhere, notably as regards technical adaptation, advances in management techniques and developments in computer-aided manufacture and ancillary services (Riddell, 1990). Further protection tended to be the quick fix which in effect retarded the response. However, the performance of the industrial sector has exhibited considerable variations among countries within Africa and, within specific countries, inter-industry and inter-firm performance differences have been quite significant. For instance, although the export promotion efforts of the 1980s had little success, some firms which were originally oriented to the domestic market have switched significantly to the export market. It is quite possible that some of these firms are exporting on the basis of marginal cost pricing, with overhead costs covered by the higher returns from the domestic market (Riddell, 1990, pp. 36–7). It is also possible that some firms have maintained increased international competitiveness over time. There are a few firms whose production has always been export-oriented, with well over 50 per cent of their output destined for export markets. There may be useful lessons to be drawn from the experience of these firms. A major concern of this book is to try to understand the process by which exporting firms maintain international competitiveness. It may be necessary to form a better understanding of the problems of comparative inefficiency and the acquisition of capabilities at the enterprise level. Such understanding could be a useful guide to finding more effective kinds of policy intervention. If technological dynamism and international competitiveness are to be achieved, then these differences in themselves ought to raise further questions regarding the constraints and opportunities on the one hand and the policy implications at macro and micro level on the other.

RESEARCH QUESTIONS

The future of traditional exports is rather bleak, considering the low income elasticities of demand associated with these products. The fact that the production of most traditional exports is associated with relatively limited technological dynamism raises doubts about their relevance for technological development in developing countries. Restructuring on the supply side needs to address the question of developing more technologically dynamic export sectors in these countries.

The main objective of this study is to understand more deeply the process of supply side restructuring and to examine the opportunities and feasible options for developing technologically dynamic and internationally competitive export industries in Africa in the context of the rapidly changing technological and world market conditions. This book will examine the process of building up and maintaining the capabilities which are necessary for maintaining competitiveness in export markets. The study examines such capabilities at firm, industry and national levels in selected countries in Africa. Since it is firms and not nations which compete on international markets, the analysis will focus on the firm level, emphasizing the process through which firms create and augment those capabilities which are necessary for acquiring and maintaining regional and/or international competitiveness over time in the context of internal and external influences (e.g. from factor markets, product markets, government interventions and institutions and policy remedies for market failures). In spite of this emphasis, the interdependence between the different levels is recognized and will be retained in the analysis.

The focus of the study is on exporting manufacturing firms, identifying and analysing the processes by which these firms have been maintaining or losing their competitiveness in international and/or regional markets. This is done by studying the capabilities of selected exporting firms with a view to understanding the process by which the creation and development of these capabilities has been promoted or inhibited over time by factors either internal or external to the firms. In this context, three main questions are addressed:

1 What factors and processes have influenced the paths which various firms have followed in attaining or losing regional and/or international competitiveness?
2 How have exporting firms been coping (or failing to cope) with changing technological and market conditions?
3 What lessons and policy implications can be drawn from the manner in which exporting firms have been maintaining (or losing) competitiveness in export markets and how have they been coping (or failing to cope) with changing technological and market conditions?

ORGANIZATION OF THIS BOOK

Recent developments in trade theory could offer useful insights into the emerging relationship between international trade and industrialization. Chapter 2 examines trade theories with a view to examining how the changing conceptualization of the relationship between trade theory and trade policy relates to the industrialization process. Chapter 3 describes the methodology adopted in this study and Chapter 4 examines some technological developments and world market conditions which are likely to be important for

Africa. Chapter 5 summarizes the major findings of the study and Chapter 6 draws conclusions and policy implication from the study. Chapters 7–12 are devoted to country case studies and Chapter 13 gives the survey questions used in these studies.

2 Trade theory
Relevance and implications for African export orientation

INTRODUCTION

Questions about the role of trade and trade policy in development represent one major factor in generalizations about macroeconomic policy and the choice of development strategy in developing countries (Colclough, 1991, p. 18a).[1] In recent years, developments in trade theory and their implications for trade policy have led to changing views on the relative importance of factors influencing trade and trade patterns and on the role of trade in economic development. This chapter examines these developments with a view to drawing out some implications relevant to development efforts in Africa. The chapter begins by examining the core of conventional trade theory, its explanatory and predictive power, and proceeds to survey briefly some critics and extensions of the theory within the conventional framework, and developments from outside it. The chapter closes with some reflections on the relevance and implications of these developments for discussions regarding the options that may be open to Africa in its development efforts in two areas: improving its position in world trade and enhancing the role of industrialization in economic transformation in a changing world economy.

CONVENTIONAL TRADE THEORY: ESSENCE AND RELEVANCE

Classical theories of trade, notably the Ricardian type, have stressed international differences in technology and real wage levels. Their focus has been on factor productivity differences. Developments in trade theories within the neoclassical framework have shifted attention from such differences in factor productivity towards differences in factor endowments. The core of the conventional trade theory is the factor proportions theory of the Heckscher–Ohlin model and its extensions. The theory is based on general equilibrium models and the assumptions associated with them, including perfect competition, concave (or at least quasi-concave) and constant-returns-to-scale production functions, and well-behaved and homothetic preference functions. Other theorems which are associated with the conventional theory are the factor equalization theorem, the Stolper–Samuelson theorem of gains accruing to the factors used in protected import-competing sectors and the Rybczynski theorem of the expansion (or contraction) of sectors which are intensive users of the abundant (or scarce) factor. As part of the general case for free markets, the case for free trade derives from the view that, as a production process, international trade is likely to be carried out more efficiently if it is left to the market mechanism.

Conventional trade theory has been questioned on methodological and empirical grounds. Critics who have emphasized the methodological problems of the conventional model are mainly associated with non-neoclassical formulations (e.g. evolutionary theory), while those who have questioned the empirical validity of the model have come from both within and outside the neoclassical framework.

The first empirical test of the Heckscher–Ohlin (H–O) model was administered by Leontief (1953).[2] Using input–output analysis, Leontief found that the US was a net exporter of labour-intensive goods and a net importer of capital intensive goods. This was not thought to amount to nullification or serious questioning of the theory. Instead, the outcome was labelled 'the Leontief paradox', reflecting the strong faith economists had in the H–O theory and their reluctance to accept the results of the test. An extensive literature on international trade has been devoted to attempts to explain the Leontief paradox – attempts in fact to find reasons why the results of the test must mean something other than the nullification of the H–O model itself. However, more recently it has increasingly been admitted that the conventional trade theory is in several ways inadequate to explain what is actually happening in the real world (e.g. Helpman and Krugman, 1985; Porter, 1990).[3]

The explanatory and predictive power of the conventional trade theory has increasingly come under attack from both inside and outside the neoclassical framework of analysis. At least three factors have influenced views on the efficacy of the conventional theory: the changing character of international trade, the changing roles and relative competitive positions of countries in the world economy (e.g.

the role of the US economy in world trade and competitiveness especially in relation to Japan) and changing views in the field of economics, especially as regards the analysis of industrial structure and competition (e.g. broadening the tool kit of economic analysis by borrowing from the field of industrial organization).

Patterns of trade have been changing in favour of North–North trade. This phenomenon, which Linder (1961)[4] observed, has received more serious attention and extensions have been made in many respects. There has been a relatively steady growth in manufacturing exports, leading to high levels of trade between countries with similar factor endowments. Three quarters of all exports from the developed countries have their destination in other developed countries, which are supposed to be relatively similar in their relative factor endowments (Yoffie, 1993).[5] The implication of these changes is that the explanation of the volume of trade on the basis of differences in factor endowments can be no more than partial. The composition of trade is also not adequately explained, since there is substantial two-way trade in goods of similar factor intensity, although it is largely true that countries' net exports seem to reflect a factor content which is consistent with underlying resources. These trends are likely to be reinforced by the on-going tendency to form larger trading blocs among developed countries (Ray, 1991).[6]

Increasing globalization has been particularly characterized by the growing role of transnational corporations (TNCs), facilitated by the explosive growth in international private financial flows. The number of TNCs has increased and the number of home bases has also increased. One consequence has been the increasing role of TNCs in exporting capital in the form of foreign direct investment (FDI). During the second half of the 1980s, FDI increased by 29 per cent annually, nearly three times the rate of growth of international trade. Further evidence from this area suggests that alliances are prevalent in global oligopolies, serving ubiquitously as vehicles for the transfer of technology between firms, achieving economies of scale, building technical standards and accessing markets, skills and resources (Yoffie, 1993). These developments have led to a new ranking of the factors creating interdependencies whereby FDI in manufacturing and services, rather than trade, is leading internationalization and is influencing location and trade patterns. During the 1980s the pattern of internationalization and globalization was further facilitated by deregulation and the globalization of finance and by the enabling features and pressure from new technologies.

These developments cannot be adequately explained in the conventional theoretical framework.

Conventional trade theory associates trade with resource reallocation, which increases aggregate national income but leaves some factors with reduced real income. However, the realities as demonstrated by the EU and the US–Canada pacts suggest that little reallocation takes place and that trade may permit increased productivity of existing resources.

Finally, increased tensions in the international trade environment and rapid technological progress, which is reflected in new products, new processes and increased productivity, have led to a reassessment of the relevance and applicability of conventional trade theory (Haque, 1991).[7] In addition, the experience of the most successful newly industrialized economies (NIEs) does not seem to conform to the traditional model of specialization. Japan, for instance, encouraged industries which are associated with high income elasticity of demand, rapid technological progress and rising labour productivity. They relied on protection, and government policy played a key role in targeting and fostering industry. They realized that the comparative cost doctrine is inherently static: clearly, comparative advantage has to be created and maintained by responding to the changing world environment in which technology is advancing and new productive capacities are being created. Success in international trade has much to do with the ability to anticipate and to be prepared to exploit trade opportunities in a dynamic context.

CRITICS AND EXTENSIONS OF CONVENTIONAL TRADE THEORY

The approach adopted by the critics is basically one of analysing the outcomes and trade implications of the behaviour of firms operating in conditions which fall short of the ideals of perfect competition (monopolistic competition, imperfect competition, increasing returns to scale). Much of the literature in this category represents sympathetic attempts to relax the basic assumptions of the H–O model and test its robustness (Kierzkowski, 1987).[8] In this context, monopolistic competition and other forms of imperfect competition have come to be central to the literature on trade theory, largely reflecting the persistence of intra-industry trade in reality. At one extreme there are those who equate countries to single firms, analyse their oligopolistic interactions, and attempt to link the instruments and concepts of industrial organization with the general equilibrium model (Caves, 1980; Brander, 1981; Brander and Krugman, 1983).[9] Other analyses have tried to formalize equilibrium trade patterns, with endogenous technological change and monopolistic competition as the innovative intermediate inputs (Ethier, 1979; Krugman, 1987; Grossman and Helpman, 1989, 1990a).[10]

The link between trade theory and industrial organization was first proposed simultaneously by Dixit and Norman (1980), Krugman (1979) and Lancaster (1980).[11] It has even been suggested that it is the contribution by Dixit and Stiglitz (1977) and Lancaster (1979)[12] that provided the foundations for a theoretical framework for analysing economies of scale and product differentiation in a general equilibrium setting (Greenway, 1991).[13] Since then, developments in this area have taken two directions: modelling the role of economies of scale and analysing market structures. In the latter case various forms of imperfect competition are taken as a starting point and the possibilities of strategic behaviour and interactions between firms are treated in the analysis.

Grappling with the presence of economies of scale

Economies of scale have recently come to be seen as more important (e.g. Scherer, 1980).[14] Various explanations for this trend have been given in the literature (e.g. Helpman and Krugman, 1985; Alcorta, 1994).[15] First, where industries produce multiple products, many products may be produced at less than optimal scale. Second, there may be important economies of multi-product operation which are not captured by plant-based estimates of scale economies. Third, there may be important dynamic scale economies internal to firms.

The existence of economies of scale provides an incentive for international specialization and trade. This incentive may complement the explanatory power of differences in factor proportions, and may even give rise to trade in the absence of such differences (Helpman and Krugman, 1985). Except under special circumstances, a world of increasing returns to scale will not be a world of perfectly competitive markets. However, in the absence of a generally accepted theory of imperfect competition, the admission of economies of scale would make it difficult to generalize on trade. More specifically, the presence of economies of scale implies that the H–O model can guarantee neither gains from trade nor the existence and uniqueness of a free trade equilibrium. The problem is that the persistent presence of economies of scale is inherently inconsistent with competitive equilibrium, as marginal cost pricing would in that case imply losses. Thus the admission of economies of scale calls for an analysis based on a market structure that allows prices above marginal cost. It is in this context that more explicit consideration has been given to alternative market structures in the analysis of international trade.

Three different approaches to the analysis of increasing returns to scale under alternative market structures (other than perfect competition) can be identified in the literature: the Marshallian approach, the Chamberlinian approach and the Cournot approach (Krugman, 1987).

The Marshallian approach

In the Marshallian approach, increasing returns to scale are wholly external to the firm. In this special case the competitive model is still operative at the level of the firm.[16] Economies of scale are then introduced in the general equilibrium models in ways which allow for the existence of a competitive equilibrium. However, the *laissez faire* competitive equilibrium is no longer Pareto optimal, to the extent that the private marginal rate of transformation deviates from the social marginal rate of transformation of any two commodities. It is in response to this rather undesirable outcome (for the advocates of free trade) that considerable literature on trade has grappled with the problem of optimal tariff policies.

It has been shown that working from the allocation of resources to production and trade rather than the other way round clarifies the role of economies of scale in determining the pattern of specialization and trade (Ethier, 1979, 1982).[17] If external economies arise from economies of scale in the production of intermediate goods which are cheaply tradable, it is argued, economies of scale should apply at the international rather than national level. Economies of scale arising from increased specialization (rather than from plant size) depend (at the aggregate level) on the size of the world market rather than on geographical concentration of industry (at national level). Such international increasing returns to scale were shown to be free of the recurrent indeterminacy and multiple equilibria characteristic of national increasing returns to scale. This implies the possibility of a theory of intra-industry trade in intermediate goods in accordance with the basic H–O model. Intra-industry trade in manufactures is viewed as complementary to international factor movements as predicted by the H–O trade theory. However, the basic assumptions, that economies of scale arise solely from fixed costs and that intermediate components are symmetric, can be questioned on empirical grounds.[18]

There is a possibility that external economies may arise from the inability of firms to appropriate knowledge completely. In such cases information may be viewed as an externality. However, innovative industries will ordinarily not be perfectly competitive. An emphasis on the generation of knowledge calls for a dynamic rather than a static model. The question of the applicable unit of analysis arises. If external economies are assumed to result from the incomplete appropriability of knowledge, the applicable unit for the analysis of externalities will depend on the details of how innovations diffuse: are they likely to be confined to a local area, to a nation, or are they international? Recent advances in information and communications technologies are likely to tilt the relevant unit of analysis towards the international arena.

The Chamberlinian approach

In the Chamberlinian approach, the possibility of product differentiation and product variety is introduced into the analysis. The resulting interaction between demand for product variety and economies of scale leads to intra-industry trade (Helpman, 1981; Lancaster, 1980).[19] Similar results have been demonstrated for differentiated intermediate goods to satisfy the demands of producers who use these diverse intermediate inputs (Ethier, 1982). Developments to the Chamberlinian approach have taken two directions. The first has assumed that each consumer has a taste for largely different varieties of product (e.g. Dixit and Stiglitz, 1977; Dixit and Norman, 1980). The second has approached product differentiation by positing a primary demand for the attributes of varieties (e.g. Lancaster, 1980). Both approaches introduce the possibility that the response to market expansion may be greater product variety. Consequently, gains from trade may occur in the form of greater choice of product varieties and in the form of lower prices. It has been shown that these basic results and their implications are retained even when demand for variety is allowed for at the level of the firm (Dixit and Norman, 1980).

The Cournot approach

The Cournot approach invokes economies of scale to explain the existence of oligopolies and treats imperfect competition as the main actor. An extension of the H–O model along these lines has introduced increasing returns to scale into the analysis and related it to the role of protection. This extension has opened up the possibility that protection of the domestic market can help the local producer to generate a higher level of output resulting in enhanced competitiveness in terms of lower average costs (Krugman, 1984).[20] This approach shows the effect of trade on increasing competition and demonstrates the possibility of interpenetration of markets, because oligopolists perceive a higher elasticity of demand for exports than for domestic sales.

The real world, characterized by economies of scale, the accumulation of knowledge and the dynamics of innovations, is not incompatible with the ideals of free trade. But if the analysis of such dynamic phenomena is formalized in static models there is a risk of major potential pitfalls where static and dynamic analyses are mixed (Helpman and Krugman, 1985). If a static model has to be used as a proxy for a dynamic world, it should be viewed as a representation of the whole time path of that world and not a snapshot at a point in time. In particular, the comparison of equilibria involved in comparative statics exercises should be understood as a comparison between alternative histories and not a change that takes place over time. Using static models to think dynamically is even more risky in imperfectly competitive markets, in which games over time can have many possibilities not seen in one-period games.

Trade theory and various market structures

The analysis of trade issues in the context of a variety of market structures has explored several issues which could not have been addressed adequately in the framework of the perfectly competitive model. The most notable approaches to the analysis of various market structures include: trade policy and the power of domestic firms, the role of price discrimination and dumping, and the role of governments in giving domestic firms a competitive advantage. Another group of analysts raise questions of the implications of the link between market structures and trade theories for new arguments for protectionism. Further extensions along these lines have attempted to capture more complex insights such as the role of intermediate goods (Ethier, 1982), non-traded goods (Helpman and Krugman, 1985), market size effects (Krugman, 1980; Helpman and Krugman, 1985)[21] and attempts to demonstrate that economies of scope and/or vertical integration lead to the emergence of multi-activity firms such as multinational corporations (Helpman and Krugman, 1985).

The literature within this strand has basically examined alternative theories of market structures which deviate from perfect competition (Helpman and Krugman, 1985). Such analyses assumed various kinds of imperfectly competitive market structures such as contestable markets[22] (Baumol *et al.*, 1982),[23] Cournot oligopoly and monopolistic competition.[24] Two main strands can be identified here: those assuming various forms of Chamberlinian monopolistic competition and those analysing various forms of oligopoly.

Various models based on Chamberlinian monopolistic competition have been developed, mainly analysing the interaction between economies of scale, product differentiation and different forms of monopolistic competition (Krugman, 1987). These models have demonstrated welfare gains from increased product variety and from lower prices. Essentially, however, the insights of the H–O model are shown to hold quite well under conditions of product differentiation and such economies of scale.

The question which the analysts of various forms of oligopoly have asked is whether firms with market power act in a cooperative or non-cooperative manner. Since formal cartel and price-fixing arrangements are generally not legal, such cooperation arrangements are to a large extent tacit. Partly for this reason, the theory of co-operative behaviour in oligopolistic industries is not well developed. Most of the contributors on this subject have therefore restricted their analysis of markets to non-cooperative behaviour.

The outcome of non-cooperative behaviour by firms has largely depended on the strategic variables with which the game is played and the conditions of entry into and exit from the industry. Most theoretical work on oligopoly has tended to take as the strategic variable either outputs (the Cournot assumption) or prices (the Betrand assumption). In more general terms, various forms of market imperfection permit firms to earn returns exceeding those that are tenable in purely competitive industries, suggesting that trade policy can be used to influence the share of international profits accruing to domestic firms (and in that way to the economy). For instance, subsidies can be used to shift profits in favour of domestic firms, implying enhancement of their strategic position versus foreign rivals in competition for world markets.

Cournot's equilibrium is tenable when each firm is doing its best to maximize profit by choosing its output level, given the output levels of its rivals. In equilibrium, no aggressive threat by any firm is likely to be believed by its rivals. However, if one firm manages to reduce its costs (or get a subsidy), a new equilibrium would be set at a higher level of output and market share for that firm. Reference has also been made to the strategic use of R&D expenditure (or subsidies) to lower costs and shift the reaction curve outward. These results open up the possibility that government action can alter the outcome of the strategic game played by rival firms. It is in this context that possibilities for strategic trade policy have been proposed. The policy of protection to promote exports is one outcome of the presence of economies of scale. Movement down the firm's learning curve, leading to higher output (facilitated by protection) and falling marginal costs, is expected to enhance the firm's competitive position in world markets (Krugman, 1984).

TRADE THEORY AND ACCUMULATION EFFECTS: INTRODUCING NEW GROWTH THEORIES

Accumulation effects in the medium term can be derived from the neoclassical models of growth. The neoclassical model without exogenous shocks (e.g. productivity increases or population changes) presents a steady state capital–labour ratio determined by equating the real marginal product of capital and the discount rate. Any policy which raises the marginal product of capital will also raise the steady state capital–labour ratio, inducing output to grow faster in the medium term as capital accumulation takes place at a higher level (Solow, 1956; Baldwin, 1993).[25] In the neoclassical model, medium-term growth results from the connection between trade and the marginal productivity of capital. Recent developments have augmented the Solow model by including human capital as a separate factor along with physical capital and unskilled labour (e.g. Mankiw *et al.*, 1992).[26] In this case, any policies (e.g. streamlining licensing procedures or easing foreign exchange restrictions) which would raise the marginal product of physical capital or human capital accruing to investors (e.g. by reducing the difficulty and expense of making investments) will also raise capital accumulation and growth in the medium term.

Although in the neoclassical growth models, continual accumulation takes the form of productivity-boosting knowledge, the rate of productivity growth is taken as given (determined exogenously). One contribution of the new growth theory is to endogenize the rate of productivity growth itself. A distinguishing feature of endogenous growth models (endogenizing investment) is that continuous accumulation requires that the return to accumulation does not fall as capital stock rises. Endogenous growth models have differed as to the type of factor which is thought to play a dominant role in the accumulation process: physical capital, human capital or knowledge capital.

The Marshallian concept, of increasing returns which are external to a firm but internal to an industry, was most widely used in static models, presumably because of the technical difficulties presented by dynamic models (Romer, 1986).[27] Following Smith and Marshall, most authors explained the existence of increasing returns on the basis of increasing specialization and the division of labour, but these cannot rigorously be treated as technological externalities.

Evidence from observations made over almost three centuries, from 1700 to 1979, shows that productivity growth rates have been increasing for the Netherlands, UK and US (Romer, 1986). Similar evidence has been found for individual countries over shorter periods. Other evidence coming from growth accounting exercises and the estimation of aggregate production functions shows that the growth of inputs alone does not fully explain the rate of growth of outputs. Interest in dynamic models of growth driven by increasing returns was rekindled by Arrow's work on learning by doing (1962),[28] in which increasing returns are supposed to arise from the new knowledge generated in the course of investment and production.

Some studies, closely related to the analysis of long-term growth, have focused on patterns of trade and their linkages with the patterns of innovation across countries, across sectors and over time. These studies have found some robust evidence regarding the impact of innovation on international competitiveness and on growth. This trend also relates to those neo-technology models which have attempted to endogenize technical progress within equilibrium open-economy development models (Krugman, 1979; Spencer, 1981).[29] Krugman's modelling of the technology gap between the North and the South and Spencer's analysis of the learning curve have contributed to bringing out some dynamic considerations in the discussions of international trade theory. Such approaches can be reduced to analyses of either learning curves or the generation of new intermediate inputs under monopolistic competition.

New growth theories which take technical progress as the driving force have extended Solow's insights by endogenizing technical progress. In the earlier models in this category, the rate of return to investment was prevented from falling due to technological spill-overs in production (Romer, 1986). The evidence on productivity growth over time coupled with the inadequacies of previous growth models motivated Romer (1986) to present a competitive equilibrium model of long-run growth with endogenous technological change, and with knowledge as an input which has increasing marginal productivity. In his model, long-run growth is primarily driven by the accumulation of knowledge by forward-looking, profit-maximizing agents. Knowledge is accumulated by devoting resources to research. New knowledge is assumed to be a product of research technology and this research exhibits diminishing returns. Romer combined three elements (externalities, increasing returns in the production of output and decreasing returns in the production of new knowledge) to constitute his competitive equilibrium model of growth. His model deviates from the Ramsey–Cass–Koopmans model and the Arrow model by assuming that knowledge is a capital good with an increasing marginal product.

A major problem with analyses undertaken in the equilibrium framework is their assumption of the existence of price- and/or quantity-based adjustment mechanisms which ensure clearing of all markets and the attainment of equilibrium in that sense. The assumptions based on the presence of maximizing agents become an inadequate representation of the general behaviour of agents when fundamental features of technological change (uncertainty and various irreversibilities) are invoked (Nelson and Winter, 1982; Dosi *et al.*, 1990; Cooper, 1991).[30] As North (1994) has suggested, the problem here reflects on the neoclassical body of theory. A theory of economic dynamics comparable to general equilibrium theory would be ideal for understanding economic change, but we do not have such a theory. The neoclassical theory is inappropriate for analysing and prescribing policy measures that will induce development. It is concerned with how markets operate rather than how they develop. Even when it attempts to take account of technological development and human capital investment, it still ignores the incentive structure, embodied in institutions, that influences societal investment in those factors.

Attempts to correct this deficiency have been based on more evolutionary micro foundations, whereby firms with different technologies and organizational traits interact under conditions of persistent disequilibrium. The essential aspects of Schumpeterian competition are highlighted, especially the diversity of firm characteristics and experience and the cumulative interaction of that diversity. Contributions in this category have focused more explicitly on the micro foundations of innovation by addressing firm-level decisions to invest in product or process innovations. The ceaseless search for better product quality and for cost-lowering process innovations continuously leads to productivity improvements. What Schumpeter referred to as 'creative destruction' is a process whereby the impulse coming from new products, new processes and new markets revolutionizes the economic structure from within, destroying the old one and creating a new one.

Contributors in this strand are more heretical and heterogeneous in nature and scope and their models are not always thoroughly formalized. Following Dosi *et al.* (1990), they may be classified into four broad groups: post-Keynesians (e.g. Posner, Vernon, Kaldor), structuralists in development economics (e.g. the dependency school), institutional economists such as Douglass North, and economic historians (e.g. Kuznets, Gerschenkron, Balough). Much of the management literature focusing on firm-level capabilities may be included in this approach (e.g. Porter, 1990). Studies which follow this approach agree on several points: that international differences in technology levels and innovative capabilities are crucial in explaining the trade flows and incomes of countries, that the general equilibrium mechanisms of international and inter-sectoral adjustment are relatively weak, that technology is not a free good and that allocation patterns induced by international trade have dynamic implications in the long term. The questions have implications regarding the causes of industrial development and growth, the linkages between these processes and their micro foundations, and the understanding of the on-going transformations and restructuring of world industry.

The evolutionary theory of economic change attempts to provide a formal theory of economic activity, driven by industrial innovation (consistent with the Schumpeterian view). It seeks to understand technical change, its sources and its impacts at micro and macro levels (Nelson and Winter, 1982). Evolutionary theory consists of heterogeneous modelling efforts which emphasize various aspects of economic change, such as the responses to market conditions of firms and industries, economic growth and competition through innovation. Many of its underlying ideas can be traced back to classical political economy (e.g. Smith, Marx, Schumpeter). In addition, contributors in this field have adopted tools of analysis from other fields. For instance, from the managerialists they have taken over a more realistic description of the motives that directly determine business decisions. From the behaviouralists they have taken an understanding of the limits of human rationality which make it unlikely that firms can maximize over the whole set of conceivable alternatives. The linkage of a firm's growth and profitability to its organizational structure, capabilities and behaviour is adopted from industrial organization (e.g. Coase, Williamson). The view that the histories of firms matter, because their previous experience influences their future capabilities, and that firms adapt to changing conditions is largely adopted from evolutionary theorists (e.g. Darwin, Lamarcker, Alchian) and economic historians (e.g. Rosenberg, David).

The version of evolutionary theory presented by Nelson and Winter (1982) questions two pillars of neoclassical theory. First, the maximization model of firm behaviour is questioned with respect to the way it specifies the objective function and the set of things that firms are supposed to know how to do. In addition, evolutionary theory objects to the way firms' actions are viewed as resulting from choices which maximize the degree to which the objective is achieved, given the set of known alternatives and constraints. Second, objections are raised to the concept of equilibrium which is used to generate conclusions about economic behaviour within the logic of the model.[31] The general term that Nelson and Winter use for all the regular and predictable behavioural patterns of firms is 'routine'. Routine consists of well-defined technical routines for producing things, procedures (e.g. for hiring and firing, ordering new stocks), policies (e.g. for investment, R&D, advertising) and business strategies (e.g. on diversification, overseas investment). These routines are categorized into the operating characteristics governing short-run behaviour, those determining investment behaviour (period-to-period changes in the firm's capital stock) and those which operate to modify over time certain aspects of the operating characteristics (e.g. market analysis, operations research, R&D). There are also aspects of the behavioural patterns of firms which are essentially irregular and unpredictable. These are regarded as stochastic elements in the determination of decisions and decision outcomes. Evolutionary theory attempts to model the firm as having certain capabilities and decision rules and choice sets (through which the main objective is pursued). These choice sets are not well defined and exogenously given. The core concern of evolutionary theory is with the dynamic process by which firm behaviour patterns and market outcomes are jointly determined over time.

The emerging theory of dynamic firm capabilities is presented by focusing on three related features of a firm (Nelson, 1991):[32] its strategy (a set of broad commitments made by a firm that define and rationalize its objectives and how it intends to pursue them), its structure (how a firm is organized and governed and how decisions are actually made and carried out) and its core capabilities (core organizational capabilities, particularly those which define how lower-order organizational skills are coordinated, the higher-order decision procedures for choosing what is to be done at lower levels, and R&D capabilities, particularly regarding innovation and how to take on-going economic advantage of innovation). Since the real world is too complicated for the firm to understand in the neo-classical way, firms will choose somewhat different strategies which will lead to their having different structures and different core capabilities.

When a new and potentially superior technology comes into existence in a relatively mature industry, the evidence suggests that what happens depends on whether the new technology is able to conform to the core capabilities of specific firms (competence enhancing) or requires very different kinds of capabilities (competence destroying) (Nelson, 1991). A change in management, and presumably a major change in strategy, is often necessary if an old firm is to survive in the new environment. Organizational change must be seen as the handmaid of technological advance and not as a separate force behind economic progress (Tidd, 1991; Nelson, 1991).[33] In the long run, what has mattered most has been the organizational changes needed to enhance dynamic innovative capabilities. However, there is little in the way of tested and proven theory for predicting the best way of organizing a particular activity, and there is considerable disagreement about what features of a firm's organization are responsible for certain successes and/or failures. These can only be unveiled in concrete situations through empirical studies which seek to understand firm-level strategies, structures and capabilities and the environment in which they are operating.

Attempts to model the way allocation patterns of international trade influence the long-term dynamics of an economy have been made, incorporating the main ideas from the two-gap models and hypothesizing that world growth is determined by asymmetrical patterns of change in technological and demand structures (e.g. Kaldor, 1970, 1975; Pasinetti, 1981; Dosi *et al.*, 1990).[34] The focus of these approaches has largely been on the relationship between trade, levels of activity and growth.

It has been pointed out that the neoclassical premise of efficient markets is undermined by the existence of transaction costs, which create a need for institutions to define and enforce contracts. If trade is to prosper, certain informational and institutional requirements become necessary. Market institutions are expected to induce the actors to acquire information that will lead to the correction of their subjectively derived models. But if institutions shape the incentive structure of society, the learning process which occurs in the interaction between institutions and organizations shapes the institutional evolution of an economy (North, 1994). Institutions may be the rules of the game but organizations and entrepreneurs are the players. While the bulk of the choices made by players are routine, some involve altering existing contracts and some may even lead to alterations in the rules of the game. Thus the most fundamental long-run source of change is learning by the players.

SOME IMPLICATIONS OF NEW TRADE THEORIES FOR AFRICA

The main contributions of new trade theories are basically in the recognition that economies of scale (and the associated market structures) and differences in technological capabilities are important. As regards technological capabilities, some strands of these theories have contributed to setting (or resetting?) the stage towards endogenizing technological development and innovations in the analysis of trade issues.

One important message which comes out of the new trade theories is that technology differences are a fundamental force in shaping comparative advantages. This implies that, in the design of trade policy and the formulation of industrialization policies, it will be necessary to give explicit consideration to the changing role and conceptualization of technological change.

In the process of industrialization in the less industrialized economies, elevating the importance given to technological change could contribute to improving the efficiency of the import substitution industries and improving the international competitiveness of the export industries. In the field of trade, in particular, lessons from the new trade theories seem to be relevant in highlighting the role of technological development and innovation and the importance of being forward-looking in assessing trade potentials, in contrast to the implications of the static comparative advantages model. In addition, the new theories demonstrate the centrality of technology in trade and, in particular, the need to gain detailed knowledge of the structures and capabilities of exporting industries and firms as a basis for formulating export promotion policies and policies intended to promote industries with dynamic comparative advantages.

Although the focus of the new trade theories is primarily on North–North trade, some elements of the role of economies of scale, product diversity and explanations for intra-industry trade may be applicable to the place of South–South trade in the world economy. As regards intra-industry trade, the available evidence suggests that the average levels of such trade have been low in developing countries and even lower if we consider only the non-NICs (newly industrialized countries) (Greenway, 1991; Havrylyshyn and Civan, 1985).[35] One problem with such evidence is that it is derived from static analysis and does not take into account the directions in which such intra-South trade could evolve. Such a dynamic conceptualization would require that consideration of South–South trade should address innovations such as the development of more appropriate products and processes for the South as a basis for South–South trade (Stewart, 1984, 1991)[36] and should pose the question of the conditions under which South–South trade is feasible and viable, drawing lessons from the emerging patterns of trade as unveiled by the new trade theories. That policy has important implications for the evolution of intra-industry trade can be inferred from the evidence that intra-industry trade tends to be higher among countries (whether developed or developing) with some kind of integration arrangement (Balassa and Bauwens, 1988).[37] This could be due to the lowering of trade barriers and/or the ability to exploit economies of scale, factors which are often associated with integration and co-operation arrangements.

The actual trade relations of SSA can be classified as a 'hub and spoke' arrangement, with Europe and North America as the hub and African countries as the spokes. The key feature of this arrangement is that trade between the hub and any spoke is easier than trade among the spokes (Baldwin, 1993). The hub-and-spoke trade arrangements exert a marginalizing effect on the African economies. Although the cost of production in SSA countries may be lower due to lower labour costs, higher trade costs (due to small markets as compared to those in the hub countries) are likely to more than offset the lower production costs. Trade liberalization between the hub and the spokes favours location of investments in the hub, especially if intra-SSA trade is not also liberalized. Hub-and-spoke trade liberalization artificially deters investment in the spoke countries. Reduction of intra-SSA trade costs would increase the chances that the lower SSA production costs will outweigh these trade costs, and so would facilitate investments in SSA.

Within the broader context of forging inter-firm linkages and cooperation arrangements, special attention will need to be paid to the possibilities of promoting investments, not only by TNCs from developed countries but also among countries in the region and with other developing countries. There is evidence that TNCs from developing countries can also have capabilities to share with other developing countries. As this study has shown, many exporting firms in Africa have undertaken various technological modifications and adaptations in response to country-specific conditions. Other studies have shown that adaptations have been made by developing country firms with respect to the characteristics of raw materials such as type, quality and input mix, scaling down, product quality and product mix, simplicity and capacity and factor intensity (Lecraw, 1981).[38] As is noted in Chapter 4, these firms have tended to produce simpler, easily marketed products.

South–South inter-firm linkages and cooperation arrangements should be viewed as complementary to the kinds of benefits which can be obtained from inter-firm networks and cooperation arrangements with TNCs from the North and not necessarily as substitutes. The Abuja declaration on the establishment of the African Economic Community is an encouraging step. Its implementation, however, should involve taking steps towards establishing the institutional framework to spearhead the development of these kinds of inter-firm linkages and cooperation arrangements, not only within Africa but between Africa and other regions.

Differences in income levels, historical backgrounds and other environmental considerations suggest that there are bound to be inter-regional, inter-country and intra-country differences in demand structures. This diversity of demand structures means that African firms could find and exploit windows of opportunities in export markets inside and outside the region.

Intra-regional trade in Africa has remained low, at perhaps 5 per cent of total African trade, and has not shown any clear signs of increasing. However, there are at least two sources of optimism regarding the prospects of growth in regional cooperation in trade and investments. First, there are indications that a substantial volume of intra-regional trade is unrecorded. Second, the degree of complementarity is often understated. That the potential for intra-Africa trade is higher than trade figures suggest is indicated by the results of demand and supply studies. For instance, the project 'Promotion of Intra-regional Trade Through Supply and Demand Surveys' was part of a more comprehensive programme aimed at promoting trade between the member states of the Preferential Trade Areas for Eastern and Southern African States (PTA) (ITC, 1985).[39] The data shows that many of the items which are imported into the PTA are also exported from the PTA, indicating that there are potentials for intra-regional trade in a wide range of sectors.[40] In spite of having the necessary raw materials, the region continues to be a net importer of various light manufactures.

Even within agriculture, which is often cited as an example of competitive structures, the potentials seem to be greater than official figures acknowledge. For instance, differences in climatic and agronomic conditions in the Eastern and Southern Africa region have been shown to be a source of complementarity of production (Koester and Thomas, 1992).[41] Similar results have been obtained in the case of West Africa, where it has been found that the differences between countries in their access to international trade, and their historical conditions, technological accumulation and consumer preferences, suggest that there is a good potential for specialization (Badiane, 1992).[42] The difference between potential and actual intra-Africa and South–South trade is due to the many obstacles to such trade: weak industrial structures, the lack of intra-industry linkages, inadequate infrastructure, tariff and non-tariff barriers, perceived unequal distribution of benefits and the instability of the real exchange rates between African countries.

The role of dynamic learning processes and the competitive pressures in export markets are relevant to the extent that such dynamic economies are industry-specific. Contrary to the neoclassical premise that all activities are equally important, new trade theories highlight the existence of strategic activities which could be developed through policy. One case is that of protection as a form of export promotion, as argued by Krugman (1984). The new trade theories' exposition of the possibility of 'import protection as export promotion' introduces a way of using trade policy strategically. The case for selectively supporting specific high-potential industries through government policy has been demonstrated to varying degrees in the experiences of the developed countries and the NICs.[43]

3   Some conceptual issues and methodology of the study

SOME CONCEPTUAL ISSUES

Chapter 1 indicated that the main aim of this book is to explore and present some insights into the process of creating and maintaining the capabilities which are needed for attaining and maintaining competitiveness in export markets. For the purposes of this study the concepts of 'capability' and 'competitiveness in export markets' will need to be clarified.

Competitiveness in export markets implies high levels of productivity. In order to understand the concept of international competitiveness it is useful to revisit the concepts of productivity and efficiency, concepts which are often taken for granted.

The productivity of a production unit is the ratio of its output to its input. Productivity differences are accounted for by differences in production technology, differences in the efficiency of the production process and differences in the environment in which production occurs. Three problems of measurement arise here: the identification of inputs and outputs to be included in the analysis, what weights (prices) should be used in the aggregation process and (if one is comparing actual productivity with what is theoretically achievable) the determination of the potential of the production unit (Lovell, 1993).[1]

The efficiency of a production unit is the ratio between the observed and the potential maximum output obtainable from a given input, or the ratio of minimum potential input to the observed input required to produce a given output. Koopmans (1951)[2] introduced a formal definition of technical efficiency, i.e. a producer is technically efficient if an increase in any output requires a reduction of at least one other output or an increase in at least one input, and if a reduction in any input requires an increase in at least one other input or a reduction in at least one output. Debreu (1951) and Farell (1957)[3] introduced a measure of technical efficiency, equal to one minus the maximum equi-proportionate reduction in all inputs which would allow the continued production of given outputs. Debreu/ Farell technical efficiency has been shown to be necessary but not sufficient for Koopmans' technical efficiency (Lovell, 1993). Variations in technical efficiency have been attributed to variations in the factors under the control of the producers (managerial input being the most common culprit), while variations in allocative efficiency have been attributed to divergence between expected and actual prices, the persistent over- or under-valuation of prices, discrimination, nepotism and satisficing behaviour.

Two important elements are often missing in discussions of efficiency in the economics literature. First, very little effort has been devoted to integrating the literature on the theory of production under uncertainty into the efficiency measurement literature. Second, the wide literature on the internal organization of the firm has not made any impression on the efficiency measurement literature, despite its obvious relevance for the measurement of producer performance (Lovell, 1993). In their efforts to develop hypotheses on efficiency variation, economists have made little use of insights from the literature on the internal organization of the firm. This book aims to make a contribution to filling this gap by examining various capabilities which are created and built up inside the firm.

International competitiveness has much to do with the ability to export, and in that process trade surpluses can be generated. However, international competitiveness is much more than simply the ability to export or generate trade surpluses, since these can be achieved temporarily through exchange rate action or the reduction of domestic expenditures. For instance, the greater utilization of capacity permitted by the foreign exchange which has become available with the implementation of SAPs in some countries in Africa may be important in the short run but may not necessarily be a source of sustained growth in TFP. In many African countries SAPs have not resulted in significantly greater capacities to produce exports, let alone the unchanged structure of the export sector. What is not yet clear is the extent to which even this availability of foreign exchange is sustainable. Sustainability would have to rest on greater capacity to earn foreign exchange, rather than more generous donor response in support of SAPs (Pack, 1993).[4]

As the experience of South Korea has shown, although export performance has been the main practical measure of progress towards international competitiveness, it has not been sufficient in itself. There are also various dynamic considerations such as the need to accept reformulations in the light of information gained (market signals, perceptions about industrial operations and potentials) during implementation (Pack and Westphal, 1986).

International competitiveness cannot adequately be explained in terms of low labour costs, especially considering the recent experience of countries such as Germany and Switzerland which are maintaining international competitiveness in spite of their high labour costs. Explanations based on natural resource endowments are put in doubt by the success of resource-poor countries such as South Korea and Japan. Explanations based on the level of productivity alone fail to deal with the problems the US economy is facing in some export markets, in spite of being the world leader in productivity levels.

The widely employed approach to the measurement of competitiveness based on prices, costs and exchange rates is losing ground, following a study by Kaldor (1978)[5] and other studies which show that a drop in relative unit wage costs and in export prices had occurred simultaneously with losses in world export market shares for manufacturing. For the US, this finding was confirmed by the Brookings Institution. Fagerberg (1988)[6] found that the main factors of international competitiveness were technological advancement and the ability to compete on delivery. In spite of these findings, much of government policy is still based on the cost price approach, neglecting these improved understandings of the role of technology, investment and organizational change.

International competitiveness is a multi-dimensional concept embracing the ability to export, the efficient use of resources and increasing productivity which ensures rising living standards for a nation. The international competitiveness of a nation is indicated by its ability to produce goods and services that meet the requirements of international markets under conditions of fair trade while maintaining and raising the real incomes of its citizens. In this context, it has been suggested that competitiveness may be indicated by at least four indicators: labour productivity, real wage growth, real returns on capital, and position in world trade (OECD, 1992a).[7]

International competitiveness is influenced by three factors: the macroeconomic environment, the ability to use and develop technology to reduce costs, improve product quality and generate new products and the ability to market products successfully. The debate on competitiveness implies a role and responsibility for government, not only in ensuring a stable macroeconomic environment but also in influencing technological development and marketing.

International competitiveness can be attained by exerting efforts at various levels: actions taken at firm level, actions and policies adopted at industry level and macroeconomic policies adopted at national level. In his review of recent writings by American authors on the competitiveness issue, Nelson (1992)[8] has recognized these three levels and classified the literature in three clusters: authors who take firms as competitors and focus on factors that are internal to firms, authors who focus on the macroeconomic policy variables, and the cluster of authors who focus on active industrial policy by governments. Nelson has rightly viewed these three clusters of literature on competitiveness as complementary. While detailed comparative studies of firms have demonstrated that many American firms can do a lot on their own to become more competitive, they have found strong similarities among firms in the same country and inter-country differences regarding the structure, behaviour and performance of firms. This points to the importance of the environment (industrial policy and macroeconomic policy) in which the firms are operating. The authors who focus on active industrial policy have demonstrated that non-convexities and externalities are present in many industries, especially where technical advance is important. The field of industrial organization has traditionally viewed an industry (its unit of analysis) in terms of the firms that constitute it and its government regulators. However, recent research results make it possible to view industries as systems involving a mix of institutions (e.g. private firms, industry associations and professional societies, public R&D institutions and training institutions) which are in many ways complementary.

Although the approach adopted in this book emphasizes factors that are internal to firms, factors that are external to the firms (at industry or national level) are addressed as important complements.

It may be difficult to obtain adequate data to measure costs or efficiency. Subject to data availability, various proxies could be used to give reasonable indications of the relative and absolute levels of efficiency. The following indicators could be used selectively, according to the availability of data: export performance over time, productivity gains over time (labour productivity, total factor productivity), domestic resource costs and the effective rate of protection. The inadequacy of some of these static measures is well known. For instance, it has been pointed out that the use of domestic resource cost measures (DRCs) to establish the extent of international competitiveness is inadequate. Even if an investment or intervention achieves a low DRC, this does not necessarily mean that the effort will be socially profitable. The present discounted value of producers' surplus after international competitiveness is achieved will need to be compared with the discounted cost of protection (representing foregone consumers' surpluses) and any excess of production cost (e.g. R&D) over the international prices of the protected commodity (Pack, 1993). However, this caution is perhaps superfluous, since such comparisons are not known to have been used to guide major investment decisions in the technologically advanced countries. The difficulty of any attempt to use this criterion would be aggravated by the need to grapple with unquantifiables such as learning effects (including intra- and inter-firm) and many R&D spill-overs. A more serious weakness of DRCs is that high DRCs do not distinguish between the various sources of inefficiency, i.e. between allocative inefficiency (along the isoquant) and technical inefficiency (outside the best-practice isoquant or inside the production frontier). In addition, the DRCs do not reveal the dispersion of TFPs within an industry. Such dispersions indicate the potentials for TFP improvement through the inter-firm diffusion of technology.

Efforts have also been made to identify patterns in the manufacturing and management processes which seem to account for differential performance and competitive gaps and to deduce how the outcome has been influenced by the histories of the firms and how they have been evolving over time. A regionally and/or internationally competitive firm is not only one which has eliminated the competitive gap but also one which has gained some mastery of the key components of its production and exporting activity. In this sense, it will be necessary to try to understand the dynamic features which reflect the presence or absence of continuous struggle to attain excellence. To the extent that this study is investigating an essentially dynamic phenomenon, static criteria such as sales, quality, return on investment or prices of stocks can at best tell only part of the story, since they will not adequately capture the dynamics of firm development of capabilities. If these measures are observed over time they may capture some of the dynamics but they will need to be supplemented by more qualitative measures. Some of these measures are: whether the firm has innovative management, whether it exhibits unique ways of doing business, its degree of flexibility in dealing with changing environments, and whether the management of the firm has a vision.

THE DYNAMICS OF FIRM CAPABILITIES

The firm as a unit of analysis

While recognizing the influence of macroeconomic policy and industrial policy, the premise adopted in this book is that it is primarily firms which compete and continue to develop the capability to remain competitive. Such firms achieve their competitiveness in a broader macroeconomic and sectoral policy context. Therefore the objective, to understand how firms have been developing their capabilities to survive and compete in export markets, is pursued within a broader macro and sectoral policy context.

In a study of this kind it is important to be cautious and to avoid taking it for granted that success of a few firms necessarily leads to success for an economy. In this context, this study tries to understand the conditions which influenced the process by which firms accumulated their capabilities to compete, with a view to assessing their sustainability and consistency with other aspects of development such as the development of indigenous skills, infrastructure and technological change in other firms in the same sector or in other sectors. It is important to establish the basis for the achievement that various firms have made over time. The study attempts to make a distinction between firms on the 'high road' to efficiency (based on improved technology, organization and marketing while maintaining or increasing real wages) and those on the 'low road' to efficiency (based on reducing real wages, tax revenues and the reward to other local factors). The guiding hypothesis here is that the sustainability of rising factor rewards will be ensured where the capacity to generate and appropriate technology rents is developed on a continuous basis.

The focus of the study is at firm level. It examines the internal and external influences on the process of acquiring and building technological and other capabilities of firms as seen from the standpoint of firms.

Studying firm-level capabilities: three components

In studying the dynamics of firm-level capabilities, attention has been given to three main components:

1 Firm histories are examined with a view to getting insights into the process through which firms have been acquiring (or losing) their competitiveness over time.

2 The present strategies and core capabilities of the firms are addressed, and also how they are being created and maintained (or lost) over time.

3 Developments in technology and world market conditions which are deemed relevant to the selected industries are addressed.

Firm histories

Firm histories are expected to shed light on the path the firms have followed over time and the historical conditions which have influenced that path towards (or away from) regional and/or international competitiveness. An attempt was made to form a picture of the evolution over time of factors such as the firm's ownership structure, technological processes, quality of production, export efforts, strategics and human resource development efforts, along with more easily quantified indicators such as size (in terms of workforce size, sales, total assets or investment), production, inputs and output mix and unit cost. The linkages between the firm and other firms and institutions were also considered. This could include, for instance, subcontracting relationships, demand conditions and types of markets, the industry structure, links with suppliers of equipment and inputs and with the providers of technical services and other services, infrastructure and government policies and regulations (macro, sectoral or specific).

Present strategies, core capabilities and levels of competitiveness

The current state of firm strategies and core capabilities were investigated and efforts have been made to identify the forces and influences which are impinging on the following: the formulation and reformulation of the strategies, the process of creating and sustaining their core capabilities, relationships with customers and competitors, linkages to supportive industries, physical configuration of the manufacturing and management process, core procedures and systems or routines and coordination of product and process design, adaptations and improvements, and related innovations.

Firm strategies consist of motivations, scope, time horizon and target segments. The following strategies have been included: investment strategies, production strategies, marketing strategies, innovation strategies (imitation, adaptations, technology search locally and in other countries, product development, internal and external linkages) and human resource development strategies. First, an attempt has been made to identify each firm's intended position. Second, the means of pursuing or implementing those intentions has been identified. Such means may include decisions to specialize or diversify, nature of product offerings, types of competitive strengths and how these are employed to compete with others in the industry and the role of technological change. In order to understand better the process of implementation, management control processes are examined. The following aspects have been addressed:

- whether standards are set.
- how performance is measured.
- how actual performance compares to the standards set.
- how decisions on corrective action and feedback are made.

Core capabilities have been categorized in terms of investment, production, organization, searching for new courses of action, marketing and linkages. Each of these will be discussed later. However, in recent years it has increasingly been realized that technological capabilities, in development and innovation, are a major determinant of international competitiveness.

Enos (1991)[9] has defined technological capability as something that enables a developing country to exploit existing techniques fully and, ideally, to improve upon those that are not perfectly suited to the country involved. He identified three components of technological capability: the individual constituents, their organization and their purpose. Technological capabilities in industry are defined as the information and skills (technical, managerial and institutional) that allow productive enterprises to utilize equipment and technology efficiently (Lall *et al.*, 1993). Technological development is the process of building up such capabilities (Lall *et al.*, 1993). Factors influencing industrial technology development are divided into three groups: the incentive framework (the demand side, largely originating from the macroeconomic environment and conditions in the major markets, such as their growth prospects), the supply factors (skills, finance, information), and institutions (the organizations set up to support the functioning of the supply factors). The process of technological development is evolutionary, involving conscious and purposeful efforts in buying some inputs from the market and providing others in-house, depending on factors such as technology, market conditions and firm strategies. In developing technological capabilities, firms also operate in a network of formal and informal relationships with suppliers, customers, competitors, consultants and various S&T (science and technology) institutions.

Technological capability may be an input into other economic activities (links formed on the input side representing the creation of technological capabilities) or an output representing the contribution it can make to the rest of the economy (Enos, 1991). Technological capability augments the firm's competitiveness in export markets in two ways: by enabling the firm to utilize the current stock of its resources more effectively or efficiently and by permitting a firm to advance more rapidly its mastery of technology. This book is concerned with the build-up of technological capabilities, possibly along with other types of capabilities (e.g. marketing, organizational), as a major contribution to improving the international competitiveness of exporting firms.

As was said above, core capabilities have been categorized into those relating to investment, production, organization, marketing and searching for new courses of action, marketing and linkages. The state of human resource development is a factor in all of these activities, in terms of types and levels of skills, recruitment policies and approaches to upgrading skills (extent and organization of in-house training, training outside the firm in local institutions and abroad), labour relations, remuneration policies and practice (absolute and relative to competitors or other sectors) and quality of working conditions.

Investment capability

The capacity to make investments includes the capacity to undertake project activities such as: project identification, feasibility studies (marketing, technical, management and financial studies), preparation, design, setting up and commissioning and the financial management and mobilization of resources (short-term and long-term finance, managerial and technical skills, technology, foreign exchange).

Production capabilities

The capacity to carry out and manage production activities consists of plant and equipment, plus human resource capabilities in production management (planning, scheduling and work procedures, execution of orders), production engineering (raw material control and material use standards, standard production times, quality control) and repair and maintenance. Access to various critical resources was examined (short-term and long-term finance, managerial and technical skills, technology, foreign exchange).

Organizational capabilities

Organization capabilities consist of capabilities to relate and coordinate all necessary functions with a view to utilizing effectively various existing capacities in the firm or outside the firm. The following capabilities have been examined: general management capabilities (sharing responsibilities for each key area, long-term direction and cohesion, definition and clarity of policies and procedures and whether they are adhered to and reviewed for effectiveness, measurement and analysis of performance, information flow and its utilization in decision-making, awareness of external factors and other linkages impinging on the firm, overall assessment of the quality of management), management of technology, division of labour, mobilization of resources and capabilities to cope with new situations.

At the level of administration and marketing, the degree and pattern of introduction of new technologies over time was studied: office work (word processing, filing, mailing), accounts (payroll, accounting), information (acquisition, storage, manipulation and distribution) and the management of the marketing function (e.g. records of clients, analysis of market trends).

Innovation capabilities

Innovation capabilities consist of search capabilities and the capacity to integrate the results of such searches. Search capabilities are those required to find new ways of carrying out the firm's investment, production, marketing and organizational activities. The search for new routines is likely to be reflected in efforts to create new patterns of human resource development (through training in-house or outside the firm), in R&D (formal and informal), in searches for technological information from local and foreign sources and in technological adaptations and market research (study of market trends and potential markets and of the possibilities of introducing new products).

In response to changing market conditions and technological developments in their industry, firms are expected to introduce changes to their products (product mix, specifications and quality) and their production process (intensity of use of the various factors of production and technology requirements, e.g. flexibility, standardization, automation, computerization). This may also involve the introduction of new technologies and other new ways of carrying out production, marketing and administration. For instance, some studies of African industry have indicated that there have been improvements in product quality and changes in product design in response to changes in market demand and tastes (e.g. Ndlela *et al.*, 1990; Amdi (n.d.); both as cited in Herbert-Copley, 1992).[10] The extent to which this has happened has been of interest for this study.

The degree and pattern of the introduction of new technologies in the various manufacturing activities, such as design, control, storage, inventory, measurement and testing, have been examined.

Marketing capabilities

Marketing capabilities have been examined in the context of domestic and export markets with emphasis on the latter. The following aspects have been covered: the ability to maintain market shares as changes in technology and demand take place, the ability to collect and analyse relevant market information, product policies (introducing new products and abandoning unprofitable ones), price policies, distribution policies, product promotion policies, efficiency of the sales force and related incentives.

Linkage capabilities

Linkage capabilities consist of linkages which are supportive to, or influence the development and utilization of, a firm's internal capabilities. The following linkages have been considered: purchasing of complementary capabilities from consulting firms; licensing, management or marketing agreements; joint ventures; linkages with other institutions providing technical services; interactions with factor market conditions and with prevailing demand conditions (aggregate demand, export demand, the structure of demand and the link with customers); interaction with local and foreign competitors; government policy (macro and sectoral policies) and regulations (whether supportive or obstructive); linkages with various input suppliers (e.g. subcontracting relations, links with local and foreign technology suppliers); interactions with domestic and international finance institutions; and any other incentive structures which influence the firm's search for new opportunities.

Developments in technology and world market conditions

Studying this component of firm-level capabilities has entailed identification of the state of the art, recent trends and prospects relating to technological and world market conditions which impinge on the industries covered in the study.

GUIDING QUESTIONS OF THE STUDY

The guiding questions of the study are as follows:

1 What factors and processes have influenced the path various firms have followed in attaining or losing regional and/or international competitiveness?
2 How have exporting firms been coping (or failing to cope) with changing technological and market conditions?
3 What lessons and policy implications can be drawn out from insights gained about the process by which exporting firms have been maintaining (or losing) their position in export markets?

THE CASE STUDY APPROACH

The case study approach can be applied to at least three different situations in evaluation research: to explain the causal links in real-life interventions that are too complex for other research strategies, to describe the real-life context in which an intervention has occurred or for illustrative purposes, and to explore those situations where a single set of outcomes is not clear (Yin, 1984).[11] This approach is particularly important when starting a new line of research and developing categories. In the process, new perspectives can be generated (Reid, 1987).[12] Case studies are the preferred approach when 'how' and 'why' questions are being posed, when the investigator has very little control over events and when the focus is on a contemporary phenomenon within its real-life context (Yin, 1984).

Studies of industrialization or trade in Africa have not paid much attention to the firm-level activities and processes which influence the path the various firms have followed and how they have been coping in changing world technological and market conditions. Thus this book seeks to examine an area in which standardized propositions and factors have not yet been identified, at least in the African context. For this reason, a case study approach has been adopted, relying principally on semi-structured interviews. With the aid of an interview guide (Chapter 13), intensive discussions were held with people who were deemed knowledgeable in the respective firms.

The case study approach has some limitations when it comes to making generalizations. Usually, case studies are generalizable to theoretical propositions rather than to populations or universes. Unlike survey research, which relies on statistical generalization, the case study approach relies on analytical generalization, in which the investigator is striving to generalize from a particular set of results to some broader theory (Yin, 1984). As has been indicated in Chapter 2, the evolutionary theory of economic and technological change has been adopted as the general theory guiding this study. The questions of the study are posed in that perspective. Generalizations from the case studies will necessarily be made with caution, realizing that the researcher is making generalizations on the basis of cases which have been selectively sampled and that inferences are being drawn from a weak or non-representative sample of cases. However, in this case we are more interested in gaining insights into the process than in producing statistically significant outcomes.

Two precautions have been taken to reduce the risks entailed in the case study approach. First, the researchers who did the country studies have track records in doing various studies on the manufacturing sectors of their respective countries. Second, taking advantage of the unique ability of the case study approach to handle a variety of evidence, the information obtained in interviews has been complemented by information from official and unofficial documents and by follow-up interviews by the principal researcher to obtain the necessary clarifications. In addition, a workshop was held in May 1993 in which selected industrialists, policy-makers, researchers and international experts in the field reviewed first drafts, and comments arising from discussions at the workshop have been incorporated in the final drafts.

In the case of Africa, the poor performance of manufactured exports may suggest that success in exporting is more of an outlier result than an average or typical situation. Even if these firms may be outliers, the approach taken in this study is that it is also important to remember that outliers can be particularly informative. As has been suggested elsewhere, information about why firms fail or achieve unusual success is more likely to come from firms at the margins than from average firms (Reid, 1987).

SAMPLING: FIRMS, INDUSTRIES AND COUNTRIES

Sample firms

Two main categories of firms were studied: those which are currently exporting manufactured products to regional and/or to international markets and firms which used to export manufactures but are being, or have already been, squeezed out of export markets.

One would expect that firms in the first category would have developed relevant core capabilities over time and that these capabilities would have been developed in response to competitive pressures from the market. The firms are also expected to be organized in such a way that they can cope with changing technological and market conditions. In addition, the linkages they have with other industries and institutions are expected to be supportive. The extent to which they are striving to sustain their international competitiveness was assessed, and the strategies they are employing to cope with the changing demands of the international market were identified, in order to gain further insights into the process by which those firms are creating and developing the necessary core capabilities. An understanding of supportive or restrictive interactions with external institutions has also been sought. Firms in this category may have acquired their success in exporting in one of two ways: by attaining international competitiveness at par with other world-class firms elsewhere, or by engaging in highly idiosyncratic exports and adapting to specific recipient environments.[13]

The second category of firms have been (or are gradually being) out-competed by other exporters. As was noted in Chapter 2, what happens when a mature industry encounters a new technology depends on whether the new technology requires changes in the core capabilities of specific firms and whether they are able to make the required changes in management and strategy. Firms in this category were expected to have failed as exporters largely because they had not managed to adjust their core capabilities to new technological and market conditions. This study addresses these processes with a view to gaining insights into the factors which have influenced their withdrawal from the race for the export market. Such factors may be domestic (e.g. developments in the domestic market, weakening of the core capabilities of the firms, or failure to cope with the growing capabilities of competitors in the world market, thus allowing the competitive gap to widen, or restrictive interactions between the firms and other government and/or non-government institutions) or they may be external (technological changes, marketing strategies and changing demands in the international markets).

The sampled firms are currently exporting manufactured products, whether to regional or international markets. Some 55 firms in 7 industries were studied: 20 in textiles and clothing, 11 in food and beverages, 4 in leather and footwear, 2 in paper and paper products, 5 in chemicals and pharmaceuticals, 3 in non-metallic mineral products and 10 in metal industries. The sample consisted of 4 small enterprises (with fewer than 50 persons engaged), 31 medium-sized enterprises (50–1 000 persons) and 20 large enterprises (over 1 000 persons). The ownership structures include public and private, and local and foreign, enterprises. The sample included 6 public enterprises, 19 local private enterprises, 9 foreign-owned enterprises and 21 joint ventures between local and foreign capital.

Sample industries

The industries studied were those which have been exporting. In each country the best export performers were included and, to facilitate inter-country comparison, the textiles and clothing industry was studied in all countries.

Sample countries

Research was carried out in a sample of six countries which are broadly representative of African countries in terms of level of development of industry and exports. The countries selected were as follows:

1 Zimbabwe: a country with one of the most diversified industrial sectors and a number of successful exporting firms. It is the most advanced in terms of technological capabilities and industrialization in Southern Africa, except for South Africa.
2 Tanzania: a country which, in its initial development, was peripheral to Kenya but which later strove to develop an industrial

sector and manufacturing exports. It faced decline in many sectors in the late 1970s and 1980s. Since the mid-1980s Tanzania has been making attempts to implement economic policy reforms and to restructure inefficient industries.

3 Nigeria: the most industrialized country in West Africa and one having the largest internal market in Sub-Saharan Africa. Nigeria is not only a large economy (by African standards), it also benefited from the oil boom in the 1970s (although that was followed by economic problems in the 1980s).

4 Kenya: the most advanced country in industrialization, industrial exports and the development of technological capabilities in East Africa.

5 The Ivory Coast: the most advanced country in industrialization and the export of manufactured products in Francophone West Africa.

6 Mauritius: a country which seems to have made considerable strides from a basically mono-crop economy in the 1960s to a diversified economy in the 1980s. Mauritius has developed its industrial sector, and in particular manufactured exports, at a faster pace than other African economies, a kind of development that is comparable to that of some lower-tier Asian NICs.

IMPLEMENTATION OF THE STUDY

Researchers in these countries were commissioned to perform the country studies. The researchers selected were known to have done substantial previous research on issues relating to industrialization and manufactured exports in those countries. In order to include international information on the changing technological and world market conditions, data on these aspects was collected, mainly in Europe. The following were the major sources of information:

- OECD industry studies
- UNIDO industry studies on Africa and technological developments in selected industries
- from the International Trade Centre in Geneva, data on trade, especially data from case studies of exporting industries and export promotion policies
- selected TNCs in Europe (e.g. Unilever) which have exporting subsidiaries in Africa
- associations of industrialists in Europe

- selected European importers of manufactured products from Africa
- UNCTAD, for trade statistics and trade-related studies
- the EU in Brussels, for information on joint ventures between EU-based companies and exporting companies in Africa.

4 The changing world economy
Market conditions and technological developments

The world economy is undergoing change in technological and market conditions which could influence the position of Africa and the role it may play in the world market. The challenge for Africa is to understand these changes as a basis for developing the ability to respond constructively and positively. This chapter addresses some of the technological and world market conditions that are likely to influence the ability of exporters to attain and maintain their position in the world markets.

CHANGING MARKET CONDITIONS

The business environment in which exporting firms must be prepared to operate is characterized by unprecedented opportunities to tap new markets, while competition in traditional markets is increasing dramatically from both traditional adversaries and new entrants and because of the evaporation of barriers to previously protected markets. With competition arising from diverse and unexpected sources, enterprises can no longer be confident about their market shares: they must constantly innovate to compete. In this new business environment the following key drivers have been gaining in importance: a focus on improving the productivity of knowledge and service workers (rather than industrial productivity), with productivity programmes shifting from cutting costs to improving organizational performance and effectiveness; a focus on quality in both products and service, with quality programmes moving from manufacturing operations to knowledge and service operations and firms building a corporate culture around quality;[1] the challenge of responsiveness, with a rising need to react rapidly to changing market conditions, competition and customer demands; the globalization of markets, operations and competition; an interest in out-sourcing certain aspects of production, distribution, sales service and support functions, resulting in a shift of enterprise focus to vertical and horizontal integration across organizations; partnering, to function on global markets by establishing alliances and joint ventures with other key players in both similar and disparate markets;[2] and greater attention to social and environmental responsibility (Tapscott and Caston, 1993; Mytelka, 1991).[3]

Overall, the trend suggests that the changing market conditions now require firms to meet more refined and personalized customer tastes, as well as society's collective needs, as expressed through a wide range of democratic and associative mechanisms (OECD, 1992b).[4] Interaction between producers and these more demanding and better informed customers is an essential factor for growth and competitiveness.

Changes in market conditions for such traditional products as textiles, clothing and footwear can be used here to make the point. The changes that have occurred in price and income elasticities of demand across products and income groups have produced a pattern of market segmentation (Mytelka, 1991). For instance, sportswear is increasingly worn in non-sport settings, leading to increasing price competition between sports speciality shops and general clothing retailers. In addition, the market has been highly influenced by developments in textile technologies (e.g. new manufacturing yarns and synthetic fibres such as Tactel, Gortex and Sympatex) and changes in fashion (CBI, 1991b).[5]

In the case of household and furnishing textiles, the traditional preference for white bed and bath linen has given way to an immense variety of colours, prints and patterns. The market has become more conscious of quality and variety, though trends are not as short-lived as those in apparel. Consumers are conscious of price, durability and fibre mixtures as well as design, colours, weight, ease of handling and product safety. The most important developments in bedroom linen have been the introduction of the fitted sheet, non-iron sheets and the eiderdown (also referred to as a duvet or quilt) together with quilt covers. In table linen the most important developments have been a decline in the daily use of tablecloths and an increase in attractive kitchen items. There is a trend away from very cheap tablecloths and towards higher-quality printed and embroidered cloths (CBI, 1991a).[6]

In the case of footwear, the European footwear importer supplies specifications, models and considerable assistance in technical know-how and quality control to the contract producer. The main suppliers are now the cheap and efficient sources in the Far East. New suppliers will have to offer the same level of competitiveness in terms of price, workmanship and timeliness (CBI, 1990).[7] Markets are becoming more segmented, with quality and timely delivery becoming important factors in competitiveness. Globally spread production networks are developing, especially in sport shoes. African countries may only be able to enter such markets by tying themselves to major names such as Adidas and meeting their requirements for production at consistent high quality (UNIDO, 1992a).[8]

THE CHANGING PROSPECTS OF ACCESS TO WORLD MARKETS

Among the external constraints on the adjustment process, access to markets and to technology could be most difficult. Protectionism is on the rise. In fact, the two principal markets for developing country clothing exports, the US and EU, have steadily increased their degree of domestic protection, mainly in the form of orderly marketing arrangements (OMAs) and voluntary export restraints (VERs). The Multifibre Agreement (MFA) has contributed to limiting opportunities for new market entrants, in particular those from developing countries (Mytelka, 1991). As the MFA became more restrictive in the 1980s, some large firms in the NICs relocated production to make use of quotas available in the less developed countries. Negotiations to relax the restrictive clauses under the MFA have not yielded fruitful results so far. With the rising regional trading blocs in the developed countries there are indications that access prospects may not improve.

Patterns of trade have been changing in favour of North–North trade so much that many recent trade theories have focused on such trade. There has been a relatively steady growth in manu-facturing exports, leading to high levels of trade between countries with similar factor endowments. Three quarters of all exports from the developed countries went to other developed countries. By 1989 only one third of developing country trade went to other developing countries (Yoffie, 1993). There are several emerging trends which suggest that this pattern is likely to be reinforced.

There is a tendency to form larger trading groups of Northern countries, a development which is likely to bring benefits of guar-anteed access to larger markets for members but with the likelihood that many poor non-members, including African exporters, will suffer from loss of access. At the same time, there is a risk that trade wars could undermine the global benefits from multilateral trade. US support for free world trade after World War II seems to have been motivated by foreign policy concerns and by the relative international competitiveness of the US economy at that time. As the foreign policy concerns have changed and the international competitiveness of the US has declined relative to Japan, support in the US for world free trade seems to be on the decline and interest in regionalism on the increase. Bhagwati (1991)[9] sees the advocacy of managed trade, and aggressive unilateralism and regionalism, as threats to GATT principles. One factor reinforcing the tendency to unfair trade is the 'diminished giant syndrome', because of the relative decline of the US within the world economy. Britain was in a similar situation at the end of the nineteenth century, as compared to the US and Germany. The other factors are the increasing criss-crossing of foreign investments, flexible exchange rates, the outbreak of protectionism in the 1980s, the increased focus on non-tariff barriers, and developments in the realms of ideas and ideology (e.g. the recognition of the irreversible gains in efficiency and competitiveness arising from learning). Bhagwati has warned that the extension of GATT rules to other areas (e.g. trade in services) may be opening up a Pandora's box and may diminish the possibility of agreeing to a rules-oriented trading system.

These developments suggest a strong case for introducing safeguards and disciplines in GATT to protect the multilateral world trading system from possibilities of damage from regional agreements. Under these conditions, the challenge seems to be whether a continuous search for new markets and market niches can be launched and sustained over time. This will have implications for the development of marketing capabilities in-house and/or appropriate linkages.

EU trade policies are essentially discriminatory against imports from the South. Even under the GSP (General System of Preferences) and Lomé Convention arrangements, the relief offered is subject to unilateral termination by the EU on grounds of 'graduation'. The EU is advocating selectivity in the application of safeguards (i.e. temporary import barriers imposed in order to protect domestic industries at risk) and is demanding that the South provides protection for intellectual property owned by nationals or companies of its member states. The question of access is particularly important for exports of manufactures. Recent intensification of protectionism in the North has subjected the South's manufactured exports to discriminatory restrictions precisely in those areas where the South has a comparative advantage. These restrictions take several forms: explicit departures from GATT (e.g. the MFA concerning textiles and clothing), VERs and OMAs.

There are further indications that the prospects of uninhibited entry of industrial products from the South to the EU are limited. One such indication is in the development and direction of R&D support. Subsidizing R&D is the core of EU industrial policy in the 1990s, as industrial policy shifts from sectoral subsidies to functional subsidies. These are used to encourage and promote the innovative capacity of firms (UNIDO, 1992a). Many EU R&D programmes are designed to improve manufacturing in traditional fields in which EU industry might otherwise lose its competitive edge (textiles and clothing, steel, and new materials such as artificial fibres which bridge the traditional separation of textile and chemical industries).

Although the Lomé Convention continues to favour African products' access to the EU market, there are reasons not to be too optimistic about this favour. First, the experience of Asian countries has shown that as soon as developing countries' progress in industry begins to threaten EU industries, quotas are often revised to limit previously favourable market access. Some of Africa's preferential provisions have been diluted in the Uruguay Round of the GATT negotiations. Second, rules of origin are likely to complicate South–South cooperation between Africa and the more advanced developing countries. Africa's favourable position in terms of access to the EU market partly derives from MFA restrictions on Asian exporters. This may induce Asian producers to relocate to Africa, as has already been occurring in Mauritius and Nigeria, as the country case studies have shown. Rules of origin, however, are likely to limit this trend as soon as it grows to a scale which threatens EU industries. Third, although this is often denied, there are indications that the former socialist countries of Eastern Europe will compete with Africa in the European scene as regards trade relations and other economic cooperation arrangements. The long-term success of the Lomé Convention as it relates to Africa should be evaluated in the light of the extent to which it has helped Africa to improve international competitiveness and change the structure of trade. It seems that, seen in these terms, it is unlikely much progress has been made.

In the Uruguay Round negotiations, there is a notable absence of agreement on specific commitments in the area of market access (UNCTAD, 1993a). The weaker trading partners have an interest in clear international disciplines to provide security of market access and to shield them from bilateral pressure from major trading powers. But the main question here is whether the market access commitments will provide improved access to markets in products of interest to Africa. It is therefore not surprising that the phasing out of the MFA, which has for years operated as a discriminatory instrument against the export interests of many developing countries, and the integration of trade in textiles and clothing in the GATT have been among the most difficult negotiations in the Uruguay Round. The outcome of the negotiations is that these sectors are to be integrated into the GATT over a 10-year period, with each party free to select specific products to be integrated at each of the four phases. Although there is provision for special treatment for the least developed countries, no specific differential or more favourable treatment has been accorded to them in the integration process. Since more advanced developing countries have moved into more sophisticated products, leaving exports of the simpler textile and clothing products to newcomers, and since the EU has been able to increase its exports of these products to developing countries, it has been suggested that a more liberal MFA would not cause much harm to producers in the industrial world (Waelbroeck and Kol, 1987).[10] The EU does not seem quite convinced that their industries in these areas are not threatened. This explains why the MFA is to be phased out over a 10-year period. Considering that the MFA was first introduced in 1974 as a temporary measure to allow time for the developed countries to adjust to the threat of competitive imports from developing countries, it has been quite long-lived. The EU is now supporting R&D investments in these industries, among others, hoping that at the end of the 10 years the threat will have been averted through technological developments.

The Uruguay Round agreement on safeguards provides for the preservation of the non-discrimination rule and the prohibition and elimination of 'grey area' measures (e.g. VERs, OMAs). There are also provisions for reducing arbitrariness in the application of anti-dumping duties. The agreement contains more defined rules and disciplines for subsidies and improved provisions on countervailing measures.

Multilateral disciplines have been extended in two areas: trade in services (GATS) and trade-related intellectual property rights (TRIPS). The GATS agreement establishes the unconditional most favoured nation (MFN) clause as the fundamental principle of agreement and provides for increased participation of developing countries in world trade in services. The TRIPS agreement involves an international upward harmonization of standards of intellectual property protection (IPP) for all countries, irrespective of their level of development. It includes the obligation to comply with the substantive provisions of the Stockholm Act of the Paris Convention.

The South Commission Report argues that applying the rules traditionally applied to trade in goods to trade in services could undermine the ability of the South to regulate and promote its services industries. Recent advances in information and communications technologies have added a new dimension to the role of services in the development process. The new producer or business services, such as the computerization of inventory control or quality control, have a profound impact on the competitiveness of a wide range of economic processes and products. In the longer term, the report argues, an excessive dependence on imported services could seriously weaken the development process to the extent that an underdeveloped domestic services sector would imply weak links between the producers and users of services. This situation is not conducive to innovation, the absorption and assimilation of new technological changes, or to benefiting from learning by doing. The thrust of this caution is supportable under African conditions, provided that lessons can be drawn from previous instances of the perpetual protection of inefficient infant activities, which never grew to maturity. Protection must be more selective and less pervasive than in the past and should be accompanied by promotional policies for the development of key service activities.

Knowledge is increasingly being privatized, and the South is being excluded. Many countries in the South find themselves increasingly unable to predict, let alone to regulate, technology flows (South Commission, 1990, p. 219).[11] The report observed that considerable progress towards facilitating the South's access to technology was made in the 1970s, with the Code of Conduct and intellectual property, so that by the early 1980s only two important matters remained to be settled in UNCTAD's code of conduct: the clause governing restrictive practices and the provision concerning applicable law and dispute settlement. The report points out that before mutual concessions by North and South on these two points could be made, further negotiations were blocked by the North and the revision of the Paris Convention was stalled for several years. The North has since used the recent acceleration of technological advances to press for a reversal of earlier negotiations (p. 254). In spite of the threatened reversal of earlier achievements, the report suggests that what is required is an international framework to regulate the activities of TNCs in developing countries, starting with the introduction of a code of conduct for TNCs.

The negotiations in the Uruguay Round have moved in the direction of greater liberalization of investments (under trade-related investment measures (TRIMS)) and greater protection of intellectual property rights. TRIMS has the effect of liberalizing investments by reducing requirements for the entry and operation of foreign firms, while TRIPS will enable investors in technology and innovating firms to capture profits from their innovations. It is feared that TRIPS is likely to reduce access to new technologies. However, since the acquisition of technology requires effort in the form of tangible and intangible investments, Africa will need to tilt the balance of the debate in favour of the design of policies which would facilitate the transfer of technology through various forms of learning, especially by African firms. The process by which firms in African countries build up and accumulate skills and acquire technological capabilities through inter-firm networks and cooperation arrangements needs to be understood better, especially in terms of the kinds of technological efforts and investments which African governments and firms need to make. Having made such technological efforts and investments in technology, obstacles to increasing international competitiveness may begin to emerge. These obstacles may or may not include those relating to the code of conduct. On that basis, the thrust of the negotiations would shift towards those practices which inhibit the process of technological learning and the accumulation of the capabilities which are required for international competitiveness.

There are indications that developing countries have made major concessions in terms of their freedom to act in trade in goods and services and of their technological and social development policies in relation to technological transfer and TRIPS (UNCTAD, 1993a). The agreement on a World Trade Organization (WTO) provides that all agreements emerging from the Uruguay Round are to be incorporated into a single legal instrument and accepted by all contracting parties. The experience of Africa and its relationship with other multilateral institutions suggests that there is a possibility that the WTO could be used to discipline the weaker players while being powerless to discipline stronger players in the game of trade. The coordination of WTO activities with those of the World Bank and IMF could also result in strong cross-institutional conditionality (Peng, 1993/4).[12]

NEW TECHNOLOGIES AND THE IMPLICATIONS OF CHANGING TECHNOLOGICAL CONDITIONS

Technological change in the developed countries has important implications for the competitiveness of manufactured exports in Africa. The policy implications of the changing technological conditions are likely to surface at two levels: a focus on monitoring new and emerging technologies with a view to making policy decisions relating to adopting and learning the new technologies at the right time, and an examination of the internal evolution of technological and demand condition.

Developments in some new technologies

During the past decade the greatest technological progress has been made in information technology (microelectronics and micro-photonics), space technologies, new materials, nuclear energy, biotechnology, and pharmaceuticals and fine chemicals (Salam, 1992).[13] Technological change can boost the growth of some industries (and even revitalize declining industries) and cause decline in others. New industries may emerge and old ones may disappear.

Recent technological developments have led to shifts in the composition of factors of production, with a considerable decline in the importance of raw materials, energy and labour inputs and an increase in knowledge intensity. Material-saving innovations have led to a decline in the consumption of natural materials and their replacement by new and advanced materials (especially engineering ceramics and polymers, composites, semi-conductors, opto-electronic materials and amorphous alloys). In addition to replacing natural materials, the advanced materials also improve strength and quality, add flexibility and cut weight. In world trade there has been an increase in the share of manufactured products and in particular high-tech products.

Technological change can result in the redefinition of industry boundaries. Where key factors of success are capable of being shared, the limits between businesses (industries) tend to be blurred (e.g. computers, telecommunications and office automation) (Dussauge *et al.*, 1992).[14] Where technological change leads to a reduction in the sharing of the costs of key resources, the result may be de-segmentation of the industry into smaller units. The distinction between manufacturing and services sectors is being blurred by their growing interconnectedness. The competitiveness of manufacturing firms now depends crucially on the quality of their interactions with the services sector, notably business services (which collect, treat and supply specialized information) and key infrastructural services (OECD, 1992a).

In reality, the pattern of manufacturing industry in the highly industrialized countries has changed considerably as services take the lead, with new skill-and-capital intensive services such as informatics gaining ground. This makes Engels' elasticities more difficult to predict and the growth of many traditional capital goods industries has slowed (e.g. construction materials, electrical machinery industries, general engineering, machine tools, iron and steel industries) (Bagchi, 1987).[15]

The most economically significant of the new technologies, in terms of the range of new products, cost savings, quality improvements and sectors of application, is information technology, followed by new materials and biotechnology (Salam, 1992). The discussion here is confined to information technology as it has been most pervasive and has the greatest economic significance.

The new paradigm in information technology (IT) is characterized by profound changes in the business application of computers, in the nature of the technology itself and in leadership in the use of technology. Tapscott and Caston (1993) have identified several shifts that are revolutionizing IT: a shift from traditional semi-conductors to microprocessor-based systems; from host-based to network-based systems[16] which allow users to access a wide range of data, applications and computing resources; from proprietary software to open software standards, which allow information to be transferred and software to be run on hardware of any size or brand; from single media to multimedia, enabling computerized documents to be exchanged containing data, text, voice and images; from account control to computer-assisted vendor–customer partnerships based on free will, with vendors now seeking partnerships with their customers based on customer choice; from craft to factory-based software development, with software developers using and reusing standardized and interchangeable modules;[17] from alphanumeric forms to a multiform graphical user interface (GUI) with icons on the screen which can be manipulated using a mouse or by touching the screen; and a shift from stand-alone to integrated software applications, with modular software built to standards that make the programs more interchangeable and integrative.

Tapscott and Caston (1993) have noted that as hardware becomes a commodity, the software proportion will continue to grow. Software, rather than hardware, is where business value is added, so software is the differentiator of competitive advantage. Software production is manufacturing with a difference: it still requires a high degree of creativity to fabricate both individual parts and broader systems. There is a growing argument for computer-aided software engineering (CASE), which enables developers to apply software engineering principles, methods, techniques and concepts such as parallel processing, object orientation and reusable code more easily.

Changes in IT use have involved a shift from stand-alone equipment and applications to computer-based networking and new information services. Telecommunications are used to connect IT equipment in the office to equipment on the factory floor. This shift is a response to changes in market conditions. Changing market demands have to be adjusted to more quickly, and just-in-time deliveries and more customized products and services impose their own requirements. The rapid feedback and response which IT permits may spur innovation processes in terms of product and/or service improvements, including improvements in R&D itself (OECD, 1992b).

The application and impact of IT have even permeated many traditional industries (e.g. textiles and clothing), where the need to improve competitiveness has led to the internalization of production and rapid increases in the knowledge-intensiveness of production. This makes the adoption of new technologies a necessary investment in competitiveness. The rapid changes in technology and globalization favour flexibility and innovativeness in the adjustment process. Low labour costs are less effective as a basis of competitiveness, while low educational levels are not conducive to the adoption of new technologies.

Clothing and textiles

Mody and Wheeler (1990)[18] found that clothing and textiles producers in the NICs are facing competition from the exports of the newly invigorated economies of Asia, e.g. China, India, Indonesia, based on low wages. Along with this increase in wage-based competition, sophisticated microelectronics-based systems for clothing and textile production are emerging in the OECD economies. Robotics, in this scenario, is a critical infant industry, with protection of the textiles market expected to give enough time and investible surplus for the OECD manufacturers to consolidate and restructure for automated production. It is hoped that 10 years of phasing out the MFA, as agreed in the Uruguay Round, will provide ample time for this infant industry to mature (Mody and Wheeler, 1990).

However, semi-automated technology is now viable for a number of operations, resulting in very low wage costs. The advantages of using advanced technologies are most likely to be reflected in shortening the production cycle, thus saving time and working capital and improving the ability to respond to customer demand at short notice. Some of the areas which are likely to be relevant for technical progress in clothing are: computer design; automatic cutting; flexible sewing and finishing technology incorporating microprocessors; robotic handling; unit production systems; shop-floor controls; logistics; supplier linkages; retail linkages and merchandise control and implementation.

The textile industry has been characterized by continuous incremental technological changes. The industry produces some final products for the consumer market but its main products are inputs (yarn and cloth) into the clothing industry, which normally imposes product and design choice. This makes engineering design more important than product design in textiles. New raw materials are continuously being introduced to the industry but the basic characteristics of the products do not change dramatically. The introduction of microelectronics to machinery control operations has contributed to productivity increases, improved effectiveness and greater reliability, quality and flexibility. While developments in the textile industry are influenced by technological change, one should not lose sight of the influences of other factors such as changes in global demand and developments in the clothing industry and, in particular, the firm strategies of large clothing enterprises.

The share of developing countries in the global textile export market increased from 18.8 per cent in 1973 to 22.7 per cent in 1982 and 28 per cent in 1988. Exports from developed market economies accounted for 62 per cent of international trade in textiles in 1970, falling to 50 per cent in 1980 and to 39 per cent in 1985. At the same time, exports from developing market economies increased from 21 per cent of world trade in 1970 to 36.5 per cent in 1980 and 50.5 per cent in 1985 (UNIDO, 1990).[19] Within the developing countries, the core of production is moving from the East Asian NICs to the second tier of lower-wage ASEAN countries such as Indonesia, Bangladesh, Sri Lanka, Thailand and the Philippines.

However, there are indications that OECD countries may be regaining competitiveness in some labour-intensive industrial activities in which they had seemed to be losing out to developing countries. For instance, in the textiles and clothing industries, the diffusion of the newest innovations has been greater in spinning and weaving technologies in OECD countries than in developing countries (UNIDO, 1990b).[20] In the late 1980s textile exports from developed countries actually increased more than from developing countries, indicating that a turning point may have been reached following a new technology boost. The case for adopting new technologies is likely to be strengthened further by the fact that profit margins in the textile industry are lower than the manufacturing industry average, implying great pressure to increase efficiency.

Recent technological developments have occurred in overall mill control, the integration of factory departments, improved quality and reliability and increased flexibility in production. The main technological changes in the past 40 years (1950–90) have been automatic bale feeders, aerofeed systems, high-draft spinning, texturizing (with the development of the air-jet method and the false twist method resulting in increases in the speed and quality of yarn), shuttleless looms[21] providing higher speed and better quality and flexibility of the woven fabric, needle-punch machines, transfer printing, rotary screen printing and increasing computer integration in the manufacturing process. The main changes in spinning have occurred in the spinning frame itself, through high-draft spinning and the development of new spinning methods (open-end spinning) which run at much higher spindle speeds. The main effect has been to reduce the number of pre-spinning steps and limit the need for roving. The newer spinning systems have also reduced the trade-off between productivity, product flexibility and quality. For instance, rotor and air-jet spinning can produce a greater number of yarn counts, of good quality and at high speed, suitable for most applications in knitting and weaving.

Rapid diffusion of some of these new technologies in spinning (see Tables 4.1 and 4.2), weaving and dyeing has led to considerable productivity gains in recent years, reducing labour time, energy consumption, materials wastage and throughput time, while improving product quality (Mytelka, 1991).

There is still a relative advantage in labour costs in developing countries, as shown in Table 4.3. However, a country such as Italy

Table 4.1 Main technological developments in various phases of short staple-spinning and their effects on output

Activity/process	Output (pounds/hr) 1969	Output (pounds/hr) 1987	Projected output (pounds/hr) 2 000	% change 1945–69	% change 1969–87
Blender	200	1 320	2 200	0	560
Cards	18	88	154	157	389
Drawings (ft/m)	800	547	874	700	–32
Lapping	500	836	990	233	67
Combing	50	110	132	78	120
Roving (warp)*	1.75	2	2	73	14
Roving (filling)*	1.30	–	–	87	–
Spinning (warp)*	0.036	0.036	0.048	66	0
Spinning (filling)*	0.023	0.036	0.048	51	55

Source: Adapted from UNIDO, 1990b, p. 202

Note: *Pounds/spindle/hour

Table 4.2 Main technological developments in various phases of short staple-spinning and their effects on capital cost per machine

Activity/process	Cost/unit (US$1 000) 1969	Cost/unit (US$1 000) 1987	Projected cost/unit (US$1 000) 2 000	% change 1945–69	% change 1969–87
Blender	4.5	103.4	206.9	228	2 198
Cards	6.0	103.4	172.4	171	1 623
Drawings	3.2	51.7	103.4	–	1 516
Lapping	14.0	124.1	172.4	183	786
Combing	14.5	137.9	172.4	285	851
Roving	26.4	124.1	310.3	212	370
Spinning	21.5	79.5	149.0	340	270

Source: Adapted from UNIDO, 1990b, p. 202

does not have low labour costs, even within the OECD, yet it was the most successful in the OECD both in textile production and exports. This suggests that labour costs do not tell the whole story. The role of technological and organizational factors (including flexible linkages and production chains and contacts with the markets)

Table 4.3 Labour costs in selected countries 1980–90

Country	1980	1990	% change 1980–90
Switzerland	9.65	19.23	99.3
Sweden	10.43	18.70	79.3
Holland	11.68	17.84	52.7
West Germany	10.65	16.46	54.6
Italy	9.12	16.13	76.9
Japan	4.35	13.96	220.9
UK	5.75	10.20	77.4
USA	6.37	10.02	57.3
Spain	4.90	7.69	56.9
Greece	4.03	5.85	45.2
Taiwan	1.26	4.56	261.9
South Korea	0.78	3.22	312.8
Brazil	1.57	1.97	25.5
Turkey	0.95	1.82	91.6
Thailand	0.33	0.92	178.8
Malaysia	–	0.86	–
India	0.60	0.72	20.0
Philippines	0.43	0.67	55.8
Indonesia	0.63	0.25	–60.3
Sri Lanka	0.16	0.24	50.0
Tunisia	1.13	2.82	149.6
South Africa	–	1.57	–
Morocco	0.85	1.28	50.6
Ethiopia	–	0.87	–
Kenya	–	0.63	–
Tanzania	–	0.32	–
Nigeria	–	0.30	–

Source: *Time Horizons*, March 1991

in ensuring flexibility, fast and timely delivery and reliable high quality needs to be appreciated.

The relative labour cost advantage is not sufficient reason to delay the selective adoption of new technologies in low-wage economies. In spite of their relative labour cost advantage, some developing countries (especially the Asian countries) are closing the technological gap with developed countries. One indicator of this process is investment in new machinery. In 1988, Asian countries accounted for 46.3 per cent of world investment, ahead of Western Europe (26.1 per cent) and North America (10.5 per cent). South America (3.4 per cent) and Africa (1.9 per cent) seem to have lagged far behind. More investment occurred in new spinning machinery

(US$2.8 billion) than for weaving (US$2.5 billion), suggesting an emphasis on modernizing yarn making rather than fabric making.

The clothing industry is not very dynamic. Its share of total manufacturing employment in the OECD declined from about 8 per cent in the 1960s to 3–4 per cent in the late 1980s (UNIDO, 1992b).[22] However, clothing has grown relatively strongly in some countries (e.g. France and Italy) until recently. Developing country exports have increased from 30.2 per cent of world clothing exports in 1973 to 42.3 per cent in 1982 and 45.4 per cent in 1988 (GATT, various reports). Clothing production in developing countries rose from 20 per cent of world clothing production in 1970 to 29 per cent in 1985, suggesting greater export orientation in developing countries. The response of the developed countries to the growing import penetration has been twofold: the rise of protectionism, and technological innovations and the use of micro-electronic-based technologies.

The clothing industry is less strongly driven by its production technology than textiles, while product design and market considerations were found to be more important. The industry is more segmented, with very differentiated products (in terms of materials, designs and production requirements) for a variety of markets (Mytelka, 1991; UNIDO, 1992b).

In one segment of the clothing industry (that producing basic products) production cost is the main competitive advantage, while in the fashionable goods segment rapid response is the main focal point of manufacture. A third segment producing high-quality clothing has its competitive advantage in variety.

Intricate formal and informal links are found between retailers, manufacturers, textile merchants, subcontracting units and home-workers. Computer-assisted design (CAD) and electronic data interchange (EDI) are becoming important in developing and retaining these relationships. CAD enables a designer to consider different weaves and colours even before weaving begins, and the possibility of quick response to the market is enhanced. Combining CAD with telecommunication networks can enable the design functions and the labour-intensive core of the clothing industry to be geographically separated. For example, the Mattel Company transmits data on clothing design to Indonesia for manufacture. However, the advantages have to be weighed against the problems of time scales for delivery, the frequency of fashion changes and transport costs.

The main phases of clothing manufacture are: the pre-production stages such as design, pattern making, grading, nesting, marking and cutting; the actual production process such as sewing and assembling the product; and the finishing operations, which consist of inspection, pressing and packaging. While technological change has occurred in all these phases, it is the pre-production activities that have seen the most important technological developments. The major microelectronic improvements have occurred in pre-assembly (design, marking, grading and cutting) and post-assembly (warehouse, distribution and management) stages. In both clothing and textile production, the advanced technologies which were observed by Mody and Wheeler (1990) are reported to be still so costly that they are optimal only in high-labour-cost environments. This finding is welcome for African countries but it is uncertain how long this situation will continue.

Developed countries have applied new technologies and organizational forms to improve flexibility, a benefit that could erode and invalidate the advantage of low wages in the developing countries. The success of the Italian networking fashion clothing companies (e.g. Benetton) is a case in point. Analyses of the costs of the various stages in the clothing industry have shown that flexible automation technology is gaining ground, especially in the pre-assembly stages, where the US now ranks first in competitive advantage in the production of women's high-style printed polyester dresses, displacing Jamaica from first position (Mody and Wheeler, 1990).

The most important technological innovations in the 1970s have been: the use of computers in marketing, inventory control and work-flow management; the use of CAD in grading and marking operations; the use of numerically controlled equipment and computer-aided laser cutting systems, which are faster, are more accurate and reduce material losses; and the use of pre-programmed, dedicated sewing machines in sub-assembly operations.

In pattern making, CAD systems are used to break down a piece of clothing to manageable components more efficiently, although there are still difficulties with tasks where optical and sensory attributes are necessary. The steps to be followed in assembling the various pieces can be defined, and the corresponding production times and costs can be calculated, using computer-based production planning. The similarity of clothing production processes allows for the use of inter-firm production planning services to improve the overall efficiency of the industry (as practised in the US). CAD and computer-assisted manufacturing (CAM) permit almost instantaneous grading for any market-specific size specifications, a task that was once tedious and time-consuming, and reduce material wastage and skilled labour requirements. The cutting process, the most highly skilled activity, underwent considerable innovations in the 1970s, with the introduction of hot wires, plasma streams, water jets and laser beams.

Sewing technology has developed slowly, with the gradual replacement of electro-mechanical systems with electronics. Three basic types of machine control applications have been developed: the dedication of microprocessors and numerical control units to the operations of specialized work stations; the use of pre-programmable convertible multi-task machines; and the use of operator-programmable sewing machines which, once programmed, take over all functions except guiding the material. Technological change in the sewing process has been essentially incremental and concentrated in three features: faster operation, the development of work aids to facilitate material handling and the mechanization of small-parts assembly.

Technological innovations in the finishing phase have been limited to pressing and repairing rejects from the inspection process.

The spread of automation has been found to be slower in small firms. Considering that many clothing firms are small (even in Germany over 50 per cent of all firms employ fewer than 50 persons), labour-intensive and operate with high flexibility in the design-based segments of the industry, the spread of new technologies is not expected to be very rapid. In Germany, for instance, only 6 per cent of firms had introduced flexible sewing units by 1987, while 8 per cent had sequential automation and 14 per cent had full cycle automation. Some 23 per cent used CAD in pattern making and grading and 36 per cent in production planning.

Footwear

The footwear industry[23] grew by only 4.1 per cent between 1983 and 1987, to 9.7 billion pairs. Global production was dominated by Asia (51 per cent), followed by Eastern Europe (18 per cent), Western Europe (12.5 per cent), South America (9 per cent) and Central and North America (6.5 per cent). World footwear exports amounted to US$20 billion, led by Italy and followed by Taiwan, Korea and Brazil. These four countries together accounted for 65 per cent of exports. Footwear exports from Korea and Taiwan increased from US$10 million in each country in 1969 to $1.5 billion and $2.3 billion respectively, in 1985 (Levy, 1990).[24] Recently, high export growth has occurred in China, Thailand and Indonesia. For the latter two, growth has resulted from a shift of high-volume, low-cost footwear manufacturing from South Korea. They have also benefited from the General System of Preferences in the EU, benefits which are not available to Taiwan, South Korea, Hong Kong and Singapore. African footwear has been insignificant and has even declined.

Technological development has been relatively slow, evolutionary and incremental, with modest automation occurring in stand-alone machines and the functions of the production process only. Machinery is quite standardized and even old machines are still in use. Microelectronic machinery controls have been applied in only a few areas such as cutting, closing, and preparing the bottom stock. Computers are used mainly in product design and management systems. New technology has had the greatest impact in the 'making' process (pulling the uppers over the last and attaching the sole), particularly in the roughing and lasting stages. Numerically controlled machines are an improvement over both the manual method and automatic machines using templates. Little technical change has taken place in finishing (examining the shoe, correcting minor faults and spraying the colour if necessary), while many technological innovations have occurred in new materials for the uppers, new insole or lining fabrics, new threads, adhesives and glues.

Towards new organizational patterns

As was noted in Chapter 2, what happens when a new technology enters a mature industry depends on whether the new technology enhances the core capabilities of extant firms or requires very different kinds of capabilities, which may entail a change of management or strategy. Organizational change must be seen as the handmaid of technological advance and not a separate force behind economic progress.

There is a growing consensus that technological developments and market trends are converging. Some refer to a transition from Fordism to neo-Fordism, characterized by more flexible production and fragmented demand. Others, such as Michael Porter, refer to the declining importance of economies of scale and the growth of flexible factories serving multi-niche markets. Yet others argue that under flexible specialization, technologically dynamic smaller firms using craft practices will challenge larger manufacturers.

Others, such as Kaplinsky (1990),[25] suggest that the greatest impact of advanced manufacturing technologies (AMT) will be in batch production, thus improving the competitiveness of small and medium-sized enterprises. Tidd (1991, p. 4) found that the management literature was unanimous in predicting that the winners in the 1990s will be smaller, more specialized, focused factories competing on the basis of quality and responsiveness to niche markets.

Tapscott and Caston (1993)[26] identify four paradigm shifts which are affecting business today: new technology (new roles for IT and open, user-centred and network computing); the new business environment (open, competitive dynamic market place); new enterprises (open, networked and information-based organization); and the new geopolitical order (open, volatile and multi polar world).

The new enterprise is becoming more open in scope, shifting from a multi-layered hierarchy to flatter networks of relatively autonomous businesses. The concept of the organization is expanding to include links with external business partners and the professional is replacing the manager as the central player, often working in multidisciplinary teams. Individuals develop strong specialized expertise and broader competencies in a working–learning environment, where the notion of life-long learning is replacing the older notion of learning job skills that require only periodic updating. The new team is self-managed, with the team members united by a common vision and individuals empowered to act responsibly and creatively. The new enterprise structure is possible when each member understands the team vision, has the required competencies, has the trust of others and has access to the information and tools required to function and collaborate within the team in a broader context.

In fact, production organization and increasing responsiveness to the market may be more important factors for competitiveness than microelectronic applications. Over time, however, microelectronics are likely to gain in importance to the extent that they enhance quality and productivity and enable more efficient control over the whole production process.

As to whether a new techno-economic system has emerged, this is debatable if a techno-economic system is defined as a bundle of technologies, institutions and forms of economic and social organization which make up a coherent whole, are mutually interdependent and enable synergies to emerge (OECD, 1991).[27] However, the mass production model is undergoing change in the direction of greater flexibility and variety, and previously separate production phases are being integrated due to generic technologies such as information technologies or new materials. Technological fusion is taking place as firms combine technologies and firms are searching for new types of relationships. Three aspects of such cooperation deserve attention: technological cooperation in relation to the diversity and variety of technological skills required, vertical cooperation between producers and users and relationships between assemblers and their suppliers. All this does not necessarily mean that a new dominant technological style has emerged; instead we may be at the beginning of a process, the elements of which are not yet wholly under control. For instance, the advances in IT have also meant an explosion in the mass of information that needs to be handled, raising problems of compatibility and bottlenecks arising from human error. Diffusion is slowed further by the high fixed costs which are involved, uncertainty, 'pure vintage effects' (the time needed to adapt the structure of capital to the demands of best practice) and the heterogeneity of firms and their environments.

It is against this background of incompatibilities and bottlenecks (at least in part) that, even in the OECD countries, there is a notable contradiction between the rapid technological progress from the end of the 1970s and the apparent failure to make a significant impact on total factor productivity. It is difficult to separate out the effect of progress made in the services sector, because its frontiers are increasingly being blurred with the manufacturing sector, but there are indications that the lack of significant impact from technical progress on total factor productivity is a reflection of the mismatch between earlier forms of corporate organization (including the public sector) and the requirements of new technologies (OECD, 1992a, 1992b). Tapscott and Caston (1993) have suggested that the main challenge for organizations is not in the area of technology but in managing change. The organizational structures for managing change, along with the knowledge, skills, resource base, approaches to systems planning and even organizational culture, are being challenged by the new era. Many of the information system (IS) professionals and managers are so buried in fighting the bush fires of the old IS world that they are unable to lead in the new era; vendors are unlikely to provide leadership because the new enterprise has relationships with multiple vendors; and third parties (e.g. consultants) are unlikely to lead the way because old approaches, knowledge, methods and attitudes die hard. The study found that leadership to manage change came from every conceivable place in every conceivable type of organization, leading to the conclusion 'leadership is your personal challenge, whatever your organizational role'.

The concept of flexible specialization (FS) has been used to capture new ways of organizing industrial production. The concept can capture changes at macro and at micro level. At the macro level, the concept of FS refers to the move from a dominant mass production system (where stable markets, factor cost reductions and economies of scale are key variables) to more diversified and ever-changing markets, products and production processes where flexibility and innovation are central (Rasmussen, *et al.* 1992).[28] At the micro level the concept captures a new type of industrial organization able to cope with the demands of increasing flexibility and innovation. In large firms FS takes the forms of decentralization into semi-autonomous specialized units, new factory layouts and just-in-time inventory control. In small firms it may take forms such as independent production, working as subcontractors to large firms and cooperative production in industrial districts.[29] Piore and Sabel (1984)[30] have used the attribute 'flexible' to refer to four aspects: technology (the multi-purpose machine), the worker (wide range of skills), the individual firm (wide range of products) and groups of firms (wide range of products and volumes).

In the neoclassical concept of the firm, flexibility is simply interpreted as the flatness of the average cost curve, implying the firm's ability to respond to changes in price and/or demand. However, in the presence of economies of scope (where the cost of the joint production of several products is less than the cost of producing each separately), the fact that the firm has end product and technology choices to confront can provide a rationale for diversification. Tidd (1991) has identified two forms of flexibility: 'active' (or adaptable), referring to the ability to respond to change by taking appropriate action; and 'passive' (or insensitive), referring to the innate ability to function well in more than one state. In the former case, three dimensions have to be considered: the range of possible states, the cost of moving from one state to another and the time taken. Tidd, drawing on earlier work by Browne *et al.* (1984),[31] has distinguished different types of flexibility: machine flexibility (ease of producing many types of products on one machine), process flexibility (ability to make a product in different ways), product flexibility (ability to switch to producing a new product), routing flexibility (ability to cope with breakdowns by processing via alternative routes), volume flexibility, expansion flexibility, operation flexibility (ability to switch the order of several different operations for each product) and production flexibility (the universe of product types that the system can produce). Since different types of flexibility may conflict in practice, the firm must decide which types of flexibility are most important and the most appropriate means of achieving them.

Innovations in firm organization in the clothing industry, characterized by the creation of firm networks, were rated as more important than technological innovations. The core of the network may be a marketing firm using outside designers and producers, or a designing firm using outside producers and marketers, or a manufacturer using outside designers, marketing agencies and other specialized subcontractors.

However, no international patterns of development or adoption of AMT have emerged, after more than ten years of diffusion, probably because different organizational and market contexts lead to divergent paths, the technologies themselves being inherently adaptable.

Changing requirements for human resource development

The move to FMS and other integrated automation technologies poses a challenge to traditional organizational patterns. Various departments need to work together and to coordinate their activities – design and production functions, and business systems engineers with manufacturing systems engineers – and to encourage coordinated and broadening skills. The trend is towards flatter and less structurally functional occupations. It has even been suggested that the benefits of FMS investment often come more from the organizational changes it induces than from the equipment as such.

The structure of employment is changing, with a shift from manual to mental work as indirect production/support work is gaining ground over direct work. Practical skills have to be complemented by higher levels of theoretical skills in science and modern technologies and there is a preference for personnel with multidisciplinary skills.

In the case of the footwear industry, for instance, changing skill requirements are apparent with deskilling in pattern making, cutting and stitching and increased skills requirements in management information and control and pre-production planning. New and better skills are required in functional management (organization and control of workers, human relations, quality control, marketing, financial planning and cost control). As a starting point, user-oriented strategies towards new technologies can result in improvements. The question is how much learning is necessary for the effective use of new technologies. Computer literacy and basic electronic hardware maintenance skills are likely to be essential.

The technical innovations in clothing have not had significant effects on the modes of manpower use or on the content of individual tasks at firm level, since the major changes have been in the initial stages of the manufacturing process. However, the division of labour between the designer and the master-tailor has become more obscure, automation of the cutting process has reduced the professional cutter to an operator and automatic conveyor systems have reduced cooperation among workers at various stages. In the process, new needs for training have emerged: needs for higher basic education, training for increased flexibility, training in machinery know-how, in production planning systems and the circulation of goods, and in electronic data processing and information and communication techniques, and training to improve quality.

Towards further internationalization and globalization

The processes of internationalization and globalization were referred to briefly in Chapter 2 (pp. 18–19) as one factor influencing views on the explanatory power of conventional trade theory. The new wave of internationalization is led by the increasing importance of TNCs and by DFI (direct foreign investment) in manufacturing and services rather than by international trade. The deregulation and globalization of finance and pressure from new technologies have led to new forms of inter-firm agreements which have developed into major means of international technology transfer. These tendencies threaten to leave many developing countries on the margins of globalized information networks and may invoke the role of the state in setting rules and codes of behaviour for firms engaged in global competition (OECD, 1992b).

In the context of globalization, computer networking extends the reach of companies and organizations, allowing better coordination of various activities at international level. Such networks may be alternatives to strategic alliances among firms and can present new opportunities which could influence the structure of industrial activities and their location (OECD, 1992b).[32] Furthermore, recent developments indicate that new technology is increasingly under commercial control and can therefore be obtained from firms and not from governments. It has also been suggested that there is a tendency for some TNCs to be more willing to locate a greater portion of their R&D activities in developing countries than they did in the past. The implications of these and related new trends for the transfer of technology are worth exploring, with a view to taking advantage of opportunities they may offer.

Africa needs to recognize these trends and respond to these changes by putting greater effort into exploring the possibilities of beneficial inter-firm linkages with TNCs from the North and from the South. New forms of networking with TNCs need to be forged and the conditions under which the role of TNCs could be complementary and supportive of the development of international competitiveness by developing countries need to be identified. However, it would appear that, if the potential benefits from TNCs are to be realized, domestic policies concerning the development of domestic firms' technological capabilities, education and vocational training, investment, trade, technology adaptation and R&D can play a crucial role. The guiding question here should be: in what ways can global trade negotiations increase the access of African firms to forging inter-firm linkages and cooperation arrangements, which can contribute to the development of the technological and other capabilities that are necessary for making gains in international competitiveness? Recent work on global trends in inter-firm partnering has raised some doubts about the usefulness of such partnerships for the less developed partner. In a recent article, Freeman and Hagedoorn (1994)[32] have concluded that inter-firm partnering has not enabled the LDCs (less developed countries), or most of the NICS, to catch up. This is because it has, on the whole, led only to the concentration of technological competence within the developed economies. They distinguish between two forms of inter-firm technology partnering: strategic technology partnering and inter-firm technology transfer agreements. Of the strategic technology alliances during the 1980s, they found 95.6 per cent to have been between firms in developed countries, 2.3 per cent between firms in the Triad (US, EU and Japan) countries and those in NICs and just 1.5 per cent were between Triad firms and LDC firms. The corresponding shares for technology transfer agreements were 90 per cent, 6 per cent and 4 per cent. Nevertheless, in their conclusions they suggest, correctly in my opinion, that the building of indigenous technological capabilities could be facilitated by capitalizing on the learning process that comes with international partnering. After all, learning by learning and learning by doing are strong elements of successful corporate innovative behaviour. Although the learning capabilities have to be built up within firms, the process can in part depend on the broader technological infrastructure.

Within the broader context of forging inter-firm linkages and cooperation arrangements, special attention will need to be paid to the possibilities of promoting investment flows among developing countries (Lecraw, 1981; UNESCAP, 1990).[33] The case for promoting inter-firm linkages within the South can be made on grounds of complementarity to other forms of networks. There is evidence that TNCs from developing countries have undertaken various modifications in response to the characteristics of raw materials (type, quality and input mix), size (scaling down), product quality and product mix (degree of diversification), machinery (simplicity and capacity) and factor intensity (Lecraw, 1981). These TNCs have tended to produce simpler, lower-technology, low-cost products which required little marketing ability to sell in world markets. They have had a higher propensity to form joint ventures with local firms, have used more local human resources and raw materials and often have down-scaled imported technologies. A case study of an Indian joint venture in Thailand showed that, since they are themselves in a learning stage, developing country firms transfer not only the know-how but also the know-why (UNESCAP, 1990). One reason why this occurs is that developing country TNCs often set up overseas enterprises using machinery imported from developed countries. This necessitates adaptation of this machinery to local conditions on site in the host country, thus providing the TNC with the opportunity to learn by doing. This would imply that developing country TNCs may be more skilled in specific technology adaptations and that they transfer those skills. Developing country firms are also associated with the ability to design smaller plants for small market segments. Through these various forms of learning, adapting and modifying imported technologies, Southern TNCs have acquired unique technological capabilities and can carry out these and related activities quite efficiently (Lecraw, 1981). This is corroborated by further indications that TNCs from the South are more appropriate for developing country needs, in terms of the characteristics of the technology with which they have expertise, integration with domestic demand and balance of payments effects (Sharma, 1993).

However, various obstacles inhibit further South–South technological cooperation: lack of information, inadequate institutional frameworks and economic and legal barriers. Some of these obstacles can be mitigated through trade policy, which needs to shift in several directions: improved South–South trading infrastructure, liberalization of intra-South trade restrictions, forging organizational ties to enhance the exploitation of economies of specialization and the creation of an effective and innovative capacity for more efficient appropriate processes and products (Sharma, 1993).

The changing characteristics of technological efforts: role of the state

Technological development requires effort. Much of this effort is expected to take the form of tangible and intangible investments. The former is the traditional investment in physical assets, while intangible investments refer to human and financial resources allocated to R&D expenditures and other forms of purchasing technology, and to training, business services, marketing expenditures and the acquisition and exploration of software (OECD, 1992a).

In recent years there has been a tendency to take a 'hands-off' attitude towards the role of the state, especially in Africa. Yet governments elsewhere are playing a leading role in shaping new trade relations. In addition to the crucial role that governments are playing in forging new trade blocs (e.g. NAFTA, EU), they have been instrumental in assisting firms to acquire international competitiveness. In the OECD there is evidence of renewed interest in funding industrial R&D, with a shift from ensuring public funding on terms favourable to enterprises to greater emphasis on the organization of capital markets and banking policies and the manner in which these influence firms' investment decisions.

Building on strategic trade theory and administrative theories of the firm, as well as the conventional explanations that focus on country characteristics, it has now become clear that when industries become globally concentrated, visible hands (of TNCs and governments) rather than the invisible hands of the market emerge to guide trade. The patterns of international trade and production are the complex outcome of several factors: traditional country advantages, the international structure of the industry, specific firm characteristics of TNCs, the style and intrusiveness of government policy and the inertia of history (Yoffie, 1993). One policy implication of these patterns is that the government can facilitate the expansion of the sources of competitive advantage over time.

The case for selectively supporting specific high-potential industries through government policy has been demonstrated to varying degrees in the experiences of the developed countries and the NICs. In the case of Japan, for instance, MITI is reported to have picked winners after ample consultation with, or the participation of experts from, diverse sectors (industry, universities, banks, trade unions and the mass media) and to have figured out which development strategy suited the capabilities of Japanese producers after paying close attention to developments in the domestic and international markets (Yamamura, 1986; Carliner, 1986).[34] In the case of South Korea, the government intervened to create and develop market agents. Its intervention was selective and favoured industries which were deemed to have dynamic comparative advantage. In selecting industries to be supported, the government consulted extensively with knowledgeable agents in the private sector (Pack and Westphal, 1986). The government operated a dual policy structure, with industries in which Korea had a static comparative advantage operating largely in a neutral incentive structure and the infant industries getting direct and indirect promotional incentives. Export performance has been the main practical measure of progress towards international competitiveness, with detailed strategy in this highly uncertain area being reformulated in the light of information gained (market signals, perceptions about industrial operations and potentials) during implementation (Pack and Westphal, 1986). Unlike most African countries, protection in Korea was not confined only to import substitution industries but went beyond and made export an ultimate target.

In mainframe computers and semi-conductors, where barriers to entry were high and the US had a first-mover competitive advantage, the government of Japan employed trade restrictions combined with limitations on FDI to encourage Japanese firms to invest aggressively in emerging technologies. The Japanese carefully limited the role of dominant foreign firms in the domestic market while providing domestic firms with incentives to export. Other governments' interventions have determined the longevity and exporting success of local industries such as textiles and apparel, steel, machine tools and colour televisions. Protectionism has kept American producers in the textile and steel business long after most free-market-based trade models would have predicted their exit (Yoffie, 1993). The governments' heavy, visible hand has often sculpted, manipulated or even directly determined the direction and volume of trade flows.

The OECD (1992a) has emphasized the role played by non-market coordination between private agents in the creation of externalities and interactive mechanisms. For countries with less developed markets, such policies may be the only way to create crucial externalities and trigger growth-generating cumulative processes. Trends in automation have shown that state intervention is necessary is various ways: in the development of education and skills; in providing consultancy assistance; in conducting awareness-raising activities, including applications and demonstration projects; in creating enabling infrastructure and information channels for technology transfer from publicly supported technology institutes and decentralized applications centres; in enhancing technology supply (upstream) by supporting domestic technology supply and improving access to foreign technology suppliers; in supporting product development and helping with organizational changes, process development and process applications; in supporting modernizing industries which have failed to adopt best-practice technologies (e.g. by providing finance to overcome their investment barriers); in organizing support programmes for diffusing new technologies; and in market identification, exploration and development (UNIDO, 1992b).

New policy challenges in the OECD countries have been in the area of policy formulation, taking into account the increasing overlap of previously distinct areas, such as industrial, telecommunications and IT policy-making, and of the institutions involved in this process. Two policy issues are relevant: industry must be supported in its efforts to develop technology, markets and competitiveness; and the legitimate regulatory functions of government must be established and maintained (OECD, 1992b).

It may be useful to emphasize that, while Africa must avoid the mistakes of the past, efforts to influence Africa's position in the new global trade relations will require that governments play an active role.

CONCLUSION

Changes in the world market and in technological conditions in the world economy in the recent past, in particular in the last decade, pose new challenges to industrialization and the development of a competitive manufacturing sector in Africa. Three main categories of changes are most relevant: changes in market conditions, in technology hardware and software and in the organization of production.

In many respects the conventional advantage of low labour cost is being undermined by the increasing importance of competitive characteristics other than cost of production, notably product/ service quality and just-in-time delivery. To cope with these requirements, greater effort will be required to develop design, marketing and new organizational and linkage capabilities, in addition to selectively acquiring new manufacturing technologies.

These market and technological changes are likely to have considerable implications for the shift in the direction of knowledge-intensive production and for the kinds of capabilities that must be developed to cope with the changing situation. First, greater effort will be needed to monitor these changes with a view to adapting to the new situation. This will often imply selective adoption of new technologies in production and marketing at the right time and in the right applications according to the dictates of quality, precision, speed and productivity requirements. Second, greater effort will be needed to create a conducive environment for the creation and development of core capabilities within firms and in the institutions that interact with those firms so as to cope with the changing conditions.

5 Main findings of the study
A synthesis

POSITION OF EXPORTING FIRMS IN THE WORLD MARKET

Type of product

The position of firms in the market is influenced by the type of product they produce. Many firms' exports are primarily common products differentiated largely by the use of brand names. Except for the subsidiaries of multinational enterprises, very few firms design and develop their own products. Most products are imitations of foreign products, usually products which were being imported and are now manufactured, following the logic of import substitution. Competition in the product market is largely based on price and quality.

Types of target markets

The exporting firms have mainly targeted regional markets, with smaller volumes being exported to international markets. Firms which target international markets are mainly resource-based manufacturers, deriving their initial comparative advantage from access to natural resources. This observation in the case studies corroborates earlier case studies in which it was noted that manufactured exports have tended to be dominated by processed goods destined for the markets outside Africa (Riddell, 1990, p. 35). If major primary processed exports are excluded then the much smaller remainder is mostly destined for neighbouring markets.

While some exporters started as export-oriented enterprises (EOEs), targeting export markets right from their inception, others started as import substitution enterprises (ISEs), targeting the domestic market and later moved into export markets. Firms took various routes in shifting or extending from domestic markets to export markets. Two categories can be identified. Some firms moved from the domestic markets to regional markets and later penetrated international markets. Others developed from domestic to regional markets and stayed there or have not penetrated international markets as yet.

The transition from domestic markets to regional markets has been influenced by the similarity between these markets. Two types of exporting firms were found to have taken advantage of this phenomenon. First, there are exporters who have found the regional market no more demanding in terms of product quality than the domestic market (e.g. steel products). Exporting based on this feature is likely to be short-lived at best, considering that quality requirements are likely to rise as economies in the region become more open. Export opportunities based on lower product quality are unlikely to be sustainable in the face of imports from elsewhere. Such less demanding export markets may produce only limited learning by exporting.

Second, opportunities in the regional markets have been tapped on the basis of product quality and appropriateness to the specific conditions in the region. For instance, regional exports in agricultural machinery and other farm implements were found to be based on products which had been developed to suit agro-economic conditions in the region. Zimbabwean firms exporting agricultural machinery had developed products which suited the soil and climatic conditions in the region. Their competitiveness was a result of many years of continuous investment in searching and learning, as indicated by their R&D activities. The firms started by copying imported designs and made efforts, in response to demands from farmers, to make innovations to suit the specificities of the region. The development of agricultural machinery suited to the conditions of Southern Africa was encouraged by the domestic demand for such innovations from the large-scale farming community. The specificity of the technological adaptations gave the firms natural protection from international competition. Because of the appropriateness of these products to the specific soil conditions in the region, they could even sell at higher prices than their imported counterparts.

However, even where there appears to be a natural monopoly, intra-regional competition has to be faced at some point, as the case of agricultural machinery from Zimbabwe and South Africa has shown. Natural protection is tenable up to a point, beyond which there is danger of losing markets to competitors from other regions. Even if imported products are not as suitable to local conditions, competitors from outside the region have sometimes penetrated the regional market by supplying their products at lower prices or by supplying products whose quality of finish looks better. Thus specific local markets can be lost to others if continuous efforts are not made to develop competitiveness in terms of quality and price.

In some cases competitors from other regions have made products specifically for the African regional market. Kangas coming from some Asian countries (e.g. India and China) or African prints from Europe have been manufactured specifically to suit the demand in the African markets. There are signs that such products are taking a share of the market from firms in the region. The evidence indicates that the specificity of regional markets may make the competition for various products less intense but it does not guarantee a monopoly. The need to exert continuous effort to attain and maintain competitiveness in such markets does not seem to be obviated by any specific characteristics of regional demand.

HISTORY OF EXPORTING: CONDITIONS AND PATH FOLLOWED

The conditions and factors which influenced entry into the export market were addressed by the case studies, shedding some light on the path which was followed in the history of exporting and providing some insights into the process and activities which led to the first entry into export markets.

Exporting strategy

The case studies have shown that most exporting firms started by serving the domestic market. The strategy of exporting came later in response to developments in their domestic markets. Most of these enterprises started exporting to regional markets, mainly in countries which did not have similar industries. The share of exports in total output is usually small (about 5–15 per cent). With such a small share of exports in their total sales, some of these firms could sell in the export market at a loss, the loss being offset by more profitable sales in the domestic market. Firms in this category have tended to position themselves with a fairly broad competitive scope, reflecting the broad competitive scope they had in domestic markets.

Import substituting firms grew up and built up various core capabilities by producing for the domestic market. The protection of the domestic market allowed them to accumulate resources, which were in turn invested in developing capabilities which enabled them to turn to exports at a later stage. ISEs were either motivated to export by export promotion incentives of various kinds or resorted to exporting as one response to saturated or collapsing domestic markets. Developments in domestic markets took several forms.

In some countries the domestic market contracted as aggregate expenditure in the economy was reduced during the implementation of economic reforms. This kind of development in the domestic markets was particularly experienced by the Ivory Coast and Zimbabwe, with the effects of drought exacerbating the contraction in the latter case. Some firms responded to the contraction of the domestic market by increasing efforts to locate new markets in other countries. The success of such attempts was limited by the fact that the transition towards exporting was rushed, without the necessary preparations. However, this survival strategy failed to compensate for the loss of domestic markets in a sustainable way. This implies that export markets are not likely to be a quick fix for the problem of contracting domestic demand.

In some cases the collapse of the domestic market occurred because a firm was established with one major local consumer in mind and that consumer collapsed. The response of the supplier firms was to turn to export markets. Morogoro Canvas of Tanzania was one such case: it had been set as a supplier of canvas to the Morogoro Shoe factory. When that factory went bankrupt, the canvas mill adjusted swiftly by changing its product mix and entering the export market (uniforms, grey cloth and bed sheets). The firm responded by making the necessary investments in technology to meet requirements of the export markets and the transition seems to have been managed quite well. Today the mill exports about 60 per cent of its output. The breakthrough in the export business is mainly attributed to special machines used for export production. This investment in technology coupled with the employment of foreign management under contract has enabled Morogoro canvas to develop a sizeable and diversified export market in the US, the UK, Canada, Holland, Germany, Saudi Arabia, the UAE and neighbouring countries.

The case studies have also shown that a few firms started as exporting firms from the outset. These firms started with an eye on the export market and showed awareness of changing market conditions from the initial stages. For these firms the export market accounted for a large share (more than 50 per cent) of their total sales. These enterprises tended to target international markets in which they occupied a specific market niche and maintained that niche by closely following changing market requirements. Some of them took advantage of preferential access to the EU markets. This strategy was adopted most conspicuously in Mauritius, for some time following the implementation of the import substitution phase. The critical measure was the Export Processing Zones (EPZ) Act (1970), which provided additional special incentives to exporting firms. The EPZ enterprises were allowed to sell their products on the local market to only a limited extent.

Some firms were motivated to pursue export strategies from the beginning because they faced small domestic markets. For instance, the radiator manufacturer in Tanzania targeted the slow end of the export market where markets are small and isolated. The firm adopted a strategy of striving to attain quality and competitiveness in export markets. However, its real breakthrough in export markets came with Original Equipment Manufacturer (OEM) certificates from well-known manufacturers such as Scania, Valmet and Landrover. Obtaining the OEM certificates facilitated exports to Europe and these achievements were used to promote exports into the region.

Previous experience of key management figures

Previous experience had prepared some key managerial and entrepreneurial personnel for conditions in the export markets and put them in contact with technology suppliers. They acquired their experience as traders in similar products or as representatives of multinational enterprises which were engaged in similar activities.

The typical local private exporting firms started as family trading enterprises and later moved into the manufacture of products which were related to their earlier trade activities. Their activities in trade had given them contacts and connections which were later useful at the manufacturing stage. The capabilities which were developed in the previous stages were put to use in the subsequent stages of development. Foreign technical assistance was sought in those areas where local capability was deficient, so that technology investments were largely in the form of more modern machinery in order to manufacture higher-quality products for the export market.

Various forms of linkages and networks

It may be unnecessary to possess all the capabilities in-house if some of them can be obtained outside the firm. However, in such cases the firm needs at least to have the capability to identify the kinds of capabilities it needs to buy from elsewhere and how best to utilize inputs and services provided by others. It was found that information provided by buyers in the export markets often influenced product specifications. Some firms entered agreements with foreign firms, under which they could have access to information about latest fashions and other market requirements. Networks and interactions with various suppliers of inputs and equipment and buyers of output had affected the choices of technology and products which enabled firms to penetrate export markets.

Foreign partners were found in many exporting firms, with their role varying according to the nature of the product, the scale of operations, the type of market and the kinds of core capabilities that the firms possessed. Typically, foreign partners supplied some form of technical assistance in aspects of technology and marketing. The various roles of foreign partners in providing these services are documented in the case studies. These foreign firms had either formed joint ventures with local firms or were hired agents for specific technology and/or marketing activities. In some cases technical cooperation agreements also involve the use of foreign brand names and trade marks. For instance, a major breakthrough for Orbitsports of Kenya occurred in 1974 when it entered into a technical cooperation agreement with Adidas, the world's largest supplier of leather balls. The firm paid royalties to Adidas for technical services, including training of the company's workers at Adidas in France, evaluating the quality of raw materials, checking the quality of final products and providing technical advice on the purchase of machinery and equipment.

The local firms located the foreign partners themselves. However, in a few cases the government and state promotion institutions played a decisive role in initiating contacts between local firms and their foreign partners. For instance, the sister industry programmes in Tanzania enabled a manufacturer of electrical goods to go into exporting.

Investments in technology

Although some regional export markets were no more demanding, in terms of product quality, than domestic markets (e.g. exports of kangas from Kenya to Tanzania), the case studies have shown that entry into export markets has often been preceded by investments in upgrading technology to meet higher quality requirements. These investments were for technological improvements to equipment and for quality control facilities. In some cases firms established new sites specifically for producing for export markets (e.g. Bata Shoes in Zimbabwe, Northern Electrical Manufacturers in Tanzania) or installed separate production lines for exports, in which special machines were installed for selected processes to guarantee export quality (e.g. Friendship Textiles and Morogoro Canvas in Tanzania, Sunflag in Kenya).

Foreign v. local investment

The positive role of foreign investment in building local technological capabilities has come out quite clearly in Mauritius, where local private capital has been progressively buying out foreign capital. This harmonious nationalization of investments has been facilitated by the existence of an entrepreneurial class which developed from the local plantocracy during the years when sugar production was dominant. The surpluses which were accumulated then were invested in industry. In addition, the macroeconomic environment and the climate for investments have been conducive for both local and foreign investment. For instance, one of the leading exporting firms in Mauritius, the knitwear firm, was established initially by Hong Kong investors with a minority Mauritian participation. After a few years the Hong Kong shareholders were bought out by Mauritians, and since 1977 the company has had an entirely local shareholding. The bulk of the shares are held by a local investment company belonging to a large sugar group. The existence of a capital market and a group of local individuals and institutions who are willing to invest seems to have favoured the process of nationalization in Mauritius.

The transfer of control from foreigners to indigenous owners has sometimes been far from smooth and possibly more destructive than constructive. For instance, the indigenization programme in Nigeria was carried out in 1974 and, together with further phases which were implemented before 1980, resulted in Nigerians taking over the control of several businesses hitherto controlled by foreigners. However, it would appear that the policy-makers overlooked the economic side-effects of the indigenization programme, especially its possible negation of the goal of economic independence. The import substitution industries which had been established were acquiring the capability to manufacture for export but this development was thwarted by the manpower dislocation caused by the indigenization programme. Several of the newly established activities experienced manpower problems and some of them failed as a result.

The contribution of foreign investment in building local capabilities has not always been positive. The case studies showed that some locally controlled firms had been bought out by TNCs in response to the threat of competition (e.g. Trituraf of the Ivory Coast). Another multinational, Saco, had a monopoly for about 10 years, after which many state-created companies started trading in the Ivory Coast. But in the middle of the 1980s nearly all of these newcomers disappeared or were taken over, leaving Saco in control of most of the local cocoa-bean processing and by-product production in the Ivory Coast.

In discussions of the role foreign investment could play in industrialization and in building technological capabilities within firms it is important that the changing forms of foreign investment be recognized. This study has shown that exporting firms in Africa have benefited in different ways from various forms of relationships with foreign firms. Foreign investment is increasingly taking forms other than the traditional direct foreign investment. There is considerable evidence that new forms of investment (NFI) will continue to gain importance in developing countries, superseding traditional FDI in some areas and complementing it in others (OECD, 1989).[1] The implication of the debt crisis and foreign exchange shortages for the balance between FDI and NFI is likely to vary from one country to another, reflecting differences in host country policies (macro-economic policies and policies on foreign investment), the host-country's market potential, perceived degree of bureaucratic red tape, political stability and the availability of local managerial skills and skilled labour. However, it is likely that, as some developing countries acquire various capabilities, they may want to bring in only those assets which they cannot obtain locally in order to minimize foreign exchange losses (through remissions abroad and payments for various services). Such long-term financial and foreign exchange considerations may lead to more selective pursuit of NFI, with government attitudes and policies tending to be more industry-specific, reflecting long-term benefits from learning by doing (OECD, 1989).

The changing perceptions of TNCs may continue to favour a relative increase in NFI, on the grounds that it increases leverage on firm-specific assets and that it has risk-shedding advantages over traditional FDI. In future, the balance between traditional FDI and NFI is likely to be influenced more by the global dynamics of inter-firm competition and by the interplay between those dynamics and host-government policies than by the latter's unilateral decisions (OECD, 1989). This underscores the importance of understanding the global trends within specific industries.

The evidence presented by the OECD (1989) suggests that there is a long-term trend in the division of risks and responsibilities between TNCs, host countries and international lenders, which is characterized by increasing emphasis by TNCs on flexibility and the development of capabilities in relatively protected industry segments (where profit potentials are high), operating upstream of production (as suppliers of technology and management) in some industries and downstream (in marketing) in others. Host-country investors are increasingly retaining partial or total ownership of investment projects, while the degree of effective control depends increasingly on factors other than host-country ownership of equity. International lenders are likely to continue to play a central role in channelling financial capital to developing countries (in the form of new loans and debt rescheduling) and in that way will exert significant control over the international investment process (OECD, 1989).

HOW FIRMS MAINTAIN OR IMPROVE THEIR POSITIONS IN EXPORT MARKETS

Having entered the export markets, maintaining and possibly improving their market position becomes a major challenge for firms. Understanding this process and gaining insights into the basis of their competitiveness has been a major interest of this study. The likely sustainability of such competitiveness over time and how consistent it is likely to be with overall increases in productivity in the economy were also of interest. Some firms have tried to maintain their positions in export markets by cutting the costs of inputs and other factors of production, while other firms have been improving productivity through searching and learning continuously over time. Only in the latter case is international competitiveness in export markets sustainable.

A competitive strategy would be expected to grow out of a sophisticated understanding of the structure of the industry and how it is changing. The changes that matter may be technological or market requirements. Firms need to maintain and improve their positions in export markets by facing the threats of new entrants and of substitutes and by coping with the rivalry among existing competitors.

The case studies have shown that the main sources of comparative advantage are in the primary activities of production and marketing, with little advantage deriving from the availability of support services such as the providers of purchased inputs and infrastructure. The advantage has been derived from lower-order factors such as low labour costs or cheap raw materials, factors which are relatively easy to imitate and therefore less sustainable. The case studies have indicated that some exporting firms have striven to develop higher-order advantages through sustained and cumulative investment in physical facilities, human resource development and searching.

Making investments in technology improvement

The case studies have indicated that exporting firms maintained and improved their market position by investing in technology and making technology improvements on a continuous basis. Improvements were made either in the production processes or in products. The processes of production were improved in order to cope with pressure to keep costs at competitive levels or to improve product quality (level and consistency). These responses were derived from signals given in export markets.

Older and simpler technology has been found to have an advantage, in that local skills can operate and maintain such equipment more efficiently. The case studies have also shown that efficiency in the use of such technologies can be pushed to its limits by the demands of export markets. For instance, much of the equipment in shoe factories in Zimbabwe is old, but it is also 'appropriate' in that it is operational and is readily maintained with local skills. Productivity, measured in units such as pairs per person per day, is low by international standards (from 7 to 45, with international levels two to three times higher for comparable styles) but the total costs of production, reflecting the written-down costs of the antiquated but operational equipment and relatively low labour costs, would appear to be competitive. This situation may have been favoured by the relatively slow pace of technological innovation in the footwear industry world-wide, as noted in Chapter 4. Productivity could be improved by reducing the number of styles being produced, while cost efficiency is already being improved through more efficient stock control, a spin-off of the present tight monetary conditions. However, given the speed at which technological development in general is moving, such efforts can at best guarantee survival for a while. In the longer run, investment in newer technologies is necessary. Some firms have started to do that already. For instance, Bata installed new export production lines in Gweru in 1993 and has just commissioned a three-colour screen printer at its Kwekwe factory. Coupled with a combined lasting and two-colour plastic sole injection moulding machine, this should make it possible to attain internationally competitive productivity levels for high-fashion sports shoes and sneakers.

Technology improvements have also been made in response to rising costs of labour. In Mauritius, for instance, as labour became less abundant and labour costs started to rise, there was a shift towards less labour-intensive processes. Owing to labour scarcity and the consequent increase in salaries, the paint manufacturing firm in Mauritius has moved to the use of more powerful equipment and less manpower. Although it has a very large share of the domestic market, the paint manufacturer faces strong competition from other domestic producers. The knitwear manufacturer in Mauritius has made significant changes in process and product technologies – the use of more sophisticated equipment and increasing automation. There have also been changes in the type and quality of its products. Fancy knitwear now accounts for 60 per cent of the firm's total output. However, unlike some large leading firms in the developed countries, these changes have not been a result of large R&D investments, since they are based on imported technologies rather than development of production processes by the firms themselves.

Some firms have introduced a number of new technologies in their production processes in order to achieve higher levels of productivity and product quality. For instance, investments in more modern spinning technology in the textile industry have led to higher production rates and higher and more uniform quality than was possible with conventional ring-spinning technology.

The use of new technologies such as computers has started to spread in various fields. Computers are used for general office work in accounting and payroll functions and in some firms they are used in projecting market demand and machine inventories. Most firms also have fax facilities. The use of computers in controlling production processes was limited, although several firms were contemplating the introduction of computer control in selected production processes as a major step towards increasing efficiency, improving quality and raising productivity. The finding that micro-electronic-based technologies are being introduced selectively in some processes suggests that the further development of these technologies in Africa itself may be appropriate and perhaps unavoidable. For instance, Pack (1993) has suggested that, in the short run, relatively low rates of effective domestic protection could be granted to production based on mechanical and chemical engineering but that no protection should be given to production based on electronics or biotechnology. The latter industries, it is feared, are associated with rapid changes in technology. However, the separability of these categories (mechanical versus electronic) is more questionable if microelectronic-based technologies are becoming widespread, albeit selectively.

Exporting firms have been investing in product design and in quality control facilities as required by export markets. Typical exporting firms have strict quality control systems in place. Quality is regarded as an important part of production, and quality standards are insisted upon at every stage of the production process. In one firm, management said that their in-house training programmes insist that quality and output go hand in hand. A trainee is only brought into the production line after achieving 75 per cent efficiency in both quality and targeted output levels. In other words, the concept of putting quality in the forefront of production is treated as a long-term strategy by companies which have been maintaining their positions in the export business. Investments in product quality sometimes involved moving from labour-intensive methods of production to more automated methods. The introduction of automatic power spraying of paint by Northern Electrical Manufacturers (NEM) of Tanzania was in this sense a necessary investment to achieve the quality standards which were required if the firm was to maintain its position in export markets.

Product design capabilities were found to be limited to copying or making minor adaptations of imported designs following the logic of import substitution. Most of the garment manufacturers said that they had no designers to speak of, except for some women's garments. The local designers generally only copy fashions and trends from overseas. Where firms have, over the years, developed design capabilities, their designs have initially been intended for the domestic market but some have been progressively adapted to the demands and specifications of external markets.

Firms which are manufacturing products whose demand characteristics are specific to the region, such as agricultural machinery, were found to have made the most consistent progress in their adaptations and design capabilities. For instance, Bain and Tinto, making agricultural machinery in Zimbabwe, have design departments staffed by highly qualified engineers and agriculturalists. Both companies have a policy of continuous improvement and innovation, not only to keep up with each other, but with an eye on the export markets in the region. During the fieldwork, it was noted that Tinto was undertaking various capital investments such as the refurbishment of the foundry at the Harare works, the installation of an arc furnace control system to improve energy efficiency and the acquisition of computer-controlled machining centres.

Larger firms have technical development departments which, beside their long-term project development, look into market requirements, especially the need for new varieties of products. However, in general R&D is done on a small scale.

Case studies revealed the introduction of new technologies such as CAD in the design functions. CAD is primarily applicable to small batch-type manufacturing organizations, since resetting becomes merely a matter of selecting and activating different computer programmes. For instance, Fashion Enterprises, the leader in women's clothing in Zimbabwe, have acquired CAD/CAM facilities for their long-run production for the export markets. The company's design capabilities have been developed jointly with overseas customers or through promoting its in-house designs for both the domestic and export markets. Both Bata and Superior Shoe manufacturers in Zimbabwe have acquired their own CAD facilities, coupled to laser pattern cutters, in recent months. This technology was first introduced to the Zimbabwean shoe industry through a grant from UNIDO to the Leather Institute, the equipment being installed in the Institute's premises in Bulawayo. It is, unfortunately, not much used at present, although it is available for use by the smaller companies in the industry. The widespread application of such new technologies is still limited by various infrastructural problems.

One major obstacle to the introduction and spread of microelectronics in industry is the lack of resources and the inadequate supportive infrastructure (e.g. constant telephone interruptions and power failures) resulting in constant machinery breakdowns. The telecommunications infrastructure needed for data transmission between user and producer is non-existent or malfunctioning. Already there are problems of inadequate software and difficulties in obtaining specialized components. Moreover, low levels of education mean that most workers are not easily trainable to handle or operate new technologies.

The case studies have shown that firms which maintained or improved their position in export markets had a way of accessing information on changes in technology. The common information channels were international industry journals, international trade fairs and membership of international industry associations. However, it was found that there is very little support by the government and other public institutions in this area. The subsidiaries of TNCs had an edge on other firms because of their connections with the parent companies abroad.

Exporting firms in which important technological functions are performed by foreign individuals and/or firms can have good export performances without necessarily building the local core capabilities which are needed to sustain exports. This phenomenon was found largely in subsidiaries of TNCs. Technological capabilities tend to be limited, since the parent company is responsible for recommending the selection of technology and the recommendations are ordinarily followed by the subsidiaries. The parent companies provide the subsidiaries with the necessary product designs and drawings (e.g. Uniwax of the Ivory Coast gets its product designs from Vlisco of Holland). The subsidiary firms therefore undertake very little technical innovation. At best they possess a technical workshop which undertakes some maintenance and the processing and preparation of designs received from the parent companies. This lack of their own technological capabilities is reflected in the high royalties and technical assistance fees paid by the subsidiary companies to their parent companies, as shown by the case study on the Ivory Coast.

However, it was found that in subsidiaries which had activities which were rather singular, in that they had no exact replica in the activities of the TNC, there was greater willingness to invest in local adaptations and in the development of local technological capabilities. The circumstances make it imperative for the local subsidiary to make modifications and innovations, as the case of Del Monte of Kenya has shown. Many vital pieces of machinery unique to the pineapple industry are made at the firm's own machine fabrication workshop. This innovative workshop produces massive, 120-feet-span boom harvesters in addition to fumigators tailored to local conditions. Some in-house modifications have also been made to mechanical slicers, crushers and sterilizers/coolers. The in-house equipment, though slightly inferior in engineering efficiency, was said to be more reliable, easily serviceable and more cost-effective. In addition, a sugar recovery plant uses waste pineapple skins to manufacture high-grade refined sugar. The refinery provides 20 per cent of the cannery's sugar needs and has helped the company to integrate its activities.

The position of those who have argued that TNCs and their subsidiaries can be effective vehicles for raising productivity because they choose appropriate factor proportions, provide advice on the purchase of appropriate equipment and can advise on marketing (e.g. Pack, 1993) is supported by evidence from this category of TNCs. But the findings from the case studies do not seem to support this position as a generalization for all TNC activities in Africa.

Human resource development as investing in learning

Improvements in the production processes or product technology need to be accompanied by a labour force which has the skills to utilize such technologies efficiently. It was found that many exporting firms maintained or improved their position in export markets by investing in training the workforce and upgrading in-house labour skills and by making efforts to engage expatriate staff for selected activities for which local personnel did not have the requisite capabilities.

It has been pointed out in the previous section that firms have maintained their positions in export markets by making continuous investments in technological upgrading. The human resource requirements to cope with these technologies are also changing. The case studies have shown that the level of formal education among the recruited workers has been rising. The firms indicated that this has been encouraged by the need for flexible labour skills and rapid learning to operate new machinery and more sophisticated technologies. Thus firms which were recruiting primary-school leavers in low-skill jobs are now recruiting secondary-school leavers (holders of 'O' level or 'A' level certificates). Graduates are increasingly replacing secondary-school leavers for middle-level jobs. These trends imply that industrial demands for higher educational levels will have to be met by further investments in education. Governments may be called on to take the lead in this respect. In the light of these findings, the suggestion that African manufacturing should make intensive use of unskilled labour (e.g. by Pack, 1993) should be received with great caution.

The case studies have shown that various forms of training, in-house, in specialized local institutions and in other countries, were used to enhance production capabilities. Many exporting firms have an elaborate training programme and their production managers indicated that trained labour was an important requirement if the firm was to achieve its production and export targets. Overseas training is expensive and has therefore largely been confined to a few managerial and specialized technical and professional skills. Local training in technical and professional institutions had catered for the training of the majority of staff. A major limitation which came out in the case studies is the absence of specialist institutions for specific industries to teach subjects such as textiles technology, and garment- and shoe-manufacturing technical skills. Lower-level skills were acquired through in-house training, either within the production facility or in the firm's training institute, for those which had one. This is an area in which investments by the state will be necessary.

Interactions with foreign partners was found to have enhanced managerial and technological capabilities but only under certain conditions. Top management or entrepreneurs who had previous experience in commerce and/or industry tended to accumulate learning faster. Their visits abroad could be a useful eye-opener when such visits were well targeted (the experience of NEM of Tanzania being a good case in point). The training of local personnel to replace expatriates was found to be more rigorous in TNC subsidiaries. These firms could take advantage of their greater size to achieve economies of training.

Where the subsidiaries were set up to do simple assembly work and sell primarily in the domestic market, very little learning took place. The main motivation in these cases was to gain access to the market of the country in which the assembly activities were located and to neighbouring countries whose domestic markets were not big enough to warrant the setting up of similar assembly activities (e.g. exports to Burundi by Matsushita Electrical Manufacturing Co. in Tanzania). The kinds and level of skills that were required were rather low and could be acquired in-house through on-the-job training without requiring any high level of formal or professional training. In spite of the emphasis these firms placed on local training, there were fewer opportunities for the indigenous workers to upgrade themselves technologically. This is partly because they worked on assembly lines which were labour-intensive and in the least skill-intensive parts of the production process. There is thus little incentive to search for or train more skilled operators and technicians. Recruitment has thus been focused mainly on primary-school leavers (seven years of schooling) who are then trained on the job. The lack of opportunities is also partly because the areas with the greatest potential for enhancing capability acquisition are reserved for expatriate personnel. For instance, in the case of Matsushita Electrical Manufacturer in Tanzania, the top management is foreign and most of the training for local workers has therefore focused on manual skills. There has been little training to enhance indigenous management, administrative and marketing capabilities.

The TNCs which were manufacturing locally for world markets were making considerable investments in training. For instance, Del Monte of Kenya placed great emphasis on training local employees in all relevant fields, on both the management and technical sides of its operations. Employees in the agricultural, canned foods processing, management, finance and accounting departments of the firm are all likely to go through the company's training department at least once in their careers. Their training needs are assessed every year. The firm uses both in-house and local training institutions and works closely with the government's Management Training and Advisory Centre, the Directorate of Industrial Training and the Kenya Polytechnic. The firm's internal courses are supplemented by on-going local management programmes conducted by reputable local firms, and several staff members are sent overseas for further training and practical experience within the Del Monte network every year. These on-going training programmes have enabled Kenyans to take up senior posts. In the past two years, the number of expatriate employees has dropped from 20 to 9, all of whom hold highly technical or senior management positions. The productivity of labour also increased. Between 1980 and 1990, the total labour force increased by 20 per cent, while canned pineapple production increased by 142 per cent, leading to a decline in the share of labour costs in total output from 10.4 per cent in 1970 to 7.1 per cent in 1990.

As the case studies have indicated, training is an important source of capability acquisition for even low-technology activities. With the emergence of new technologies, the demands for higher levels of education and professional training are increasing. Many firms have made investments in staff training but this is largely on-the-job training and other kinds of short-term training which may not be sufficient to develop the capabilities to handle the more demanding stages of industrial development. Many firms could not train their staff at a higher technical or professional level because they lack resources and face the risk of losing staff after training them. Training within firms can expand the base of required human resources but it cannot be a substitute for investment in basic and higher formal education for higher-level managerial and technical personnel. At higher levels of industrialization, the demands for government intervention in investment on education, especially in technical and engineering areas, is likely to increase. There is a strong case for the government to provide the levels of formal education and training needed to acquire industrial capabilities.

Organization of production

A new technology may or may not conform to the core capabilities of a firm. If it does not, a change in some of the core capabilities may be required. A change in management and organization systems is often necessary. In the long term, organizational changes are needed to enhance dynamic innovative capabilities.

The case studies show that some of the firms which were maintaining their positions in the export markets through undertaking continuous investments in technology, training and marketing had also taken initiatives to change the way they organized production. For example, Bain of Zimbabwe has benefited in recent years from an International Trade Centre project which seconded a master welder to assist in improving performance on the shop floor. Apart from offering training in welding skills and suggesting changes in component design to improve weld strength and overall finish, the person concerned also made suggestions about plant layout, handling equipment and maintenance. The changes implemented have had a marked effect on efficiency. In response to increasing competition, Tinto has taken steps to improve its production management system. By employing a local consulting organization, the Kawasaki Production System has been introduced. This is essentially a 'just-in-time' production system, which has been particularly successful in improving productivity and efficiency at the Norton factory. There have been significant financial savings from reducing the amount of work in progress, which has also allowed for a 60 per cent reduction in working space.

Investing in marketing capabilities

Firms which invested in marketing, either by building in-house capabilities or by engaging various types of marketing services, managed to follow changes in the export markets and to make adjustments in response to the signals which came from the market.

Investments in marketing have taken the form of building in-house capabilities by strengthening marketing departments. Firms chose one or more of the following channels for marketing their products in export markets: using overseas agents, making direct contacts with some chain stores, posting their own agents in export markets and relying on the assistance of national external trade institutions.

Larger companies were more likely to be able to afford to set up their own agents in marketing offices in the export market. The subsidiaries of TNCs had an advantage in that they already had established offices which could handle marketing functions in many countries.

Some firms continued to sell in export markets, even at a loss, for the sake of maintaining their market positions while they were making the investments in technology necessary to improve their competitiveness. This kind of exporting at a loss is an investment, provided it is a matter of temporarily holding onto export markets while specific core capabilities are being built or strengthened.

Small and medium-size firms may find the investments needed to build core capabilities in marketing beyond their means. In these cases public institutions for handling trade matters such as organizing trade fairs and establishing contacts can be very useful. Institutions such as ZimTrade of Zimbabwe, the Board of External Trade in Tanzania and the Kenya External Trade Authority were established to play that role. Many firms in the case studies benefited from the services of these institutions but it was often said that their effectiveness needs improvement.

The trade–production nexus

The trade–production nexus was manifested in two forms. First, the contacts which were made in the trading phase with consumers or with suppliers enabled firms to accumulate capabilities and knowledge about the characteristics of the markets and of suppliers. These contacts were a useful asset when these firms entered the manufacturing stage. Second, as some firms shifted from trading to manufacturing, part of the family continued with trading activities and some of them were located abroad. The local manufacturing firms then made use of the family connections, who acted as trusted agents and 'marketing offices' abroad. Networking with family members in foreign countries has been useful in getting access to information about market opportunities and sources of technology. Such family connections were found very effective in Mauritius, in Zimbabwe within the white community and in Tanzania and Kenya within the Asian community. A large number of these contacts were retained and operated as networks through which new ideas about changing technological and marketing conditions were disseminated, contributing to the improvement of firms' positions in export markets.

Exporting firms which are subsidiaries of TNCs have benefited from a production–trade nexus of a different kind. Through their global networks of companies, TNCs in resource-based activities have engaged in the production and processing of primary resources and trading in the final products. Either they control the source of raw materials by developing their own plantations or, by establishing processing activities at the source of the raw materials, they have priority over procurement. For instance, the production of cotton is highly dispersed world-wide but its marketing is concentrated in the hands of a few big traders (notably 15 cotton traders of whom two are European companies, eight are US companies and five are Japanese trading houses). The coffee market is dominated by a few trading companies (General Foods, Nestlé, Suchard).

Even in areas where TNCs used to procure the raw materials from local producers, technological developments are opening up possibilities for them to establish their own plantations. For instance, tissue-culture coffee trees have already been planted in large plantations (mainly by multinationals such as Nestlé) in Malaysia, Singapore and Indonesia with an eye on the Japanese market (Brown and Tiffen, 1992). Trading activities are also carried out by their own companies.

In clothing production, barriers to entry are low, but in the garment trade large OECD-based buying groups dominate the market, using their vast purchasing power to influence the design, quality and price of garments. The degree of concentration in international buying is very high, so, instead of making direct investments, buying groups use their assets to undertake non-equity forms of investment in developing countries, mainly in the form of international subcontracting and licensing of trade marks and brand names (OECD, 1989).

HOW SOME FIRMS LOSE GROUND IN EXPORT MARKETS

The case studies have yielded some insights into the conditions under which firms which were once exporters to regional and international markets have lost or are losing ground in these markets.

Failure to cope with changing technology

Failure to keep pace with changes in production process technology was often reflected in uncompetitive costs of production and/or deficiencies in product quality. Some firms had made initial investments in labour-based production processes to take advantage of relatively low labour costs. However, the state of technology changed and such methods could not provide the quality and precision now required in finished products. Investment in more automated production methods became necessary. Those firms that failed to make these investments lost their markets because they could not meet the product quality demands of export markets.

There are several factors which inhibited investments in improved technologies. Some firms did not have search mechanisms for information on changing technological and market conditions and did not keep abreast of the technological trends in their industries. The gap had not been filled by any institutional arrangements initiated by governments or industry associations. Some firms had not made any investments in improved technology for lack of foreign exchange or of accumulated profits which could be ploughed back into the enterprises. Such firms had either accumulated losses or had failed to generate profits for a long time. Some firms had suffered from the effects of rigid price controls but others had been operating at low capacity utilization rates for a long time for various reasons. Firms which had been in financial problems for a long time had eroded their capacity to make any significant investments in capital equipment, training and innovations. Investment in general had been low or stagnant.

For instance, it was found that Tanganyika Textiles used to export vikoy, mainly to the Muslim community in Kenya, but it has been pushed out of that export market mainly because it could not modernize its 1959 labour-intensive textile technology. Capacity utilization rates have been falling during the last decade, from about 41 per cent in 1980 to around 20 per cent in 1993, leaving the firm too under-capitalized to modernize its technology in any substantial way. Competitors' finished products were perceived as being of higher quality and the export price could not cover the firm's costs of production. Although the collapse of its export market (in Kenya) was triggered by the collapse of the East African Community in 1977, this may have been only the last straw. In fact the firm has not recovered since then and in the meantime Kenya has developed its own textile base. Even in the domestic market this firm is losing its market share to imports from Southeast Asia.

After 1985, one manufacturer of kangas in Kenya (Rivatex) started to lose its markets in the Middle East and to some extent in Tanzania to the Far East, where prices were more competitive. While Rivatex was selling kangas at US$3.20 per pair, similar products from the Far East were selling at US$1.70 per pair. This loss of competitiveness is partly due to lack of technological improvements or innovations over time. The firm's ability to make investments in technology had been eroded by the rising costs of debt servicing on loans denominated in foreign exchange (between 1976 and 1992 the Kenya Shilling depreciated substantially against the Deutschmark). The firm has failed to inject new capital, to modernize its machinery, or to finance training programmes for its staff.

In the import liberalization phase, some firms which had operated profitably in protected domestic markets found it difficult to compete with imports. In response, instead of making efforts to improve their competitiveness, some firms resorted to export markets with the help of channels which were not strictly commercial, e.g. religious groups or charity organizations. This strategy seemed to work for a while but it could not be sustained. This indicates that losers in the domestic markets are not likely to succeed by seeking refuge in export markets, even if it may seem possible at first.

Some firms were found to be putting considerable effort into improving their competitiveness but the results in terms of export performance did not seem to be commensurate to their efforts. Two categories of reasons were identified in the case studies. First, it was found that the efforts these firms were making were blunted by the inadequacy of infrastructural and institutional support, which ordinarily originates from outside the firms. Second, the basic limitations in the technologies the firms were using were not being tackled. Instead, futile efforts were made in more peripheral aspects of technology. This situation was particularly present in areas in which technology had changed to the extent that high product quality was no longer being attained by highly skilled labour working with labour-intensive technologies but rather by the use of microelectronic controls. In such cases, further investment in training labour and perfecting skills in the labour-intensive methods could not yield much fruit. These firms succeeded in reducing costs and improving product quality but these achievements did not meet the requirements of international markets. This points to the limitations of small-scale, labour-intensive operations, in specific industry contexts, in producing high-quality products for the international market. Investments in more radical changes in technology were needed. This underscores the importance of understanding the pace and trends of technology development elsewhere, as a guide to the kinds of investment that must be made to create and develop new technological capabilities.

The case studies have also shown that technological changes in the materials used in production have undermined the competitiveness of firms which had based their competitive strength on cheap local resources. For instance, Orbitsports of Kenya had gained a competitive advantage in exporting balls under licence from Adidas. This advantage was based on the domestic availability of cheap, high-quality leather. As a consequence of technological developments in materials, Adidas recommended a shift from leather to synthetic, non-woven fabrics. The problem has been aggravated by high import duties on imported synthetic materials. The firm has been losing some export orders to competitors from Asia and Europe.

Import substitution in importing countries

The countries which had made an earlier start on industrialization in Africa found their export markets in the neighbouring countries, whose level of industrial development was lower. Some of these regional markets have been lost as neighbouring countries decided to establish and protect their own industries. While this may be a necessary step towards industrialization, it poses the question of whether industrialization might not be better pursued within regional cooperation arrangements which could reduce duplication of productive capacities within the cooperating regions.

Problems of reliability of supply and quality of local inputs

Substitution of local inputs for imported inputs has been one innovative step taken to cut down costs or as a survival strategy in the face of import controls. For example, the shift in textiles in Tanzania, from using imported rayon to local cotton, and from imported starch to local cassava starch, was stimulated by cost-cutting considerations and responses to import controls. These modifications have resulted in a considerable reduction in production costs, as import content was lowered. But these are one-off cost cutting innovations and do not necessarily represent continuous efforts. In the past some of these innovations were made in response to foreign exchange constraints. As competitive pressures build up, with import liberalization and competition from export markets, product quality considerations are gaining in importance. Where such import substituting innovations had compromised product quality, these innovations are being reversed.

The case studies have shown that some exporting firms failed to meet product quality requirements or delivery times because of the low quality of local inputs and unreliability of supply. Firms which could not obtain good-quality inputs found it difficult to maintain their position in export markets. This has some similarities to findings on the Colombian clothing industry by Morawetz (1981).[2] He made a comparison of Colombian and East Asian clothing exporters and found that, in early 1977, Colombian exporters were offering prices for jeans and shirts which were 44 per cent higher than prices from Korea, 25 per cent higher than Hong Kong and 11 per cent higher than Taiwan. One explanation of the lack of competitiveness of Colombian firms was the price and quality of their inputs. While East Asian firms obtained good-quality fabrics at world prices, the Colombian firms bought from domestic producers at prices 50–108 per cent higher than the world prices. These producers were protected and were too small to take advantage of economies of scale. Locally made zippers and threads in Colombia were two to three times the world price. The case studies suggest that the African situation is quite close to the Colombian one.

The industries which are supplying inputs to the exporting firms have more often developed monopolistic and protectionist structures than competitive ones. In Zimbabwe, for instance, there are about 250 garment manufacturing firms which get their fabrics from only five textile firms. There is little competition between these firms, since two of them account for 60 per cent of the total output of the sector. The local grey cloth which the textile mills manufacture is not competitive in the world market and it is difficult for those using this grey cloth as an input to face competition in export markets successfully.

This implies that local availability of inputs and linkages in the domestic economy are not always a blessing. If the firms using local inputs have to be competitive, the efficiency of the supplying firms and supporting institutions also needs to be ensured.

The lack of specialization

The case studies have indicated that the degree of specialization in many firms was limited by two considerations: the size and stability of the markets which the firms had decided to target and the supply conditions in the supportive industries, especially those producing inputs.

Target market conditions were crucial determinants of specialization for firms which were primarily targeting domestic markets and became exporters at a later date. While supplying the domestic markets, these firms adopted the diversification strategy as a growth path where domestic markets for particular products were very small (e.g. NEM and Themi in Tanzania and the fertilizer and paints manufacturers in Mauritius). While these firms extended from domestic markets to exports they retained the wide variety of products they were manufacturing. Firms which targeted the export market from the outset tended to be more specialized than those which were primarily catering for the domestic market.

Product diversification has presented further challenges: shorter production runs, the associated loss of economies of scale and having to cope with requirements of marketing. The case studies have identified the lack of specialization as one factor which inhibited attainment of international competitiveness. The textile firms (e.g. those owned by the government in Kenya) had a low average size, of about eight thousand spindles per mill, compared to the minimum economic size of a spinning plant of 25–30 thousand spindles. These findings are corroborated by a previous study of the textile industry in Kenya (Pack, 1987).[3] That study employed engineering and economic data to analyse the deviation of textile plants (in Kenya and Philippines) from international best practice. The lack of specialization was identified as the main source of such deviation. Excessive diversification of products (partly reflecting tariff protection) and the consequent short production runs accounted for considerable inefficiency.

Facing the absence of reliable networks for input supplies, some firms have taken steps in-house to tackle the problem. Diversification in the form of vertical integration has been adopted as one way of ensuring reliability in the supply of inputs. For instance, some clothing firms (e.g. Fashion Enterprises of Zimbabwe) have solved the problem of unreliable supply of fabrics by establishing their own fabrics-manufacturing units to guarantee quality and reliability of supply. While this kind of diversification increases reliability of input supplies, it has often led to higher costs. Where the domestic market has been protected, such costs could be passed on to consumers. In the export business, however, this may not be possible. Some firms have tried to check costs by creating autonomous production units under one group of companies. While this option has been feasible for large corporations operating a group of companies, it is more difficult for smaller firms.

Failure to cope with changing market conditions

Employment of high technology may be a necessary condition but it is by no means sufficient. Faulty marketing strategy and failure to develop the necessary marketing capabilities have led to disaster in spite of having invested in modern and advanced technology. For instance, the manufacture of cloth for shirts and trousers started in Mauritius in 1990 as a significant move towards high fashion and high-technology production in clothing manufacture and exports. The firm was equipped with the latest textile machinery available on the European market. However, due to a defective marketing strategy and a narrow and excessively concentrated customer base, sales collapsed and the firm was placed in receivership barely two years after its creation.

LINKAGES AND SUPPORTING INDUSTRIES

Inter-firm linkages

The study found that internal linkages (i.e. within the country) are limited. While there were some linkages among firms which shared premises in the industrial estates, there were only isolated cases of subcontracting arrangements outside these networks. There is little subcontracting or local procurement of manufactured inputs in the exporting firms. Large firms have only infrequent relations with small firms except for the purchase of some repair and maintenance services. Information and technology diffusion among firms is minimal except for very informal channels.

Several factors explain this situation. First, import dependence over a long time has pre-empted the search for local alternative linkages. For instance, in the cases of NEM, Afrocooling and Matsushita, the lack of linkages reflects the pattern of import substitution industrialization which emphasizes import-dependent assembly. Second, access to tied donor finance reduced the need to search for local sources of supply. Third, the capability to search for various local suppliers had not been developed. Fourth, some firms competed with their potential suppliers of technological services rather than being assisted by them. For instance, Themi of Tanzania produced farm implements, some at least of which were also being produced for the domestic market by two research and development institutions. The competitive relationship between the firm and the institutions which are supposed to provide technological services was not conducive to the development of technological linkages between them. Lastly, poor inter-sectoral linkages may reflect poor infrastructural facilities for small firms, biases in policies and in credit markets and the lack of an extension network.

Industry associations had made attempts to promote interactions among local firms by harmonizing production processes (e.g. identification of excess capacity in individual firms and possibilities of subcontracting, trading in spares, joint quality control, etc.). The case studies showed that in isolated incidents firms which receive large export orders have subcontracted some of the work to other firms. Inter-firm trade in unfinished products is very rare.

The creation of linkages or establishment of input-producing activities have been influenced by government policy. For instance, in the case of textiles and brewing, the establishment of some input-supplying activities was influenced by government policies discouraging imports (e.g. yarn and malt in Nigeria). Some of these firms have achieved such tremendous expansion that they now export as well as selling on the local market. In the case of the brewing industry in Nigeria, the search for local alternatives was intensified with the introduction of restrictions on importing barley. Increasing success with local substitutes for barley malt improved the capacity utilization rate for the industry. The search for local substitutes for imported barley malt involved most of the firms in investment in R&D, as well as substantial plant conversion. Their efforts were complemented by the independent research endeavour at the Federal Institute of Industrial Research, Oshodi (FIIRO), which, through some of its research report series, demonstrated that lager beer could be produced using only sorghum. Today, most of the more successful firms use maize and sorghum in their beer production process.

Buyer–consumer links

The case studies found that buyers and consumers of the firms' products provided useful market information. They were very instrumental in inducing product quality improvements. The interaction with export markets, which are more demanding, was particularly effective in this respect.

Linkages with marketing agents have been common among exporting firms which are not large enough to afford large investments in building their marketing capabilities. The role of marketing agents had been observed to be important in South Korea but there seems to be one difference; that is, Korean firms selectively let foreign buyers do much of the marketing during the early stages of export development but this role was gradually transferred to the firms or to local trading institutions. This progressive transfer process does not seem to have taken place as yet except for some firms in Mauritius.

Infrastructural problems

Various problems of infrastructure have been pointed out in the country studies as obstacles to the attainment and maintenance of competitiveness in export markets. Supportive infrastructure is an important prerequisite for successful exporting. Expensive, sporadic and unreliable transport and communications are a serious impediment to the exporters of non-traditional goods. Reliability of delivery is also critical. High transport costs contribute greatly to the lack of competitiveness of exports. Poor telecommunications and constant power and water interruptions also raise the costs of doing business and compound the problem of lack of information. To obtain electricity, some firms had to purchase generators or other equipment which is ordinarily supposed to be purchased by the national electricity supply authorities. This added unnecessary costs to the operations of the firms.

Information flow is very important if firms are to respond to opportunities which arise from time to time. It was one thing to introduce supportive facilities, it is another to make full use of the facility. Some firms were found not to be aware of the existence of some of the facilities which were supposed to assist them.

THE INFLUENCE OF POLICY ON FIRMS' EXPORT ACTIVITY

The macro and sectoral policy environment in which exporting firms have been operating has an influence on decisions taken by firms.

Import policies

Import policies have been mentioned as important in influencing the performance of exporting firms. The competitiveness of some exporting firms was undermined by high duties on imported inputs or difficulties of access to quality inputs required to meet export orders. This study has also revealed that there are cases in which government support had favoured subsidiaries of TNCs which were in competition with local firms. For instance, Cosmivoire would have performed better if the government had been able to guarantee fair competition within its sector: its main competitor is a subsidiary of a powerful multinational which receives many advantages from the government. In the case of Kenya, Sharpley and Lewis (1990)[4] have pointed out that the rate of effective protection for foreign private firms (averaging 57 per cent) and especially parastatal enterprises (65 per cent) was considerably higher than for local firms (35 per cent).

One major problem mentioned by all firms in the sample is that of cumbersome, bureaucratic and lengthy procedures for licensing, access to credit and foreign exchange, and export documentation. Some exporters have to travel long distances from the regions to the capital city simply to register themselves. There are also still tight bureaucratic bottlenecks in foreign exchange allocation, resulting in long lead times for imports. Such long and cumbersome procedures involving many institutions impose extra implicit costs (in terms of delays, etc.) on exporters. Delays could be even more disastrous for risk exports such as fresh fruits and fish. Some country studies have proposed the establishment of some kind of export centre which would offer at one location a package of relevant export services such as registration, licensing, proofs of ownership, export advice and export promotion.

Bureaucratic delays at Customs and related obstructionist tendencies increased the operating costs in many ways, making it less attractive for exporting firms to export, or to import in order to export. For instance, several respondents complained about Customs' insistence on sticking to the letter of their duties, even when there is little or no customs revenue involved and delays could cost the country not just one particular export order but perhaps a valuable relationship with an overseas client. For example, in preparing an export order for the UK, Bata was requested to tag the shoes with bar codes. As these could not be produced in Zimbabwe, Bata requested their UK customer to supply the tags, which were duly sent but then seized by Customs and held while they decided what tariff to apply. In the process Bata's ability to meet the deadline was threatened. Similar experiences have been cited in respect of the Customs handling of samples.

Under very restrictive import control regimes, the incentive offered by export retention schemes (where exporters could retain a portion of their foreign exchange earnings to pay for imported inputs) was quite effective (e.g. Tanzania, Zimbabwe). While export retention schemes (ERSs) made it easier for exporting firms to import the inputs they required, the consequences of the schemes were not always positive. Their implementation had side-effects associated with market distortions. The case studies showed that some exporting firms had 'over-responded' to this kind of incentive by selling to the export markets at a financial loss (at the official exchange rate) and by diverting a greater part of their output to exports even if the domestic market was deprived.

The handling of foreign exchange by individual units raises some longer-term concerns. For instance, the case of Zimbabwe has shown that the trend towards individual farmer control over foreign currency could undermine the capacity to support agriculture on a sector-wide basis with adequate supplies of inputs. Not only is it inefficient for companies to go through all the export procedures for each individual farmer, but individual access to foreign currency is leading individual farmers to keep significant stocks of spare parts, while the agent has virtually none. From all points of view (the individual farmer, the agricultural support sector and the nation), this case study found that these unintended consequences of the ERS system amount to a highly inefficient use of foreign exchange resources. The weakening of agricultural support companies not only makes it more difficult for them to compete in export markets, it also disadvantages farmers who produce mainly for the domestic market and do not have access to ERS funds. These disadvantages have led to some policy changes in which tradable ERS funds have become available and are widely used, alleviating these problems.

Trade liberalization

Trade liberalization measures were found to have been implemented in most case study countries in the 1980s. Trade liberalization introduces competitive pressures which may stimulate firms to build capabilities to cope with the new situation but it also carries the potential dangers of deindustrialization, exposes the fragile manufacturing sector to the danger of dumping and other external trade practices and may make it difficult to address major gaps in the sector. The implications of liberalization measures and their impact on the competitiveness of exporting firms varied. Three types of import liberalization regimes were identified in the case studies.

The first regime is represented by countries like the Ivory Coast and, to a lesser extent, Kenya, which were already fairly open. Import liberalization merely lowered and rationalized some tariffs but did not represent a major shock for industrial firms. The second regime is that of countries like Tanzania, where quantitative restrictions on imports had been quite pervasive, so that import liberalization came as a major policy shift. Competition from imports came suddenly, not giving much time for adjustment to the new competitive environment. In the case of Nigeria, the end of the oil boom around 1980 led to extensive use of tariffs and quantitative restrictions. The various foreign exchange conservation measures implemented in the period 1982–85 meant that several industries which were dependent on imported inputs had to operate considerably below capacity, hence reducing growth and worsening unemployment. The adoption of the SAP in 1986 represented a fundamental shift in the basic philosophy of economic management at the national level. The reforms include the adoption of a largely market-determined exchange rate and the removal or relaxation of quantitative restrictions on many tradable goods.

The third regime is represented by Zimbabwe and Mauritius, in which the implementation of trade liberalization was managed more selectively in a situation where the export sector was already quite diversified and firms had attained a reasonable degree of competitiveness. Trade liberalization had a constructive effect in that firms were given adequate time to make adjustments. In Zimbabwe, for instance, import liberalization started with imported inputs through some form of an open general import licence system. The users of these inputs were made aware that the next phase of import liberalization would be applied to outputs. This message induced many firms to invest in technological improvements of various kinds in anticipation of a more competitive environment. Managed import liberalization stands a better chance of providing an opportunity and incentive for firms to build up capabilities which can cope with a more competitive environment.

The influx of imports in the liberalization phase took part of firms' market shares, forcing them to look for new markets abroad. This could be the beginning of intra-industry trade as practised in the more developed countries, or it could be a futile attempt to conceal inherent inefficiency. In the latter case, such survival would at best be short-lived. In the former case, the level of competitiveness of the firm could be raised if this move meant that less efficient lines of production contracted while more efficient lines expanded and further improved their competitiveness.

Pricing policies

Pricing policies may influence the prices of inputs or outputs of firms. Price controls on inputs affect the cost competitiveness of firms, while price controls on outputs affect the revenue side. The case studies showed that some exporting firms had to procure local inputs (e.g. cotton, palm oil) at prices well above their world market prices, putting users of these inputs at a relative disadvantage to their competitors in export markets. It was pointed out that local users of cotton (e.g. textile firms in Zimbabwe) and steel (e.g. manufacturers of agricultural machinery in Zimbabwe) were paying more for these local inputs than their competitors (in the importing countries) were paying for the same inputs.

Some firms had access to inputs at prices which were lower than the world market prices. For instance, in addition to the fiscal advantages provided by the 1959 investment code, a setting-up agreement signed between Capral–Nestlé and the Ivory Coast government allowed the firm to buy green coffee at local prices, which are sometimes as low as one third or one quarter of world prices. However, in 1984 the government put an end to this arrangement and the fiscal advantages under the investment code expired at the same time.

Rigid price controls on output can run down an otherwise profitable firm to near collapse by depriving it of the resources to plough back into investment in general and technology in particular. For example, in one case it was pointed out that for over eight years the government had failed to adjust prices to levels that would turn around the firm's performance, making it difficult for the firm (Bamburi of Kenya) to secure financial assistance to refurbish the plant. Continuing under-capitalization of the firm placed it in an increasingly poor position, threatening to wipe out its exports.

Pricing, however, has also been used positively to encourage firms to increase efficiency and attain competitiveness in export markets, as in the case of agricultural machinery manufacturers in Zimbabwe. Altering the generous cost-plus pricing system (by allowing lower prices) exposed long-term weaknesses in the firms, which led to the adoption of more cost-effective production methods (Riddell, 1990, pp. 354–8). Some of the actions taken include expansion into the export market, reorganizing production lines to a continuous flow system, staff training and recruitment of more skilled personnel, leading to higher-quality products and improved designs of traditional lines.

Fiscal and monetary policies

High interest rates reduced economic access to export finance and other working capital requirements. High interest rates made working capital and fixed investments more expensive, leading to the postponement of some investments in technology. Affordability becomes more of a problem than availability. In such situations subsidiary companies have an advantage in receiving soft loans from their mother companies.

Provisions for tax rebates or drawback schemes were evidenced in the country case studies. However, implementation has not been commensurate with the intentions of such schemes. The problem of bureaucratic delays in paying export incentives was particularly noted in the case of exporting firms, in all country case studies except Mauritius. The effect of bureaucratic delays was to reduce the effectiveness of whatever export incentives had been put in place.

Relationship between government and the enterprise sector

The relationship between government and the enterprise sector influences cooperation with the enterprise sector and the effectiveness of government policy. In three cases it was found that the rapport between the government and the enterprise sector was good and consultations were made between them on a regular basis. In the case of Zimbabwe during the Unilateral Declaration of Independence (UDI) period, the industrialists and the government of the day shared a determination to overcome the impact of sanctions which the international community had imposed on the then Rhodesia. The system of controls was made to operate effectively and the highly protected system that they constituted did not lead to the gross inefficiency which has characterized other import substitution regimes. The need to adapt and innovate led to the development of a wide range of technical skills, particularly in various branches of engineering. The strong orientation to market requirements led to a proliferation of products, often produced within large, vertically integrated conglomerates.

In the case of Mauritius the government and the enterprise sector cooperated in many ways and held consultations on matters affecting industry. Government policy facilitated the process by which local entrepreneurs continuously gained control of industrial development. In the Ivory Coast the government worked with and was supportive of enterprise sector development in a way which did not threaten the main actors in industry, even if they were non-Ivorians.

In the other three countries (Tanzania, Kenya and Nigeria) and the post-independence Zimbabwe, the relationship between government and the enterprise sector (or significant parts of it) was less cordial. Government intervention in industrial development was perceived as intending to address imbalances in society, as a result of which some leading actors in industrial development could be losers. In Tanzania the nationalization policy and the socialist policy were perceived as a threat to the private sector. In Kenya the way the Africanization policy was introduced and practised was perceived as a threat to the Asian community, who were the leading local private-sector industrialist group. The indigenization policy in Nigeria posed a threat to some foreign investors. In post-independence Zimbabwe, too, the relationship between government and sections of the enterprise sector became less cordial as the government began to address some imbalances in society. The leading white community entrepreneurs perceived that they would be the losers. The application of controls in the absence of the rapport with the private sector that had existed under the previous regime, and the introduction of new controls on wages and labour relations, led to a situation in which bureaucracy became a major obstacle to the running of any kind of economic enterprise.

6 Conclusions and policy implications

BUILDING CORE CAPABILITIES: TOWARDS COMPETITIVENESS

In the context of new technologies and the rapidly changing world market conditions, the process of restructuring for export orientation poses a challenge to Africa. Constraints are bound to arise but opportunities could also emerge for these economies as they set out to restructure and develop their industrial sectors towards export orientation.

One major consideration which will influence the way the industrialization problem is conceptualized relates to the changing character of innovations and their role in international trade and competitiveness. Industrialization, for the less industrialized countries in Africa, will have to take place under conditions of accelerating technical change and the pervasive application of new technologies. The evidence presented in this book supports the Schumpeterian conceptualization of technological change, which emphasizes learning and the accumulation of technological capabilities. This is bound to have considerable implications for the conceptualization of the industrialization problem in Africa.

The findings of this study support the thrust of recent trade and growth models which have focused more explicitly on the micro-foundations of innovation by addressing firm-level decisions to invest in product or process innovations. The case studies have shown that ceaseless search for improvements in technology (especially product quality and cost-lowering process innovations) has been most instrumental in improving productivity. Productivity growth, in turn, was a most important factor enabling exporting firms to succeed in the changing technological and market conditions. Exporting firms maintained and improved their market position by investing in technology and continuing to improve on it. Improvements were made not only in the firm's products but also in the processes of production, in order to cope with pressure to keep costs at competitive levels or to improve product quality (level and consistency). These responses were derived from signals given in export markets.

A major policy implication suggested by these findings is that, in conceptualizing the industrialization problem in Africa, fuller recognition will need to be given to the altering nature of technological change, with an emphasis on learning and the accumulation of technological capabilities within firms, with the requisite support from the state in the form of various supportive infrastructural investments. This contrasts with the previous emphasis on the transfer of the capital and know-how required for an industrialization process which was primarily directed at import substitution.

ECONOMIC REFORMS AND INDUSTRIALIZATION

The poor record of many developing countries can be explained by their inability to create internationally competitive industry. One criticism of the structural adjustment programmes which many of the countries in Sub-Saharan Africa adopted during the 1980s has been their over-emphasis on 'getting prices right' to the neglect of other things that governments ought to be doing. The nature of the problems that exporting firms face in their struggle to remain competitive in world markets suggests that, although exchange rate action and import liberalization and incentives for improving tradables can help, it is difficult to sustain an export recovery without additional steps being taken to assist firms in the export sector to improve their international competitiveness. Some firms have found it difficult to maintain their position in export markets because of a lack of complementary supportive investments by government. In fact, references often made to the deindustrialization consequences of economic reforms in Africa could be a reflection of this lack of complementary supportive intervention by governments. As the Chinese example has shown, the withdrawal of the state, combined with active intervention in infrastructural support, can lead to a booming non-state sector (Qian and Xu, 1993).[1]

The findings of this study suggest that economic reform policies can enhance the industrialization process and restructuring of the export sector in Africa, provided that these policies incorporate a considerable element of government support, in particular complementary investments to assist firms to build the technological capabilities which are necessary for attaining and maintaining competitiveness.

EXPORT ORIENTATION OR IMPORT SUBSTITUTION?

The case studies have shown that most exporting firms started by serving the domestic market. Import substituting firms grew up and built up various core capabilities by producing for the domestic market. The protection of the domestic market allowed them to accumulate resources, which were in turn invested in developing capabilities which enabled them to turn to exports at a later stage. In this sense, the findings of this study have underscored the point that import substitution and export orientation are complementary in the African context. Import substitution has preceded exporting and has, under certain circumstances, formed an important basis for export orientation. At firm level, the experience and capabilities which were developed during the import substitution phase became useful in the next phase, when the firms were shifting to or extending to export markets. At the broader level, export orientation programmes such the Mauritian EPZs built on the capabilities which had been accumulated during the import substitution phase. The policy implication in this is that, if import substitution is effective in providing for the development of technological capabilities, it can establish the basis for building a competitive export sector. In the process of exporting, firms can develop efficient linkages and acquire technological capabilities. The challenge is to blend efficient import substitution and export orientation through a mix of policies which aim at maximizing the benefits from increased domestic demand and at stimulating both substantial (and efficient) import substitution and increased export orientation on the basis of growing technological capabilities.

LOCAL OR FOREIGN INVESTMENT?

This study shows that outsiders (foreign firms in some form of partnership with local firms, or non-indigenous entrepreneurs) have sometimes been instrumental in initiating the process of building up the capabilities that are necessary for improving competitiveness. This occurred where these outsiders were incorporated into the national accumulation process and their capital and know-how were transferred to others.

The case studies revealed an array of relationships between foreign capital and local capital. In some cases foreign investment preceded investment by local firms but the latter developed and gradually took over ownership from foreign-controlled firms. In other cases, foreign firms had been buying out local firms. Foreign investment and other industrialization agents have a role in building technological capabilities. Foreign investment, in particular, could make a contribution to filling some important gaps in the capabilities of African firms.

REGIONAL COOPERATION AND TRADE AGREEMENTS

The volume of trade to countries in the region was found to be influenced by the nature of the regional cooperation and trade agreements. This finding is grounds for a reassessment of the viability of small-scale import substitution and far more consideration for regional cooperation and regional trade, which enable economies of scale to be tapped.

The exporting firms have mainly targeted regional markets, with smaller volumes being exported to international markets. This study has found that even to sustain regional markets, competition with other regions of the world will have to be faced sooner or later. There is always a danger of losing the regional markets to competitors from other regions. Even if imported products are not as suitable to local conditions, competitors from outside the region have sometimes penetrated the regional market by supplying their products at lower prices or by supplying products with a better finish. Thus specific local and regional markets can be lost to others if continuous efforts are not made to develop competitiveness in terms of quality and price. The study has revealed some cases in which competitors from other regions have made products specifically for the African regional market. Thus the specificity of regional markets may make the competition for various products less intense but it does not guarantee a monopoly. The need to exert continuous effort to attain and maintain competitiveness in such markets does not seem to be obviated by any specific characteristics of regional demand.

Africa has demonstrated the slowest progress in developing regional integration and cooperation arrangements (UNCTAD, 1993b). The challenge which emerges from this study is whether regional cooperation arrangements can be designed for Africa to facilitate (through investments, joint technological activities and trade) the process by which firms and other institutions in Africa build up technological capabilities. The African Economic Community and existing sub-regional economic cooperation arrangements should accord high priority to promoting trade expansion, based on both exports and imports, by removing distortions, avoiding the duplication of large investments where national markets are small, reducing transaction costs (e.g. by trading arrangements which guarantee market access, regional marketing intelligence, improvements in the marketing infrastructure) and by redirecting trade flows.

Notes to Part I

1 INTRODUCTION

1 UNECA, *Beyond Recovery: ECA-revised Perspectives of Africa's Development*, 1988–2008, E/ECA/CM.14/31, Addis Ababa, March 1988.
2 World Bank, *Accelerated Development in Sub-Saharan Africa*, Washington, D.C., 1981.
3 During 1980–88, 33 countries in Africa had agreements with the IMF and 12 had extended fund facilities, while 15 had Strategic Adjustment Loans with the World Bank.
4 UNCTAD, *Developments and Issues in the Uruguay Round of Particular Concern to Developing Countries*, Note by the UNCTAD Secretariat, TD/B/39(2)/CPR 1, 15 March 1993a.
5 UNIDO, *African Industry in Figures*, Vienna, 1993.
6 Sharma, R., *The 'Missing Middle' in Sub-Saharan Africa: Role of South–South Cooperation, Research and Information for the Non-aligned and other Developing Countries*, New Delhi, Interest Publications, 1993.
7 Riddell, R.C. (ed.), *Manufacturing Africa: Performance and Prospects of Seven Countries in Sub-Saharan Africa*, London, James Curry, etc., 1990.
8 UNCTAD, *Follow-up to the Recommendations Adopted by the Conference at its Eighth Session: Evolution and Consequences of Economic Spaces and Regional Integration Processes*, TD/B/40(1)7, 23 July 1993b.
9 Husain, I., Structural Adjustment and Long-term Development in Sub-Saharan Africa, in van de Hooven, R., and van de Kraaj, F. (eds) *Structural Adjustment in Sub-Saharan Africa*, London, James Curry, 1994.
10 *Sub-Saharan Africa: From Crisis to Sustainable Growth, A Long-term Perspective Study*, Washington, D.C., 1989.
11 Prebisch, R., Five Stages in My Thinking about Development, in Bauer, P., Meier, G., and Seers, D. (eds), *Pioneers in Development*, New York, 1954.
12 Nurkse, R., *Patterns of Trade and Development*, Wicksell Lectures, Stockholm, 1959.

13 The main exports in order of importance are: cocoa, coffee, timber, cotton, sugar, live animals and meat, tobacco, tea, fish products, rubber, groundnuts, palm oil, bananas, sisal, spices and fruits.

14 Brown, M.B. and Tiffen, P., *Short Changed: Africa and World Trade*, London, Pluto Press, 1992.

15 ITC, *Cocoa: Traders' Guide*, Geneva, International Trade Centre, 1987.

16 Killick, T., Explaining Africa's Post-independence Development Experiences. Paper presented at the Second Biennial Conference on African Economic Issues, Abidjan, 13–15 October, 1992

17 North, Douglass C., Economic Performance through Time, *American Economic Review*, 84 (3), June 1994.

18 However, over time there has been a shift in this approach towards recognition of institutional and enterprise-level actions as a complement to macroeconomic and sectoral policies [Lieberman, I., *Industrial Restructuring Policy and Practice*, Research and Policy Series, Washington, D.C., World Bank, 1990].

19 Weiss, J., *Industry in Developing Countries: Theory, Policy and Evidence*, London and New York, Routledge, 1988.

20 Bhagwati, J.N. and Srinivasan, T.N., *Foreign Trade Regimes and Economic Development: India*, National Bureau of Economic Research, New York, Columbia University Press, 1975.

21 World Bank, *Capital Accumulation and Economic Growth: The Korean Paradigm*, World Bank Staff Working Papers, No. 712, Washington, D.C., 1985.

22 Westphal, L., *Empirical Justification for Infant Industry Protection*, World Bank Staff Working Paper No. 445, Washington, D.C., 1981; Pack, H. and Westphal, L.E., Industrial Strategy and Technological Change: Theory versus Reality, *Journal of Development Economics*, 22, 1986; Jacobsson, S. and Alam, G., *Liberalization and Industrial Development in the Third World: A Comparison of the Indian and South Korean Engineering Industries*, New Delhi, Sage, 1994.

23 Lall, S., Navaretti, G.B., Teitel, S. and Wignaraja, G., *Technological Capabilities and Industrial Development in Ghana*, Study prepared for the World Bank, Washington, D.C., March 1993.

2 TRADE THEORY: RELEVANCE AND IMPLICATIONS FOR AFRICAN EXPORT ORIENTATION

1 Colclough, C., Structuralism versus Neo-liberalism: An Introduction, in Colclough and Manor, p. 18a, 1991.

2 Leontief, W.W., *Studies in the Structure of the American Economy*, New York, Oxford University Press, 1953

3 Helpman, E. and Krugman, P., *Market Structure and Foreign Trade: Increasing Returns, Imperfect Competition and the International Economy*, Brighton, Wheatsheaf, 1985; Porter, M., *The Competitive Advantage of Nations*, London and Basingstoke, Macmillan, 1990.

4 Linder, S.B., *An Essay on Trade and Transformation*, Stockholm, Almquist and Wikell, 1961 (reprinted New York, Garland, 1983).

5 Yoffie, D.B. (ed.) *Beyond Free Trade: Firms, Governments and Global Competition*, Boston, Mass., Harvard University School Press, 1993.

6   Ray, E.J., US Protection and Intra-industry Trade: The Message for Developing Countries, *Economic Development and Cultural Change*, 40 (1), October 1991.
7   Haque, I.U., International Competitiveness: Public Sector/Private Sector Interface, in Haque, I.U., (ed.) *International Competitiveness: Interaction of the Public and Private Sectors*, collected papers from an EDI policy seminar in Seoul, Republic of Korea, 18–21, April 1990.
8   Kierzkowski, H., Recent Advances in Trade Theory: A Selected Survey, *Oxford Review of Economic Policy* 3 (1), 1987.
9   Caves, R., International Trade and Industrial Organization: Introduction, *Journal of Industrial Economics*, 29, 1980; Brander, J.A., Intra-industry Trade in Identical Commodities, *Journal of International Economics*, 11, 1981; Brander, J.A. and Krugman, P.A., A Reciprocal Dumping Model of International Trade, *Journal of International Economics*, 1983.
10 Ethier, W.J., Internationally Decreasing Costs and World Trade, *Journal of International Economics*, 9, 1979; Krugman, P.R., Increasing Returns and the Theory of International Trade, in Bewley, T. (ed.), *Advances in Economic Theory*, Cambridge, 1987; Grossman, G. and Helpman, E., Product Development and International Trade, *Journal of Political Economy*, 97, 1989; Grossman, G.M. and Helpman, E., *Trade Innovation and Growth,* American Economic Review, Papers and Proceedings, May 1990a.
11 Dixit, A.K. and Norman, V., *Theory of International Trade*, Cambridge, Nisbet, 1980; Krugman, P.R., A Model of Innovation, Technology Transfer and the World Distribution of Income, *Journal of Political Economy*, 87, 1979; Lancaster, R., Intra-industry Trade under Perfect Monopolistic Competition, *Journal of International Economics*, 10, 1980.
12 Dixit, A.K. and Stiglitz, J., Monopolistic Competition and Optimum Product Diversity, *American Economic Review*, 67, 1977; Lancaster, R., *Variety, Equity and Efficiency*, New York, Columbia University Press, 1979.
13 Greenway, D., New Trade Theories and Developing Countries, in Balasubramanyam, V.N. and Lall, S. (eds), *Current Issues in Development Economics*, London, Macmillan, 1991.
14 Scherer, F., *Industrial Market Structure and Economic Performance*, Chicago etc., Houghton Mifflin, 1980
15 Alcorta, L., The Impact of New Technologies on Scale in Manufacturing Industry: Issues and Evidence, *World Development*, 22 (5), May 1994.
16 The traditional formulation assumed that the output of the domestic industry is the source of external economies via the larger demands for intermediate inputs (presumably produced at lower cost).
17 Ethier, W.J., National and International Returns to Scale in the Modern Theory of International Trade, *American Economic Review*, 72, 1982.
18 The assumption of symmetry requires that all intermediate goods (components) be producible from capital and labour via identical production functions and that all these components contribute in totally

symmetric fashion to the finished manufactured goods, implying that all components are produced in equal amounts.

19 Helpman, E., International Trade in the Presence of Product Differentiation, Economies of Scale and Monopolistic Competition, *Journal of International Economics*, 11, 1981.

20 Krugman, P.R., Import Protection as Export Promotion, in Kierzkowski, 1984.

21 Krugman, P., Scale Economies, Product Differentiation and the Pattern of Trade, *American Economic Review*, 70, 1980.

22 The concept of contestable markets combines the Betrand behaviour of firms and costless unrestricted entry and exit.

23 Baumol, W.J., Panzar, J.C. and Willig, R.D., *Contestable Markets and the Theory of Industrial Structure*, New York, Harcourt Brace Jovanovich, 1982.

24 Monopolistic competition is like contestable markets, with the possibility of product differentiation.

25 Solow, R.A., Contribution to the Theory of Economic Growth, *Quarterly Journal of Economics*, 71, 1956; Baldwin, R.E., Review of Theoretical Developments on Regional Integration. Paper presented at the first Project Workshop on Regional Integration and Trade Liberalization in Sub-Saharan Africa, African Economic Research Consortium, Nairobi, 2–4 December 1993.

26 Mankiw, G., Romer, D. and Weil, D., A Contribution to the Empirics of Economic Growth, *Quarterly Journal of Economics*, 107, 1992.

27 Romer, P. Increasing Returns and Long-run Growth, *Journal of Political Economy*, 94, 1986.

28 Arrow, K., The Economic Implications of Learning by Doing, *Review of Economic Studies*, June 1962.

29 Spencer, M., The Learning Curve and Competition, *Bell Journal of Economics*, 12, 1981.

30 Nelson, R. and Winter, S., *An Evolutionary Theory of Economic Change*, Cambridge, Mass., Belknap Press of Harvard University Press, 1982; Dosi, G., Pavitt, K. and Soete, L., The Economics of Technical Change and International Trade, London, Harvester Wheatsheaf, 1990; Cooper, C., Are Innovation Studies on Industrialized Economies Relevant to Technology Policy in Developing Countries?, Maastricht, INTECH Working Paper, No. 3, 1991.

31 In mathematical terms, the addition of an equation specifying equilibrium conditions is a way of providing for the model's 'determination' or 'closing the model'.

32 Nelson, R., The Role of Firm Differences in an Evolutionary Theory of Technical Advance, *Science and Public Policy*, 18 (6), December 1991.

33 Tidd, J., *Flexible Manufacturing Technologies and International Competitiveness*, London, Pinter, 1991.

34 Kaldor, M., The Case for Regional Policies, *Scottish Journal of Political Economy*, 17, 1970; Kaldor, M., What is Wrong with Economic Theory?, *Quarterly Journal of Economics*, 89, 1975; Pasinetti, L.L., *Structural Change and Economic Growth, A Theoretical Essay on the Dynamics of the Wealth of Nations*, Cambridge, Cambridge University Press, 1981.

35 Havrylyshyn, O. and Civan, E., Intra-industry Trade among Developing Countries, *Journal of Development Economics*, 18, 1985. Greenway (1991) evaluated the extent of intra-industry trade in developing countries as a way of determining how widespread economies of scale and product differentiation are. Two categories of intra-industry studies are invoked: documentary studies recording the incidence of intra-industry trade at a given level of aggregation, and econometric studies identifying the determinants of a given level or change in intra-industry trade.

36 Stewart, F., Recent Theories of International Trade: Some Implications for the South, in Kierzkowski, 1984; Stewart, F., A Note on 'Strategic' Trade Theory and the South, *Journal of International Development*, 3 (5), 1991.

37 Balassa, B. and Bauwens, L., *Changing Trade Patterns in Manufactured Goods*, Amsterdam, North-Holland, 1988.

38 Lecraw, D., Technological Activities of LDC-based Multinationals, *Annals of the American Academy of Political and Social Science*, 458, November 1981.

39 ITC, *Supply and Demand Surveys: Indicative Value of Imports and Export Trade in Selected Products for Member Countries of the PTA (1981–1985)*, Geneva, ITC/UNCTAD/GATT, December 1985.

40 The COMTRADE data base was used. This contains foreign trade statistics for 199 countries and customs areas. In the absence of sufficient data for all PTA countries, the official statistics of the countries' trading partners were systematically scanned. The data series relate to 17 countries: Angola, Burundi, Comoros, Djibouti, Ethiopia, Kenya, Madagascar, Malawi, Mauritius, Mozambique, Rwanda, Seychelles, Somalia, Uganda, Tanzania, Zambia and Zimbabwe. Data for Botswana, Lesotho and Swaziland had to be excluded as their trade flows are recorded as part of the Southern African Customs Union. Trade with South Africa and the then USSR is not reflected in the data base. However, the data displays a high degree of volatility from year to year: often a country changes from a large exporter of a product one year to a non-exporter in the following years. This could be a reflection of the quality of data.

41 Koester, U. and Thomas, M., *Agricultural Trade among Malawi, Tanzania, Zambia and Zimbabwe*, IFPRI, Washington, D.C., February 1992.

42 Badiane, O., *Macroeconomic Policies and Inter-country Trade in West Africa*, IFPRI, Washington, D.C., 1992.

43 See, e.g., Spencer, B.J., What Should Trade Policy Target?, in Krugman, 1986. The point has been disputed in Srinivasan, T.N., Recent Theories of Imperfect Competition and International Trade: Any Implications for Development Strategy? *Indian Economic Review*, 24 (1), 1989.

3 SOME CONCEPTUAL ISSUES AND METHODOLOGY OF THE STUDY

1 Lovell, K.C.A., Production Frontiers and Productive Efficiency. In Fried, Harold O., Lovell K.C.A. and Schmidt, Shelton S. (eds), *The Measurement of Productive Efficiency: Techniques and Applications*, Oxford, Oxford University Press, 1993.

2 Koopmans, T.C., An Analysis of Production as an Efficient Combination of Activities, in Koopmans T.C., (ed.), *Activity Analysis, Production and Allocation*, Cowles Commission for Research in Economics, Monograph No. 13, New York, John Wiley, 1951.

3 Debreu, G., The Coefficient of Resource Utilization, *Econometrica*, 19 (3), July 1951; Farell, M.J., The Measurement of Productive Efficiency, *Journal of the Royal Statistical Society*, series A, General, 120 (3), 1957.

4 Pack, H., Productivity and Industrial Development in Sub-Saharan Africa, *World Development*, 21 (1), 1993.

5 Kaldor, N., The Effect of Devaluations on Trade in Manufactures, in *Further Essays on Applied Economics*, London, Duckworth, 1978.

6 Fagerberg, J., International Competitiveness, *Economic Journal*, 98 (391) 1988.

7 OECD, *Technology and the Economy: The Key Relationships*, Paris, OECD, 1992a.

8 Nelson, R., Recent Writings on Competitiveness: Boxing the Compass, *California Management Review*, 34, (2), Winter 1992.

9 Enos, J.L., *The Creation of Technological Capability in Developing Countries*, Pinter, London, 1991.

10 Ndlela, D.B., Kaliyathi, J.W.E., Mutungwazi, D. and Zwizwai, B.M., A Study of the Transfer of Technology and Technology Acquisition in the Metals and Metal Goods Sector in Zimbabwe, in East Africa Technology Policy Studies Network (EATPS), *Technology Policy Studies in Eastern and Southern Africa*, Nairorbi, International Development Research Centre (IDRC), 1990; Amdi, I.E.S., *Government Policy and Assistance in the Development of Technological Capacity of the Metalworking Cabottage Sector on Benue State of Nigeria*, Zaira, Nigeria, Department of Political Science, Ahmadu Bello University (n.d.); Herbert-Copley, B., Technical Change in African Industry: Reflections on IDRC Supported Research, *Canadian Journal of Development Studies*, 13 (2), 1992.

11 Yin, R.K., *Case Study Research: Design and Methods*, Applied Social Science Research Methods Series, Vol. 5, London and New Delhi, Beverly Hills, 1984.

12 Reid, G.C., *Theories of Industrial Organization*, Oxford, Blackwell, Oxford, 1987.

13 Competitiveness based on minor, locally generated adaptations and improvements specific to recipient environments has been cited in the case of Argentina's international sale of industrial plants and engineering works.

4   THE CHANGING WORLD ECONOMY: MARKET CONDITIONS AND TECHNOLOGICAL DEVELOPMENTS

1   The concept of 'quality' has been broadened to encompass consistency, predictability, employee motivation, supplier involvement and performance measurement.

2   Partnering can involve R&D consortia, joint ventures and cross-licensing arrangements.

3   Tapscott, D. and Caston, A., *Paradigm Shift: The New Promise of Information Technology*, New York, McGraw-Hill, 1993; Mytelka, L.K., *Strategic Partnerships: States, Firms, and International Competition*, London, Pinter and Cranbury, N.J., Fairleigh Dickinson University Press, 1991.

4   OECD, *Information Networks and New Technologies: Opportunities and Policy Implications for the 1990s*, Information Computer Communications Policy, No. 30, Paris, OECD, 1992b.

5   CBI, *Active Sportwear: A Survey of the Netherlands and Other Major Markets in the European Community*, Rotterdam, CBI, September 1991b.

6   CBI, *Household and Furnishing Textile: A Survey of the Netherlands and Other Major Markets in the European Community*, Rotterdam, CBI, January 1991a.

7   CBI, *Footwear: A Survey of the Netherlands and Other Major Markets in the EC, Rotterdam*, CBI, 1990.

8   UNIDO, *The Implications of the Single European Market for Industry in Developing Countries*, PPD.229 (SPEC.), Vienna, 6 October 1992a.

9   Bhagwati, J.N., *The World System at Risk*, London, Harvester Wheatsheaf, 1991.

10   Waelbroeck, J. and Kol, J., *Export Opportunities for the South in the Evolving Pattern of World Trade*, Brussels, CEPS, 1987.

11   South Commission, *The Challenge to the South*, The Report of the South Commission, Oxford, Oxford University Press, 1990.

12   Peng, Martin Khor Kok, The End of the Uruguay Round and Third World Interests, *South Letter*, Winter 1993/Spring 1994.

13   Salam, M.A., *Science and Technology: Challenge for the South*, Trieste, Third World Academy of Sciences and Third World Network of Scientific Institutions, 1992.

14   Dussauge, P., Hart, S. and Ramanantsoa, B., *Strategic Technology Management*, Chichester, John Wiley, 1992.

15   Bagchi, A.K., *Public Intervention and Industrial Restructuring in China, India and the Republic of Korea*, Geneva, IL-ARTEP, 1987.

16   This computing architecture goes by various names, such as network computing, cooperative processing and client/server architectures.

17   This is a fundamentally different approach called object-oriented software, which enables the developer to inherit all the expertise of those who used and improved the object in the past. It reduces the number of design and programming errors by reducing the number and complexity of the programming operations required to develop an application.

18 Mody, A. and Wheeler, D., *Automation and World Competition: New Technologies, Industrial Location, and Trade*, Basingstoke and London, Macmillan, 1990.

19 UNIDO, *Industry and Development, Global Report 1989/90*, Vienna, 1990a.

20 UNIDO, *Industry and Development, Global Report 1990/91*, Vienna, 1990b.

21 There are three types of shuttleless looms, each featuring some form of specialization. Air-jet looms are used on plain fabrics, while rapier and projectile looms can weave more complicated types of fabrics (e.g. colour stripes and designs).

22 UNIDO, *Trends in Industrial Automation*, PPD 231 (SPEC.), Vienna, 1992b.

23 Information on footwear is largely drawn from UNIDO (1992b).

24 Levy, B., Transactions Costs, the Size of Firms and Industrial Policy: Lessons from a Comparative Case Study of the Footwear Industry in Korea and Taiwan, *Journal of Development Economics*, 32 (1/2), November, 1990.

25 Kaplinsky, R., Firm Size and Technical Change in a Dynamic Context, in Freeman, C. (ed.), *The Economics of Innovation*, Aldershot, E. Elgar, 1990.

26 Their findings are based on a study of several thousand organizations in North America, Europe and the Far East. The main objective of the study was to investigate the nature and impacts of changes in technology, including emerging applications, organizational benefits and management implications.

27 OECD, *Technology and Productivity: The Challenge for Economic Policy*, Paris, OECD, 1991.

28 Rasmussen, J., Schmitz, H. and Dijk, M.P. van, Introduction – Exploring a New Approach to Small-scale Industry, *IDS Bulletin*, 23 (3), July 1992.

29 On this point Rasmussen *et al.* (1992) have made reference to Pyke, F., Becattini, G. and Sengenberger, W. (eds), *Industrial Districts and Inter-firm Cooperation in Italy*, Geneva, International Institute for Labour Studies, 1990.

30 Piore, M. and Sabel, C., *The Second Industrial Divide: Possibilities for Prosperity*, New York, Basic Books, 1984.

31 Browne, J., Dubois, D., Rathmill, K., Sethi, S.P. and Stecke, K.E., Classification of Flexible Manufacturing Systems, *The FMS Magazine*, April 1984.

32 Freeman, C. and Hagedoorn, J., Catching up or Falling behind: Patterns in International Inter-firm Technology Partnering, *World Development*, 22 (5), May 1994.

33 UNESCAP, Technology Flows in Asia – Strategies for Enhancing the Flow of Technologies among Regional Developing Countries (Prepared by Prasada Reddy), Bangkok, 1990.

34 Yamamura, K., Caveat Emptor: The Industrial Policy of Japan, in Krugman, 1986; Carliner, G., Industrial Policy for Emerging Industries. In Krugman, 1986.

5   MAIN FINDINGS OF THE STUDY: A SYSTHESIS

1   OECD, *New Forms of Investment in Developing Country Industries: Mining, Petrochemicals, Automobiles, Textiles, Food,* by Charles Oman in collaboration with others, Paris, Development Centre of the OECD, 1989.

2   Morawetz, D., *Why the Emperor's New Clothes are Not Made in Colombia: A Case Study in Latin American and East Asian Manufactured Exports,* New York, Oxford University Press, 1981.

3   Pack, H., *Productivity, Technology and Industrial Development,* New York, Oxford University Press, 1987.

4   Sharpley, J. and Lewis, S., *Kenya: The Manufacturing Sector to the Mid-1980s,* see pp. 211 and 232, in Riddell, 1990.

6   CONCLUSIONS AND POLICY IMPLICATIONS

1   Qian, Yingyi and Xu, Chenggang, Why China's Economic Reforms Differ: The M-form Hierarchy and Entry/Expansion of the Non-state Sector, *The Economics of Transition,* 1 (2), 1993. China's economic reforms differ from those of Eastern Europe and the then Soviet Union in the way they have permitted on-going entry and expansion of the non-state sector, resulting in economic growth averaging 8.6 per cent during 1979–91, and a substantial improvement in the standard of living.

Bibliography

Alcorta, L., The Impact of New Technologies on Scale in Manufacturing Industry: Issues and Evidence, *World Development*, 22 (5), May 1994.

Amdi, I.E.S., *Government Policy and Assistance in the Development of Technological Capacity of the Metal-working Cottage Sector in Benue State of Nigeria*, Zaria, Nigeria, Department of Political Science, Ahmadu Bello University (n.d.).

Arrow, K., The Economic Implications of Learning by Doing, *Review of Economic Studies*, June 1962.

Badiane, O., *Macroeconomic Policies and Inter-country Trade in West Africa*, IFPRI, Washington, D.C., 1992.

Bagchi, A.K., *Public Intervention and Industrial Restructuring in China, India and the Republic of Korea*, Geneva, IL-ARTEP, 1987.

Balassa, B. and Bauwens, L., *Changing Trade Patterns in Manufactured Goods*, Amsterdam, North-Holland, 1988.

Baldwin, R.E., A Critique of Infant Industry Protection, *Journal of Political Economy*, 17, 1969.

Baldwin, R.E., Review of Theoretical Developments on Regional Integration. Paper presented at the first Project Workshop on Regional Integration and Trade Liberalization in Sub-Saharan Africa, African Economic Research Consortium, Nairobi, 2–4 December 1993.

Baumol, W.J., Panzar, J.C. and Willig, R.D., *Contestable Markets and the Theory of Industrial Structure*, New York, Harcourt Brace Jovanovich, 1982.

Bhagwati, J.N., *The World System at Risk*, London, Harvester Wheatsheaf, 1991.

Bhagwati, J.N. and Srinivasan, T.N., *Foreign Trade Regimes and Economic Development: India*, NBER, New York, Columbia University Press, 1975.

Bhalla, A., James, D. and Stevens, Y. (eds), *Blending New and Traditional Technologies: Case Studies*, Dublin, ILO, Tycooley, 1984.

Bozeman, B. and Link, A.N., *Investments in Technology: Corporate Strategies and Public Policy Alternatives*, New York, Praeger, 1983.

Brander, J.A., Intra-industry Trade in Identical Commodities, *Journal of International Economics*, 11, 1981.

Brander, J.A. and Krugman, P.A., A Reciprocal Dumping Model of International Trade, *Journal of International Economics*, 1983.

Brown, M.B. and Tiffen, P., *Short Changed: Africa and World Trade*, London, Pluto Press, 1992.

Browne, J., Dubois, D., Rathmill, K., Sethi, S.P. and Stecke, K.E., Classification of Flexible Manufacturing Systems, *The FMS Magazine*, April 1984.

Buckley, P. and Casson, M., *The Future of the Multinational Enterprise*, London, Macmillan, 1976.

Buckley, P. and Casson, M., The Optimal Timing of a Foreign Investment, *Economic Journal*, 91, 1981.

Cantwell, J.A., *Technological Innovations and Multinational Corporations*, Oxford, Blackwell, 1989.

Carliner, G., Industrial Policy for Emerging Industries, in Krugman, 1986.

Carlsson, B., Industrial Dynamics: an overview, in Carlsson, B. (ed.), *Industrial Dynamics: Technological, Organizational and Structural Changes in Industries and Firms*, Studies in Industrial Organization, Vol. 10, Boston etc., Kluwer Academic Publishers, 1989.

CASTAFRICA II: Second Conference of Ministers responsible for the Application of Science and Technology to Development in Africa, Final Report, July, 1987.

Caves, R., International Trade and Industrial Organization: Introduction, *Journal of Industrial Economics*, 29, 1980.

CBI, *Footwear: A Survey of the Netherlands and Other Major Markets in the EC*, Rotterdam, CBI, 1990.

CBI, *Household and Furnishing Textiles: A Survey of the Netherlands and Other Major Markets in the European Community*, Rotterdam, CBI, January 1991a.

CBI, *Active Sportwear: A Survey of the Netherlands and Other Major Markets in the European Community*, Rotterdam, CBI, September 1991b.

Chandler, A.D., *Scale and Scope*, Cambridge, Mass., The Belknap Press and Harvard University Press, 1990.

Colclough, C., Structuralism versus Neo-liberalism: An Introduction, in Colclough and Manor (1991).

Colclough, C. and Manor, J. (eds), *States or Markets? Neo-liberalism and the Development Policy Debate*, Oxford, Clarendon Press, 1991.

Cooper, C., Are Innovation Studies on Industrialized Economies Relevant to Technology Policy in Developing Countries?, Maastricht, INTECH Working Paper, No. 3, 1991.

Cornwall, J., *Modern Capitalism: Its Growth and Transformation*, London, St. Martin's Press, 1977.

David, P., *Technology, Resource Endowments, Property Rights and Trade: An Open Developing Country's Viewpoint*, Stanford, Center for Economic Policy Research, No. 278, December 1991.

Debreu, G., The Coefficient of Resource Utilization, *Econometrica*, 19(3), July 1951.

Dixit, A.K. and Norman, V., *Theory of International Trade*, Cambridge, Nisbet, 1980.

Dixit, A.K. and Stiglitz, J., Monopolistic Competition and Optimum Product Diversity, *American Economic Review*, 67, 1977.

Dosi, G., Perspectives on Evolutionary Theory, *Science and Public Policy*, 18 (6), December 1991.

Dosi, G., Pavitt, K. and Soete, L., *The Economics of Technical Change and International Trade*, London, Harvester Wheatsheaf, 1990.

Dussauge, P., Hart, S. and Ramanantsoa, B., *Strategic Technology Management*, Chichester, John Wiley and Sons, 1992.

Enos, J.L., *The Creation of Technological Capability in Developing Countries*, London, Pinter, 1991.

Ethier, W.J., Internationally Decreasing Costs and World Trade, *Journal of International Economics*, 9, 1979.

Ethier, W.J., National and International Returns to Scale in the Modern Theory of International Trade, *American Economic Review*, 72, 1982.

Evans, D., *Comparative Advantage and Growth: Trade and Development in Theory and Practice*, Hemel Hempstead, Harvester Wheatsheaf, 1989.

Evans, D., Visible and Invisible Hands in Trade Policy Reforms, in Colclough and Manor, 1991.

Fagerberg, J., International Competitiveness, *Economic Journal*, 98 (391) 1988.

Farell, M.J., The Measurement of Productive Efficiency, *Journal of the Royal Statistical Society*, series A, General, 120 (3), 1957.

Fransman, M., *Biotechnology-generation, Diffusion and Policy: An Interpretive Survey*, INTECH Working Paper, No.1, Maastricht, 1991.

Fransman, M. and King, J., (eds), *Technological Capability in the Third World*, London, Macmillan, 1984.

Freeman, C. and Hagedoorn, J., Catching up or Falling behind: Patterns in International Inter-Firm Technology Partnering *World Development*, 22 (5), May 1994.

Greenway, D., New Trade Theories and Developing Countries, in Balasubramanyam, V.N. and Lall, S. (eds), *Current Issues in Development Economics*, London, Macmillan, 1991.

Griliches, Z., (ed.), *R&D: Patents and Productivity*, Chicago and London, University of Chicago Press, 1984.

Grossman, G.M., Strategic Export Promotion: a Critique, in Krugman, 1986.

Grossman, G.M. and Helpman, E., Product Development and International Trade, *Journal of Political Economy*, 97, 1989.

Grossman, G.M. and Helpman, E., Trade Innovation and Growth, *American Economic Review*, Papers and Proceedings, May 1990a.

Grossman, G.M. and Helpman, E., Comparative Advantage and Long-run Growth, *American Economic Review*, 80, 1990b.

Handousa, H., Nishimiau, M. and Page, J.M. Jr., Productivity Change in Egyptian Public Sector Industries after the 'Opening', 1973–79, *Journal of Development Economics*, 20, 1986.

Haque, I.U., International Competitiveness: Public Sector/Private Sector Interface. In Haque, I.U. (ed.), *International Competitiveness: Interaction of the Public and Private Sectors*, collected papers from an EDI policy seminar held in Seoul, Republic of Korea, 18–21 April, 1990.

Havrylyshyn, O. and Civan, E., Intra-industry Trade among Developing Countries, *Journal of Development Economics*, 18, 1985.

Helpman, E., International Trade in the Presence of Product Differentiation, Economies of Scale and Monopolistic Competition, *Journal of International Economics*, 11, 1981.

Helpman, E. and Krugman, P., *Market Structure and Foreign Trade: Increasing Returns, Imperfect Competition and the International Economy*, Brighton, Wheatsheaf, 1985.

Herbert-Copley, B., Technical Change in African Industry: Reflections on IDRC Supported Research, *Canadian Journal of Development Studies*, 13 (2), 1992.

Hiey, P.J., *Stabilization and Adjustment Policies and Programmes*, WIDER Country Study 16, Helsinki, 1988.

Holmstrom, B.R. and Tirole, J., The Theory of the Firm, in Schmalensee, R. and Willig, R.D. (eds), *Handbook of Industrial Organization*, Amsterdam and New York, North-Holland, 1989.

Husain, I., Structural Adjustment and Long-term Development in Sub-Saharan Africa. In van de Hooven, R. and van de Kraaj, F., (eds), *Structural Adjustment and Beyond in Sub-Saharan Africa*, London, James Curry, 1994.

ITC, *Supply and Demand Surveys: Indicative Value of Imports and Export Trade in Selected Products for Member Countries of the PTA (1981–85)*, Geneva, ITC/UNCTAD/GATT, December 1985.

ITC, *Cocoa: Traders' Guide*, Geneva International Trade Centre, 1987.

Jacobsson, S. and Alam, G., *Liberalization and Industrial Development in the Third World: A Comparison of the Indian and South Korean Engineering Industries*, New Delhi, Sage, 1994.

James, J., *Microelectronics and the Third World: An Integrative Survey of Literature*, INTECH Working Paper, 2, Maastricht, 1991.

Kaldor, M., The Case for Regional Policies, *Scottish Journal of Political Economy*, 17, 1970.

Kaldor, M., What is Wrong with Economic Theory?, *Quarterly Journal of Economics*, 89, 1975.

Kaldor, N., The Effect of Devaluations on Trade in Manufactures. In *Further Essays on Applied Economics*, London, Duckworth, 1978.

Kaplinsky, R., Firm Size and Technical Change in a Dynamic Context. In Freeman, C. (ed.), *The Economics of Innovation*, Aldershot, E. Elgar, 1990.

Keller, R., *Technological Capability and Development: A Study of India and Korea*, Nationalekonomiska Institutionen, Handelshogskolan vid Goteborgs Universitet, Memorandum No. 156, Göteborg, 1991.

Kendrick, J.W. and Grossman, E.S., *Productivity in the United States: Trends and Cycles*, Baltimore, Johns Hopkins University Press, 1980.

Kierzkowski, H. (ed.), *Monopolistic Competition and International Trade*, Oxford, Clarendon Press, 1984.

Kierzkowski, H., Recent Advances in Trade Theory: A Selected Survey, *Oxford Review of Economic Policy*, 3 (1), 1987.

Killick, T., Explaining Africa's Post-independence Development Experiences. Paper presented at the Second Biennial Conference on African Economic Issues, Abidjan, 13–15 October 1992.

Koester, U. and Thomas, M., *Agricultural Trade among Malawi, Tanzania, Zambia and Zimbabwe*, IFPRI, Washington, D.C., February 1992.

Koopmans, T.C., An Analysis of Production as an Efficient Combination of Activities. In Koopmans, T.C., (ed.), *Activity Analysis, Production and Allocation*, Cowles Commission for Research in Economics, Monograph No. 13, New York, John Wiley, 1951.

Krugman, P.R., A Model of Innovation, Technology Transfer and the World Distribution of Income, *Journal of Political Economy*, 87, 1979.

Krugman, P., Scale Economies, Product Differentiation and the Pattern of Trade, *American Economic Review*, 70, 1980.

Krugman, P.R., Import Protection as Export Promotion, in Kierzkowski, 1984.

Krugman, P.R. (ed.), *Strategic Trade Policy and the New International Economics*, Cambridge, Mass., MIT Press, 1986.

Krugman, P.R., Increasing Returns and the Theory of International Trade. In Bewley, T. (ed.), *Advances in Economic Theory*, Cambridge, 1987.

Krugman, P.R., New Trade Theory and the Less Developed Countries, in Calvo, G., Findlay, R., Kowi, P. and Braga de Macedo, J., (eds.), *Debt, Stabilization and Development: Essays in Memory of Carlos Alejandro*, Oxford, Blackwell, 1989.

Lall, S., *Building Industrial Competitiveness in Developing Countries*, Paris, OECD, 1990.

Lall, S., Navaretti, G.B., Teitel, S. and Wignaraja. G., *Technological Capabilities and Industrial Development in Ghana*. Study prepared for the World Bank, Washington, D.C., March 1993.

Lancaster, R., *Variety, Equity and Efficiency*, New York, Columbia University Press, 1979.

Lancaster, R., Intra-industry Trade under Perfect Monopolistic Competition, *Journal of International Economics*, 10, 1980.

Lecraw, D., Direct Investment by Firms from Less Developed Countries, *Oxford Economic Papers*, 1977.

Lecraw, D., Technological Activities of LDC-based Multinationals, *Annals of the American Academy of Political and Social Science*, 458, November 1981.

Leontief, W.W., *Studies in the Structure of the American Economy*, New York, Oxford University Press, 1953.

Levy, B., Transactions Costs, the Size of Firms and Industrial Policy: Lessons from a Comparative Case Study of the Footwear Industry in Korea and Taiwan, *Journal of Development Economics*, 32 (1/2), November, 1990.

Levy, B. and Kuo, Wen-Jeng, The Strategic Orientations of Firms and the Performance of Korea and Taiwan in Frontier Industries: Lessons from Comparative Case Studies of Keyboard and Personal Computer Assembly, *World Development*, 19 (4), April 1991.

Lieberman, I., *Industrial Restructuring Policy and Practice*, Research and Policy Series, Washington, D.C., World Bank, 1990.

Linder, S.B., *An Essay on Trade and Transformation*, Stockholm, Almquist and Wikell, 1961 (reprinted New York, Garland, 1983).

Link, A.N., *Technology Change and Productivity Growth*, Chur and London, Harwood Academic Publishers, 1987.

Lipton, M., Market Relaxation and Agricultural Development, in Colclough and Manor, 1991.

Lovell, K.C.A., Production Frontiers and Productive Efficiency, in Fried, Harold O., Lovell, K.C.A. and Schmidt, Shelton S., (eds) *The Measurement of Productive Efficiency: Techniques and Applications*, Oxford, etc., Oxford University Press, 1993.

Mankiw, G., Romer, D. and Weil, D., A Contribution to the Empirics of Economic Growth, *Quarterly Journal of Economics*, 107, 1992.

Mody, A. and Wheeler, D., *Automation and World Competition: New Technologies, Industrial Location and Trade*, Basingstoke and London, Macmillan, 1990.

Morawetz, D., *Why the Emperor's New Clothes Are Not Made in Colombia: A Case Study in Latin American and East Asian Manufactured Exports*, New York, Oxford University Press, 1981.

Mytelka, L.K., *Strategic Partnerships: States, Firms and International Competition*, London, Pinter and Cranbury, NJ, Fairleigh Dickinson University Press, 1991.

Ndela, D.B., Kaliyathi, J.W.E., Mutungwazi, D. and Zwizwai, B.M., A Study of the Transfer of Technology and Technology Acquisition in the Metals and Metal Goods Sector in Zimbabwe, in East Africa Technology Policy Studies Network (EATPS), *Technology Policy Studies in Eastern and Southern Africa*, Nairobi, International Development Research Centre (IDRC), 1990.

Nelson, R., The Role of Firm Differences in an Evolutionary Theory of Technical Advance, *Science and Public Policy*, 18 (6), December 1991.

Nelson, R., Recent Writings on Competitiveness: Boxing the Compass, *California Management Review*, 34, (2), Winter 1992.

Nelson, R. and Winter, S., *An Evolutionary Theory of Economic Change*, Cambridge, Mass., Belknap Press of Harvard University Press, 1982.

North, Douglass C., Economic Performance through Time, *American Economic Review*, 84 (3), June 1994.

Nurkse, R., *Patterns of Trade and Development*, Wicksell Lectures, Stockholm, 1959.

OECD, *New Forms of Investment in Developing Country Industries: Mining, Petrochemicals, Automobiles, Textiles, Food*, by Charles Oman in collaboration with others, Paris, Development Centre of the OECD, 1989.

OECD, *Technology and Productivity: The Challenge for Economic Policy*, Paris, OECD, 1991.

OECD, *Technology and the Economy: The Key Relationships*, Paris, OECD, 1992a.

OECD, *Information Networks and New Technologies: Opportunities and Policy Implications for the 1990s*, Information Computer Communications Policy, No. 30, Paris, OECD, 1992b.

Pack, H., *Productivity, Technology and Industrial Development*, New York, Oxford University Press, 1987.

Pack, H., Productivity and Industrial Development in Sub-Saharan Africa, *World Development*, 21 (1), 1993.

Pack, H. and Westphal, L.E., Industrial Strategy and Technological Change: Theory versus Reality, *Journal of Development Economics*, 22, 1986.

Pasinetti, L.L., *Structural Change and Economic Growth, A Theoretical Essay on the Dynamics of the Wealth of Nations*, Cambridge, Cambridge University Press, 1981.

Pavitt, K. and Patel, P., Technological Strategies of the World's Largest Companies, *Science and Public Policy*, 18 (6), December 1991.

Peng, Martin Khor Kok, The End of the Uruguay Round and Third World Interests, *South Letter*, Winter 1993/Spring 1994.

Pennings, J.M. and Arend, B., (eds), *New Technology as Organizational Innovation*, Cambridge, Mass., Ballinger Publishing Co., 1987.

Piore, M. and Sabel, C., *The Second Industrial Divide: Possibilities for Prosperity*, New York, Basic Books, 1984.

Porter, M., *The Competitive Advantage of Nations*, London and Basingstoke, Macmillan, 1990.

Prebisch, R., Five Stages in My Thinking about Development, in Bauer, P., Meier, G. and Seers, D. (eds), *Pioneers in Development*, New York, Oxford University Press, 1954.

Pyke, F., Becattini, G. and Sengenberger, W., (eds), *Industrial Districts and Inter-firm Cooperation in Italy*, Geneva International Institute for Labour Studies, 1990.

Qian, Yingyi and Xu, Chenggang, Why China's Economic Reforms Differ: The M-form Hierarchy and Entry/Expansion of the Non-State Sector, in *The Economics of Transition*, 1 (2), 1993.

Rasmussen, J., Schmitz, H. and Dijk, M.P. van, Introduction – Exploring a New Approach to Small-scale Industry, *IDS Bulletin*, 23 (3), July 1992.

Ray, E.J., US Protection and Intra-industry Trade: The Message for Developing Countries, *Economic Development and Cultural Change*, 40 (1), October 1991.

Reid, G.C., *Theories of Industrial Organization*, Oxford, Blackwell, 1987.

Riddell, R.C., (ed.), *Manufacturing Africa: Performance and Prospects of Seven Countries in Sub-Saharan Africa*, London, James Curry, etc., 1990.

Romer, P., Increasing Returns and Long-run Growth, *Journal of Political Economy*, 94, 1986.

Rosenberg, N., Critical Issues in Science Policy Research, *Science and Public Policy*, 18 (6), December 1991.

Salam, M.A., *Science and Technology: Challenge for the South*, Trieste, Third World Academy of Sciences and Third World Network of Scientific Institutions, 1992.

Scherer, F., *Industrial Market Structure and Economic Performance*, Chicago etc., Houghton Mifflin, 1980.

Sharma, R., *The 'Missing Middle' in Sub-Saharan Africa: Role of South–South Cooperation, Research and Information for the Non-Aligned and Other Developing Countries*, New Delhi, Interest Publications, 1993.

Sharpley, J. and Lewis, S., Kenya: The Manufacturing Sector to the Mid-1980s, In Riddell, 1990.

Simon, H., *Administrative Behaviour*, New York, Free Press and London, Collins Macmillan, 1947, 1976.

Simon, H., Theories of Decision Making in Economics, *American Economic Review*, 49, 1959.

Solow, R.A., Contribution to the Theory of Economic Growth, *Quarterly Journal of Economics*, 71, 1956.

South Commission, *The Challenge to the South*, The Report of the South Commission, Oxford, Oxford University Press, 1990.

South Letter, Nos. 9 and 10, Geneva, South Commission, 1991.

Spencer, B.J., What Should Trade Policy Target? In Krugman, 1986.

Spencer, M., The Learning Curve and Competition, *Bell Journal of Economics*, 12, 1981.

Srinivasan, T.N., Recent Theories of Imperfect Competition and International Trade: Any Implications for Development Strategy?, *Indian Economic Review*, 24 (1), 1989.

Stewart, F., Recent Theories of International Trade: Some Implications for the South. In Kierzkowski, 1984.

Stewart, F., A Note on 'Strategic' Trade Theory and the South, *Journal of International Development*, 3 (5), 1991.

Tapscott, D. and Caston, A., *Paradigm Shift: The New Promise of Information Technology*, New York, McGraw-Hill, 1993.

Tidd, J., *Flexible Manufacturing Technologies and International Competitiveness*, London, Pinter, 1991.

UNCTAD, *Transfer and Development of Technology in Least Developed Countries: An Assessment of Major Policy Issues*, UNCTAD/ITP/TEC/12, 17 August 1990.

UNCTAD, *Transfer and Development of Technology in a Changing World Environment: The Challenges of the 1990s*, UNCTAD/TD/B/C.6/153, 25 January 1991.

UNCTAD, *Developments and Issues in the Uruguay Round of Particular Concern to Developing Countries*, Note by the UNCTAD Secretariat, TD/B/39(2)/CPR.1, 15 March 1993(a).

UNCTAD, *Follow-up to the Recommendations Adopted by the Conference at its Eighth Session: Evolution and Consequences of Economic Spaces and Regional Integration Processes*, TD/B/40(1)7, 23 July 1993b.

UNECA, *Beyond Recovery: ECA-revised Perspectives of Africa's Development*, 1988–2008, E/ECA/CM.14/31, Addis Ababa, March 1988.

UNESCAP, Technology Flows in Asia – Strategies for Enhancing the Flow of Technologies among Regional Developing Countries (Prepared by Prasada Reddy), Bangkok, 1990.

UNIDO, *Industry and Development, Global Report 1989/90*, Vienna, 1990a.

UNIDO, *Industry and Development, Global Report 1990/91*, Vienna, 1990b.

UNIDO, *The Implications of the Single European Market for Industry in Developing Countries*, PPD.229 (SPEC.), Vienna, 6 October 1992a.

UNIDO, *Trends in Industrial Automation*, PPD 231 (SPEC.), Vienna, 1992b.

UNIDO, *African Industry in Figures*, Vienna, 1993.

Valk, P. de, *A General Framework for Evaluating the Performance of Textile Enterprises in LDCs: With Application to Tanzania Under Structural Adjustment*, (forthcoming).

Waelbroeck, J. and Kol, J., *Export Opportunities for the South in the Evolving Pattern of World Trade*, Brussels, CEPS, 1987.

Wallack, A.S., O'Halloran, J.D. and Leader, C.A., World Class Manufacturing: Benchmarking World Class Performance, *The McKinsey Quarterly*, 1, 1991.

Warren, B., *Imperialism: Pioneer of Capitalism*, London, New Left Books, 1980.

Weiss, J., *Industry in Developing Countries: Theory, Policy and Evidence*, London and New York, Routledge, 1988.

Westphal, L., *Empirical Justification for Infant Industry Protection*, World Bank Staff Working Paper, No. 445, Washington, D.C., 1981.

World Bank, *Accelerated Development in Sub-Saharan Africa*, Washington, D.C., 1981.

World Bank, *Capital Accumulation and Economic Growth: The Korean Paradigm*, World Bank Staff Working Papers, No. 712, Washington, D.C., 1985.

World Bank, *Sub-Saharan Africa: From Crisis to Sustainable Growth, A Long-term Perspective Study*, Washington, D.C., 1989.

Yamamura, K., Caveat Emptor: The Industrial Policy of Japan. In Krugman, 1986.

Yin, R.K., *Case Study Research: Design and Methods*, Applied Social Science Research Methods Series, Vol. 5, Beverly Hills, London and New Delhi, Sage, 1984.

Yoffie, D.B., (ed.) *Beyond Free Trade: Firms, Governments and Global Competition*, Boston, Mass., Harvard University School Press, 1993.

Part II
Country studies

7 Zimbabwe

Dan Ndlela and Peter Robinson

INTRODUCTION

Phases of industrialization

Beginnings of industrialization

Industrialization began in what was then Southern Rhodesia in the early decades of the twentieth century. By the early 1940s the country had a relatively sophisticated industrial base, ranging from the only integrated iron and steel plant in Sub-Saharan Africa to basic consumer goods industries. Around 10 per cent of GDP and 8 per cent of exports were derived from the manufacturing sector (Riddell, 1988, p. 2).

During the Second World War further import substitution took place. The establishment of the Federation of Rhodesia and Nyasaland created a common market in what is now Malawi, Zambia and Zimbabwe. Much of the manufacturing investment to serve this market was located in Southern Rhodesia and the enterprises concerned became accustomed to serving markets in the other two countries.

The UDI period

The breakup of the Federation in 1963 was followed in 1965 by the Unilateral Declaration of Independence (UDI) by the minority government in Southern Rhodesia. Trade sanctions led to a new era of inward-looking import-substituting industrialization. In 1965 manufacturing accounted for just 17 per cent of GDP. By the end of this period, in 1980 this figure had risen to 24 per cent and the range of products produced had risen dramatically. Significantly, however, the ratio of manufactured exports to gross output dropped from about 27 per cent to 15 per cent (in 1992 this ratio was expected to be about 20 per cent), while the sector's utilization of foreign currency for raw material and capital equipment imports rose sharply.

Several features of the growth of the manufacturing sector during this period are important in understanding subsequent developments. The government created an extensive set of controls to ration foreign exchange (forex), for both investment and recurrent expenditure. With forex allocation reinforcing the tendency to monopolization in a small market, price controls were also established. These were intended to protect both producers, purchasing capital and inter-mediate goods from the manufacturing sector, and final consumers, especially regarding foodstuffs. Due to the political and economic repression of the black majority, a significant part of the consumer goods sub-sectors developed to serve an extremely narrow market with a surprising range of goods.

With the industrialists and the government of the day sharing a determination to overcome the impact of international sanctions, the system of controls was made to operate effectively and the highly protected system that they constituted did not lead to the gross inefficiency which has characterized other import substitution regimes. The need to adapt and innovate led to the development of a wide range of technical skills, particularly in various branches of engineering. The strong orientation to market requirements led to a proliferation of products, often produced within large, vertically integrated conglomerates.

With the strong domestic market orientation and international sanctions in place, the development of exports from the manufacturing sector was limited. The main market was South Africa, which did not abide by sanctions. Trade between the two countries was fostered through the 1964 bilateral trade agreement. This allowed Rhodesian manufacturers of items such as textiles, clothing, leather and footwear, processed food and furniture to export under preferential conditions to South Africa.

Post-independence

At independence, the new government maintained the panoply of controls over the economy, with the apparent intention of using state intervention to redirect development to benefit the mass of the population. However, the application of the controls in the absence of the rapport with the private sector that had existed under the previous regime, and the introduction of new controls on wages and labour relations, led to a situation in which the bureaucracy became a major obstacle to the running of any kind of economic enterprise. As foreign currency availability emerged as the main macroeconomic constraint, competition for access to imports became a major pre-occupation for economic entities in all sectors, whether private or public.

The government's initial response was to introduce new incentives for exporters. The Export Incentive Scheme, whereby an exporter is paid 9 per cent of the f.o.b. value of exports (in Zimbabwe dollars), was introduced in the early 1980s. This was followed in 1983 by the Export Revolving Fund (ERF), which allowed exporters to have access in advance to the foreign currency needed to purchase the imported inputs required to manufacture goods for specific export orders (the ERF was scrapped in the first quarter of 1993). The ERF was targeted at the manufacturing sector; the Export Promotion Programme (EPP) catered for the mining and agricultural sectors. The Industrial Bonus Scheme allows a supplementary foreign currency allocation to be made on the basis of incremental exports achieved.

During the 1980s there had been a running debate with external agencies, particularly the World Bank, on the merits or otherwise of scrapping the foreign currency controls inherited at independence and adopting a programme of trade liberalization. The intention of such a programme would be to move towards a more open economy, forcing industries which had grown up under sanctions to face international competition and become more export oriented.

An initial study undertaken at the instigation of the Bank concluded that a high proportion of Zimbabwean industry *was* inefficient and should be closed down, including the iron and steel plant. The government found the conclusions unacceptable, and examination of the report revealed a poor application of domestic resource cost methodology, which would not anyway give definitive answers about long-term comparative advantage. Later and more careful studies by the Bank itself found Zimbabwean industry to be remarkably efficient, the operation of foreign exchange allocation and investment licensing having avoided many of the problems found in other countries with similar trade regimes. Even capital goods received a positive verdict. 'The conclusion that the capital goods industry in Zimbabwe is largely efficient is puzzling, since the same pervasive policy interventions in other African countries have led to disastrous results' (World Bank, 1989, p. 46).

The Bank's surprise has not led it to abandon its call for trade liberalization, or, for that matter, to draw any useful lessons for other African countries about what can be achieved by way of industrialization under a carefully managed import substitution regime. The argument for trade liberalization in Zimbabwe has just shifted ground: 'since most industries are efficient, they no longer need protection.'

Although it was not in a situation of economic crisis, in which the Fund/Bank would be able to set the main lines of policy, Zimbabwe itself has decided to embark on a comprehensive structural adjustment programme, of which trade liberalization constitutes a central element. The government's decision does not seem to have been directly related to efficiency considerations but was motivated by the political threat from the rapidly growing number of unemployed, many with a relatively high level of education, and the consequent need to move the economy from a lacklustre 3 per cent p.a. GDP growth rate to at least 5 per cent p.a., with a much higher rate of job creation than was achieved in the 1980s.

The strategy now being pursued is to borrow the foreign currency needed for investment, reduce bureaucratic requirements for investment and the conduct of business, while also liberalizing trade in order to make the productive sectors far more outward-looking and to improve the availability, price and quality of goods (consumer and producer goods) on the local market. The overall success of the programme hinges on whether the export response is adequate and sustainable, enabling repayment of the borrowed funds and a diminution of the foreign currency shortage which in the past has been the major constraint on growth and development.

The phasing of liberalization was designed to maximize export performance, while giving industries time to adjust before facing competition from competitive imports. Thus the importation of production inputs was to go onto Open General Import Licence (OGIL) before outputs, with priority for inputs for sectors in which export volumes are assured or for 'linkage' sectors which do not directly export but are important in the export chain. Sectors where the export price has traditionally been lower than the domestic price are to have their inputs liberalized last, the intention being that they should earn the foreign currency they need through an Export Retention Scheme (ERS).

The ERS was thus introduced at the same time as a start was made on putting imported productive imports onto OGIL, from mid-1990. The ERS allows exporters to retain a proportion of the foreign currency earned to be used to import raw materials, spare parts or capital equipment. For the manufacturing sector, the retention rate was initially set at 7.5 per cent but was raised to 15 per cent from the end of 1991 and 25 per cent and 30 per cent for the two halves of 1992. It was increased to 50 per cent in April 1993. The restrictions on the use of ERS funds were removed (except for a small negative list) and trading was allowed from January 1992.

The ERS has clearly been intended as a major inducement to Zimbabwean firms to seek out export markets. Another important factor has been exchange rate policy. Since a devaluation in 1982, Zimbabwe has operated on a sliding peg exchange rate, which has served to offset an inflation rate of 15–20 per cent, generally higher than Zimbabwe's trading partners. In the third quarter of 1991, however, the Zimbabwe dollar was devalued drastically, moving from Z$3 to Z$5 to the US dollar, but was kept at that level during 1992.

Inflation rose rapidly, however, reaching 40–50 per cent by the end of 1992, and further depreciation of the currency was undertaken in early 1993. By February, the rate was Z$6.3 to the US dollar and since then it has been at around Z$6.5 to the US dollar. If exports are to be kept competitive, continued high inflation will require further devaluations to be made. Fortunately, in the first and second quarters of 1993, inflation fell to around 30 per cent.

Finally, mention should be made of post-independence trade agreements which have a bearing on exports. Zimbabwe has joined the Lomé Convention between the African and Caribbean States and the European Community and also the Preferential Trade Area for East and Southern Africa (PTA). Lomé has been extremely important for exporters of manufactured goods but the PTA agreement has had little overall impact on trade.

Other arrangements were disturbed by the PTA, however. In particular, when both Malawi and Zimbabwe joined the PTA the bilateral agreement between those two countries was dropped, resulting in a sharp fall in Zimbabwe's exports to Malawi. On the other hand, the bilateral agreement with South Africa was continued and consolidated in 1987 and another round of negotiations to extend the agreement is presently in progress.

As Botswana is not a member of the PTA, the bilateral trade agreement with Botswana has continued and has provided an important opportunity for Zimbabwean exporters. The Botswana agreement has also, however, provided opportunities for Zimbabwean companies (particularly in textiles and clothing sub-sectors) to expatriate capital through transfer pricing, and has thus been controversial. A move by the Zimbabwean authorities to insist on the payment of a surtax which effectively removes the preferential access that Botswana-made goods previously enjoyed in Zimbabwe has resulted in retaliatory action by Botswana. This has had severe implications for Zimbabwean exporters.

Context of the study

Economic conditions in 1992

Even without experiencing one of the most severe droughts this century, 1992 would have been a difficult year for the economy.[1] A critical element of the Economic Reform Programme is that government should significantly reduce its budget deficit through contraction of the public sector and the elimination of subsidies to parastatals. While progress was made on the elimination of subsidies, the additional burden imposed by the drought resulted in a much higher deficit during 1992 than had been planned, with the result that government appropriated an excessive share of liquidity in order to finance the deficit.

With the simultaneous opening up of the money market and the rapid escalation of inflation, interest rates rose to unprecedented levels (40 per cent as compared with the 10–15 per cent that had prevailed between 1965 and 1991). Delays in the payment of export incentives exacerbated the liquidity situation of many firms. With delays of six months not being uncommon, the value of the incentives was eroded. When the amount involved is as much as 5 per cent of annual turnover, which is not uncommon, this has had a negative effect on performance, including a company's ability to compete effectively in export markets.

While the liquidity squeeze led to much more efficient holding of stocks by the manufacturing sector, it also led to postponement of the investments which were meant to provide growth under the structural adjustment programme and, in many cases, a contraction in current production. Contract workers and some full-time workers were laid off during 1992 and short-time working was introduced. Tracing the economic links back, it is clear that government's reluctance to shed jobs in the bureaucracy led directly to conditions of high inflation and tight liquidity, resulting in companies in the productive sectors laying off workers. The loss of productive sector jobs, rather than unproductive bureaucratic jobs, is a major source of concern.

Besides the problems of liquidity and interest rates, production and investment were also limited by the state of infrastructures such as electricity, telecommunications and rail transport. Poor performance in these areas is a legacy of the neglect of maintenance, investment and management of key parastatals during the 1980s. The Zimbabwe Investment Centre (ZIC), which was meant to overcome the bureaucratic impediments to investment, has failed to do so. While ZIC procedures are acceptable for a large project and may produce faster results than a few years ago, this is not the case for small projects. Having to complete ZIC's 20-page questionnaire for a Z$100 000 import order (as cited by one of the respondents) was an unacceptable and unnecessary burden. Some changes to improve this have been introduced during 1993.

Other problems faced by the manufacturing sector, specifically highlighted by sample firms, were endless delays and obstructionism from the Department of Customs and the new policy on pre-shipment inspection of imports, which was seen as causing delays and unnecessarily raising the costs of imports. On the growing shortage of skills, the productive sectors were concerned that, while tax and other policies were encouraging a 'brain drain' of Zimbabwean skills, the policy on the recruitment of expatriate workers (on a short- or long-term basis) continued to be unnecessarily restrictive. Allowing ERS funds to be used for this purpose was seen as one way of reducing the impact of this constraint. This has not yet been implemented.

Although most of these problems ought to be resolvable by decisive government action, in practice they remained in 1992 an on-going drain on the energies of the productive sector. Over and above these issues, the impact of the drought in 1992 was devastating. From being an exporter of foodstuffs such as maize and sugar, and self-sufficient in most other food items, the country was obliged to find the resources to import two million tonnes of maize (the staple), plus sugar, cooking oil and a range of inputs to manufacturing that normally derive from the agricultural sector, including cotton lint. Mismanagement of the dwindling water resources in Kariba led to severe curtailment of hydro-electricity generation, requiring periodic load shedding and the subsequent implementation of a rationing system that cut supplies to manufacturing sector enterprises by 20–30 per cent as compared with their averages for the previous year.

Official estimates of economic performance are that GDP in 1992 fell by 7.7 per cent in real terms. The contribution of manufacturing fell by a larger amount (9.5 per cent), a reflection of a combination of the supply constraints such as water and electricity shortages and a precipitous fall in domestic demand. One of the legacies of the previous trade regime is the conviction that export performance should be subsidiary to a solid foundation in the domestic market. So, although some firms responded to the decline in the domestic market by aggressively seeking out compensating exports, others were more hesitant.

Priority issues for investigation

Considering that the tight protection which has been in place at least since international sanctions were imposed against Rhodesia in 1965 is being rapidly dismantled, with the monetary and fiscal environment simultaneously altered, it is not surprising that a major preoccupation of exporters in Zimbabwe is with the policy framework. The emphasis in the current study is not on policy but on the areas of technology, product development and the firm's ability to adapt to changing world market conditions.

Although these issues are of considerable interest from the viewpoint of economic theory,[2] as will be seen from the case studies, these are areas in which Zimbabwean companies, or at least the larger ones, are confident. They see the challenge of exporting to be more one of finding a niche in overseas markets (or, to be more accurate, a series of niches) and ensuring that stringent delivery time and product quality standards are met, or of competing, increasingly with South African companies, for scarce foreign currency held by importers in regional markets. As trade liberalization proceeds, however, and Zimbabwean companies have to compete with imports of final goods, the challenge of achieving sustained productivity increases will be a real one. In the past, the protected domestic market was always available to cross-subsidize exports implicitly, the motivation for exporting lying in the incentives on offer, particularly the foreign currency incentives.

Manufacturing sector in Zimbabwe and choice of sub-sectors

In 1992, manufacturing constituted about 24 per cent of GDP when measured in constant (1980) prices, or 30 per cent in current prices. Manufactured exports, which included semi-processed minerals and agricultural products such as ferrochrome and cotton, are estimated to have accounted for 33 per cent of merchandise exports.

Recurrent imports for the manufacturing sector were larger than this, however. The proportion of productive sector employees working in manufacturing was estimated at 37 per cent.

Manufacturing had been set to expand rapidly under the structural adjustment programme but, as already mentioned, the drought led instead to a sharp reduction, with the volume of production falling by over 9 per cent. Not only sub-sectors dependent on agricultural inputs were directly affected: all of industry suffered from the sharp fall in incomes and hence reduction in domestic demand, while on the supply side firms had to contend with shortages of electricity and, in cities such as Bulawayo and Mutare, severe shortages of water.

As regards the choice of sub-sectors for the study, textiles and clothing were required to be chosen for comparison purposes, and are anyway critical sectors in Zimbabwe's drive to increase manufactured exports. Due to the strong linkages between them, it was found convenient to discuss textiles and clothing together (see pp. 152–68). Footwear, with backward linkages to leather production, was chosen because it is a commodity being exported into both regional and overseas markets. While entry barriers are relatively low in footwear exporting, competition is fierce (see pp. 171–3). Finally, agricultural machinery was chosen so as to include some aspect of Zimbabwe's engineering capabilities. Zimbabwean agricultural machinery has been developed for local conditions and the export market is limited to regional markets in which similar conditions apply (pp. 181–5).

To provide some quantitative measure of the size of the sub-sectors being studied, Table 7.1 gives an estimated breakdown of the manufacturing sector's contribution to GDP, exports and

Table 7.1 Estimated contribution of sample sub-sectors to manufacturing GDP, exports and employment 1992

Sub-sector	Contribution to GNP		Exports		Employment	
	Z$m	%	Z$m	%	Z$m	%
Textiles and clothing	1 475	19	518	20	59 000	29
Footwear and leather	165	2	130	5	9 000	4
Agricultural machinery	89	1	120	5	1 200	1
Total manufacturing	7 760	–	2 587	–	199 200	–

Note: Exchange rate during 1992 was approximately Z$5 = US$1

employment. This clearly shows that textiles and clothing are very significant in the manufacturing sector, particularly as regards employment. Footwear and leather, and agricultural machinery, on the other hand, are relatively minor sectors, with modest contributions to GDP, exports and employment.

TEXTILES AND CLOTHING

Background

The textile and clothing sub-sectors have played, and continue to play, a major role in the Zimbabwean economy. In addition to providing one of the most important consumer goods for the population, these sub-sectors generate significant amounts of employment and are critical sectors in Zimbabwe's drive to increase manufactured exports.

The textile and clothing sub-sectors consist of three components: production and ginning of cotton, transformation of lint into yarn and fabric, and the conversion of fabric and yarn into garments. Our attention will be focused on the last two components which, with some other sub-sectors, form the hub of technologically dynamic exports from the country's manufacturing sector.

The parastatal Cotton Marketing Board (CMB) has an exclusive monopoly over the processing and marketing of cotton in both domestic and foreign markets. While in the past most lint has been exported, there has also been an increasing absorption of cotton domestically, as the local textile industry has grown. The CMB has always given priority to domestic users, exporting only what was not needed by the domestic textile industry (Mead, *et al.*, 1992, p. 2). The Board employs about 1 500 people on a full-time basis and an additional 2 500 seasonal workers.

The price of lint paid by local spinners and weavers was subsidized to the tune of Z$2–6 million per year in the early 1980s and the subsidy rose to Z$75 million in 1990–91. While part of the cost of this subsidy was born by the government, over the years the largest share of the subsidy for spinners and weavers has come from the price they were able to pay to growers, which was lower than it would otherwise have been. Partly as a result of this, the number of commercial farmers growing cotton declined by 20 per cent between the mid-1980s and 1990. While this slack was at first taken up by small-scale communal farmers, since 1988/89 the number of communal farmers growing cotton has also declined (Mead, *et al.*, 1992, p. 3).

The spinning and weaving industry is dominated by five large companies, two of which produce 60 per cent of the total textile output of the country and account for close to 75 per cent of the fabric supplied to domestic users. These five firms together employ about 12 000 people and the value of their sales is about Z$500 million. In addition there are 45–50 registered small and medium-size enterprises engaged in spinning, weaving and finishing off textiles and knitting cloth, providing employment for an additional 9 000 people; giving a total of 21 000 employees engaged in spinning, weaving, knitting and finishing textiles.

Employment within the clothing sub-sector has increased by over 65 per cent since 1984. In 1982 there were 113 clothing manufacturers; by June 1992 the clothing sub-sector consisted of over 250 companies employing over 24 000 people. Knitted clothing, including T-shirts, underwear, hosiery and jerseys, is also manufactured, employing about 9 000 people. There are also small and medium-size garment manufacturers who operate without registration. Whilst it is difficult to estimate the number of such enterprises or the employment they provide, the numbers are not insignificant.

The figures quoted here do not include some thousands of people engaged in retail dressmaking and tailoring, or the large number of garment cooperatives established in rural areas. An estimated 100 000 people are employed by these small firms as tailors and dressmakers. The clothing sub-sector is thus one of the most labour-intensive sub-sectors in Zimbabwe's manufacturing sector.

The clothing sub-sector manufactures a wide range of garments including work clothing, menswear, children's wear and women's clothing from housecoats to high-fashion garments. Some items have very low mark-ups which are counter-balanced by other, more fashionable and higher-risk garments which require higher prices to be viable. This is particularly so in the fashion industry where prints and colours change from season to season and year to year, making unused fabrics and undelivered garments saleable in succeeding seasons only at very heavy discounts.

Some of the garment manufacturing firms are highly export-oriented, not only to the South African market and the countries of the East and Southern African sub-region but also to the more sophisticated and competitive European and North American markets. These firms have enjoyed considerable growth in exports in recent years in spite of the sub-sector's inability to obtain competitive raw materials and the rising input costs, which cannot be passed on because both the home and export markets have become increasingly competitive. These difficulties have been further exacerbated by the current drought and high interest rates pervading the economy.

History of firms in the sample

Origins, ownership and structure

The six firms surveyed in the present study have production experience ranging from 24 years to over 50 years. Four were established during the 1950s (Table 7.2).

All but one of the firms were established as family enterprises to supply the domestic market. Family ownership appears to have contributed to the steady growth of some firms. Most often the dynamism has come from the family members who provided the vision, the will to survive and continuity of management.

The oldest firm in the sample, Bernstein Clothing, was established in 1939 by the Meyer family to manufacture clothing, mainly shirts, for the domestic market. It has experienced all the phases of industrialization described on pp. 143–8.

The growth in manufacturing and exporting activities can be illustrated by the case of Concorde Clothing Company, which developed from a wholesale business established by the Lessem family in 1944. Along with their wholesale business, they established a small workshop for the manufacture of khaki shorts and shirts. In the early 1950s they were already exporting garments to the UK. By 1959 both the wholesale and manufacturing operations had grown substantially and the business was transformed into a clothing company by the name of Concorde Clothing. This was done with the assistance of a French company, Boussac, which provided short-term technical assistance in setting up the new company. The technical assistance took the form of providing technology and machinery. Experts were sent from France to guide the movement into manufacturing better-quality shirts, lounge shirts, trousers, etc. Personnel from Boussac stayed for about six months at a time, and the French company continued for some years to sell high-quality fabrics to the Zimbabwean firm and to provide the much-needed technical assistance.

Fashion Enterprises, established in 1959, started as a small manufacturing enterprise to supply the domestic market, while exporting small numbers of garments to Zambia and South Africa. Exports to South Africa, however, constituted the first serious attempt to develop the firm's export markets. There was little difficulty in entering the South African market in both the big chain stores and the small boutique shops. From the start Fashion Enterprises set up a comprehensive agency to promote its exports into South Africa. This was the major initial investment by the firm in the South African market.

The only enterprise in the sample which was not initially a family business was David Whitehead Textiles Limited, established as a textile mill in Chegutu, Zimbabwe, in 1952. The company was established as part of a strategy to set up textile mills in the British colonies by a Lancaster-based textile company, David Whitehead – UK.[3] Following the takeover of David Whitehead – UK by Lonrho in 1970 the latter acquired a 65 per cent holding in David Whitehead Textiles.[4]

In terms of structure, the larger and more entrepreneurial firms have a high degree of vertical integration. The two textile firms in the sample are typical of the larger firms in the sub-sector. These firms started with the manufacture of fabrics and gradually integrated backwards into spinning and weaving. For instance, in the case of David Whitehead Textiles, its raw material – cotton yarn – was initially purchased from what was then Rhodesian Spinners in Kadoma. The main production activity of the firm was to weave and dye fabrics for the domestic market and neighbouring countries. In 1960 David Whitehead Textiles purchased Rhodesian Spinners, which is now its spinning division, from the government. Two years after going public on the local stock exchange in 1968 the company purchased C.W. Hall in Gweru, which became its hosiery division.

The largest clothing firm in the sample, Fashion Enterprises, also started as a manufacturer of garments but with time became vertically integrated. Under the Fashion Industrial Holdings Group of Companies, there are two garment manufacturing firms (Fashion Enterprises and Julie Whyte) serviced by an in-house textile printing and dyeing firm (Screentone).

Thus, compared to their counterparts elsewhere in the third world, many large clothing producers in Zimbabwe – like large producers in other sectors of the economy – are highly vertically integrated, undertaking many peripheral or non-core activities rather than purchasing from more specialized outside suppliers. Two factors help to explain this tendency. First, the shortage of raw materials and other inputs since 1965, at the onset of UDI, has eroded the firms' trust in domestic markets to supply the much-needed inputs of goods and services. The Zimbabwean economy is still a shortage economy. In this situation, large firms have been under considerable pressure to take whatever steps were necessary to ensure that they had access to a regular supply of inputs. Secondly, the often non-competitive environment in which large companies operate has meant that, to be assured of a more reliable supply, they have been able to get away with paying a risk premium; the resulting higher costs being easily passed on to final consumers.[5]

There is reason to believe that both these factors should be changing. Some vital inputs continue to be placed under the OGIL, and the operation of the ERS has enabled firms to procure a wide range of inputs on easier terms than before. But because of the current drought, the rather slow liberalization of the supply of the required inputs and the continued monopolistic tendencies, especially among the large suppliers, the existing vertically integrated structure of the large firms is likely to persist among the textile and garment producers.

Export history

Though originally established for the domestic market, Zimbabwean companies in the textile and clothing sub-sectors carried out some export activities from the 1960s and 1970s, albeit at very low levels. For example, Concorde Clothing became the first local clothing company to export garments by airfreight to the London C&A shops in 1963. These exports continued for only three years. During the UDI period the company switched its exports to South Africa.

The two textile mills in our sample have exported since the 1960s but their export growth has been lacklustre. For example, in the early 1970s David Whitehead Textiles had insignificant exports to South Africa. In the mid-1970s, because of the shortage of foreign exchange, the government agreed to let the company export yarn to Europe and retain the proceeds in order to purchase machinery. That market was retained for a while but because of the thriving domestic market around 1980 the company concentrated on supplying the domestic market. Only small amounts of canvas and yarn were exported to South Africa. Cotton Printers, the other textile mill in the sample, exported cheap bed sheets to South Africa in the 1960s. By 1982 its exports amounted to Z$1 million – all to South Africa.

Table 7.2 Profile of Zimbabwean textile and clothing firms

Firm	Year established	No. of employees	Main products
Textile firms:			
David Whitehead Textiles	1952	4 900	Loomstate fabrics, and some yarn
Cotton Printers	1952	1 500	Yarn, loomstate fabric, bed linen, indirect fabrics exported through other firms
Clothing firms:			
Fashion Enterprises	1959	2 500	Women's and children's dresses, pants, skirts, blouses, unstructured jackets, men's shorts
Concorde Clothing	1959	450	Men's trousers, shirts, suits, casual wear
Bernstein	1939	385	Shirts and men's trousers – dresses were produced in the past
Femina Garments	1968	136	Women's wear (skirts, blouses, maternity) and children's wear

Source: Fieldwork interviews

Most companies only started thinking about promoting exports in earnest around 1988. After 1990 exports started rising substantially in both volume and value terms. One of the firms' exports rose from Z$0.5m in 1980 to Z$10.5m in 1990 and to Z$44.6m in 1992. In volume terms its exports of fabric increased from 4.2 million metres in 1991 to 7.8 million metres in 1992. Domestic sales revenues dropped from Z$120 million in the first half of 1992 to Z$83 million in the second half, while exports increased from Z$17 million to Z$27 million in the same period. Another textile firm's exports amounted to 40 per cent of total production in value terms and 55 per cent in volume terms in 1990/91. In certain production lines as much as 90 per cent of the fabric (in volume terms) was exported, but this is likely to come down to 70–75 per cent when the domestic market picks up.

Zimbabwe's clothing companies, like the textile mills, have been exporting piecemeal since the 1960s and the 1970s, but the more serious drive towards export-led growth started in the second half of the 1980s and the early 1990s. Thus Concorde Clothing exported garments to the UK between 1963 and 1965, thereafter switching exports to South Africa until 1981, when the company turned to the domestic market. The current export drive by Concorde Clothing began in 1985 when 15 000–20 000 units were exported to the UK. By 1992 export volumes to the UK market had risen to 100 000 units and new markets were being opened up in France and Holland. The two companies, Concorde Clothing and Bernstein, had an average export growth rate of 55 per cent from 1991 to 1992.

In 1978/1979 Fashion Enterprises, the largest exporter in the clothing sub-sector, started exporting to Western Europe and these exports had increased by 1980. The firm's exporting activities were greatly assisted by the introduction of the ERF. In 1986, 11 000 units were sent to the USA, rising to 250 000 in 1992. In value terms Fashion Enterprises' clothing exports increased by 400 per cent from 1980 to 1990, and since then by an average of 65 per cent per year.

Largely because of the slump in the domestic market, export production has risen as a proportion of total production. One of the clothing company's exports represented 22.5 per cent of total production in 1992. In terms of units, another firm's exports represented 70–75 per cent of total production, while in value terms they represented 50–55 per cent of total production during the same year. This increase in the export share came about as a replacement for the loss in the local market.

The smallest firm in the sample, Femina Garments, concentrated solely on the domestic market until 1987, when small numbers of garments were exported to Germany. A serious export drive started only in 1990, with increased exports to Germany and small volumes going to Botswana.

The sudden rise in exports in recent years can in part be explained, paradoxically, by the drying up of foreign currency allocations to importers by 1988/89 and by the introduction of the ERS (see pp. 146–7). The ERS enabled exporters to earn the much-needed foreign currency. In other words, in order to get imports, companies had to be exporters. The introduction of the Economic and Structural Adjustment Programme (ESAP) and the decline in the domestic market as a result of the current drought have helped to accelerate the programme.

External factors affecting export growth

As shown above, the recent growth in exports in the textile and clothing sub-sectors has been quite impressive despite the difficult circumstances faced by individual companies. The principal external factors that were found to be adversely impacting on the export growth of textile and clothing sub-sectors are (1) inability to obtain export finance at a competitive cost and (2) problems of obtaining competitively priced raw materials. Other factors adversely affecting firms' export growth are connected with infrastructural problems and bureaucratic and policy obstacles. Whilst the supply side of the most important inputs is not competitive, the companies cannot pass on these high and rapidly rising input costs because both the domestic and export markets are intensely competitive.

Ability to mobilize export finance

In the Zimbabwean case, company size is a significant factor in determining the firm's ability to mobilize financial resources in general, including export finance. This is mainly because the larger companies deal with larger volumes compared to their small counterparts. Thus whilst the smallest firm in the sample (Femina Garments) increased its exports by an astronomical figure of 218 per cent from 1990 to 1991, this was in value and volume terms far less than the larger firms in the sample. During the same period, the slowest export growth in the sample, in percentage terms, was that of Concorde Clothing at only 8 per cent but because of Concorde's size this represented a greater increase in terms of value than Femina achieved.

On the other hand, Fashion Enterprises combines both large volumes and high export growth: 129 per cent from 1990 to 1991 or an increase of US$31 million compared to Femina Garments' increase of US$48 000. In Zimbabwe, where resources, and especially finance, are not freely available in the market on a competitive basis, larger companies have more access to these resources than the smaller firms. A company that has successfully exported before is further assured of the critical foreign exchange resources for upgrading and replacing its machinery and equipment and procuring spare parts through its utilization of the ERS. Such resources are not easily available to new exporters and especially not to small firms, which can only obtain ERS funds at a premium price. At the prevailing interest rate of over 30 per cent, access to export finance becomes prohibitive.

However, all exporters face similar problems with regards to mobilizing export finance, which is a major problem for textile and garment exporters. It normally takes 90 days for export orders to be paid, and local companies insist on obtaining an irrevocable letter of credit. But in practice textile mills say that it takes up to 9 months from the time cotton is purchased from the CMB to the time when export proceeds are received. Cotton purchases have to be paid for within 7 days. One garment manufacturer said it normally has an 8-month cycle for exports to the US and 2–3 months for Europe because of airfreight arrangements. In the meantime the companies have to finance their production through bank bills, which is expensive given the high interest rates prevailing in the economy. Before the domestic market collapsed, companies financed export activities from the more lucrative domestic market.

Raw material problems

Both the textile mills and clothing companies face problems with regard to raw materials, although in different ways. The main raw material problem faced by textile mills appears to be the pricing structure of cotton from the CMB, while that of the clothing companies is related to the price and delivery quality of fabrics from the textile mills.

As shown above, the problem of cotton prices and deliveries from the farmers is an historical one dating from the 1980s, when a number of farmers abandoned cotton growing because of the low price paid by the CMB. This in turn has led to rationing of cotton to the textile mills. By June 1992 they were allocated only 60 per cent of their requirements.

The problem has been further compounded by the commitment of the CMB to export part of the lint instead of supplying all that is available to the local mills. The export parity price of cotton has been more attractive than the domestic price paid by the mills.[6] On the other hand, the clothing sub-sector's biggest and most long-standing problem is obtaining suitable raw materials, especially fabrics for both the local and export markets. The position faced by the clothing manufacturers was recently summarized by the Zimbabwe Clothing Council as follows:

> Locally-produced fabrics are in the main unsuitable for the clothing export market, increasingly so since world fashion trends have dictated a swing to fabrics with a high proportion of special weaves, blends and finishes not available from local textile mills. Even the few types of fabric local textile mills can produce frequently cannot be used for export because of unreliable quality and deliveries and the unfortunate practice adopted by most mills of refusing to hold prices at contracted levels.
>
> (Zimbabwe Clothing Council, 1992, p. 2)

This creates insurmountable difficulties for clothing manufacturers attempting to cost their exports in a rational manner. An equally insurmountable problem is the high reject rates on local fabrics, which can exceed 15–20 per cent. These rates have become a norm and sometimes as much as 50 per cent of fabric delivered is unusable even at the lowest-budget end of the local market. The two firms interviewed confirmed these high rejection rates. Reject garments due to fabric flaws, especially poor weaving and dyeing standards, often lead to the cancellation of export orders. Even in the local market, such garments are sold at a considerable discount and in some cases at well below cost.

Such problems would generally not exist where there is competition among producers. Free competition would normally ensure that suppliers would adhere to quoted prices irrespective of subsequent increases in their own input costs, and that their products would be competitive in terms of quality and delivery times. Lack of competition in the textile sub-sector is likely to permit the industry to continue to increase prices at will without any improvement in quality, variety and reliability in deliveries.

However, as a result of the rationing of foreign exchange, local clothing manufacturers cannot readily obtain the imported fabrics which are demanded by both domestic and export markets. The representatives of the clothing sub-sector are, therefore, arguing that their inputs should be brought under OGIL as soon as possible, so there can be a realistic adjustment period before they have to face competition from imported finished clothing when that is finally put on OGIL.

In the Zimbabwean case these problems are made possible by the foreign exchange shortages and an almost monopolistic textile industry, in which over 250 clothing firms are effectively supplied by just five textile companies, of which two provide 60 per cent of the total textile output of the country.

Some of the textile mills recognize some of the problems faced by the clothing industry. As a step towards supplying the varieties of cloth required by local clothing firms, at least one textile mill has contemplated reducing style choice at the level of spinning and weaving by concentrating on continuous processing, while introducing more varieties or ranges at the level of dyeing and finishing. In Zimbabwean production conditions, to be competitive in terms of cost-effectiveness, a mill must produce a minimum run of 3 000 metres of fabric at a time. This strategy is meant to enhance the competitiveness of textile mills by responding to customer requests within the minimum threshold of a company's production programme.

Textile mills confirmed that 30–35 per cent of the fabrics they produce would not pass international standards. As a result these are normally sold to local clothing firms. Their suggested solution is to invest in laboratory and shade-matching equipment. Two of the firms interviewed claimed that they already had plans to improve the quality of their products, as demanded by local garment manufacturers. This is becoming more important given the lack of competitiveness of local grey-cloth fabrics in the world market, a situation which is turning more textile mills to develop 'indirect exports': supplying good-quality fabrics to local clothing firms which, in turn, manufacture garments for export.[7]

Technology, productivity and human resources

Characteristics of demand in target markets

In the past, Zimbabwean textile and garment manufacturers failed to take advantage of the abundant raw cotton, low labour costs and reasonably good experience of textile manufacturing to exploit international markets. Only towards the end of the 1980s were the more entrepreneurial firms prodded into action by the decline in sales on the domestic market and the desire to earn more foreign currency, which could be obtained through the export incentive scheme and more recently through the ERS. But by this time the availability of raw materials had become a major problem and domestic labour costs had escalated following the introduction of minimum wages and a general increase in wages during the 1980s.

Production costs escalated during the 1980s, mainly due to increases in wages and other inputs. The opening up of the economy and general reduction in subsidies paid to public utilities (e.g. energy and transport) have also contributed to rising costs of production. This is in addition to the unpredictable price hikes by the local textile mills and the 1991 devaluation of the Zimbabwean dollar, which has increased the cost of imported raw materials, mainly fabric and the trim content of the garment.

Despite these problems, the textile and garment firms, especially the larger and more entrepreneurial ones, are aggressively seeking and establishing contacts in both the regional and overseas markets. Various methods have been used in order to penetrate these markets. Export contracts have been obtained through personal contact with overseas agents, chain stores, or posting independent agents in those markets. The more established enterprises have their agents in these markets, while others are in direct contact with the importers. More recently Zimtrade, a trade promotion organization co-sponsored by the government and the private sector, has assisted newcomers in the export market by organizing exhibits for Zimbabwean exporters in both the regional and overseas markets.[8]

Whilst in certain cases such markets are receptive, Zimbabwean manufacturers come under tremendous price pressure. More subsidized products from countries such as Pakistan and China take advantage of the falling price of fabrics in overseas markets. For example, the price of grey-cloth fabric has fallen from US$1.15 in 1987 to US$0.79 in 1992, a situation that is not helped by the near-monopolistic price of raw materials in Zimbabwe.

The firms interviewed are succeeding in varying degrees: exports accounted for between 20 per cent and 75 per cent of their production. Besides maintaining market shares in the more established markets, both textile and clothing firms are establishing footholds in new markets, especially in European and North American markets, where some of the larger firms have established solid export contracts. All the firms are seeking to raise their market share urgently in order to replace the shrinking local market.

Companies involved in the search for these markets are confident of increasing their market shares. Wage rates at least became competitive following the currency devaluation of September 1991, although this has been eroded by recent pegging of the exchange rate during a period of significant inflation. Managers are confident of maintaining the present levels of skills and production quality in Zimbabwe's textile and garment industry. The larger companies with access to modern equipment and technical expertise are able to maintain market shares and even increase them.

However, only the larger white-owned enterprises are in a position to take advantage of such opportunities, because of the concentration of experience, skills and overseas contacts required to make export contracts possible. The smaller operations do not have the resources to engage consultants to explore overseas markets. Because the price of exports must cover all the exporter's direct costs, including administrative costs, the higher the volumes exported the lower the production costs. Even when they are able to get export orders, small delivery volumes mean they cannot use containerized cargo, which is cheaper than airfreight cargo. There is, therefore, a need for government policy to facilitate the development of exports among the smaller enterprises.

Design capabilities

Zimbabwean textile and garment manufacturers have, over the years, developed design capabilities. Design was initially for the domestic market but some of these designs have been progressively adapted to the demands and specifications of external markets. Textile mills often have technical development departments which, beside their long-term project development, look into market requirements, especially the need for new varieties and styles of fabrics. In general R&D is done on a small-scale basis.

Most of the garment manufacturers said that they had no designers to speak of, especially in men's garments. Instead, a typical Zimbabwean firm needs a good merchandiser to put together a collection of colours and new styles for each approaching season. On the basis of this market information and trends the designer and factory pattern makers put up new patterns for the market. Once the market needs are identified and assessed, development takes the form of designing the product to suit the specification of the market. In other words, the local designers only copy fashions and trends from overseas.

Fashion Enterprises, the leader in women's clothing, have, however, acquired CAD/CAM facilities for their long-run production for the export markets. The company's design capabilities have been developed jointly with overseas customers or through promoting its in-house designs for both the domestic and export markets. Alternatively the exporter's own designed ranges can be promoted side by side with those of the customer. Because of changes from season to season, the companies maintain their in-house capability to design and develop new products in accordance with the desires and whims of the market.

Technology and productivity

In most of the textile and clothing firms, management positions are occupied by people who have been with the firms for a long time. In one garment manufacturing firm, the production manager has been with the firm for over thirty years and has thus seen all the changes and transformations in the production processes over time.

These have involved changes in aids to manufacture, fusing processes and the introduction of automatic markers.

There are, however, quite glaring differences in the technological processes adopted by companies in the sample. They range from firms with outdated plant and machinery to a few companies that can boast of the most modern plant by any standards. For instance, the Fashion Enterprises plant is comparable to any plant of its kind in Europe and North America. Modernization has not been limited to processing fabrics: advances have also been made in the area of merchandising, which is crucial for the development of the firm's own export ranges and when working with overseas-based agents to develop and quickly respond to customers' requirements.

Productivity has steadily improved because of improvements in technology and management techniques. One textile mill reported that in those areas where labour accounts for around 90 per cent of value added, e.g. in hemming, there have been many improvements in labour productivity. Both the textile mills said that the wage cost of the conversion of raw materials into finished products has been kept low while volumes produced have increased. This has been made possible by a number of factors including improved training of labour, improvements in production programming and reducing the varieties and styles produced in the production runs.

Two companies in the sample reported using an incentive bonus system to achieve higher levels of productivity. In one, the management sets an output target for every section. Any production above this point is rewarded by a bonus system on a percentage basis. The second bonus system rewards the department that achieved the best results at the end of each year. A third is the general bonus, which is awarded to all the workers depending on the general performance of the firm. This is given at the discretion of the board of directors of the company.

There are, however, still problems of low production quality because of old machinery, which would have been replaced long ago if foreign currency had been available. This is especially the case in the spinning of yarn. Despite these problems, in the regional context Zimbabwean textile firms have a competitive edge, even over their South African counterparts. This is mainly due to a prolonged history of protection of the textile industry in that country.

The production costs of clothing firms which have the larger portion of their production geared for the domestic market are badly affected by the uncompetitive prices and unpredictable quality of local fabrics. Though their wage rates and unit costs are not comparable to those in Asian countries, local garment exporters are fairly competitive in the context of Sub-Saharan Africa, including South Africa.[9] The strength of local firms has been their reliability in producing quality products and delivery on time.

All the companies in our sample have strict quality control systems in place. Quality is regarded as an important part of production. There is a quality control department in each of these firms, but in addition quality standards are insisted upon at every stage of the production process. In one firm, management said that their in-house training programmes insist that quality and output go hand in hand. A trainee is only brought into the production line after achieving 75 per cent efficiency in both quality and targeted output levels. In other words, the concept of putting quality in the forefront of production is treated as a long-term strategy for companies in the export business.

Production linkages and subcontracting

Though the textile and clothing sub-sectors have quite well-developed forward and backward linkages, most of these linkages are limited to purchasing raw materials and other inputs between enterprises. Companies within the sub-sectors also cooperate closely in the event of machine breakdowns and exchange technical expertise among themselves. One large firm has a record of passing on to other firms those export enquiries they cannot handle.

This leaves out one kind of link between firms – the inter-firm trade in unfinished inputs in the form of Cut-Make and Trim (CMT). CMT is a system under which a producer is subcontracted by another producer or, more generally, a distributor to produce garments to the latter's precise specifications, with the fabric and designs being supplied by the distributor. It has gained importance in recent years but is largely limited to subcontracting between local distributors and micro and small enterprises (MSEs), rather than among exporting firms.[10]

Most of the larger firms in the textile and garment sub-sectors are less likely to be involved in any form of production linkage because of the high level of vertical integration in their production. Among the garment manufacturers, the more vertically integrated ones (such as Fashion Enterprises), which combine under one roof garment manufacturing, fabric processing and textile printers and dyers, have had more success in processing their export orders. This is because they have better control of their stocks, quality of fabric and delivery times than firms dependent on textile mills for all their raw materials.

Firms are also afraid that if they subcontract on a CMT basis to a competitor, they may in the process lose their market to the competitor. Moreover, the non-exporting firm has no incentive to support an exporter because it will not share the export incentive. The compensation for this must, therefore, be an attractive price for the CMT. Two garment manufacturers confirmed that they have engaged in CMT business when the price offered for subcontracting was attractive.

Human resources and development of skills

Most of the general skills required in both the textile mills and garment manufacturers are obtained internally within the firms. The companies have adopted aggressive training programmes and retain their skilled personnel for as long as possible. In addition to in-house training programmes, promising middle-level personnel are often sent abroad on secondment and for formal training. Taking advantage of its overseas connections, David Whitehead has sent most of its high-level people to obtain the Higher National Diploma in Textiles in Lancaster in the UK

One Bulawayo-based company, Cotton Printers, prides itself on recruiting graduates of the Textile Designing Department of the Bulawayo Technical College. At higher levels the textile mills recruit people with basic skills such as loom mechanics and chemical and electrical engineers. These receive in-house training to become textile specialists. They are often sent for specialized training in South Africa, the UK and other countries. At the management and supervisory levels companies make use of training opportunities provided by the Institute of Management.

In general, the skilled workers required by the clothing sub-sector are designers, pattern makers, cutters and machinists. These core skills are complemented by experienced supervisors and middle and senior management personnel. Skill development is mainly by in-house training. Recruits with either 'O' or 'A' level qualifications are taken on at the lowest levels and are given routine tasks before being trained to perform tasks in all sections of the firm starting. Middle and senior management positions have often been filled by people who started from the lower echelons of the shop floor. There were exceptions to this rule in the past, especially before independence when middle and senior positions were filled by personnel recruited overseas, often people with family connections.

Since the early 1980s this source of recruitment has almost dried up and a shortage of well-trained people at middle and senior levels has become a serious problem. A major problem facing the clothing industry is inappropriate training. The current training undertaken at local public and private colleges does not produce suitable candidates for the industry. These colleges do not use the standard industrial machines employed by firms, a situation that results in college graduates arriving at factories without experience in handling state-of-the-art machinery and equipment.

In order to fill this gap, the Zimbabwe Clothing Council (ZCC) is in the process of setting up a training school for the clothing sub-sector which will complement training at the factory level and provide further sophisticated training for the sub-sector. The new school will concentrate on providing appropriate training in project management, designing and maintenance.

FOOTWEAR

Background

Shoe production must have been amongst the earliest industries established in Rhodesia, but large-scale factory production only took off after the Second World War. As cattle breeding has always been important, the availability of leather stimulated the development of the industry. The other major raw materials are canvas, which is locally produced, together with imported rubber and more recently plastic.

Hide production is dominated by the parastatal Cold Storage Commission (CSC), although in recent years private abattoirs have become increasingly important as a source of hides. At the next stage of leather production there are six tanneries, the four main ones being owned by three shoe manufacturers: Bata, Superior and G&D Shoes. These three vertically integrated enterprises, with combined employment of about 5 500, thus dominate the sub-sector. There are also four medium-size shoe manufacturers with about 250 workers each, five small but mechanized shoe manufacturers with about 50 workers each and a large number of artisan enterprises, mainly involved in repair but also in the manufacture of shoes (Mead and Kunjeku, 1992, p. 21).

The demand for shoes in Zimbabwe would appear to be in excess of one pair per person per annum, although the actual consumption is highly dependent on economic conditions. This year, with the combined effects of the drought and the downturn induced by structural adjustments, domestic demand has dropped precipitously except for the high end of the market. In that segment, there is a remarkable range of locally made shoes on offer, as diverse a choice of styles as is available in many industrialized countries. Bata alone is presently making 3 000–4 000 styles in a country with a population of only 10.4 million.

Since the initiation of trade liberalization, a significant proportion of raw materials needed in the shoe industry, such as chemicals, has been put onto OGIL. This has considerably eased input supply problems. Domestic input supply has also improved in some respects. Competitive imports of finished shoes will only be allowed in the closing phases of the liberalization process. It is local production of cheaper footwear, such as plastic and canvas shoes, which will be most under threat from imports from the Far East, especially China. Manufacturers of high-fashion leather footwear believe that, if they use the intervening years to improve productivity, they will be able to compete with comparable imports with little or no tariff protection.

History of firms in the sample

Origins, ownership and structure

The three main firms studied have very different origins and resulting structures. The Zimbabwe Bata Shoe Company (henceforward referred to as Bata) is a wholly owned subsidiary of Bata International, based in Canada. Despite its vast size (Bata has a presence in over a hundred countries), the Bata empire is still in some ways run along the lines of a family business, with one of the Bata family visiting Bata in Zimbabwe at least once a year. In other ways, it is a sophisticated modern multinational, with considerable autonomy being given to local management in order to provide the requisite motivation and setting to maximize creativity and productivity.

In Zimbabwe, Bata consists of a vertically integrated leather and shoe manufacturing concern, together with the largest chain of wholesale and retail shoe outlets in the country. Zimbabwe Bata is the third largest Bata subsidiary internationally. The production side consists of three units on the same site as the head office in Gweru (tannery, canvas and rubber, leather shoes), a sports shoe factory in Kwekwe (manufacturing, *inter alia* Adidas shoes under licence) and a plastic shoe factory in Mutare.

Superior Footwear was started in 1967 by da Costa, an immigrant from Portugal. It is now part of a group of companies with specialized functions, including a leather tannery (Imponente Tanning), shoe component manufacturers and an engineering workshop for machinery construction and maintenance. The group is controlled by the da Costa family through Superior Footwear Holdings, which was registered in 1991. In addition to members of the family making decisions at board level, key management positions are held by them.

Cathula Sandals is a more recent company, formed in the 1970s by Mr Mpofu, at a time under the UDI government when it was difficult for blacks to go into business. Starting from hawking leather goods after hours while still in full-time employment, Mr Mpofu moved through successive stages: setting up of a production unit in his home, opening a retail outlet in town, expansion of the production unit into successively larger hired premises, opening further retail outlets, building a retail outlet and finally building a factory. At the time of the interview, the construction of the new factory was stalled at window height, due to financing difficulties. To carry out the building, Mr Mpofu had started a construction company, and in order to overcome difficulties in obtaining imported raw materials, he had also set up a buckle manufacturing concern. Besides marketing through their own outlets, Cathula also sells to large chains, including Bata.

As Table 7.3 shows, the three companies are of very different sizes and capacities. The figures are not directly comparable, because the product ranges are very different. The majority of Bata's large output consists of canvas, plastic and rubber shoes, with only a relatively small proportion of leather and fashion footwear. By contrast, Superior concentrates only on the upper end of the market for high-quality leather shoes. Cathula only manufactures sandals, which are much less demanding from a production viewpoint than shoes. Superior and Cathula are in the process of establishing new factories; planned capacities for these are given as well as current capacities.

Shorter interviews were held with officials of two other companies: Footwear and Rubber in Bulawayo and Italian Styles in Harare. Both of these companies have been hit by the decline in domestic demand. Footwear and Rubber has laid off 160 workers and has reduced production from 2 000 to 600 pairs per day; Italian Styles is working a 3-day week, producing 150 pairs per day. This contrasts

Table 7.3 Employment and production capacity of sample firms

| Firm | Employment | | Capacity |
	Shoe production	Total	(pairs/day)
L Bata	1 650	3 500	50 000
Superior Footwear:			
present	190	450	800
planned: shoes	210	470	1 500
plus uppers	–	–	3 000
Cathula Sandals:			
present	30	42	400
planned	125	138	2 000

Source: Company interviews

with Bata, which has managed to avoid any lay-offs or short-time operations, in no small measure because of its ability to export, in particular to increase its exports to South Africa rapidly to make up for the shortfall in domestic demand. Prior to independence, Footwear and Rubber used to be a major exporter of footwear to the region, before UDI maintaining a branch office in Lusaka; exports now are mainly to South Africa, with about 16 per cent of normal production going to this market.

Export history

Within the sample, Bata is the main company exporting footwear. Superior has exported shoes in the past but these have mainly been small, sporadic consignments. Cathula has been approached by potential customers from the region but is yet to export.

Internationally, Bata's main objective is to provide affordable footwear for the people of the countries in which it operates, so that exports are secondary. In Zimbabwe's case, apart from exports to South Africa under the bilateral trade agreement, there was little scope for exports during the UDI period. Since independence, Bata has responded to downturns in domestic demand, and to the growing array of export incentives, by attempting to break into new export markets. These efforts have not always been successful: mistakes were made in exports to France and Italy a few years back, resulting in the loss of those markets. The lessons from this experience are being applied to the European markets presently being developed (principally the UK).

With the advent of the ERS and the present downturn in the domestic market, production for export is being given priority. As a result, the domestic market tends to suffer shortages of particular styles and sizes but one of the advantages of being vertically integrated and dominant in the domestic market is that Bata retail outlets and the ordinary Zimbabwean customer have to put up with this. At present, Bata exports approximately 20 per cent of its production (10 000 pairs per day or about 3 million pairs per annum). Export value has grown rapidly in recent years (partly as a result of devaluation) to about Z$30 million (US$6 million) in 1992 and was expected to reach Z$40 million (US$8 million) in 1994.

Bata's main export markets are in South Africa (60 per cent of total exports), Botswana (10–15 per cent) and the UK (10 per cent), with the balance being spread over a variety of countries. These include Namibia, Angola, Zambia, Malawi, Tanzania, Burundi, Ghana and Uganda in Africa, and Australia, New Zealand, the US, Ireland, France and Italy elsewhere in the world. In African countries, exports are generally made either to agents or to other subsidiaries of Bata. In the UK, exports are made directly to suppliers of large retail chains.

During the 1980s Superior became a major exporter of leather, the approach adopted being to start at the lowest level (wet blue) and, working with established customers abroad, to add value progressively by exporting product that has been through further stages of production (to crust and then to finished leather). Shoe manufacture is seen as the final stage in this process and, in order to make the sort of concerted effort that is required for the successful export of footwear, a new factory has been built and is presently being commissioned. Superior plans shortly to expand its footwear exports significantly, starting with exporting shoe uppers and moving into the export of finished shoes. Ultimately footwear exports will be a major component of the company's activities.

The reasons for Cathula not exporting, despite enquiries about its products from potential customers in Africa (Nigeria, Kenya, Swaziland, South Africa and Botswana), are significant. Cathula would have liked to respond but did not have the foreign currency needed to purchase the imported inputs which would have been required. The company was unaware until very recently of the existence of the ERF, which was specifically set up to overcome this problem. Cathula did spend some time lobbying the Ministry of Industry and Commerce for an increased foreign exchange allocation but was not during that period informed by Ministry officials of the existence of the ERF. The lobbying was successful, so much so that in the present period of poor liquidity, the company is unable to access all of its foreign currency allocation because it is unable to put up the corresponding amount in Zimbabwe dollars.

The record of Cathula has some clear lessons for support agencies set up to assist companies to become established and to export. These would include the Indigenous Business Development Centre and Zimtrade, both of which have been alerted to the experience documented in this study.

External factors affecting export growth

Ability to mobilize export finance

Provided that companies are well run, size has numerous advantages when it comes to competing in export markets. One obvious aspect is the ability to mobilize export finance. A company such as Bata can more readily raise export finance from banks than less well-established concerns, or can simply absorb the costs of foreign market development, including having to wait for payments for goods exported.

While neither Bata nor Superior specifically complained of lack of finance as a constraint to expanding exports, both companies are experiencing some difficulties with the tight monetary conditions currently prevailing. Cathula, however, has over-extended itself in constructing a new factory, to the extent that money borrowed for working capital has been used, to the bank's displeasure, for fixed capital purposes. With the rise in interest rates, Cathula is now unable to do more than make the required monthly repayments. As the bank has refused to make further loans so that the new factory can be completed and used, the future is gloomy. As the company is unable to make full use of its existing foreign exchange allocations and is not significantly constrained on the domestic market, and since margins on exports would be unlikely to be as high as domestic ones, Cathula does not see any reason to pursue export markets actively.

Raw material problems

In the past, the availability and price of imported raw materials have been problems. In recent months, however, many of the required inputs have been put under OGIL, allowing currency allocations to be used for the remainder, topped up, if necessary, by ERS allocations earned from exporting, or from buying surplus ERS from others at a premium. While availability has improved through these mechanisms, prices have also gone up markedly, partly through the sharp devaluation of 1991 and partly through new taxes which have been introduced to curb imports and raise revenues; these include a 20 per cent duty on all goods brought into Zimbabwe on OGIL.

The quality and reliability of supply of domestic raw materials remains problematic. This applies particularly to leather, where the following underlying causes can be noted:

- lack of care of hides by cattle owners, the premium system introduced by the CSC of Z$10 per hide being insufficient to change practices such as branding in the rump rather than the neck and not protecting the animals from damage on barbed wire fencing.
- deterioration in the services and supervision in government departments such as veterinary services and parastatals such as the CSC.
- additional deterioration in the current year due to drought stress on the animals.
- the large-scale production orientation of the country's tanneries, which are not geared to produce the quality that is needed to make shoes for export to sophisticated markets.

In the past, smaller consumers of leather felt that too much leather was being exported, in particular the better-quality leather. There was some justification for this assertion, as the workings of the exchange control regulations at the time made it imperative for the CSC to export untreated hides and for the tanneries to export treated hides and finished leather, even when there was a shortage of leather on the local market. This situation was clearly irrational from a national economic viewpoint and one of the benefits of trade liberalization will be to eliminate such anomalies. With 70 per cent of the imported inputs to the tanning industry now on OGIL, and new equipment installed to bring capacity in the later stages of tanning into line with the capacity to produce wet blue hide, the situation should improve markedly.

For the small shoe manufacturer, problems with leather availability and quality are compounded by the fact that the three tanning groups are also vertically integrated with major shoe companies: Bata, G&D Shoes and Superior Footwear. The tanners counter that their own shoe factories suffer the same problems that outside shoe companies do in securing regular supplies of high-quality leather.

This may in general be true but it is none the less the case that when a special order of leather is required to meet an export contract, the vertically integrated enterprise is in a much better position to put pressure on the tannery to produce the quality and colour of leather required in time. A particular example was cited in the interviews: a European client had approached both Superior Footwear and Italian Styles but only Superior was able to respond, as Italian Styles found itself unable to obtain the requisite colour leather from its normal supplier, Imponente, the tannery belonging to the Superior Footwear Group. There is no suggestion that Superior had tried to sabotage Italian Style's efforts but simply that Imponente was not geared to provide what was required in this particular case.

Italian Styles sees the availability of leather as the primary constraint in pursuing export markets. Since it cannot guarantee the quality of leather which may be available, the company feels it should not accept export orders. The present situation is that some consignments of leather are first rate but others are 'shocking'; reliability is essential if companies are to succeed in exporting high-quality (high-value added) footwear. The solution may eventually lie in placing leather on OGIL (hides have already been put on OGIL but not finished leather). In the meantime, some of the second-tier shoe manufacturers are looking to small, independent tanneries to produce the quality of finished leather needed to meet export orders for shoes.

Once finished leather is on OGIL, shoe manufacturers will be able to choose between locally produced and imported leather. This will force local producers to be more competitive in quality and service, with price determined by the world price plus duties on imports. Shoe manufacturers should not then have grounds to complain of discrimination and inability to produce the highest-quality goods for export due to shortages of leather. For the exporter, able to claim duty rebates, the price should also be close to the price faced by competitors in other countries. Already, with the possibility of using ERS funds for importation, some of the shoes being made for export are using imported leather, although Zimbabwe itself is a significant producer and exporter of leather.

Infrastructural problems

As mentioned on p. 149, deterioration in the quality of infrastructural services and failures to expand supplies fast enough to cater for demand are beginning to impact directly on productive activities. Besides the problems now common in Zimbabwe of making contact with suppliers and customers by telephone or other forms of telecommunication and of obtaining reasonable transport services, and the challenge of managing production within the monthly quota of electricity allocated by the supply utility ZESA, there are specific problems encountered by companies in the sample.

Specific instances of the general problems cited in the interviews will illustrate their importance. For example, the new factory being built by Superior has had to contend with considerable problems with respect to electricity and telephones. In order to obtain an electricity connection, the company itself had to purchase the equipment that ZESA would normally be expected to supply. As far as telephones are concerned, the PTC has not allocated any lines to a factory which will employ over 200 people, producing for export as well as the domestic market. Requests to have lines transferred from the old factory 4.5 km away have been turned down. It is hard to accept that the technical difficulties cited would be insurmountable if the PTC (Post and Telecommunications Corporation) were to adopt a more constructive and determined posture.

Superior is also considering the purchase of stand-by electricity generators to obviate the risk of an unscheduled power cut resulting in an entire consignment of hides and tanning chemicals having to be destroyed. With nine tanning drums operating simultaneously in the tannery, the risk is substantial. A single such incident would justify the purchase of the stand-by equipment (approximately Z$1 million). The company is reluctant, however, arguing that the country surely should have higher priorities for the expenditure of foreign currency, not least being the need to allocate sufficient quantities of foreign currency to ZESA for effective maintenance to reduce the risk of unscheduled load shedding or blackouts.

Bureaucratic and policy obstacles

While welcoming improvements as imported inputs go onto OGIL, the companies continued to identify bureaucratic and policy issues as major problems inhibiting export growth. Again, the problems being faced, whether on-going or related to the 1992 drought-distorted economic climate, are general to the manufacturing sector (see the list on pp. 148–50) but some concrete examples may serve to bring home their significance.

For instance, several respondents complained about the Department of Customs. Customs' insistence on sticking to the letter of their duties, even when there is little or no customs revenue involved and delays could cost the country not just one particular export order but perhaps a valuable relationship with an overseas client, goes beyond being exasperating into the realm of economic sabotage.

For example, in preparing an export order for the UK, Bata was requested to tag the shoes with bar codes. As these could not be produced in Zimbabwe, Bata requested their UK customer to supply the tags, which were duly sent but then seized by Customs and held while deciding what tariff to apply. Although these were of no intrinsic value and destined anyway for re-export, Customs refused to release the tags for long enough to threaten Bata's ability to meet the deadline for the export order, in a situation where meeting the deadline was one of the primary demands of the customer.

Another example is the trade practice of sending samples to manufacturers, asking them to return 'counter-samples' and quotations, which might then lead to export orders. When such a parcel is received by Customs, it sends notice to the recipient of the need for an import licence, which requires application to the Reserve Bank through a commercial bank and thereafter application to the Ministry of Industry and Commerce. As the counter-sample is typically required within days, such procedures rule Zimbabwean firms out of consideration.

Technology, productivity and human resources

Characteristics of demand in target markets

Bata's main regional markets (South Africa and Botswana) are not dissimilar to the Zimbabwean domestic market. Bata supplies its agents in those countries, who are also major manufacturers in their own right, with styles in canvas and leather which complement their own ranges. In the case of South Africa, Bata puts forward suggested designs for each season (twice per year) and manufactures those selected by its agent. Deliveries are made to final customers in South Africa, with a small commission being paid to the agent. Bata is sufficiently well known in the relatively large South African market for export business to be secured at short notice. Thus during 1992, Bata was able to arrange additional export orders to South Africa to compensate for the decline in the domestic market in Zimbabwe.

Overseas markets are far more demanding in terms of style, finish, overall quality and delivery time than the regional markets. This is because Zimbabwe cannot become a large volume exporter in Europe or America, so it must find special niche markets, often involving developing a personal rapport with customers. Zimbabwean companies are prepared to supply small orders (10 000 pairs or less), while companies in other countries are said to be interested in much larger orders (e.g. Indonesia, supplying an order of 1 million pairs). Zimbabwe is thus well placed to serve some of the smaller developed markets, such as Australia with a population of 14 million.

In the UK market, in which Bata and Superior are presently active, the companies have to be able to offer alternative designs, responding to subtle changes in style and fashion. On the production side, quality depends both on careful production management to achieve the required craftsmanship and on supplies of uniformly high-quality inputs. Finally, adhering to agreed delivery dates is considered to be particularly important by the UK importers, because the marketing of shoes is carefully phased and any unforeseen delay is likely to result in reduced sales and being left with unwanted stocks.

Reliability, in terms of quality and delivery times, is thus the watchword for Zimbabwean shoe exports to overseas markets. *Inter alia*, this implies that orders whose quality and delivery cannot be assured have to be turned down. Bata made several errors during the 1980s in exports to France and Italy: the company now regularly carries out a critical path analysis for the production of an export consignment and carefully monitors each of the critical activities to ensure successful completion of the work.

Design capabilities

Both Bata and Superior have acquired their own CAD facilities, coupled to laser pattern cutters, in recent months. This technology was first introduced to the Zimbabwean shoe industry through a grant from UNIDO to the Leather Institute, the equipment being installed in the Institute's premises in Bulawayo. It is unfortunately not much used at present but is available for use by the smaller companies in the industry.

Bata already has a very strong product development department, with a staff of 11, together with a sample factory with a staff of 35. This has enabled Bata to offer prospective buyers visiting Gweru a wide range of styles which have been discussed and agreed, with samples being produced during the visitor's stay. In one case, it is reported that the visitor returned to Europe with 1 000 samples! The CAD equipment will facilitate interaction with the client and help to speed up the whole process. As is clear from the discussion in the previous section, speed of response is an important attribute which overseas shoe importers are looking for.

Technology and productivity

As is typical in Zimbabwean manufacturing, much of the equipment in shoe factories is old enough to be considered museum pieces elsewhere in the world. It is, however, also 'appropriate' in that it is operational and is readily maintained with local skills. Productivity, in units such as pairs per person per day, is low by international standards (from 7 to 45, with international levels two to three times higher for comparable styles) but the total costs of production, reflecting the written-down costs of the antiquated but operational equipment and relatively low labour costs, would appear to be competitive. Productivity could be improved by reducing the number of styles being produced, while cost efficiency is already being improved through more efficient stockholding, a spin-off of the present tight monetary conditions.

Despite the continued productivity of old machinery, it is none the less significant that the footwear companies in a position to do so are importing modern, sophisticated equipment with a view to being able to compete not only on export markets but with imported footwear once the final product is put onto OGIL. Bata, for example, will be installing new export production lines in Gweru in 1993 and has just commissioned a three-colour screen printer at its Kwekwe factory. Coupling this with a combined lasting and two-colour plastic sole injection moulding machine, it should be possible to attain internationally competitive productivity of high-fashion sports shoes and sneakers. The German technicians who come out regularly to ensure that production standards for the Adidas footwear being made under licence are adequate are well satisfied with the performance of the Kwekwe factory. Bata will be introducing an across-the-board efficiency improvement programme (the Swiss USO–9 000 system) during 1993.

In its new shoe factory, Superior Footwear has installed an ultramodern 'rink' system to be used particularly for export production. A computer-based diagnostic and training system has also been commissioned. This enables a supervisor to view on a computer screen the performance of a trainee during a session of work, identify problems and suggest ways in which improvements to quality and productivity can be made. The company foresees improvements in skills, productivity and hence the quality and price competitiveness of the final product. This will benefit the local market as well as the export market.

The third company studied, Cathula, uses far less sophisticated machinery, producing a product (sandals) for which indications of being hand-made may often be a positive marketing trait, rather than a negative one. Like many companies during the UDI period, Cathula has reacted to problems associated with a shortage of foreign currency by innovating. For example, the machine in use for printing transfer patterns on shoes, and much of the equipment in the buckle making plant, have been designed and built by the company. The drive and skills required for such innovation are thus not confined to the old established companies.

Human resources and the development of skills

Now that the supply of materials, especially imported inputs, has become easier, the availability of skills is emerging as the limiting constraint. On the shop floor, several companies are experiencing difficulty in finding suitable supervisory staff, and skilled personnel are also needed, particularly for product design. In order to keep abreast of developments, regular exchanges need to be made, with Zimbabwean designers travelling abroad and overseas designers visiting Zimbabwe. Under current foreign exchange regulations, such visits are apparently difficult to arrange but the benefits could be quite considerable in terms of maximizing value added in export markets. International organizations such as UNIDO have supplied consultants from time to time (e.g. to assist Superior in commissioning its new shoe factory), but it is generally felt that the limited duration of such visits has restricted their usefulness.

Since there is no formal training, such as polytechnic courses on footwear design and production, available in Zimbabwe, all of the companies interviewed have some means of providing in-house training. Due to its size and corporate culture, in-house training is most comprehensive at Bata, which offers various kinds of training programmes to all its staff and has developed the infrastructure necessary to do this. The Leather Institute would like to see regular training being offered for the benefit of the industry as a whole.

Up to 1991, the British Council gave scholarships for Zimbabweans to study leather technology in the UK. At present, both Superior and Cathula are themselves sponsoring employees or family members undertaking courses in leather technology and shoe design in the UK.

Zimbabwe shoe manufacturers attempt to keep abreast of the latest developments in styles, production processes and equipment by subscribing to international industry journals, belonging to international associations of leather and footwear institutes (such as the Shoe and Allied Trade Research Association, based in the UK), and attending trade fairs where new equipment can be viewed and selected. Bata, as part of a multinational, has the advantage of getting much of this information through Bata's international network but the local company is not obliged to take the parent company's advice on issues such as the choice of equipment.

Subcontracting

There is strong resistance to the idea of subcontracting. Companies are used to having tight control within their organization of each stage of production and the idea of putting out work to others and then being reliant on their performance to meet quality standards and delivery requirements is anathema. The suggestion that production for the domestic market might be subcontracted if there were to be a surge in export demand which would require the full capacity of the company's own facilities is also not appealing. There is a fear that markets would be lost to subcontractors, who would in time make contact and establish relations with the ultimate client, whether this be an export or a domestic market customer. This has in fact been the experience of some firms which have experimented with subcontracting (Mead and Kunjeku, 1992, p. 25).

The only example given of subcontracting by the companies interviewed is the stitching of moccasins for Bata in Gweru. This is regularly undertaken by cooperatives, which may legally be paid on a piece-work basis. The first time a cooperative was approached by Bata was during a boom period, when the company found it did not have the personnel to carry out this function. While subcontracting this particular function has apparently been very successful, the idea has not been carried across to other functions which might profitably be handled in the same manner. This reluctance to subcontract is one of many barriers to entry that a small producer is faced with in a market dominated by efficient enterprises.

AGRICULTURAL MACHINERY

Background

The agricultural machinery industry goes back to the early years of the century. Initially based on importation and assembly during the Second World War and subsequently the UDI period, the industry has developed not only into full manufacture but also into the design and development of new equipment appropriate to the changing conditions and trends in agriculture in Zimbabwe.

Precisely because the equipment is designed and built for Southern African conditions, export markets are limited to the region. However, Zimbabwean agricultural equipment enjoys a degree of natural protection against imports from other parts of the world, as experience has indicated that the equipment is appropriate and rugged.

Similar comments may be made about South African agricultural equipment, and as that country becomes even more aggressive than in the past in exporting to the region it will emerge as the major competitor. One of the problems faced by Zimbabwean manufacturers is unreliable and increasingly expensive supplies of raw materials.

A high proportion of the steel required by the industry is produced by the Zimbabwe Iron and Steel Corporation (ZISCO), but supplies have become increasingly irregular (mainly due to deterioration of equipment through lack of investment but also to loss of skills as people of ability get fed up and leave), while prices have increased dramatically as subsidies have been removed under the structural adjustment programme. ZISCO does not produce steel plate, which is usually imported from South Africa at prices which, surprisingly, tend to be lower than those faced by South African manufacturers. Labour costs are, however, considerably lower in Zimbabwe and efforts to increase productivity will continue in order to remain competitive (see pp. 190-2).

History of firms in the sample

Origins, ownership and structure

There are four main manufacturing concerns in the agricultural machinery sub-sector. The market for tractor-drawn equipment is dominated by Tinto Industries, with competition being provided by Bain Manufacturing Company. In respect of animal-drawn equipment, there are two manufacturers, Zimplow and Bulawayo Steel Products. All but the last were covered in this study.

The longest established of these companies is Bain, which started as a distributor of tractors and farm equipment in 1922 and diversified into producing its own range of equipment in 1968. The original British owners of the company were bought out in 1989. The company is now owned by the government through Willowvale Motor Industries (50 per cent), by a workers' trust company (33 per cent) and by the directors (17 per cent). The present structure is a holding company, W. Bain Holdings, under which the main subsidiary companies are Bain Manufacturing, Bain Farm Equipment (sales and distribution) and Fiatagri (an agency for Fiat tractors). Total employment within the group is 320, with 86 workers directly involved in manufacture.

Zimplow was started in 1939 in order to achieve self-sufficiency in agricultural implements in the face of the threat of import disruptions at the start of the Second World War. The plant was located in Bulawayo to take advantage of the availability of foundries and engineering works which could supply components which it would not be economical to produce in-house, and because Bulawayo was the hub of the rail network. 'At that time, rail offered the only reliable means of transport for the fast and efficient distribution of goods to the local market and to markets in neighbouring countries – including Botswana, Mozambique, Malawi, South Africa and Zambia' (Zimplow, 1989).

At the time of independence, when the company's name was changed from Rhoplow to Zimplow, it was externally controlled through a majority shareholding by the South African company Fedmech Holdings. In 1983 Fedmech released its shares for purchase by Rothmans of Pall Mall (Zimbabwe) Ltd, which had the effect of making the company locally controlled. There is now a diverse ownership through the Zimbabwe stock exchange, although Rothmans is dominant with 49.2 per cent of the shares. The company has 122 permanent workers (14 of whom are skilled toolmakers and fitters and turners). There is little labour turnover and the majority of the permanent workers have completed more than 15 years of service. During a busy season up to 150 additional workers may be employed on a contract basis.

Tinto Industries is of more recent origin than the other two companies, although it developed by purchasing existing concerns. It was the result of a large mining house (Rio Tinto) not being able to repatriate its profits during the UDI era. In 1971, a foundry, agricultural machinery, irrigation and trailer manufacturing concerns were acquired and merged to form Tinto Industries. Since that time, further acquisitions have been made, raising Tinto's market share in tractor-drawn agricultural equipment to a dominant level of around 80 per cent. The company has also diversified (into textile and mining chemicals) in order to reduce its extreme vulnerability to downturns in the agricultural sector. The company now consists of seven operational divisions: Tinto Discs (the sole source of plough discs in Zimbabwe), Tinto Foundries, Tinto Trailers, Tinto Water Engineering and Tinto Implements are the main manufacturing divisions, with Tractor and Equipment (Pvt) Limited as a distributor of tractors and implements and Tinto Chemicals as supplier of chemicals.

Tinto Industries is a division of Rio Tinto (Zimbabwe), which is a public company with 46 per cent local shareholding and 54 per cent held by RTZ (London). Until recently, Tinto Industries employed 900 workers but the downturn in the domestic economy has led to the laying off of 155 workers.

Export history

All of the agricultural equipment manufacturers are extremely vulnerable to the success or otherwise of the agricultural season. To an extent, exporting has been viewed as a means of compensating for downturns in the domestic market, although this strategy has been limited by the fact that drought conditions have typically prevailed simultaneously across the whole region. The effect of the government's export incentive policies, particularly the ERS, has certainly been to enhance export orientation but the companies remain committed first and foremost to the Zimbabwean farmers, commercial and communal.

Bain began exporting in 1974 with substantial orders to Zambia and Mozambique. These markets disappeared as the liberation struggle intensified, and exporting resumed only after independence in 1980. Bain's main export market is Zambia but exports are also made to Malawi, Mozambique, Tanzania, Zaire and Botswana. Up to 20 per cent of production has been exported in some years but generally this proportion has been lower, especially when domestic demand has been buoyant.

The history of exporting by Tinto Industries is very similar. Within Tinto Industries, it is really only the agricultural implements division which exports. As that division accounts for only 11 per cent of company turnover and about 20 per cent of its output is exported, overall exports constitute a small proportion of company turnover. The main destinations for its exports are Zambia, Malawi and Tanzania, with sporadic export orders to Angola. Before Zimbabwe's independence, South Africa was also a significant export market.

As indicated previously, Zimplow has had an export orientation from the company's inception but the primary market has always been domestic. From independence to 1986/87, exports by value constituted up to 20 per cent of turnover, with the exception of 1983/84 when the proportion rose to 31 per cent in the face of a sharp decline in the domestic market. From 1987/88, the export proportion has been over 30 per cent, with a peak of 36 per cent in 1988/89. In the last completed financial year (1991/92) exports were over Z$5 million out of a turnover of Z$15 million.

Three factors have stimulated export growth since independence. The first is the state of the domestic market, export effort and results going up when drought reduces purchasing power in the domestic market. Related to this is the question of price control, which was introduced by the government in 1982 and finally removed in 1990. As shown by Riddell (1988), the profit squeeze that price control implied revealed the inefficiency and hence vulnerability of the company but this led to considerable efforts to improve productivity and to increase exports. Finally, the growing number of export incentives has also been significant. In particular, the ERS is regarded as a means of earning the foreign currency the company needs to replace its antiquated plant and machinery. The combination of these factors explains both the growth and the fluctuations in export sales over the past twelve years.

In 1982, Botswana was virtually the only Zimplow export destination. Since that time, marketing trips to all parts of Africa have been made and also some to Europe in the hope of selling hoes. However, the main markets remain confined to the Southern Africa region: Zambia, Lesotho, South Africa, Namibia, Angola and Tanzania in addition to Botswana. Besides direct exports to these countries, the company's products are also exported indirectly by entities such as commercial agents and aid agencies, which buy large consignments for shipment to neighbouring countries (such as Mozambique). A large proportion of Zimplow's exports are funded by donors in the importing countries but orders are also received from stockists in Botswana, South Africa and Zambia.

External factors affecting export growth

General

Most of the constraints described for the textile, clothing and footwear sectors apply equally to agricultural machinery manufacturers and need not be analysed again in detail. These include the mobilization of finance in the current restrictive monetary conditions, compounded by delays in the payment of export incentives, infrastructural problems, delays and obstructionism by the Department of Customs and reduced demand from Botswana because of the debacle over the bilateral trade agreement (this having a major adverse effect on Zimplow in particular). Transport is a particular problem, as road hauliers do not like transporting agricultural equipment, which is awkward in shape, and railways have started charging for a full wagon even though consignments may be much smaller.

As with the other sub-sectors studied, one of the main problems is obtaining basic raw material supplies from a parastatal whose efficiency has for various reasons declined sharply in recent years. In this sub-sector, it is supplies of steel from ZISCO which are at issue. The government has put pressure on ZISCO to expand its product range to include any sections it could possibly manufacture and which are required by the domestic market. This pressure came at the same time as ZISCO's ability to produce was declining. The result was that the time between ordering and delivery of particular sections began to increase, with even common sections only being produced once or twice per annum. The outcome was that production in the engineering sector has often been held up for lack of raw materials.

The companies responded by building up large stocks of raw materials, a necessary hedge against supply disruptions but a policy which became very expensive when interest rates rose dramatically under structural adjustment. Costs rose especially when the requirement that parastatals should become commercially viable led ZISCO to increase its domestic prices by more than 200 per cent over 1991 and 1992. Despite the large devaluation in 1991, the Zimbabwe dollar export price of steel is still well below the domestic price. Rival companies in other countries (for example, Agrimol in Malawi, which is a direct competitor with Zimplow) can purchase ZISCO steel more cheaply than Zimbabwean companies can.

Partly in recognition of this and partly to increase its own margins, ZISCO introduced an export incentive scheme in the last quarter of 1992. This allows companies exporting ZISCO steel in finalized form to claim a rebate on the purchase price of the ZISCO steel input. This results in the effective price coming down from the regular domestic price of an average of Z$2 000 per tonne to as low as Z$1 600 per tonne, as compared with ZISCO's average export realization of Z$1 000 per tonne. With the differential remaining large, and given the benefits to the country of exporting steel in a higher-value-added form after manufacture into final products, consideration should be given to offering even larger discounts on steel for export manufacture under this scheme.

Government pricing and procurement policies also have an important role to play in creating the conditions under which companies will increase exports. This arises partly from the entrenched perception amongst the firms in the industry that exports should be based on a sound domestic market performance: 'Fundamental to success in the export market is the necessity for reasonable and fair profits in the local market so as to enable manufacturing exporters to meet external competition on a competitive basis.' (Chairman's Review, Zimplow, 1985). Besides price controls on the output of the sector itself, which have now been lifted, the prices of agricultural commodities, the availability of agricultural credit through parastatals such as the Agricultural Finance Corporation and from the commercial banks, and the government's own agricultural and rural development support policies all have an effect on domestic turnover and hence on companies' ability to compete on domestic markets.

It is not only the companies which stand to benefit but also the rural communities which government programmes are supposed to serve. For example, in the current drought relief ploughing programme, more effort should have been made by government to have donor funds released in time for an adequate range of implements to be provided with the tractors which have been purchased to assist peasant farmers with ploughing. Similarly, the project put forward by Bain for dam scoops to be purchased for use with government-owned tractors deserves support, as the concept is to utilize the huge capital investments already made in mechanized power during periods when the tractors are not in use for agricultural purposes. The benefits of constructing a large number of small dams at minimal expense would not be difficult to demonstrate, even in the absence of the extreme drought conditions experienced in the current year.

Export retention schemes

One of the main problems for Zimbabwean exporters is the availability of foreign currency in the target markets. As mentioned previously, this is often strongly influenced by the willingness or otherwise of the donors to provide finance for imports of equipment from Zimbabwe. The fact that Zimbabwean products are superficially not price competitive is significant in a market where the decisions are often made by rotating expatriates, rather than by the farming community itself, which would be aware from experience of the logic of paying a higher price for products that are significantly more appropriate and longer-lasting than products developed for conditions in other parts of the world. It is in circumstances such as these that a significant market in Tanzania was lost by Tinto Industries.

With the advent of ERSs, the above pattern is beginning to change and, at least in respect of tractor-drawn implements, much of the export business is now handled directly with individual commercial farmers. This applies particularly to the Zambian market, where there is now 100 per cent export retention for farmers. The immediate effect of this has been to expand a market which had contracted sharply in the face of extreme foreign currency shortages, but the trend towards individual farmer control over foreign currency (in Malawi, Mozambique and Zimbabwe as well as Zambia) is one that raises longer-term concerns.

This is because the agricultural support industry needs to operate on a sector-wide basis, with adequate supplies of inputs, whether domestic or imported, in order to fulfil its critical supporting role to the agricultural sector. Not only is it inefficient for companies to go through all the export procedures for each individual farmer, individual access to foreign currency is leading individual farmers to keep significant stocks of spare parts, while the agent has virtually none. For example, for a particular tractor model, Bain is aware that there are now over 600 overhaul kits sitting on individual farmer's shelves in Zimbabwe, while the company has fewer than the 20 which they would aim to have in stock to serve the existing national fleet. Buying to best advantage and maintaining what amounts to a shared pool of spares are key roles which the agricultural support sector is meant to perform.

From all points of view (the individual farmer, the agricultural support sector and the nation), these unintended consequences of the ERS system amount to a highly inefficient use of foreign exchange resources. The weakening of agricultural support companies not only makes it more difficult for them to compete in export markets, it also disadvantages farmers who produce mainly for the domestic market and do not have access to ERS funds.[11]

Technology, productivity and human resources

Characteristics of demand in target markets

As mentioned previously, export markets are limited to the Southern African region, plus to some extent East Africa. Attempts to market Zimbabwean products further afield, for example in West and North Africa, have been complete failures, as agricultural conditions are so different in those areas and existing suppliers are very well established.

The strategy of Zimbabwean exporters has been to market sound equipment, suitable for African conditions. Success in exporting has arisen from having a strong, robust and appropriate product. Where companies have failed to gain access to markets or have lost markets, they say customers have been taken in by superficial characteristics, such as the superior finish of much of the equipment imported from elsewhere as compared with the Zimbabwean product, and its lower initial price. The Zimbabwean companies believe they will ultimately regain any markets lost as the superiority of their products and after-sales service becomes evident. The companies are not, however, resting on their laurels, as they realize that price is important and productivity and efficiency have to be improved in order to offer a competitive price. The export incentives provide some flexibility, allowing the export price to be lower than the domestic market price if this is necessary to secure an export deal. The companies find it demoralizing to be competing against firms from countries such as Brazil and India, where the export incentives offered by their governments enable products to be landed at prices which are sometimes below the input costs of the Zimbabwean manufacturer.

In respect of animal-drawn and hand implements, Zimbabwe's well-publicized success in peasant farming helps to promote a positive image of Zimbabwean implements. In addition, in the market for animal-drawn implements there is a lot of conservatism, based presumably on the good performance of a mature product. The customers are said to like what their grandfathers bought, even as far as the colour is concerned, a green plough being considered stronger than a red one. These perceptions seem to apply as much in export markets as in the domestic market. In foreign markets, care has been taken to deliver always on time and to choose agents who will always carry a full range of parts and provide proper after-sales service.

Design capabilities

Bain and Tinto have design departments staffed by highly qualified engineers and agriculturalists. Both companies have a policy of continuous improvement and innovation, not only to keep ahead of one another but with an eye on the fact that with export retention, Zimbabwean farmers are now in a position to import equipment from elsewhere if they so choose.

Bain, for example, has five people in its R&D department but expects ideas also to come forward from other parts of the company and from contacts with the farming community and other agricultural researchers. Within the Bain product range there are items which are produced on licence but many items are the result of their own development. The reversible disc plough, chisel tiller, ridge hog, seed press, tandem dam scoops and crumbler provide examples. Recent development work has concentrated on equipment for reduced tillage systems, which are gaining acceptance as research results have proved promising.

Tinto is also working in this area and is justly proud of a recently developed pneumatic direct seeding drill, which leads the world in zero tillage planters. It is being successfully used in Zambia as well as Zimbabwe. Interest has been shown from as far away as the US and Canada and world-wide patents have been taken out.

Because of the extreme conservatism mentioned in the previous section, Zimplow has scant need for product development, although a plough suitable for use by women has been developed in recent years. Export orders have occasioned some development work, however. For example, for the Botswana market Zimplow developed a range of equipment for flood plain cultivation. With only a 60-cm depth, the conventional ploughs and cultivators had to be modified quite considerably.

Technology and productivity

As with other industries in Zimbabwe, much of the equipment used to produce agricultural machinery is antiquated and inefficient from a technical viewpoint, if not necessarily from an economic one. With the pressures induced by restrictions on the domestic market, including in the case of Zimplow price control on its output and the need to compete on export markets and become more efficient as protection is lifted under the Economic Reform Programme, all the companies have made strenuous efforts to increase efficiency and productivity.

Bain, for example, has benefited in recent years from an International Trade Centre (ITC) project which seconded a master welder to assist in improving performance on the shop floor. Apart from offering training in welding skills and suggesting changes in component design to improve weld strength and overall finish, the person concerned also made suggestions about plant layout, handling equipment and maintenance. The changes implemented have had a marked effect on efficiency. In addition, in the last two years a start has been made on replacing equipment which was second-hand in 1966, when production was started. At the same time, with the change in ownership, directors and workers have acquired a direct share in the business and the effect of this on productivity, although difficult to measure, should also be significantly positive.

Tinto, with the foresight to anticipate the changes that structural adjustment would require, has gone further in changing its production management system. By employing a local consulting organization, the Kawasaki Production System has been introduced. This is essentially a 'just-in-time' production system, which has been particularly successful in improving productivity and efficiency at the Norton factory. This may be because of the 'collegiate' atmosphere at that plant (most of the workers live together close to the works), or because the types of processes at the Harare plant are less amenable to the changes that the system requires.

Significant financial savings have arisen from cutting down on work-in-progress, which has also allowed for a 60 per cent reduction in working space. In addition to improving production management, the company is undertaking various capital investments such as the refurbishment of the foundry at the Harare works, the installation of an arc furnace control system to improve energy efficiency and the acquisition of computer-controlled machining centres.

As mentioned previously, Zimplow increased its productivity markedly during the 1980s in order to increase profitability in the face of price controls on the domestic market. Referring to Bulawayo Steel Products as well as Zimplow, Riddell notes that:

factories were radically reorganized, with production lines altered from a series of separate and uncoordinated operations to a continuous flow system; more rapid throughput meant that stock levels could be reduced; staff training education was initiated to upgrade workers and identify particular tasks in the overall production process; new skilled staff were employed on the shop floor, leading to higher quality products being produced and to improved designs of traditional lines ... the squeezing of profit margins induced the most dramatic increases in manufacturing efficiency that the firms had experienced in 15–20 years.

(Riddell, 1988, pp. 37–8)

By 1992, however, Zimplow reported that productivity had declined relative to 1988 levels, despite the replacement of equipment during those years. This is attributed partly to the general malaise in the country, perhaps affecting people in Bulawayo more than most due to the on-going water crisis, and to problems in obtaining raw materials from ZISCO. To overcome the latter, the company is now holding up to two years of stocks of some items, which is extremely expensive in current financial market conditions.

Human resources and the development of skills

From the viewpoint of the availability of skills, engineering industries are much better off for skilled labour than specialized industries such as textiles or footwear. This is because there is an established national system of apprenticeship and formal education for artisans through the technical colleges and for qualified engineers through the University of Zimbabwe (in future to be complemented by the National University of Science and Technology in Bulawayo). There have been persistent reports that the standards of technical education have been falling in recent years, the effects being more severe in some areas than in others. For example, personnel for machine shops, such as fitters and turners, are far easier to find than those needed for foundries, such as pattern makers.

The incentive structure in the general economic environment (including factors such as high personal taxes, restricted access to imported goods and foreign currency for travel, and high inflation) is leading to a significant brain drain of Zimbabwean skills. Countries such as Botswana and South Africa are providing opportunities for employment, undermining the value for Zimbabwe of its considerable investment in the education and training of engineering staff.

Subcontracting

At present Bain and Zimplow have all their foundry work done outside the company. Bain gave careful consideration in recent years to establishing its own foundry but the problem of obtaining the skilled personnel necessary and the fact that a good deal of outside work would have had to be obtained for the foundry to be viable, argued against the project. Bain is pleased about its negative decision now, because it would otherwise have been saddled with much higher prices than originally envisaged due to devaluation and very high interest charges.

Other than foundry work and Bain's purchase of plough discs from Tinto, none of the companies in the sample is regularly involved in subcontracting. Particularly at present, when demand is depressed and companies are seeking to find sufficient work to keep their production staff occupied, subcontracting would not make sense. Even in boom conditions, subcontracting is not a mode of operation that has been adopted in the past.

This could well change in the future. The unfolding of the structural adjustment process is having a marked effect on the way businesses are run. For example, tight liquidity and expensive credit have led to much more careful management of stocks and of work-in-progress. Subcontracting would be merely a further step in reducing overhead and inventory costs and may thus come to be adopted in the future.

CONCLUSIONS

The aggregate performance of the manufacturing sector since the start of the structural adjustment programme has been poor. In terms of volume of output, for example, the Central Statistics Office reports a rise of 9 per cent between February 1991 and February 1992, but then a fall of 25 per cent between February 1992 and February 1993 (February is used in preference to January because many firms shut down for part of January). Manufactured exports increased each year in Zimbabwe dollar terms but declined when measured in US dollars, by nearly 20 per cent between 1990 and 1991 and a further 5–6 per cent between 1991 and 1992. This poor export performance is particularly worrying since the start of the SAP marked an intensification of export incentives for manufacturers, rather than a change in direction which might have been expected to be disruptive.

There are no data on investment but indications are that investment in manufacturing has been very low. There was a large backlog of project submissions to the ZIC in 1991 but the sharp increase in interest rates and later exchange rates caused many investors to reassess their projects, and a large proportion was scaled down or shelved.

In contrast to the macro figures, a more positive picture has emerged from interviews at the micro level. While it is still too early to make a definitive judgement, in general it would appear from the survey that the major intentions of trade liberalization and ESAP do seem to have been realized, at least in the larger companies.

Improvements in productivity and competitiveness have come about as a result of investment in equipment and through better production management and training, sharpening of technical skills and a greater orientation to exports. Many companies in the sample, for example Bata in leather and footwear, Cotton Printers in textiles and Fashion Enterprises in clothing, invested in new machinery and equipment in the period leading up to the commencement of ESAP in 1990. They also undertook export market development, which in turn stimulated the other positive changes which have taken place.

The introduction of the ERS, enabling exporters to earn much-needed foreign exchange, has been of central importance in reorienting industry towards exports. However, the liberalization of imports which the free use and tradability of the ERS have made possible has had some negative effects on the drive to increase manufactured exports. Firstly, access to imported raw materials has led companies in sectors such as clothing and footwear to use imported fabrics and leather increasingly as raw materials, rather than the Zimbabwean-based products, which would maximize the value-added content of exports for the country. While some import content in raw materials would make sense, this tendency has arisen in part because the existing export incentive structure rewards only final exporters, so textile and leather producers would rather export their products directly than strive to provide the range and quality of inputs required by clothing and footwear exporters.

The second factor is that competitive imports have penetrated domestic markets much earlier than had been envisaged in the original design of the trade liberalization process. Proponents of early across-the-board import liberalization argue that it gives rise to the sort of competitive pressures which lead to enhanced productivity, the ability of domestic producers to compete in terms of quality and production costs in export markets, and hence to higher national income. Experience from other countries fails to bear this out, however. In Zimbabwe's case the immediate effect of early liberalization has been to cut the turnover of many firms, increasing the amount that has to be recovered per unit to cover overheads and thus putting upward pressure on the pricing of exports.

The use of ERS funds to import competing products has increased sharply in the period since the survey was carried out, in part because the retention proportion was raised to 50 per cent from April 1993. In view of the problems outlined above, there have been calls for the government to overhaul the export incentive structure so as to cater for indirect exports and encourage greater utilization of Zimbabwean raw materials (Robinson, 1993). While no action has yet been taken by government on this, the other issue, the liberalization of competitive imports, is now a *fait accompli*.

Companies with foresight had already begun to act on the realization that once the domestic market was no longer protected, survival would depend on their competitiveness both in the domestic and in the export markets. The question is whether the *majority* of companies will come to the same realization quickly enough to survive the onslaught of competitive imports. As foreign currency becomes more readily available, as indicated by the falling premium on ERS funds (down to 16 per cent by the end of July 1993), the ERS may lose its potency as an incentive to export. New policy measures may then have to be introduced to sustain export growth.

Providing companies are well managed, size was found to have numerous advantages when competing in export markets. Larger companies such as David Whitehead, Cotton Printers, Bata and Fashion Enterprises are more able to mobilize export finance than the less established firms. The larger firms can also meet the costs of foreign market development, including having to wait for payments for goods exported. This puts the smaller companies at a disadvantage.

The textile, leather and footwear and agricultural machinery sub-sectors are highly oligopolistic. The larger companies are vertically integrated, which places them in a better position to organize raw materials than that of the smaller concerns. For example, as they are in control of most of their inputs, the vertically integrated companies can put pressure on their sister companies to deliver the quality and colour of fabrics and leather needed by the export market.

In 1992 this has meant that only the larger companies have managed to avoid significant lay-offs or short-time operations, because of their rapidly increased exports, which have compensated for the sudden decline in the domestic market. The smaller companies found it less easy to respond to downturns in the domestic market by expanding exports, despite the growing array of export incentives. To overcome the problems of obtaining raw materials for the smaller exporters, the government would do well to allow the raw materials needed for exports, such as leather and fabrics, to come onto OGIL quickly. Even before OGIL applies to all steel products, the ZISCO scheme to give rebates on steel used to produce high-value-added goods for export should be made more generous.

Zimbabwean companies were found to have a good deal of expertise available locally, although specialized skills remain a problem. At the same time, companies are in reasonable control of the technologies they need for export development. For the established companies, this has been added onto existing technologies over time. In these circumstances there may be no need either for state intervention in R&D (as has been argued by Mhone, 1992) or for direct foreign investment by multinationals (as argued by Hawkins, 1992) for established Zimbabwean firms to compete in export markets.

These markets are either regional, similar in many ways to the domestic market, or moving niche markets in the industrialized countries. Zimbabwe can muster the skills and technology to export into these markets. State money in R&D would probably best be used to support private companies' efforts in these areas and at the same time to assist new entrants in accessing and unpackaging the technologies needed to compete in domestic and export markets.

In the case of Zimbabwe, the policy environment remains important for sustained export development. Government should ensure that obstacles are removed, instead of exhorting companies to export and at the same time tripping them up at each stage. Policy should also be supportive to the small and medium-scale manufacturing enterprises, which cannot at present handle the raw material problems, the financial squeeze, especially as it affects the mobilization of export finance, and the spider's web of bureaucratic procedures.

In the case of sub-sectors supporting major productive sectors, such as agricultural machinery, government needs to ensure that policies made in other contexts, such as the ERS, do not undermine such support services. Resources for service industries need to be pooled. Government should also use its procurement policies to ensure that throughput is maximized, reducing overhead cost contributions per unit, thereby assisting companies to compete on export markets.

NOTES

1 The interviews on which this study is based were carried out during the last quarter of 1992. The paper has been revised in July 1993, incorporating comments from the workshop held in Arusha in May. With significant changes being made by government to the policy environment, the general lessons and conclusions noted in the final section have been updated and expanded from those presented in the original draft.
2 Mhone (1992) analyses the Zimbabwe case.
3 David Whitehead UK set up textile mills in Zimbabwe (then Southern Rhodesia), South Africa, Kenya, Uganda, Nigeria and Mauritius. All these mills have continued to operate, albeit under different ownership structures, with the exception of the Mauritius company, which closed down in the 1960s mainly due to the absence of local raw materials (cotton) in that country.
4 The rest of the shares are held by the Industrial Development Corporation (10 per cent) and the public through the Zimbabwean Stock Exchange.
5 For similar conclusions, see Mead and Kunjeku (1992).
6 The textile mills' current raw material problem may actually get worse, given the current pre-planting producer price that the government has promised to the growers. Members of the Central African Textile Manufacturers' Association (CATMA), the trade association representing textile manufacturers, are arguing that if cotton is purchased at the projected price of Z$2.95 per kilo from the grower, the CMB will be compelled to sell it to the textile mills at between Z$9.00 and Z$9.50 per kilo in order to make profit, but this would be above the world parity price.
7 One textile firm said that in the year ending September, 1992 'indirect exports' were estimated at Z$65 million, which was over 40 per cent more than the company's direct exports and a quite significant contribution for one company.
8 The primary objectives of Zimtrade are to gain an effective central role in the development of exports from Zimbabwe through enhancing the implementation of ESAP, to promote self-reliance in export management through the development of human resources, to support new entrepreneurs and establish structures to support the development of appropriate industrial design in Zimbabwe and to assist in achieving export targets.
9 The competitiveness of Zimbabwe's clothing products in the South African market has been affected by the latter's so called anti-dumping

tariffs, brought in on 1 May 1992, to protect that country's garment industry against countries which South Africa claims are dumping clothing products. This has seriously affected Zimbabwe, though it was not meant to do so. The current confusion and temporary exemptions for Zimbabwe's garments will only be finally resolved with the conclusion of the current renegotiation of the Zimbabwe–South Africa trade agreement.

10　A recent survey reported that the CMT system was responsible for the subsistence of about 50 per cent of the MSEs surveyed, at least during the first few years of their operations. See Imani Development, (1992). See Mead and Kunjeku, (1992), for a discussion of the four aspects of business linkages.

11　Since the fieldwork was carried out, tradable ERS funds have become available and are widely used, alleviating these problems.

BIBLIOGRAPHY

Hawkins, Anthony, Lessons from Zimbabwe. Paper prepared for Regional Economic Integration Conference, Harare, December 1992.

Imani Development, Sub-Sector Study: Textiles and Clothing. Mimeo prepared as background for Zimconsult study for UNIDO of Small-Scale Enterprises, Harare, March 1992.

Mead, D.C. and Kunjeku, P., Business Linkages and Enterprise Development in Zimbabwe. Mimeo, Harare, 1992.

Mhone, Guy, A Macro-economic Strategy for Industrialisation and Indigenization of Technology. Paper prepared for the Third Symposium on Science and Technology, Research Council of Zimbabwe, Harare, October 1992.

Riddell, Roger, *Industrialisation in Sub-Saharan Africa, Country Case Study – Zimbabwe*, ODI Working Paper, No. 25, London, Overseas Development Institute, 1988.

Robinson, Peter B., Adjustment and Long-Term Industrial Development. Mimeo prepared for International Labour Office, May 1993.

World Bank, *Zimbabwe: The Capital Goods Sector, Investment and Industrial Issues*, Washington, D.C., 1989.

Zimbabwe Clothing Council, *Survey of Problems Currently Facing the Zimbabwean Clothing Industry*, Bulawayo, 5 June 1992.

Zimplow, *50 Years of Service to the Agricultural Sector*, Annual Report, 1989.

Zimplow, Annual Report, 1985.

8 Tanzania

M.S.D. Bagachwa and A.V.Y. Mbelle

INTRODUCTION

Firms in developing countries are increasingly striving to export their products. However poor quality, high prices brought about by high production costs, and unreliable deliveries have eroded competitiveness. These firms seek to improve their competitiveness in a number of ways, which include searching for new technologies and internal reorganization. The outcome has, despite these efforts, not been very encouraging.

This study examines the technological responses of firms in Tanzania in the face of declining competitiveness. The analysis uses information from a survey of nine firms: four from the metals and engineering sector and five from the textile industry. It was found that technological adaptations and improved capabilities (both technological and human) are necessary but not sufficient conditions for improved export competitiveness. Factors such as a 'hostile' macroeconomic environment, a weak industrial base and the lack of resources, especially foreign resources, impose serious limits.

Trends and performance of export manufacturing 1966–90

Three phases of export history

The trend and general performance of Tanzanian manufactured exports are summarized in Table 8.1 (p. 205). Three main development phases can be identified over the period 1966–90. The first phase, 1966–80 was a period of gradual but continuous growth in manufacturing exports. This growth was consistent with the growth in overall manufacturing output, which grew from 4 per cent of GDP at independence (1961) to a peak of 12 per cent in 1977. The major manufactured exports at the time included textiles, cigarettes, canned food, cement, non-ferrous metals and batteries. The main markets for these products were in East Africa, and these markets were lost when the East African Community broke up in 1977.

The second phase, 1981–85, was a period of significant decline in manufactured exports. Apart from the loss of traditional markets, there were pressures on foreign exchange, necessitated by a decline in the volume of exports, drastic cuts in net foreign resource inflows and a steep decline in the net barter terms of trade. The resulting low import capacity combined with an overall decline in output to reduce significantly the supply of raw materials and intermediate inputs to industry. This led to extremely low levels of capacity utilization, which averaged 10–20 per cent. As a result of this 'deindustrialization' process, manufacturing activity fell to 7 per cent of GDP in 1985. Manufacturing's share of national exports also shows a decline from an annual average of 15.6 per cent during 1975–80 to 13.1 per cent during 1981–85. The degree of export orientation (measured as the percentage of manufacturing output which was exported), which had begun to decline steeply during the late 1970s, remained very low at 4.6 per cent. The overall growth rate measured in 1966 purchasing power parity dollars (PPP$) was –16.6 per cent during the 1981–85 period.[1]

During the third phase, 1986–90 manufactured exports recovered and benefited from the Economic Recovery Programme (ERP) and the healthy state of the economy whose real annual GDP growth averaged about 4 per cent for the period. Even higher annual growth, averaging about 7 per cent, took place in the manufacturing sector. This was a reversal of the trend between 1981 and 1985, when manufacturing's value added declined by 4.2 per cent per annum. In real terms the growth of manufactured exports averaged 14.1 per cent per annum for the period 1986–90 and the portion of output which was exported increased to a historical high of nearly 18 per cent.

The resurgence in export growth during the recent period can be attributed to several factors. They include a package of export incentives (e.g. adjustment in the exchange rate, a foreign exchange retention scheme, the seed capital revolving scheme, the presidential export award, export drawback scheme and export credit guarantee scheme); the 'own funds' scheme which has resulted in repatriation of capital; a fall in the real price of petroleum and related products; temporary improvement in the terms of trade due to the coffee boom in 1986; and increased donor aid as a result of adopting economic reforms (Bagachwa *et. al.*, 1990; World Bank, 1991).

While Table 8.1 shows a significant increase in export orientation, especially after the mid-1980s, Table 8.2 (p. 206) reveals the further broadening of the export base during the same period. The increasing diversification of exports is clearly reflected in the doubling of the shares of the non-traditional exports[2] in total exports between 1986 and 1990. If gold is included as a non-traditional export, this share reaches about 50 per cent in 1992 (Ndulu and Semboja, 1992).

The changing policy context: towards export orientation

Until the mid-1980s, development policies and the system of production and export incentives in Tanzania (e.g. an over-valued currency, import controls, administrative allocation of foreign exchange and high protective tariffs) tended to discriminate against exports and to benefit import substituting crops and products. Tanzania has therefore relied on growth in domestic demand and import substitution as the basis for industrial development. As late as 1986 an estimated 60 per cent of Tanzania's total supply of manufactured products were produced and consumed locally, 5 per cent were exported and 35 per cent imported. This contrasts with figures at independence (1961), when 30 per cent was domestic production, 8 per cent was exported and 62 per cent was imports (Wangwe and Bagachwa, 1990).

However, the policy of import substitution was reversed with the adoption of the ERP in 1986. Under the ERP the policy emphasis on the supply side of the economy has shifted from an import substitution strategy (ISS) to an export orientation strategy (EOS) and in particular towards export diversification. The new policy advocates the shifting of resources from non-tradables to tradables by changing the structure of incentives, i.e. through devaluation and exchange rate unification, changes in domestic prices and the relaxation of wage control policies. Measures which allow private importers to use their own funds to import goods and exporters to retain a portion of foreign exchange for importing goods have also contributed to the reversal.

The emphasis on export orientation is known to have a number of advantages, some of which have been demonstrated empirically. Some analysts contend that policies which do not discriminate against exports allow the realization of economies of scale, permit the exploitation of comparative advantage, foster greater capacity utilization, facilitate employment creation via market expansion and are a major source of enhanced industrial skills, productivity increases and technological improvement (Krueger, 1978; Rati, 1985; Bhaghwati, 1987).

In other quarters however, preoccupation with the EOS has been criticized for (1) failing to recognize the untenability of the static equilibrium and the pervasive market failures arising from dynamic and unpredictable learning, externalities or complementarities, (2) lacking strong empirical evidence to justify the link between export performance and productivity increases and (3) failing to recognize other key factors that influence efficiency and productivity, especially the role of capabilities in terms of skills and technological endowments (Helleiner, 1986; Weiss, 1988; Lall, 1992).

The strict separability between ISS and EOS has also been strongly questioned. As the experience of South Korea has shown, EOS can be preceded by, and can even build upon, the achievements of ISS (Jacobsson and Alam, 1992). Moreover, the Chilean experience has demonstrated the insufficiency of market forces alone in effecting shifts from ISS to EOS (Weiss, 1988; Cooper, 1992). Furthermore, some countries pursuing ISS have managed to develop more dynamic industrial sectors than others, and in fact some of the highly export-orientated NICs have built up a major part of their competitive strength by protecting selected industries (Lall, 1992). This study is based on the premise that ISS and EOS are not necessarily competing alternatives but can actually converge and reinforce each other.

The issue of the diversification of Tanzania's export base is quite crucial. In 1991 the six traditional crops accounted for 55 per cent of the total merchandise export earnings. Prices for these primary products have generally been very unstable. The terms-of-trade index for Tanzania deteriorated from 100 in 1980 to 73 in 1989. The purchasing power of exports index also declined from 100 in 1980 to 68 in 1989 (UNCTAD, 1990). Worse still, the raw material content in modern products is declining and there are gluts in some commodities (such as coffee) which are produced in Tanzania. At the same time, sisal fibre continues to face stiff competition from polyethylene, while coffee may soon face competition from manufactured biocoffee. These trends spell disaster for Tanzania, especially when its three largest export crops (coffee, tea and sisal) are reported to have low income and price elasticities (Islam and Subramanian, 1989). Moreover, to the extent that the promotion of most traditional exports is associated with relatively limited technological dynamism, the feasibility of some of the SAP policies which are designed mainly to facilitate the expansion of traditional primary commodities is highly questionable. In the circumstances, if the restructuring process is to bring about sustainable development it should emphasize the diversification of traditional primary exports into the technologically more dynamic non-traditional crops and manufactured exports.

A framework for analysing export competitiveness

A firm as a unit of analysis

A typical African industrial firm is described as one that lacks international competitiveness, dynamism and strong linkages (Lall, 1992). These weaknesses cannot simply be blamed on the lack of imported inputs and domestic recession, nor on the lack of incentives due to distorting trade and industrial policies as the current ERP supposes. These are only a part of the problem. A major structural weakness for African industrial firms has been their failure to build up an indigenous technological capacity which is capable of acquiring technological capabilities (Lall, 1992; Wangwe, 1992). Technological capabilities (TCs) are defined in this context as a set of skills and information needed to operate a given technology and its associated organizational system efficiently (Lall *et al.*, 1991, p. 2).

The main objective of this study is to examine the process of building and maintaining competitiveness in export markets. Recent research on the acquisition of technological capabilities in developing countries (Katz, 1987, in Latin America; Lall, 1987, in India; Pack and Westphal, 1986, in Korea; Lall, 1992 and Wangwe, 1992, in Africa) and the earlier work on the evolutionary theories of growth by Nelson and Winter (1982) have underscored the point that any meaningful analysis of the determinants of industrial performance should initially focus at the firm level. The extrapolation of firm-level factors should then be used to develop broader explanations of industrial performance at the sectoral or national levels. The unit of analysis in this study is the exporting firm. The focus will be on how different firms strive to build up technological capabilities.

The nature of capabilities

Lall et al., (1991) have conveniently summarized and classified the various capabilities and their functions in the form of an illustrative matrix akin to Table 8.3 (p. 212). The columns explain the major technological capabilities by function. The rows indicate the degree of complexity or difficulty. The major categories of capabilities are investment, production and linkages. The acquisition of technological capabilities therefore involves a number of things such as making some adaptations to suit local conditions, i.e. gaining mastery, making minor improvements and creating new technologies or innovating through R&D. In the case of small firms some of these functions may be performed by the entrepreneur. But as the firm expands it may develop dynamism by deepening its capabilities, and most of the functions become formalized as separate units are set up to deal with each.

The firms in the sample

Nine firms were selected: four from a heterogenous set of industries and five from the textile industry. Detailed firm histories are presented in the next section. One of the firms, Northern Electrical Manufacturers Ltd (NEM), is an indigenous privately owned firm, located in Arusha town in northern Tanzania. It has been selected because it started in 1979 as a small firm with state support, producing electrical products for the domestic market with just 12 employees. It gradually acquired modest technological capabilities and grew into a moderately successful exporting firm with 120 employees by 1991. Themi Farm Implements Ltd (Themi), another firm in our sample, presents a contrast to NEM. It also started, in 1981, as a small firm with state support, employing 10 persons, and is located in the same town of Arusha. It has, however, failed to acquire substantial technological capabilities and has remained a small firm, with 15 employees in 1991. Its export performance has been unimpressive.

A third firm in our sample is Afrocooling Systems Ltd, based in Dar es Salaam. The firm started as a small unit with 45 employees and with solid investment capabilities. It gradually deepened its technological capabilities and grew to become a medium-sized exporting firm with modest success. Matsushita Electric (EA) Company, a subsidiary of Matsushita Electric Industries of Japan, is a foreign-owned and relatively old firm established in 1967. The firm is fairly large and currently employs 500 workers. It assembles Japanese components to make dry cell batteries, radios, torches and fans. It has depended mainly on training to develop very limited local capabilities. The firm exports batteries to Rwanda, Burundi, Zaire and Malawi. It is exploring the possibility of manufacturing radios.

Table 8.1 Summary performance indicators for manufactured exports 1966–90

	Share of manufactured in total exports	Growth rate of total manufactured exports in PPP$*	Growth rate of manufactured exports except petroleum in PPP$	Share of exports in total manufactured output
1966–70	13.5	10.1	–10.1	16.8
1971–75	14.5	14.6	20.7	12.4
1975–80	15.6	15.5	23.3	0.8
1981–85	13.1	–16.6	–20.1	4.6
1986–90	21.2	56.6	62.4	17.9
1991–92	17.3	–8.6**	–	13.0

Sources: Bank of Tanzania, *Economic and Operations Report*, various issues; University of Dar es Salaam (1991); URT: *Economic Surveys*; various issues; URT, *Foreign Trade Statistics*, various issues; URT, *Annual Trade Reports*; cited in Ndulu and Semboja, 1992.

Notes: * Exports in PPP$ at 1966 prices computed as Exports (in Tshs)/PPPNOER, where PPPNOER is the nominal official exchange rate that would maintain purchasing power parity with the major trading partners with 1966 as a base. PPPNOER = NOER/RER*100.
**Measured in current US$.

The firms from the textile industry were chosen to reflect two main strata: exporters and non-exporters. One firm, Tanganyika Textile Industries Ltd, a private company, started as an exporter but failed in that field. It is currently concentrating on the domestic market only. Another private firm, JV Textiles, started as an export firm and has maintained export business throughout. Three publicly owned firms, Friendship, Morogoro Canvas Mill and Morogoro Polyester Textiles, were established to supply the domestic market. Due to an interplay of factors these firms have entered the export business and have successfully maintained a hold.

THE DYNAMICS OF FIRMS' CAPABILITIES

This section focuses on the dynamics that shape capabilities at the firm level. These dynamics relate to three interrelated aspects: (1) the processes through which firms have evolved over time and the historical conditions which have shaped their particular development paths (i.e. firm histories), (2) firms' strategies and capabilities and (3) the implications of global technological developments for firms' flexible and adaptive capabilities.

Table 8.2 Export diversification in Tanzania, 1966–92

	Share of non-traditional exports in total exports		Share of manufactured exports in total exports	
	(a)	(b)	(c)	(d)
1966–70	0.2486	0.3594	0.0754	0.1346
1971–75	0.2350	0.3221	0.0871	0.1452
1976–80	0.2562	0.3258	0.1122	0.1567
1981	0.2961	0.3885	0.0923	0.1103
1982	0.3092	0.3938	0.0846	0.1124
1983	0.2402	0.3550	0.1148	0.1528
1984	0.2240	0.3098	0.9852	0.1437
1985	0.2404	0.3158	0.1144	0.1622
1986	0.2101	0.2475	0.1125	0.1258
1987	0.3572	0.4205	0.1814	0.2017
1988	0.3545	0.3972	0.1938	0.2266
1989	0.4081	0.4395	0.2407	0.2806
1990	0.4209	0.4883	0.2254	0.2673
1991	0.3260	0.4470	0.1920	0.2120
1992	0.3000	0.4260	0.1540	0.1800

Sources: Bank of Tanzania, *Economic and Operation Report*, various issues; University of Dar es Salaam, (Economic Research Bureau), 1992; URT, *Economic Surveys*, various issues; URT, *Foreign Trade Statistics*, various issues; URT, *Annual Trade Reports*. Figures up to 1990 were cited from Ndulu and Semboja, (1992); those for 1991–92 were obtained from the Bank of Tanzania (see Table 8.6).

Notes: (a) Non-traditional exports excluding minerals. (b) Non-traditional exports including minerals but excluding gold. (c) Petroleum not included in manufactured exports. (d) Petroleum included in manufactured exports.

FIRM HISTORIES

Northern Electrical Manufacturers Ltd (NEM)

NEM is a private company, owned by six indigenous entrepreneurs. The firm started its operations in Arusha in 1979 under the sister industry programme (SIP)[3] managed by the Small Industry Development Organization (SIDO). Under the SIP, NEM (the junior sister) is linked to the Eldon Company of Sweden (the senior sister). Initially, like many other firms working under the SIP, NEM's office and factory were located in SIDO's Arusha Industrial Estate (AIE).[4] At present NEM operates from two sites: the old factory in the AIE produces for the domestic market while the new site in the Themi Industrial Area (TIA) produces for the export market.

Initial capital funds for equipment and machinery were provided as a low-interest loan by SIDO through funds provided in turn by the Swedish International Development Authority (SIDA). SIDO also provided a highly subsidized industrial building to house NEM's operations and paid for related local infrastructural services. The senior sister, Eldon Company, provided the initial raw materials and technology support (i.e. design and specification of equipment needs, installation and commissioning) as well as initial and continued training.

NEM has a formal organization and dynamic leadership. At present the board of directors is composed of six directors, four of whom are shareholders who work within the company, while the other two are outsiders. The general manager is the chief executive with overall charge of operations in the company. He is assisted by three departmental directors for marketing and finance, production, and technical matters. The stability of the ownership structure has allowed the company to enjoy an atmosphere of continuity and stability and has given it time enough to build up experience.

NEM began by producing only fuse boards and later introduced other products. Today NEM produces over 25 products. Some of these are sold in the domestic market and others are destined for export markets. At present, NEM's major products include fuse boards, switch boxes, cable trunkings, wall lights, brackets, fluorescent fittings and ceiling lamps. The company also imports and carries out installations of industrial power distribution panels. The firm's basic production operations involve sheet metal fabrication (which includes shearing, punching and welding), spray painting and the assembly of parts.

NEM's operations have increased substantially since its inception (see Table 8.4, p. 213). Sales have expanded rapidly, especially during the 1980–86 period when NEM was the sole domestic producer of electrical goods and domestic demand was well in excess of NEM's capacity to supply. In practice, until the mid-1980s NEM received direct protection, in that importation of similar products was prohibited. It also enjoyed indirect protection from having access to foreign exchange through Swedish import support while potential local competitors' access to raw materials was limited by lack of foreign exchange. However, liberalization measures under the ERP have increased competition. Products from the Far East, in particular, are making it difficult for NEM to dispose of all its production. Employment has grown from 12 in 1979 to 120 in 1991.

NEM has experienced consistent growth in exports. The dollar value of its exports increased 2.7 times between 1986 and 1991, rising from 14.3 per cent of total sales in 1986 to 58.2 per cent in 1991. Despite the strategy of reducing the import content per unit of product, import content still averages 86 per cent of the total raw material costs. There is little diversification in terms of input sourcing: as late as 1991 over 90 per cent of the total raw materials were being provided by the Swedish company Eldon. There are now initiatives to find alternative sources of raw materials. About 97 per cent of NEM's total exports are sold to one market – IKEA, a chain of Swedish furnishing stores with outlets throughout Europe. There are quality problems and the level of rejects is considered to be high (about 35 per cent).

Themi Farm Implements Company (Themi)

Themi is located in Arusha Town and was established in 1981. The project was capitalized by the Arusha Regional Government through a loan with USAID funds made available through the Arusha Planning and Village Development Project (AP/VDP). It was started mainly to supply the local market with ox-drawn tool bars and ox-carts and was designed to use simple fabrication technology. The factory equipment is simple and suited for most general engineering work.

The firm is privately owned. The management of the project was selected in competitive interviews as a partnership from among 62 other group applications. The group contracted to supervise the establishment of the industry and its production plan, and was responsible for machinery installation, tooling and other start-up processes. The seven partners contributed 15 per cent cash equity and after one year of grace began to repay the loan equity of the project.

The major activities of Themi include:

- the manufacture and sale of animal-drawn farm implements;
- fabrication and sale of hand-operated oil presses, decorticators and settling tanks;
- conducting short term training courses designed to provide practical training and know-how to village communities in the use and maintenance of agricultural implements;
- offering consultancy services and designing;
- casting and machining all kinds of shafting brackets, hockers, pulleys, etc.; and
- manufacturing all kinds of spares for ploughs and ox-carts.

Themi's most important products include ox-drawn tool bars, ox-carts, hand planters, maize and nut shellers, plough parts and spares, wheelbarrows, oil presses, hand pumps, storage tanks and brick-making machines.

The overall management of the company is directed by the board of directors under the chairmanship of the regional development director (RDD) for Arusha region. The day-to-day management of the company is in the hands of the managing director, who is assisted by six directors, heading the six departments of research and planning, finance and administration, production, maintenance and foundry, fabrication and assembling, and ox-cart production.

In the first four years of operation Themi performed very well. Output exceeded targets in both major categories of production and several minor ones. Sales increased six times between 1981 and 1985 while employment more than trebled (Table 8.4). During this time all output was sold locally. Between 1985 and 1991, however, the numbers employed have fallen to half while domestic sales have declined steeply from TSh30.8 million in 1985 to only TSh20 million in 1991. In real terms the decline was even more pronounced, falling from TSh4.3 million to 0.2 million. This negative performance was in spite of the firm's successful attempt to reduce the import content from 90 per cent in 1981 to 10 per cent in 1991.

Themi's officials attribute the decline in output to the liberalization measures introduced under the ERP in 1986. The major raw material used by Themi is mild steel. This is distributed by a local firm (the National Steel Corporation) which imports most of it. Devaluation raised the domestic price of steel from TSh7 000 in 1985 to TSh200 000 in 1990. The increase in steel prices has been compounded by increases in transport costs (resulting from increases in the domestic price of oil). As a result, Themi's price for a plough shot up from TSh1 800 in 1985 to TSh8 000 in 1991. Since farmers' incomes have not risen by as much, the demand for these products has fallen significantly. Sales have also dropped because under the 'Own Funds' imports scheme, large-scale importers have been importing and distributing ploughs at lower prices. The strategies adopted by Themi in response to these problems are discussed in detail in the section below on firm strategies (p. 217). These include product diversification, exploring export markets, improved product delivery systems and the rationalization of management and production.

Afrocooling Systems Ltd (Afrocooling)

Afrocooling is a local private firm specializing in the manufacture of car radiators. It was established in 1979. The firm has dynamic and efficient management under the overall direction of a board of directors. The managing director is the executive head in charge of day-to-day company business. There are three main departments: production, finance, and administration and marketing.

The overall performance of Afrocooling has been rather mixed. Sales have been rising consistently: turnover increased by 4.9 times in nominal terms and 2.1 times in real terms between 1979 and 1989. The corresponding figures for the period 1985–91 were 5 and 1.9 times (Table 8.4). Exports, however, have declined from US$256 000 in 1985 to US$137 000 in 1991. As a proportion of sales, exports peaked at 23.6 per cent in 1986, declined to 14.6 per cent in 1990 and rose to 16.7 per cent in 1991. Employment has increased consistently from 45 in 1979 to 130 in 1991, commensurate with the expansion in sales.

Afrocooling's success in the domestic market reflects high-quality, efficient and innovative management which has always emphasized strict quality control and competitive pricing. It also reflects the firm's success in reducing costs (e.g. by substituting domestic for imported inputs, increasing capacity utilization, etc.). However, the decline in exports highlights the need to have an effective institutional and infrastructural network (e.g. functioning export service institutions, efficient transportation and communications, etc.). It also under-scores the limitations of small-scale, labour-intensive operations in producing high-quality products for the international market.

Matsushita Electric Company (EA) Ltd (Matsushita)

Matsushita was established in 1967 as a subsidiary of the Matsushita Electric Company of Japan. Between 1958 and 1964 Japan's share in the Tanzanian market for wireless sets had risen sharply from 1.4 per cent to 68 per cent, due to the relatively low prices of its products and the aggressive marketing strategies of Matsushita Electric Co. However, in 1964 Phillips of the Netherlands formed Phillips Electronics Ltd, and with 50 per cent tariff protection was able to take much of Matsushita's market. Matsushita Japan, having lost its radio market, decided to counter the threat indirectly by establishing a battery factory in Dar es Salaam in 1967 and a radio assembly unit a few years later.

Today Matsushita is a relatively large firm employing about 500 persons. It produces a wide range of products including dry cell batteries, radios, radio cassettes, torches and fans. Most of the work involves assembling Japanese components produced in CKD (completely knocked down) form. Almost all the equipment and machinery (e.g. rolling machines, furnaces, injection moulds and battery sealers) are supplied by the parent company. Parts for assembly are obtained from the company's headquarters or other subsidiaries such as the Asia Matsushita Electric Company. The bulk of the packaging materials (e.g. boards, paper, boxes, metal jackets, caps, etc.) is supplied locally, by Kibo Paper Industries and Tanzania Eyelets.

The company has an elaborate management organization headed by the managing director, who has always been a Japanese. The three directorates of planning and production, finance and administration, and marketing are also headed by Japanese. There are seven departments and 15 sections.

Matsushita's sales volume has been increasing consistently in both nominal and real terms since 1980. Between 1980 and 1991 sales increased by about 24 times in nominal terms and by almost four times in real terms. Export performance, which peaked in 1985 at US$3.4 million, has since been declining, reaching as little as US$0.3 million in 1990. The increase in domestic sales, even during the recent liberalization period, is mainly attributed to offering economical but high-quality products, aggressive marketing and a competitive price strategy. The decline in exports partly reflects a diversion of exports to the domestic market, where demand is greater. The decline is also to a limited extent due to the loss of market share in the major importing countries of Burundi and Rwanda, which in turn have opened up their economies to cheaper imports from Southeast Asia.

The firm has already developed two new models of radio sets for export and has recently penetrated the Malawian market. The company has plans to move from radio assembly to manufacturing. Matsushita has already embarked on research into the product demand in Kenya, Zaire and Zimbabwe.

The Friendship Textile Mill (Friendship)

The civil works for this public firm were undertaken by the Chinese and were completed in 1966 at a cost of TSh50 million. The firm was commissioned in 1968 as a public company, with an installed

Table 8.3 Illustrative matrix of technological capabilities

Degree of capability	INVESTMENT		FUNCTIONAL PRODUCTION			Linkages within economy
	Pre-investment	*Project execution*	*Process engineering*	*Product engineering*	*Industrial engineering*	
Basic: Simple routine (experience based)	Pre-feasibility and feasibility studies; site selection, scheduling of investment	Civil engineering, associated services, equipment installation, commissioning	Debugging, balancing, quality control, preventive maintenance, assimilation of process technology	Assimilation of product design, minor adaptation to market needs	Workflow scheduling, time–motion studies, inventory control	Local procurement of goods and services, information exchange with supplier
Intermediate: Adaptive, Duplicative (search based)	Search for technology source, negotiation of contracts, bargaining for suitable terms, info systems	Equipment procurement, detailed engineering, training and recruitment of skilled personnel	Equipment stretching, process adaptation and cost saving, licensing new technology	Product/quality improvement, licensing and assimilating new imported product technology	Monitoring productivity, improved coordination	Technology transfer to local suppliers, coordinated design; S&T links
Advanced: Innovative, risky (research based)		Basic process design, equipment design and supply	In-house process innovation, basic research	In-house product innovation, basic research		Turn-key capability cooperative R&D, licensing own technology to others

Source: Adapted from Lall *et al.*, (1991), Table 1 p. 21.

Table 8.4 Size and performance indicators of non-textile sample firms over time

	First year of operations	1980	1985	1986	1989	1990	1991
NEM:	(1979)						
Employment	12	12	30	78	114	120	120
Sales (TSh x 1 000)	1 500	3 911	30 000	56 000	152 800	160 000	180 500
Real sales (1976 prices)	1 095	2 573	9 345	13 025	24 255	20 515	21 235
Exports (US$ x 1 000)	–	–	–	155	164	311.0	420
Exports as % of sales	–	–	–	14.3	20.6	38.2	58.2
Import content (%)	100.0	88.0	86.0	n.a.	86.0	86.0	86.0
Themi:	(1981)						
Employment	10	–	38	30	28	25	15
Sales (TSh x 1 000)	5 000	–	30 770	6 280	15 000	30 850	20 000
Real sales (1976 prices)	2 645	–	9 585	1 460	2 380	3 953	2 350
Exports (US$ x 1 000)	–	–	–	–	–	1.2	0.9
Exports as % of sales	–	–	–	–	–	29.5	11.2
Import content (%)	90.0	–	80	–	–	20.0	10.0
Afrocooling:	(1979)						
Employment	45	85	120	125	129	128	130
Sales (TSh x 1 000)	8 500	16 900	41 600	52 500	197 000	189 900	206 200
Real sales (1976 prices)	6 205	11 118	12 960	12 209	31 285	24 345	24 260
Exports (US$ x 1 000)	–	–	256	240	216	142	137
Exports as % of sales	–	–	10.2	23.6	21.1	14.6	16.7
Import content (%)	95.0	85.0	75.0	75.0	70.0	60.0	50.0
Matsushita:	(1967)						
Employment	–	866	625	618	540	424	458
Sales (TSh x 1 000)	5 130	210 317	265 743	360 500	772 232	1 420 376	2 000 500
Real sales (1976 prices)	–	138 365	82 785	83 837	122 576	182 099	235 353
Exports (US$ x 1 000)	–	2 798	3 469	1 045	50	31	107
Exports as % of sales	–	10.6	21.5	15.0	1.2	0.4	1.3
Import content (%)	100.0	25.0	20.2	20.0	20.0	20.0	20.0

Source: Interview data

capacity of 35 million square metres of cloth per annum. Rates of capacity utilization have declined from up to 92 per cent in 1980 to about 60 per cent currently. Though this firm was originally intended to produce canvas products for the local market, the firm managed to change its product mix and penetrate the export market in 1979. Today the mill exports about 40 per cent of its total production, mainly yarn and grey cloth, with a profit margin of 10 per cent. The exports achieved momentum after the firm installed a new machine (from Japan) for export products only.

Friendship's textile mill is the most labour-intensive in the industry, with 4 000 employees. Its organizational structure is by business functions (production, finance, engineering, personnel sales, purchasing). The basic input, cotton, accounts for about 23 per cent of production costs and salaries and wages account for about 26 per cent. One interesting development in the costs is the declining share of imported dyes and chemicals, from about 12 per cent in 1980 to about 7 per cent at present, partly due to the shift in emphasis from producing mainly finished textiles to semi-processed grey cloth and yarn. There has been no change in ownership structure (100 per cent government ownership). There are however, plans to sell some of the shares to the private sector.

JV Textiles

The JV Textiles mill, established in 1971, is part of the JV conglomerate (in textiles, beverages, etc). It is 100 per cent privately owned, with 900 employees, about 600 of whom are on a permanent basis. The management is mainly expatriate. There are two types of plant, old and new. The installed production capacity is 4 million linear metres of cloth (processing). The mill employs some recent weaving technologies such as airjet looms and rapiers.

JV Textiles started exporting in 1980 to neighbouring countries. Today about 15 per cent of total production is exported, mainly T-shirts, towels, cotton fibres and other manufactures going to the UK, Germany and Sweden. It has links with other firms on sub-contacting terms (e.g. Henkel chemicals, other textile mills, etc.).

Current capacity utilization rates are 45 per cent for weaving, 35 per cent for knitting and 42 per cent for processing. The decline in production has mainly been attributed to the change in inputs from polyester to cotton (since 1980), since the machines were originally designed to process polyester.

The Morogoro Canvas Mill

Established in 1979 (production starting in 1985), the Morogoro Canvas Mill is the only public textile firm being run under a foreign management contract (M/S Hebox Holland Engineering BV).

The installed capacity is about 4.6 million square metres of assorted canvas products, with a labour force of 1 032 employees (850 working in the factory). Morogoro Canvas Mill was originally planned as a supplier of canvas to the Morogoro Shoe factory. When that factory went bankrupt, the canvas mill adjusted swiftly by changing its product mix and entering the export market (uniforms, grey cloth and bed sheets). Today the mill exports about 60 per cent of its output. The cost structure is dominated by cotton, followed by chemicals. Unlike other public textile firms, Morogoro Canvas is not a member of the holding corporation TEXCO. Autonomy in decision-making is quite high.

The breakthrough in the export business is mainly attributed to special machines used for export production. Morogoro Canvas has quite a sizeable and diversified export market (the US, the UK, Canada, Holland, Germany, Saudi Arabia, the UAE and neighbouring countries).

Tanganyika Textiles Industries Ltd

Tanganyika Textiles was established as a private company in 1959 and has remained wholly private since then. The employment level is currently around 450 employees. Inputs have changed from rayon yarn to cotton yarn, which now accounts for about 70 per cent of total production cost. Capacity utilization rates have been falling during the last decade from about 41 per cent in 1980 to around 20 per cent at present. Export performance has not been good. The only export market was Kenya, and when the East African Community collapsed in 1977 the firm completely lost its export market and has not recovered it, mainly because Kenya has developed its own textile base.

Morogoro Polyester Textiles Ltd (Polytex)

The firm was established in 1985, mainly to supply the domestic market. It is publicly owned, with a labour force in 1990 of 1 890. The main inputs are cotton, polyester, rayon, dyes and chemicals. Capacity utilization is about 40 per cent (processing). The quality

of its grey cloth has gradually been improved. Exports include yarn
and blended fabrics.

It has subcontracting links with other firms (e.g. Hoechst and
CIBA-Geigy for dyes and chemicals, Dawooe for rayon and polyester) and a service contract with International Computers Limited
(ICL). The company runs a workshop for making and repairing some
spare parts.

Firm strategies

The strategy of a firm covers the explicit or implicit plans adopted
by an enterprise to achieve certain targets and the means to be
pursued to achieve such ends. Targets may include levels of growth,
the range of products to be produced or marketed, markets to be
penetrated, skills to be enhanced or acquired, processes to be used
or developed, etc. Enterprise strategy is crucial because it may determine performance and the pace and extent of the acquisition
of technological capabilities.

NEM's strategies

NEM has always had a vision of becoming a leading supplier of electrical fittings to East Africa. A number of strategies have been
pursued to achieve this end, notably an export marketing strategy
which aims at earning foreign exchange to ease the chronic shortages of raw materials and other imported inputs which the company
has faced and at providing alternative outlets given the competitive
character of the domestic market, especially since the mid-1980s.
Efforts to enter the export market have been successful. What
remains is to work hard on quality control and to secure markets
other than Sweden.

Other strategies used by NEM to avoid raw material and foreign
exchange shortages have included: (1) the development of new products using local raw materials, (2) concentrating on products that
have a relatively lower import content and (3) attempting to increase
the local content in existing products. One marketing strategy that
gives NEM a competitive edge is its ability to provide a full range
of electrical fittings.

The success of these strategies has been enhanced by NEM's
active and continuous search for new product ideas from many
sources, its ability and willingness to subcontract other firms and a
flexible technology that can be used for a wide variety of products.

Themi's strategies

During its first five years, Themi Farm Implements seems to have been lacking a clear operating strategy. The demand for its two major products, ploughs and ox-carts, was high and Themi was satisfied with the *status quo*. There is no evidence of a conscious search for new ideas and initiatives or a deliberate strategy to innovate. The absence of a competitive environment seems to have acted as a disincentive to innovate.

However, the liberal and competitive environment after the mid-1980s cost Themi market shares for its two major products. To cope with the problem Themi has adopted survival strategies. One strategy focused on product diversification. Themi has embarked on the production of new products including hand-operated oil presses, oil expellers, manual water pumps, water storage tanks, manual and electric drill presses, presses for making cement and soil bricks, and hay bailers.

To expand its market and generate foreign exchange, Themi, through the Catholic Religious Services, has searched for and secured new export markets for its products in Uganda, Rwanda and Burundi. It has also introduced a strategy of improved product delivery services, involving setting up independent satellite units to supply spares for fast-wearing parts and to repair customers' implements. The strategy has boosted demand because the firm's major competitors, Ubungo Farm Implements (UFI) and Mbeya Farm Implements Co., do not offer such services. Domestic sales have been further boosted by the use of the Tanganyika Farmers Association as distribution agents.

Rationalization of management and production has been another strategy. Initially, production and marketing decisions were centralized. To increase motivation and encourage an aggressive search for alternative markets, there are now three autonomous product departments, for ploughs and ox-carts, oil presses and drill presses. Each department has to be aggressive in innovating and looking for markets for its respective product.

Afrocooling's strategies

Afrocooling Systems has a vision of producing, marketing and exporting high-quality products. This vision was also prompted by shortages of raw materials and foreign exchange and by competition from imported products. In pursuit of this objective Afrocooling has adopted four main strategies in the fields of appropriate technology, innovative production, innovative marketing and quality control. The technology used by the enterprise is relatively small-scale, simple, labour-intensive and flexible. These attributes have enabled the firm's engineers to adapt, assimilate and standardize it. The technology is flexible in the sense that it can be used to produce over 500 varieties of radiators.

The firm's major technological improvement has been the standardization of the design for radiator tubes and structures with the assistance of a design engineer imported from India. Other innovations have included the substitution of local brass and bronze fittings for imports and the making of its own toolings, spares and industrial heat exchangers in-house. Rigorous quality control has been the major source of Afrocooling's competitive edge. Change in product design is a continuous process based on customers' needs and product performance. Its products have been approved by Sweden to be used in the Tamco truck assembly plant, which is a joint venture between a local parastatal firm (State Motor Corporation) and a Swedish firm (Saab-Scania). Similarly, the Valmet Company of Finland has approved the firm's radiators for use as original equipment in its tractor assembly plants in Tanzania and Brazil. Afrocooling markets its products aggressively at home and overseas. It now exports radiators to Sudan, the UK, Egypt, Kenya and the Gulf States.

Matsushita's strategies

Consistent with the Japanese tradition, the operations of Matsushita have been guided by the vision of producing high-quality competitive products. Another factor has been the fear of being pushed out of the market by either genuine competitive pressures or a monopolistic situation developing within Tanzania. The firm has developed explicit strategies in the areas of utilizing mass assembly lines, skill enhancement and aggressive marketing.

The assembly of components and parts into finished products is extremely labour-intensive and would be expected to benefit from the low wages prevailing in Tanzania. Furthermore, the assembly of standard products and components in large volumes is considered the key to the realization of economies of scale. To achieve and maintain high levels of quality in the products, the workers have to be skilled. Matsushita has thus placed strong emphasis on local training. Of all the workers who have received training, in-house (on-the-job) training has accounted for 50 per cent, training in local institutions accounts for 35 per cent and training abroad (in Japan, Sweden and Pakistan) has accounted for 15 per cent. There is a strong quality control department and the company has a systematic and aggressive marketing strategy. It is continuously carrying out product market research, conducted in most cases by consultancy firms. Aggressive marketing is also reflected in regular advertising in both local and regional media and a systematic collection of customer enquiries. Matsushita exports batteries to Rwanda, Burundi, Zaire and Malawi.

The textile firms' strategies

Four of the five textile firms in our sample were established as part of the import substitution strategy. Most of these firms attempted to export only after several years of operation: Friendship Mill after eleven years; JV Textiles after nine years, Polytex after two years. Their entry into the export business came in response to two factors: the loss of local markets, especially after the liberalization of trade which saw an influx of second-hand clothes (see Table 8.6) and new opportunities arising out of new contacts and market research.

When these changes started to be felt, firms started targeting the export market. However, a number of problems were experienced: poor quality, due mainly to old machinery, and high costs, partly reflecting the technology in use and partly due to high costs of operation, which in the past were easily recovered given the monopoly position of these firms and the 'cost plus' pricing method in use. These problems necessitated changes in strategy if these firms were to survive, changes which are currently being coordinated by TEXTMAT (Textiles Manufacturers' Association of Tanzania).

One common factor is that all textile firms import technology. The first strategic response was then to effect changes in the technology used. Specific machines were imported to cater for export production with an emphasis on automation. Changes have taken place in the processes of printing (replacement of roller and flatbed printing with rotary screen machines), winding (with the introduction of electronics) and in weaving (airjet looms and rapiers). The introduction of these new machines has been relatively easy due to the reorientation of human resources development in response to the market changes. The emphasis has shifted slightly from in-house training to high-level training, in some cases overseas. In addition, the accumulated skills of the past, in areas such as the fabrication of spaces, tooling, etc., have greatly helped in enabling firms to modify certain machines. They have, for example, gone from using imported rayon to local cotton and from imported starch to local cassava starch. These modifications have resulted in a considerable reduction of production costs, as import content was lowered. Operational costs have been further lowered through streamlining employment.

One area which has seen great strategic response has been marketing, with the goal of targeting the export market. Through individual firm efforts and TEXTMAT, firms have established an export 'desk' within their organizational structure and have even been able to penetrate the highly competitive markets of the West, where specialized products are sold, although on a small scale. Specific new marketing strategies have included the appointment of marketing agencies abroad, effective participation in trade fairs abroad, a close working relationship with the Board of External Trade in the search for new markets, market visits and advertisements in mass media overseas.

Despite these strategic responses there are certain limiting factors to exports (even where firm orders have been secured). These include low production levels (see Table 8.7) attributed to old machinery, despite the introduction of new machines at certain stages; insufficient working capital (Mbelle, 1992; Nelson and Persson, 1992; de Valk, 1992); poor quality control and the 'hostile domestic operating environment' (unfavourable fiscal policy and tight monetary policy).

The domestic market, which in the past was assured regardless of the quality and price of the textiles produced, has experienced some dynamism with the liberalization of the economy, especially after 1986.

Firms' investment capabilities

One structural weakness of Tanzanian industry has been its lack of investment capabilities (Mlawa, 1983; Bagachwa, 1991, 1992; Wangwe, 1992). Firms lack the skills needed (1) to identify and evaluate projects, (2) to specify the appropriate and correct location, scale, and product and input mixes, (3) to research, select, bargain for, purchase and transfer the appropriate technology and (4) to participate in carrying out basic and detailed engineering functions, e.g. equipment specification, procurement and testing, civil construction, mechanical erection and commissioning, and to execute the start-up and training functions.

It is possible to hire some of these skills from specialized engineering or consulting companies or the manufacturers of capital goods in developed countries. However, the cost involved is likely to be heavy. Moreover, as the case of the milling industry has shown, the lack of active local participation in the design and execution of certain critical investment functions may lead either to inappropriate technology choices and the subsequent failure to master, adapt and improve upon imported technologies, or to failure to establish linkages with local suppliers of capital goods (Bagachwa, 1991, 1992). These major sources of industrial inefficiency happen because valuable opportunities for technological learning and spill-over are lost (Lall, 1992). It is therefore important that such skills be developed, either through past experience or through conscious training.

NEM's investment capabilities

Under SIP, NEM, like many other 'junior sister' firms, was not given the opportunity to participate in the early entrepreneurial investment functions such as the selection of the products and technology, or in the negotiations with a senior Swedish firm. During the first phase these functions were performed by SIDO, with assistance from FIDE. SIDO conceived of the investment idea and carried out a market search to identify products. It then secured Sweden as a donor of technology and technical assistance. SIDO, together with the technology supplier and FIDE, agreed on the type of products to be produced and the type of technology to be used. FIDE then identified a medium-sized Swedish firm, Eldon, which produces similar products, to act as a senior sister in transferring the production technology to NEM. The contract between the NEM and Eldon was formalized by SIDO. SIDO, through public advertisements, invited entrepreneurs to bid for the running of NEM. The present NEM entrepreneurs were selected by interviews and entrusted with the management of the firm. SIDO used funds provided by SIDA to procure equipment and deliver it to NEM under a low-interest hire purchase arrangement.

In addition, SIDO provided a low-rent shed, electricity and water to NEM. The role of Eldon was to install and commission the machinery, to guarantee its functioning, to make regular visits to oversee operations, to continue assistance with marketing and product development and to provide technical training in Sweden and on the job.

Thus NEM's entrepreneurs missed the opportunity to participate in and learn from the key initial entrepreneurial tasks. When selecting the entrepreneurs, SIDO considered their formal education and past experience. In effect the selected entrepreneurs were like 'hired managers'. But what is important is whether these selected managers assumed the typical roles of entrepreneurs, i.e. developing new ideas, testing them and put them into operation.

Themi's investment capabilities

Themi's entrepreneurs, like those of NEM, were brought into a ready-made project. SIDO and the USAID-sponsored AP/VDP conceived of the project to produce ox-drawn tool bars and ox-carts for the local market. They then advertised for entrepreneurs to manage the project. Out of a total of 62 groups, one partnership group of seven indigenous entrepreneurs was selected. In contrast to NEM, these entrepreneurs were then responsible for the procurement of machinery, installation and tooling. Funds for equipment were provided as a low-interest loan by USAID through AP/VDP and channelled through the RDD's office. The Tanzania Rural Development Bank (TRDB) provided a short-term loan to procure raw materials.

The choice of technology and its supplier (in the UK) was made by the entrepreneurs themselves after receiving several quotations from various suppliers. They were also responsible for procuring the equipment and participated fully in the installation and commissioning of the plant. Some assistance was obtained from SIDO and AP/VDP technicians. This investment capability was possible because three of the entrepreneurs, though not very experienced, held a degree (BSc) in engineering. It was said that this direct participation facilitated the procurement of simple technology which is suited for most general engineering works. And, unlike most equipment procured by SIDO, this equipment was not mis-specified. Although the product had been chosen by SIDO and AP/VDP, which limited the type of technologies which could be used, Themi's entrepreneurs could still make their choice from various equipment suppliers offering significant sophistication, price and quality differences. It was therefore possible for them to negotiate for the best terms.

Afrocooling's investment capabilities

Unlike the entrepreneurs of NEM and Themi, who were assisted by the state (through SIDO) in performing certain early entrepreneurial functions, those in Afrocooling had to undergo the long and difficult but instructive process of feasibility studies, project identification and execution. The feasibility study and civil works were contracted to local firms. The entrepreneurs hired consultants from India to specify and supervise the construction of the factory and install and commission the plant. The entrepreneurs obtained quotations for the supply of equipment from the leading radiator equipment manufacturers in the world. Equipment from a variety of suppliers in the UK, the then West Germany and India was selected. The entrepreneurs participated fully in all these negotiations, showing a grasp of pre-investment tasks rare in Tanzania. The equipment selected is considered appropriate to the Tanzanian condition, given the firm's flexible, small-scale and labour-intensive operations.

Matsushita's investment capabilities

In the case of Matsushita, all the investment functions, such as feasibility studies, site selection, technology research, negotiation of contracts, civil construction, equipment erection, commissioning and procurement, were performed by the parent company, Matsushita Electric Industries of Japan. It was claimed that at that time (the mid-1960s) there were no Tanzanians with sufficient engineering capability to participate in the decision-making process.

The textiles firms' investment capabilities

Investment capabilities in the textile firms vary mainly according to the nature of ownership. While the government made all the decisions in the case of the public firms Friendship, Polytex (through the parastatal holding company TEXCO) and Morogoro Canvas, for JV Textiles and Tanganyika Textiles the decision was made by the (private) managing director.

The feasibility studies for the public firms were undertaken through bilateral donor arrangements (e.g. the Chinese for Friendship) or under multilateral arrangements (e.g. Canvas Mill). Even in the case of the two private firms, foreign consultants were invited in. This reflects the absence of indigenous capacity at that time, though such capabilities now exist even within the firms.

The choice of technology (machinery, product range, etc.) in the case of public firms was mainly dictated by the source of finance (e.g. the Chinese government in the case of Friendship) while private firms had their choices made by the managing director. Civil works were done by foreign firms in all cases.

One factor which is common to all public firms is that the current management is not knowledgeable of what transpired at the crucial early stages (feasibility, construction, commissioning), except for the Canvas Mill, which still has a foreign management contract.

Production capabilities

Production capabilities are the skills necessary for: (1) process engineering, i.e. specifying equipment, laying out raw materials, setting engineering and maintenance routines to ensure efficient plant operation, making adaptions and material substitutions, energy conservation, process improvement and the introduction of new techniques; (2) product engineering, i.e. establishing the optimum product design, modifying purchased designs (acquiring know-how), introducing new products (acquiring know-why), basic research; and (3) industrial engineering, i.e. overall planning of production, determination of batch sizes, sequencing and scheduling, make-or-buy decisions, materials planning and inventory control.

NEM's production capabilities

If one were to judge NEM's production capability by its formal qualifications then the stock is unimpressive. There are two graduate engineers, four diploma holders, three FTC (Full Technician's Certificate) holders and four certificates in business. The rest of the workforce of 107 do not have any recognized formal certificates. Of the 70 workers in the production department, only four have recognized formal credentials, i.e. one has an advanced diploma and three are FTC holders.

However, if one takes into consideration experience and on-the-job training, then the production capabilities at NEM are not as low as they appear. Two of the entrepreneurs (shareholders) of NEM had 13 and 10 years, respectively, of work experience in business and industry at both supervisory and managerial levels before starting NEM. The other five also had a considerable industrial experience and business knowledge of six or more years as owners of small enterprises before joining NEM. Two of the entrepreneurs also underwent training in Sweden before the machinery was installed. The heads of the three departments have all undergone training at least once in Sweden. Regular on-the-job training has also been provided for 48 workers, and 20 other workers have been trained in local institutions. The combination of prior experience, short-term in-house and external training, learning by doing and frequent contacts and advice given by the senior sister and consultants have helped to enhance the workforce's production capability acquisition.

NEM has acquired some limited capabilities to perform some of the elementary process engineering functions. A recent evaluation report found all of the five machines bought ten years ago looking 'fairly new' and functioning properly (INTERMACOS, 1991, p. 5). This suggests that the machines have been properly maintained. The machines have adequate stocks of spare parts to cope with any major breakdown. The supplier of machines still exists and is a reliable source of spares.

NEM has developed its capacity to carry out both preventive and corrective maintenance. It has maintenance manuals for all core equipment. During the early years, preventive maintenance and regular overhauls were carried out with the senior sister's assistance. However, through experience and training, there is now an in-house capacity to perform such functions. The involvement of NEM's technicians during the expansion phase is said to have been instrumental in the selection of flexible technologies that are capable of producing a large variety of products.

Information generated from interviews and corroborated by evidence elsewhere (Alänge, 1987) suggests that NEM has the capacity to perform some of the tasks of product engineering. This is reflected, for example: in (1) new initiatives such as a systematic and active search for new product ideas from a wide range of sources, customers, product catalogues, imported products, the senior sister, etc.; (2) innovative activities such as the development of their own tools, modification of assembly workplaces, establishment of new production lines, introducing new local components in existing programmes and minor adaptations to imported product designs; and (3) a product market search which has included diversification from production for domestic to export markets to avoid raw material shortages associated with a lack of foreign exchange, lowering of import content from 100 per cent at the time of inception to about

86 per cent in 1991 and a recent initiative to look for alternative sources of imported inputs and for export markets besides Sweden.

Themi's production capabilities

Themi has not been able to acquire appreciable production capabilities. Although it started with three graduate engineers, these did not have significant industrial or business experience. From the outset the management of the firm lacked vision, determination and drive. Themi is particularly weak in administrative capabilities. The managing director of the firm is an engineer who had had neither prior management training nor previous experience in managing a small or large firm. The firm would certainly have benefited a lot if it had hired an experienced manager. The department of finance lacks qualified personnel. The accounts section is disorganized and functions on an *ad hoc* basis. One is struck by the absence of a section or department of marketing. At present each of the three departments (ploughs and ox-carts, oil presses and drill presses) is supposed to market its own products. The firm does not have any marketing strategy. Marketing and sales are probably the weakest parts of Themi.

It is obvious that Themi lacks the capability to perform even some of the industrial engineering functions. The department of research and planning exists only on paper, having had no qualified personnel since its inception. There is no evidence of raw material or inventory control systems. Information on production and sales is not easily accessible.

Themi has, however, some limited inventive capabilities. It has made some modifications in imported designs for hand planters, groundnut shellers, hand operated presses, hand pumps and ox-carts. It has the capacity and ability to maintain, service and repair almost all equipment. Themi's inventive capability is also reflected in the more than 15 new products it has introduced into the market.

The process of capability acquisition has been rather slow in Themi due to various factors. Foremost has been the lack of management with significant industrial or business experience who would be able to take the initiative in training and product development. Other factors include the failure to hire qualified personnel to handle the various specialized functions of the different departments, the lack of training and marketing strategies and a lack of entrepreneurial vision.

Afrocooling's production capabilities

Afrocooling's production capabilities are very impressive. The firm's top management group already had considerable industrial experience, business knowledge and more formal technical and commercial education prior to joining the company. All the shareholders held shares in other companies before forming the company. They also manage a successful firm, Auto Mech Ltd, which rehabilitates automotive engines. Today the company has five graduates, three holding BSc degrees in engineering and the other two in finance and business management. There are two expatriates from India: an engineer and a financial advisor. There are five diploma holders: four in engineering-related fields and one in finance. There are 47 other skilled workers holding certificates in engineering trades, with 10 holding FTCs.

Besides prior industrial and business experience, the process of capability acquisition has been enhanced through learning by experiencing, i.e. managing their own firm, and by intensive training in both the plant and outside institutions. Although most of the training is aimed at developing further manual (production) skills, there is also limited training in management and marketing. Between 1981 and 1991 the firm trained 50 workers on the job, 20 in local institutions and two in India. The firm also imported a design engineer from India, who has taught other engineers how to standardize the design for radiator tubes and structures. Some technicians have been trained in preventive and corrective maintenance and in fault diagnosis through simulation of faults in some equipment. Experience accumulated over time, high formal qualifications and learning-based knowledge have all enabled Afrocooling to design appropriate future strategies and to acquire considerable production capabilities.

Matsushita's production capabilities

In spite of Matsushita's emphasis on local training, there seem to be less opportunities for the indigenous workers to upgrade themselves technologically. This is partly because the assembly line is one of the most labour-intensive and least skill-intensive portions of the production process. There is thus little incentive to search for or train more skilled operators and technicians. Recruitment has thus been mostly based on primary-school (Standard VII) leavers, who are then trained on the job. The lack of opportunities is also partly because areas with the greatest potential for enhancing capability acquisition are confined to the expatriate personnel. Besides, the managing director is a Japanese, which means a lost opportunity for a Tanzanian manager to learn from experience. Moreover, the responsibility for new product design and market research are limited to the directors of planning and production and marketing departments, who are Japanese. Most of the training for local workers has therefore focused on manual skill development and there has been little training to enhance management, administrative and marketing capabilities. Perhaps the process of indigenous capability acquisition will be enhanced now that Matsushita intends to move into the manufacturing of radios. But this will also depend on the division of labour between the Japanese and Tanzanian workers.

The textile firms' production capabilities

Skills development in the textile industry was traditionally focused on training employees in trade skills, especially at the shop-floor level. This has recently changed to training middle- and senior-level personnel, with greater weight being given to production, technical and engineering departments. Professional skills are also being emphasized.

In the past, training was done mainly by public firms (partly out of government funds) and the private sector had no major formal training programmes. The private sector, however, got publicly trained professionals through attractive incentive schemes. Some private firms (e.g. JV Textiles) now have comprehensive training programmes within the country and even abroad.

The end results of the past and current programmes are that there are personnel with high-level skills (at least a first degree in the relevant field) to head departments, and firms have also acquired capabilities to fabricate a wide range of spares, etc., which has improved maintenance and enabled them to carry out important modifications to machinery, such as conversions from imported to local inputs.

Except for the Canvas Mill, the textile firms have acquired the local capability to oversee the entire production line and beyond to marketing.

Determinants of production capabilities

The examples of NEM and Afrocooling suggest that a major source of production capabilities is the accumulation of entrepreneurial, technical and managerial skills from previous experience in commerce and industry. Where such experience is absent (as with Themi), industrial performance and hence export competitiveness are bound to be very weak. The case of Themi also demonstrates quite well that the existence of entrepreneurs, even those driven by the profit motive, eager to take risks and with higher formal education, may not in itself be a sufficient condition for the development of dynamic capabilities unless it is associated with the capability required to organize and manage the production process.

Training is another important source of capability acquisition. As Lall (1992, p. 117) notes, even the operation of the easy, low-technology activities with which industrialization generally starts requires literacy and schooling, a range of basic skills and some high-level technological and managerial skills. The government must therefore provide the base of literacy or formal training needed for industrial capabilities. Training within firms can expand the base but cannot be a substitute for basic formal education. Some private firms which have their own resources (such as Matsushita) or access to foreign technical assistance (such as NEM) have managed to train their staff. But even in such cases, the training has been on a short-term basis and is certainly insufficient for developing capabilities to handle the advanced and more demanding stages of industry. Themi has failed to train its staff because it lacks resources. Firm-level training is also bound to be limited because private firms may fear losing their trainees once they are sufficiently qualified. Thus, as industrialization develops, it will not be enough for the government to provide primary and secondary education as a broad base for industrial skills. Further formal technical education will be needed.

Flexible and adaptive capabilities

Flexible and adaptive capabilities are skills and abilities that enable an enterprise to cope with rapidly changing global market conditions and technological developments. One of the major recent global technological changes has been the introduction of new technologies, especially the major technological breakthroughs in the fields of microelectronics and IT, biotechnology, material sciences and renewable energies. A major consequence of the technological revolution is that comparative advantage, international competitiveness and the international division of labour are now determined not so much by natural endowments or the invisible hand as by (1) access to new technologies, (2) capacity to respond to rapidly changing consumer tastes with new and differentiated products, (3) the ability to seek out new market niches and (4) improvements in productive efficiency.

The non-textile firms' flexible and adaptive capabilities

Access to new generic technologies, i.e. technologies that are potentially applicable as inputs across a broad spectrum of industries, is crucial, because they can drastically improve possibilities for upgrading existing technologies and for extending the range of organizational innovations. Three of the sample firms, NEM, Afrocooling and Matsushita, use computers in certain aspects of firm operations. Mostly, however, computers are used for general office work in accounting and payroll functions. In Matsushita they are also used in projecting market demand and machine inventories. None of the firms uses computers to control processes. The three firms also have fax facilities. Themi has no access to fax and computer facilities. Matsushita is contemplating automation in some of its assembly processes to increase efficiency, improve quality and raise productivity. Afrocooling has plans to modernize its equipment.

All firms have shown some flexibility in responding to rapidly changing consumer tastes by introducing new and sometimes differentiated products. NEM has introduced automatic power spraying of paint instead of manual painting to improve quality. Themi had to introduce marketing agents and zonal services and repair units to streamline its marketing operations. Afrocooling made a market breakthrough by standardizing its radiators. Matsushita maintains a strong department of quality control.

These flexible and adaptive abilities, however, are still at an elementary level. Access to new technologies is still difficult due to the lack of sufficient resources (e.g. Themi). Where resources are available there are still formidable obstacles to be overcome. Supportive infrastructure is still very weak (e.g. constant telephone interruptions and power failure), resulting in constant machinery breakdowns. Linkages between the users and producers of new technologies are weak because all the new technologies are imported and the market is still too small to motivate the supplier to provide back-up support. The telecommunications infrastructure which could have permitted data transmission between user and producer is non-existent or malfunctioning. Already there are problems of inadequate software and specialized components. Moreover, low levels of education mean that most workers are not easily trainable to handle or operate new technologies.

The textile firms' flexible and adaptive capabilities

The need for flexibility and adaptability to global developments is enormous in the textile world. The global environment has witnessed changes in many fields, e.g. production and trade relations, management practices and industrial organization, market characteristics, hardware and software technology, etc.

The textile industry has been influenced by these developments to a great extent. At the spinning stage the development has mainly been in the form of automation using single roving technology. The latest in this respect is the open-end spinning spindle, which processes rough yarn into individual fibres ready to be made into ready-to-use yarn. At the weaving stage the technological developments have included moving to fully automated looms as well as developments within the loom technology itself. The latter has led to a number of options: shuttle systems, projectile looms, rapier looms, airjet and wetjet looms. Weaving is the most important stage. It demands flexible adaption to technological and market changes.

The introduction of microelectronics (computers) at the finishing stage has brought about a great change in finishing, increasing precision and time control and reducing the labour input. The response to these global technological developments in the textile industry has varied from firm to firm. The main limiting factor is finance, since the desire to acquire technology and the necessary information are there. By the very nature of textile processing, the piecemeal introduction of new technologies at separate stages is possible and need not create pressure at the subsequent stage, as semi-finished products can be exported.

Linkage capabilities

Linkage capabilities relate to specific skills which enable the enterprise to locate and interact with efficient input and technology suppliers, product customers and various institutions providing credit, technical, research, R&D and infrastructural support services.

The non-textile firms' linkage capabilities

Generally speaking, linkage capabilities were observed to be weak in the four non-textile firms under study. Limited subcontracting arrangements exist between NEM and three other SIP firms: i.e. Arusha Metal Industries (AMI) provides NEM with galvanizing services; Kilimanjaro Metal Shapers (KIMESHA) makes wall brackets for lights for NEM; and Uhandisi Industrial Fasteners makes special screws and rivets for NEM. There were no subcontracting arrangement outside the SIP network of firms. The bulk of intermediate inputs for NEM's operations are supplied by a single Swedish firm and almost all its exports go to a single Swedish firm. This implies the absence of significant forward and backward linkages within the economy and reflects a limited ability to locate customers and input suppliers outside the SIP arrangement. The firm needs to diversify input and technology sources and export markets to minimize the vulnerability that comes with dependence on a single customer or supplier. When the supplier is also a competitor the risks become much greater (Ernst and O'Connor, 1989).

Themi does not have any subcontracting activities with other industrial firms. The absence of linkages between Themi and other larger firms such as UFI and Mbeya Farm Implements is especially striking. The firm is, however, linked back to the National Steel Corporation of Dar es Salaam, which provides most of Themi's mild steel. Themi has also forged some forward linkages with the agricultural sector via sales of ploughs and ox-carts.

Afrocooling has managed to establish significant forward linkages through its sales of radiators to the local automobile industry, including vehicle assembling firms such as TAMCO (Scania trucks), TRAMA Valmet (tractors), Landrover and several vehicle repair units. There is no evidence, however, of significant subcontracting arrangements with other domestic firms. Likewise, domestic backward linkages appear to be weak. The bulk of inputs such as brass strips, copper strips and brass sheets are imported from Outokuspan, Sweden.

Matsushita's internal linkages are equally weak. Most of the work involves the assembly of parts and components imported from Japan. Limited backward linkages have been created with Kibo Paper Industries (which provides packing materials) and Tanzania Eyelets (which supplies battery caps).

Other forms of linkages such as economic spin-offs have also been limited. An economic spin-off is defined as a spontaneous outgrowth (in the form of a new enterprise) from a previous activity. NEM has been active in this sense. It has established a new unit on a new site outside its previous location in the industrial estate area to cater for exports. NEM has also established a joint venture with two foreign companies, Finnveden Development and Swedfund, to establish a new company, Arusha Precision Tools and Die Makers Company (ATOMAC). The new company serves as a highly sophisticated tool-and-die workshop. In addition NEM has joined forces with two other SIP firms, Kimesha and the Arusha Galvanizing Company Ltd (AGACO), to establish Galkin, which produces lamps for export. There is no evidence of spin-offs for Themi and Matsushita. The owners of Afrocooling, however, have established a new company, Auto Mech Ltd, which rehabilitates automotive engines.

The absence of significant inter-sectoral linkages can be explained from four perspectives. First, in the cases of NEM, Afrocooling and Matsushita, it reflects the pattern of IS, which emphasizes import-dependent assembly. Second, the case of NEM shows that ease of access to donor funding may discourage producers from actively looking for locally available parts or materials. Third, the case of Themi demonstrates management's inability to search for or appreciate the positive role which can be played by subcontracting, and equally that the large public firms such as UFI and Mbeya Farm Implements lack the resources and technological capabilities needed to set up subcontractors. Lastly, poor inter-sectoral linkages may reflect poor infrastructure facilities for small firms, biases in policies and in credit markets and the lack of an extension network.

Similarly, in all four cases linkages with research institutions were almost non-existent. Themi, for example, viewed the Institute of Productivity Innovation (IPI) at the University of Dar es Salaam and the Centre for Agricultural Mechanization and Rural Technology (CAMARTEC) as competing rather than collaborative institutions (IPI and CAMARTEC make prototypes of agricultural equipment and are supposed to disseminate the technologies to the rural areas). In all four firms there were no cooperation or close links with: (1) institutions charged with applied research and training such as universities, (2) technology generating and design institutions such as IPI, CAMARTEC and the Tanzania Engineering and Manufacturing Development Organization (TEMDO), (3) institutions for industrial standards, testing and quality assurance such as the Tanzania Bureau of Standards (TBS), (4) institutions for technological information such as the Tanzania Science and Technology Commission, or (5) institutions for consultancy, export market information and support such as the Tanzanian Industrial Studies and Consultancy Organization (TISCO) and the Board of External Trade (BET).

Failure to forge close links with industry-related institutions can be attributed to two key factors. First, some firms (e.g. Themi) may not be aware of the usefulness of such links. Secondly, in most cases existing institutions in Tanzania are ill-equipped and poorly funded, staffed and managed and are assigned conflicting objectives. For example, the government's continuous reduction in funds for R&D activities has forced IPI, CAMARTEC and TEMDO to spend less on the development of appropriate technologies and their dissemination in rural areas and increasingly to produce technologies for sale.

The textile firms' linkage capabilities

The textile firms surveyed revealed some limited forms of linkages with other local institutions outside the industry, in most cases of a service nature. TISCO is among the institutions often referred to in plans for future linkages, while training institutions such as the University of Dar es Salaam carry out some consultancy work (with the Institute of Production Innovation of the university being called in for technical services). TEXTMAT attempts to promote interactions among local textile firms by harmonizing production processes (e.g. identification of excess capacity in individual firms and possibilities of subcontracting, trading in spares, joint quality control, etc.).

The firms are strongly linked to the suppliers of their technology, who happen to be foreign. For example, the Friendship Mill is embarking on modernization with the Chinese government, the supplier of its original machines, charting the technology supply programme. The factor limiting links with local firms was said to be that these have little to offer (especially in technology, the crucial area).

DETERMINATION OF ENTERPRISE PERFORMANCE AND EFFICIENCY

A useful quantitative tool for assessing a firm's efficiency is the domestic resources cost (DRC). The DRC is the cost of the domestic resources (factors) that are necessary to save or earn one unit of foreign exchange by producing a unit of value added (valued at border prices). Unfortunately the data collected in this study is not detailed enough to permit use of the DRC methodology. A crude indicator of firm-level performance has been used instead, namely the labour surplus, or value added per worker.

Table 8.5 (pp. 238–9) provides information on surplus generation in the sample firms in the metals and engineering sector for the years for which data was available. Themi has the worst performance in the sample. Even in nominal terms it had a negative value added and hence negative surplus and productivity in 1985 and in 1990. In real terms the situation is even more alarming. NEM's performance has been rather mixed. The firm's real value added per worker declined from TSh50 000 in 1983 to TSh5 500 in 1986. It has since recovered and rose to TSh85 800 in 1990. The best performers are Afrocooling and Matsushita, which show rising surplus levels and real value added per worker, especially after 1985.

But when Table 8.5 is read alongside Table 8.4 the emerging picture is rather confusing. Trends in export performance in the most productive firms have not been encouraging. Afrocooling's exports has declined between 1989 and 1991, Matsushita's exports declined from US$1 045 000 in 1986 to a low of US$31 000 before rising marginally to US$107 000. Export earnings for the worst performers rise between 1986 and 1991.

The overall picture that emerges is that, despite an increasingly favourable macropolicy environment for export enterprises and modestly successful attempts to acquire and build technological capabilities within Afrocooling, Matsushita and NEM, these relatively efficient non-textile firms are losing their export market shares.

The textile industry in Tanzania has, in the 1980s, expanded its productive capacities. Despite the expansion, output has been declining, from 93.0 million square metres of cloth in 1980 when industry capacity was 200 million, to 62.5 million in 1992, when capacity had reached 252 million[5] square metres of cloth per annum (see Table 8.7). The poor performance of the industry has been attributed to lack of foreign exchange for inputs and spares, frequent interruptions in the supply of electricity and water, aged plant and machinery, inadequate credit facilities, an inappropriate or hostile macroeconomic environment which gives an unfair competitive edge to textile imports, unhelpful rules and regulations, etc. (see e.g. Mbelle, 1992).

The export performances of the individual firms covered in this study have also not been very good. Three firms which are apparently the frontier firms in the industry (Canvas, Friendship and JV), recorded average capacity utilization rates of 80 per cent, 49.9 per cent and 45.3 per cent respectively in 1990. Polytex and Tanganyika had utilization rates of less than 30 per cent.

A logical conclusion of the above trend is that proper export incentives, a realistic exchange rate, a competitive pricing regime and a stock of technological capabilities are essential but not sufficient conditions for sustainable export growth. Other factors certainly matter. As pointed out earlier, significant advances have been achieved in establishing an exchange rate regime that would serve as an incentive to exporters. However, a number of anomalies persist in the regulatory environment which urgently need to be rectified if successful exporting is to take place. One major problem mentioned by all firms in the sample is that of cumbersome, bureaucratic and lengthy procedures for licensing, access to credit and foreign exchange, and export documentation. Some exporters have to travel long distances from the regions to Dar es Salaam simply to register themselves. Those based in Dar es Salaam have to commute from one corner of the city to another seeking approval from various institutions such as the Ministry of Lands and Natural Resources, the Ministry of Industries and Trade, BET, the NBC (National Bank of Commerce), the Investment Promotion Centre (IPC) and the Bank of Tanzania (BOT). There are also still tight bureaucratic bottlenecks in the administration of foreign exchange allocation, resulting in long lead times for imports. Such long and cumbersome procedures involving many institutions impose implicit extra costs (in terms of delays, etc.) on exporters. Delays could be even more disastrous for risk exports such as fresh fruits and fish.

All this suggests the need to establish some kind of an export centre that would offer at one location a package of relevant export services such as registration, licensing, proofs of ownership, export advice and export promotion. Delays in allocating foreign exchange could be substantially reduced if the OGL (Open General Licence) and import support funds were merged and their allocations were issued under similar conditions, and if forex facilities were made available through commercial banks only where letters of credit could be issued against their equivalent value in Tanzanian Shillings.

Supportive infrastructure is another important prerequisite for successful exporting. Expensive, sporadic and unreliable transport and communications are a serious impediment to the exporters of non-traditional goods. Reliability of delivery is also critical. High transport costs contribute greatly to the lack of competitiveness of exports. Poor telecommunications and constant power and water interruptions also raise the costs of doing business and compound the problem of lack of information.

There are serious weaknesses in the existing supportive institutional infrastructure as well. A survey of selected non-traditional exporters carried out in 1990 revealed that seven out of ten firms faced problems in accessing information about markets or lacked skills in designing products, packaging and controlling quality. Moreover, most of the exporters interviewed were ignorant about the modalities of exporting to the PTA member countries (Bagachwa *et al.*, 1990). Some of these deficiencies can be remedied by private agents as they build up experience but others require the establishment of specialized and informed service institutions. As already pointed out, some relevant institutions exist in Tanzania but these seem to provide only limited support as far as technical services, training, information and export standards are concerned.

Successful exporting requires a conducive macroeconomic setting and a functioning infrastructure. Once these are in place, adequate incentives and the right capabilities and support institutions are required. Proper export incentives, a realistic exchange rate and a competitive pricing regime are essential in increasing the profitability of exports. The dynamic process of acquiring technological capabilities through learning, adaptation and improvements will be the key to efficiency and productivity gains over time. With the appropriate superstructure of specialized and informed institutions, there will be opportunities for exporters to get the necessary advice on market outlets, product quality, standards, packaging, etc. Policymakers must seriously address these needs if they wish to make a positive contribution to the promotion of non-traditional exports in Tanzania.

EMERGING ISSUES AND THE CHALLENGES AHEAD

The preceding discussion presents two main challenges facing Tanzanian manufacturing firms seeking international competitiveness in exports. The first challenge is to acquire the capabilities to search actively for relevant and flexible technologies, secure the best sources and negotiate the best possible terms of acquisition. The second challenge is how to accelerate the process of technological mastery. There are two main actors in this game of technological capability acquisition, the firms and the government.

The role of government will certainly be crucial in creating conditions conducive to exploiting new technological opportunities. One of the key policy areas in which government should intervene is the development of the human resource base needed for industrial

Table 8.5 Performance indicators for sample non-textile firms for selected years (TSh × 1 000)

	1980	1983	1984	1985	1986	1987	1988	1989	1990
NEM:									
Gross output	3 911	38 742	—	28 613	48 845	53 439	—	177 447	167 535
Total costs	3 261	31 363	—	25 198	38 885	46 158	—	155 251	77 173
Value added	222	6 831	—	2 756	8 719	4 885	—	18 937	90 362
Real value added	148	2 970	—	861	2 028	688	—	3 006	11 585
Labour costs	180	1 276	—	2 937	3 839	6 201	—	14 135	10 117
Surplus	42.0	5 555	—	(181)	4 880	(1 316)	—	4 802	80 245
Value added per worker	18.5	128.9	—	91.9	111.8	39.4	—	166.1	668.7
Real value added per worker	12.0	56.0	—	28.7	26.0	5.5	—	26.4	85.8
Themi:									
Gross output	—	—	4 717	2 953	6 281	—	—	—	26 850
Total costs	—	—	2 821	2 701	3 367	—	—	—	20 130
Value added	—	—	1 587	(17)	2 542	—	—	—	(635)
Real value added	—	—	588	(5.3)	1 591	—	—	—	(81.4)
Labour costs	—	—	768	579	1 160	—	—	—	535
Surplus	—	—	819	(596)	1 382	—	—	—	(1 170)
Value added per worker	—	—	51.2	(0.45)	90.8	—	—	—	(25.4)
Real value added per worker	—	—	19.0	(0.14)	21.1	—	—	—	(3.26)

Table 8.5 (continued)

	1980	1983	1984	1985	1986	1987	1988	1989	1990
Afrocooling:									
Gross output	–	–	–	–	56 701	83 407	106 661	200 300	–
Total costs	–	–	–	–	39 565	63 150	70 291	171 605	–
Value added	–	–	–	–	16 524	19 662	35 843	27 779	–
Real value added	–	–	–	–	3 842	2 769	5 689	4 409	–
Labour costs	–	–	–	–	5 916	5 836	9 402	8 640	–
Surplus	–	–	–	–	10 608	12 826	26 441	19 139	–
Value added per worker	–	–	–	–	132.2	166.6	254.2	215.3	–
Real value added per worker	–	–	–	–	30.7	23.5	31.3	34.2	–
Matsushita:									
Gross output	210 591	–	–	273 901	–	–	–	781 790	–
Total costs	191 145	–	–	227 677	–	–	–	562 914	–
Value added	16 688	–	–	24 398	–	–	–	210 407	–
Real value added	11 125	–	–	7 624	–	–	–	33 398	–
Labour costs	15 962	–	–	21 995	–	–	–	74 348	–
Surplus	726	–	–	20 169	–	–	–	136 059	–
Value added per worker	19.4	–	–	39.0	–	–	–	389.6	–
Real value added per worker	18.6	–	–	12.2	–	–	–	61.8	–

Source: Survey data, Bureau of Statistics

development. Training is an important source of capability acquisition. Government should provide both the literacy base in the general population and the formal training needed for industrial training. In-firm training, either on the job or in a more formal framework, would then supplement, but cannot substitute for, such training. In-firm training is bound to be limited. The government will therefore have to subsidize firms or provide training facilities directly, or assist in securing foreign technical assistance.

The other area for government intervention is the provision of an environment in which flexible adjustment of production structures in the face of changing demand conditions is made possible. The provision of efficient infrastructure in the form of functioning water and electricity supplies and efficient telecommunications and transportation facilities would reduce firms' operating costs significantly. Government should also facilitate access to information about, and the acquisition of, technologies by domestic firms. It should promote contacts between domestic firms and foreign technology suppliers. Support in these efforts might significantly reduce search costs.

Most of the firms in Tanzania are still too small and ill-equipped to make any meaningful expenditure on R&D. The state, while stimulating R&D activities among industries, will initially have to mobilize and pool resources and then to decentralize such resources to individual firms. The examples of NEM and Themi have shown that government can play an important role in stimulating technological activity, by intervening more directly and taking the initiative. The state can also assist in the early phases of investment by carrying out feasibility studies, identifying products and production processes, estimating market potential and securing equipment suppliers. It is important, however, that government should involve potential entrepreneurs when making such decisions.

There are also some technological functions that cannot be performed adequately in-house. As already pointed out, the Tanzanian government has set up relevant institutions for research and extension, quality control, design, training, technology information and industrial standards. These institutions, however, need to have adequate manpower and financial resources if they are to perform their functions properly.

Finally, provision of incentives in the form of protection for strategic industries, which, for example, generate higher externalities, use flexible or difficult technologies, or have high linkages, will be necessary. Such protection, however, should be industry-specific and properly phased.

APPENDIX

Tables 8.6–8.8 give information on the textile industries' consumption structure, capacity and output and exports.

The authors would like to thank all those who assisted in one way or the other towards the production of this paper.

Table 8.6 Comparative structure of textile consumption in Tanzania 1985 and 1988

Type of production	1985	1988
Local manufactures:	61	43
% of total	49	10
Imported textiles:	63	383
% of total	51	90
of which second hand	36	287
% of total	29	67
Others:	27	96
% of total	22	23

Source: Mbelle (1992), Table 3, p. 189

Note: Consumption in million square metres of cloth.

Table 8.7 Capacity and output of the textile industry in Tanzania for selected years

	Installed capacity			Output			Capacity utilization		
	Industry	Public	Public %	Industry	Public	Public %	Industry	Public	Private
1980	200.0	145.6	72.8	93.0	83.8	90.1	46.5	57.6	16.9
1985	200.0	145.6	72.8	66.0	39.4	59.7	26.2	27.1	25.0
1990	252.0	199.0	79.0	65.2	32.5	51.5	25.0	16.3	58.1
1991	252.0	199.0	79.0	66.5	38.5	57.9	26.4	29.1	52.8
1992	223.5	157.0	70.4	62.5	31.7	50.7	28.0	20.1	46.3

Source: Mbelle (1988, 1992) – 1980 and 1985 figures; URT *Economic Survey* (1991, 1992); URT Ministry of Industries and Trade 1993/94 budget speech

Note: * Capacity and output in million square metres of woven cloth.

Table 8.8 Exports of textile products in Tanzania (US$million) 1985–92

	1985	1986	1987	1988	1989	1990	1991	1992*
Total	86.24	85.93	146.05	148.48	166.86	201.77	163.50	177.35
Manufactured	32.94	43.39	69.15	80.97	91.39	103.36	70.25	64.19
Textiles:								
As % of total	9.56	9.60	9.12	12.89	13.35	14.17	13.16	12.81
As % of	11.1	11.2	6.2	8.7	8.0	7.0	8.0	7.2
manufactured	29.0	22.1	13.2	15.9	14.6	13.7	18.7	20.0

Source: Bank of Tanzania

Note: * Provisional.

NOTES

1 According to Ndulu and Semboja (1992), measuring exports in purchasing power parity dollars (PPP$) facilitates comparisons over time, especially given the serious depreciation of the domestic currency in the 1966–90 period. See notes to Table 8.1 for the definition of PPP$.
2 Traditional exports include the six major agricultural cash crops, i.e. coffee, cotton, sisal, tea, tobacco and cashew nuts, along with traditional mineral exports of diamonds.
3 The SIP is a Swedish aid-financed programme for establishing small-scale industries in Tanzania (junior sisters) through international technology transfer by Swedish small or medium-sized industries (senior sisters). The programme began in 1977. SIDO selects products and technology and with the aid of a Swedish consulting firm, FIDE, identifies the senior sister. The senior sister is responsible for designing and specifying production equipment, its installation and commissioning, training junior sisters, supplying the necessary raw materials and other back-up support services during the agreed (5–10 years) term of cooperation. To date the SIP has resulted in 34 projects (junior sisters) located in five of the 20 regions, i.e. Kilimanjaro (13) Arusha (12), Mbeya (7) and one each in Tanga and Iringa.
4 All SIP projects are situated in SIDO's industrial estates, which generally provide infrastructure such as roads, water and electricity connections, common workshop facilities and industrial sheds.
5 Some sources give 223.5 million.

BIBLIOGRAPHY

Alänge, S., *Acquisition of Capabilities through International Technology Transfer*, Gotebörg, Department of Industrial Management, Chalmers University of Technology, 1987.

Bagachwa, M.S.D., *Choice of Technology in Industry: The Economics of Grain Milling in Tanzania*, Ottawa, International Development Research Centre (IDRC), 1991

Bagachwa, M.S.D., Choice of Technology in Small and Large Firms: Grain-Milling in Tanzania, *World Development*, 20 (1), 1992.

Bagachwa, M.S.D., Luvanga, N.E. and Mjema, G.D., A Study on Non-Traditional Exports. Report to the Government of Tanzania and the World Bank, 1990.

Bhaghwati, J., Outward Orientation; Trade Issues, in Corbo, V., Goldstein M. and Khan, M., (eds), *Growth-oriented Adjustment Programs*, Washington, D.C., IMF/World Bank, 1987

British Textile Technology Centre (BTTG), Industrial Rehabilitation Study of the Textile Sub-sector of Tanzania. Report to the Ministry of Industries and Trade, Dar es Salaam, 1990.

Cooper, C., Are Innovation Studies on Industrialized Economies Relevant to Technology Policy in Developing Countries? Paper presented to INTECH Seminar, January 1992.

Ernst, D. and O'Connor, D.O., *Technology and Global Competition*, Paris: OECD, 1989.

Helleiner, G.K., Outward Orientation, Import Instability and African Economic Growth: An Empirical Investigation'. In Lall, S. and Stewart, F., (eds), *Theory and Reality in Development, Essays in Honour of Paul Streeten*, London, Macmillan, 1986.

INTERMACOS, Tanzania Northern Electrical Manufacturers Limited. Report on the Review of Operations (August), Arusha, 1991.

Islam, N. and Subramanian, A., Agricultural Exports of Developing Countries: Estimates of Income and Price Elasticities of Demand and Supply, *Journal of Agricultural Economics*, 40 (2), 1989.

Jacobsson, S. and Alam, G., *Liberalization and Industrial Development in the Third World: A Study of Government Policy and Performance of the Indian and Korean Engineering Industries*, (forthcoming).

Katz, J., (ed.), *Technology Generation in Latin American Manufacturing Industries*, London, Macmillan, 1987.

Krueger, A.O., *Liberalization Attempts and Consequences*, New York: National Bureau of Economic Research, 1978.

Lall, S., *Learning to Industrialize*, London: Macmillan, 1987.

Lall, S., Structural Problems of African Industry', in Stewart, F., Lall, S. and Wangwe, S.M., (eds), *Alternative Development Strategies in Sub-Saharan Africa*, London, Macmillan, 1992.

Lall, S., Navaretti, G.B. and Wignaraja, G., The Dynamics of Enterprise Development in Africa, World Bank RPED Study Concept Paper, Oxford, Oxford University, mimeo, 1991.

Mbelle, A.V.Y., Efficiency Performance Under Structural Adjustment Programmes: The Case of Textile Manufacturing in Tanzania, *Tanzania Journal of Economics*, Vol. 2 (1), 1990.

Mbelle, A.V.Y., Restructuring the Public Textile Industry in Tanzania: Nature and Prospects. In Bagachwa, M.S.D., Mbelle, A.V.Y. and van Arkadie, Brian (eds), *Market Reforms and Parastatal Restructuring in Tanzania*, Dar es Salaam, Economics Department, ERB, 1992.

Mbelle A.V.Y. and Sterner, T., Foreign Exchange and Industrial Development: A Frontier Production Function Analysis of Two Tanzanian Industries, *World Development*, 19 (4), 1991.

Mlawa, H.M., The Acquisition of Technological Capability and Technical Change: A Study of Textile Industry in Tanzania. Doctoral dissertation, University of Sussex, Brighton, 1983.

Ndulu, B.J. and Semboja, J., The Development of Manufacturing for Export in Tanzania Experience, Policy and Prospects. Dar es Salaam, mimeo, 1992.

Nelson, A. and Persson, H., The Tanzanian Textile Industry: Is there a Connection between Organizational Structure, Environment and Effectiveness? Unpublished MBA Thesis, Department of Management and Economics, University of Linköping, 1992.

Nelson, R.R. and S.J. Winter, S.J., *An Evolutionary Theory of Economic Change*, Cambridge, Mass., Harvard University Press, 1982.

Pack, H. and L.E. Westphal L.E., Industrial Strategy and Technological Change: Theory Versus Reality, *Journal of Development Economics*, 22, 1986.

Rati, R., Exports and Economic Growth: Some Additional Evidence, *Economic Development and Cultural Change*, 33, 1985.

Shaaeldin, E., Manufactured Exports from Sub-Sahara Africa: Performance, Constraints and Prospects. Economic Research Paper, No. 14, Abidjan, African Development Bank, 1991.

Stewart, F., Lall, S. and Wangwe, S.M., (eds), *Alternative Development Strategies in Sub-Saharan Africa*, London, Macmillan, 1992.

UNCTAD, *Handbook of International Trade and Development Statistics*, New York, UNCTAD, 1990.

United Republic of Tanzania, *Economic Survey 1991*, Dar es Salaam, Planning Commission, June 1992.

United Republic of Tanzania, *Economic Survey 1992*, Dar es Salaam, Planning Commission, June 1993.

United Republic of Tanzania, Ministry of Industries and Trade, 1993/94 Budget Speech, Dar es Salaam, July 1993.

University of Dar es Salaam (Economic Research Bureau), *Tanzania Economic Trends*, 4 (3), October 1991.

University of Dar es Salaam (Economic Research Bureau), *Tanzania Economic Trends*, 4 (4), January 1992.

Valk, P., de, and Mbelle, A.V.Y., *Textile Industry under Structural Adjustment in Tanzania 1980–1990*, The Hague and Dar es Salaam, Institute of Social Studies, Department of Economics, 1990.

Valk, P., de, *A General Framework for Evaluating the Performance of Textile Enterprises in LDCs, with an Application to Tanzania under Structural Adjustment*, The Hague, Institute of Social Studies, 1992.

Wangwe, S., Building Indigenous Technological Capacity: A Study of Selected Industries in Tanzania, in Stewart, F., Lall, S. and Wangwe, S.M, (eds), *Alternative Development Strategies in Sub-Saharan Africa*, London, Macmillan, 1992.

Wangwe, S.M. and Bagachwa, M.S.D., Impact of Economic Policies on Technological Choice and Development in Tanzanian Industry, in Stewart, F., Thomas, Henk and de Wilde, Ton, (eds), *The Other Policy*, London and Washington, D.C., IT Publications, 1990.

Weiss, J., *Industry in Developing Countries: Theory, Policy and Evidence*, London and New York, Routledge, 1988.

World Bank, Towards Sustainable Development in the 1990s, Report No. 9352-TA, Vol. II, Washington D.C., World Bank, 1991.

9   Nigeria

Oluremi Ogun

INTRODUCTION

This report focuses on Nigeria, as a case study within the context of an Africa-wide analysis of new technologies and export-oriented growth. The introductory section provides information on the structural composition of the economy, the composition and destination of exports, the relationship between the economic environment and industrial policies and export incentives and institutions. This is followed by three sections giving the results of a survey of three major manufacturing sub-sectors which engage in exporting: textiles, brewing, and food and beverages.

Structure of the economy

Before the oil boom of the 1970s, the Nigerian economy could be described as predominantly agrarian, with agriculture accounting for an average of over 60 per cent of its national output between 1950 and 1965. The oil boom transformed the economy drastically: by 1985 agriculture was 26 per cent of GDP, while oil and mining, which had contributed only about 1 per cent of GDP in 1960, accounted for about 20 per cent. The detailed picture of the transformation which occurred in this period can be gauged from Table 9.1. In brief, manufacturing has experienced rather sluggish growth since around 1970, while infrastructure and services appear to have experienced persistent growth interrupted only by the economic recession of the 1980s. Another marked trend is the general improvement in agriculture's share of GDP since 1985, standing at about 40 per cent in 1990. Over the same period, oil and mining fell to about 14 per cent of GDP, while infrastructure and services appear to stabilize at lower levels of about 9 per cent and 28 per cent, respectively, between 1987 and 1990.

Table 9.1 Distribution of gross domestic product in Nigeria for selected years (%)

Sector	1960	1965	1970	1975	1980	1985	1987*	1990
Agriculture	64.1	55.4	44.7	26.5	21.1	26.6	40.2	40.8
Oil and mining	1.2	4.7	11.9	23.9	24.1	19.8	13.4	13.8
Manufacturing	4.8	7.0	7.5	4.5	8.9	9.3	9.7	8.5
Infrastructure	8.9	10.4	9.1	15.4	17.6	12.8	8.0	8.6
Services	21.0	22.5	26.8	29.7	28.3	31.5	28.7	28.3
Total	100	100	100	100	100	100	100	100
Value (₦m)	2 493.4	3 146.8	4 219.0	26 283.3	30 808.3	26 159.0	79 270.0	89 100.0

Sources: Central Bank of Nigeria, *Annual Report* and *Statement of Accounts*, various issues

Note * The naira value of GDP since 1987 reflects a significant policy shift, with the adoption of an extensive liberalization policy.

Except for the 1980s, when the economy experienced zero average growth, the general growth in real output has been impressive, averaging 6 per cent and 5 per cent respectively in the 1960s and 1970s. Oil and mining grew the fastest between 1960 and 1990, at an average rate of 11 per cent, with manufacturing averaging about 6 per cent, agriculture and services about 3 per cent and infrastructure at –0.2 per cent. The oil boom of the 1970s tremendously influenced the growth of the oil sector, which achieved an unprecedented growth rate of about 47 per cent, at a time when agriculture was contracting by about 2 per cent annually.

Composition and destination of exports

Nigeria's exports have always been mostly unprocessed raw materials but their composition has by no means remained unaltered. As can be seen from Table 9.2, food and inedible crude materials dominated the export structure in the 1950s. Their shares of total exports declined markedly after 1960, and by 1985 their export shares had become virtually insignificant. The export share of animal and vegetable oils and fats followed a similar trend. In contrast, exports of mineral fuels and related materials rose from an insignificant level in the 1950s to dominate the export structure in the 1980s. Manufactured exports grew impressively in the 1960s after a stagnant period in the 1950s, but then fell persistently in the 1970s, recording only slight improvements in the 1980s.

A sharper picture of these changes is revealed by Table 9.3, which classifies exports according to economic sectors. Agriculture's share of total exports declined persistently between 1960 and 1980, with a somewhat sluggish recovery thereafter. On the other hand, oil and mining's share of total exports generally increased over the same period. Manufacturing's export share fluctuated widely but declined fairly constantly in the 1970s and the early 1980s.

A closer look at the composition of the manufacturing sector, as in Table 9.4, reveals changes over time. For example, manufactured and semi-manufactured agricultural products, principally cocoa butter, cake and powder, groundnut cake (until 1977), cocoa liquor and cocoa kernel expellers (both in 1985 and 1986 only), palm kernel expellers, oil and pallets (all three, only in 1985 and 1986) dominated the structure of manufactured exports until the late 1980s when a new entry, textiles, temporarily took the lead, after which another new entry, chemicals, took over in the 1990s.

Table 9.2 Exports by commodity groups in selected years

Commodity group	1950 ₦'m	1950 %	1955 ₦'m	1955 %	1960 ₦'m	1960 %	1965 ₦'m	1965 %	1970 ₦'m	1970 %	1975 ₦'m	1975 %	1980 ₦'m	1980 %	1985 ₦'m	1985 %
Food	58.4	33.0	61.1	23.5	86.0	26.0	99.4	18.9	167.7	19.1	216.8	4.4	221.1	1.6	243.8	2.1
Beverages and tobacco	0.1	0.1	0.2	0.1	0.04	*	0.08	*	0.01	*	–	–	0.01	*	–	–
Crude materials (inedible) except fuels	92.9	52.5	160.3	61.7	188.7	57.0	200.4	38.1	122.8	14.0	57.7	1.2	44.0	0.3	15.2	0.1
Mineral fuels, lubricants and related materials	–	–	0.5	0.2	9.1	2.7	136.2	25.9	510.0	58.1	4 590.1	93.3	13 330.7	97.4	11 335.8	96.7
Animal and vegetable oils and fats	24.2	13.7	32.6	12.6	38.6	11.7	48.5	9.2	32.9	3.8	11.4	0.2	15.9	0.1	0.4	*
Chemicals	0.2	0.1	0.3	0.1	0.4	0.1	0.1	*	0.3	*	1.2	*	0.9	*	1.4	*
Manufactured goods (classified by materials)	0.9	0.5	2.4	0.9	3.0	0.9	35.4	6.7	39.1	4.5	27.5	0.6	17.5	0.1	6.3	0.1
Machinery and transport equipment	–	–	–	–	–	–	–	–	–	–	–	–	0.6	*	0.8	*
Miscellaneous manufactured goods	–	–	0.02	*	0.01	*	0.1	*	0.2	*	0.1	*	0.5	*	–	–
Miscellaneous exports	0.2	0.1	2.3	0.9	5.3	1.6	6.1	1.2	4.1	0.5	15.4	0.3	56.2	0.5	114.2	1.0
Total	176.9	100	259.7	100	331.1	100	526.4	100	877.1	100	4 920.2	100	13 687.4	100	11 717.9	100

Source: Federal Office of Statistics, *Digest of Statistics*, various issues

Note: – Negligible amount. * Zero entry.

Table 9.5 shows that the developed countries of the West and Japan bought over 90 per cent of Nigeria's total exports in 1989. The European Community's (now EU's) importance has been falling, and that of the US and the ECOWAS (Economic Community of West African States) countries rising, since the late 1980s.

The economic environment and industrial policies

Two major economic problems confronted Nigeria at the time of independence in 1960. These are (1) the near absence of industrial structures in the economy and (2) a deteriorating balance of payments position which had emerged from the continuous imbalance between the rate of growth of imports and the rate of growth of exports. Nigeria explicitly adopted an import-substitution industrialization strategy in 1961, in line with its economic objectives.[1] The assumption behind this policy appears to have been that import substitution (IS) would reduce the amount of imports necessary to maintain output at any given level and thereby help to conserve foreign exchange. Import substitution was also expected to speed up industrialization as more industrial activities would be performed domestically.

The main instrument employed under the policy was tariff protection, variously combined with quantitative restrictions and industrial incentives. Before independence, tariffs had been used mainly as a means of generating revenue. They now became the main instrument for solving the balance of payments problem and protecting domestic industry. Tariff rates were raised substantially on increasing numbers of finished goods, while duties on imported raw materials and capital equipment were reduced (Ogun, 1987).[2] Import licensing requirements, which were already in place at the time of independence, were used to restrict further the importation of some finished goods. By the end of the 1960s, imports of capital equipment and raw materials constituted over 70 per cent of the country's total imports, as compared to less than 50 per cent in 1960.

As a result, the rate of growth of imports actually fell towards the end of the 1960s. The number of industrial activities performed domestically witnessed an impressive growth. However, one major failing of this industrialization strategy was already becoming evident. It had been hoped that import substitution would reduce the volume of imports, thereby conserving foreign exchange. This, however, did not come to pass. The newly established import substituting industries (ISIs) were making increasing demands on foreign reserves.

Table 9.3 Exports by economic sectors in selected years (%)

Sector	1950	1955	1960	1965	1970	1975	1980	1985	1990
Agriculture	92.1	89.0	89.7	60.6	33.0	5.5	2.0	2.2	2.6
Oil and mining	7.2	9.1	7.8	31.5	62.0	93.6	97.4	96.7	97.0
Manufacturing	0.5	0.9	0.9	6.8	4.5	0.6	0.1	0.1	0.2
Others	0.2	1.0	1.7	1.1	0.5	0.3	0.3	1.0	0.2
Total (%)	100	100	100	100	100	100	100	100	100
Value (US$m)	253	371	475	752	1 240	8 001	25 946	12 548	13 671

Sources: Federal Office of Statistics, *Digest of Statistics*, various issues; Central Bank of Nigeria, *Annual Report* and *Statement of Accounts*, various issues; *International Financial Statistics*, various issues

Table 9.4 Composition of manufactured exports (%)

Sector	1975	1980	1985	1989	1990	1991
Manufactures and semi-manufactures of agricultural products:						
Cocoa butter	37.9	28.2	67.8	34.9	13.7	9.0
Cocoa powder	0.6	6.0	–	–	–	–
Cocoa cake	7.8	5.8	–	–	–	–
Cocoa paste	–	–	–	–	–	–
Cocoa liquor	–	–	5.5	–	–	–
Cocoa kernel expellers	–	–	14.6	–	–	–
Palm kernel expellers	–	–	5.2	–	–	–
Palm kernel oil	–	–	5.2		–	–
Palm kernel pallets	–	–	1.6	–	–	–
Groundnut cake	1.1	–	–	–	–	–
Wood products	–	–	–	4.2	3.4	8.7
Textiles	–	–	–	43.9	13.1	29.4
Chemicals	–	–	–	–	18.8	38.2
Tin metals	37.9	20.0	–	2.0	0.7	1.2
Precious metals	–	–	–	0.4	–	–
Other manufactures	14.7	40.0	–	14.7	50.3	13.6
Total (%)	100	100	99.9*	100.1*	100	100.1*
Value (₦m)	53.8	71.0	69.0	291.4	784.8	781.5

Source: Central Bank of Nigeria, *Annual Report* and *Statement of Accounts*, various issues

Note: * Rounding error.

Table 9.5 Total exports by destination, 1980–89 (%)

Period	EEC	US	Japan	ECOWAS	Others	Total
1980	50.4	33.2	no data	1.7	14.7	100
1981	50.5	29.3	1.5	4.4	14.3	100
1982	41.8	34.8	0.1	2.4	20.9	100
1983	59.0	21.6	0.1	2.8	16.5	100
1984	62.7	13.3	0.1	4.5	19.4	100
1985	66.2	18.1	0.1	3.5	12.1	100
1986	47.8	35.0	0.1	3.9	13.2	100
1987	41.9	47.0	0.1	6.2	4.8	100
1988	36.3	49.8	0.2	7.0	6.7	100
1989	38.5	51.1	2.7	7.0	0.7	100
Average	49.5	33.3	0.6	4.3	12.3	100

Source: Nigerian Export–Import Bank, *1991 Annual Report & Statement of Accounts*

The problem was compounded by the inefficiency inherent in tariff protection, which made it difficult for domestic industries to acquire the capability needed for competition in foreign markets.

In addition, the exchange rate policy had by the late 1960s become protectionist and by the early 1970s the domestic currency was over-valued. The country twice refused to devalue in tandem with the devaluations of the British pound and the US dollar, to which its currency had been tied.[3] These protectionist policies led to an outflow of foreign exchange. As a result, the balance of payments was negative for the greater part of the 1960s.

The main lesson that emerged from the economic policies implemented in this period was the need for an ample supply of foreign exchange in order to prosecute a programme of import substitution successfully. The negative effects of these policies were, however, effectively cushioned by the oil boom that was to commence in 1973.

The primary effect of the boom of 1973–80 was the flow of huge foreign exchange resources (over US$100 billion) into the country. Naturally, the government hoped to quicken the pace of economic development on the one hand and achieve a reasonable degree of economic independence on the other hand. Accordingly, overly ambitious economic programmes were designed and implemented. An indigenization programme was carried out in 1974 and, together with further phases which were implemented before 1980, it resulted in Nigerians taking over the control of several businesses hitherto controlled by foreigners.

It would appear that the policy-makers overlooked the economic side-effects of the indigenization programme, especially its possible negation of the goal of economic independence. The ISIs which had been established were acquiring the capability to manufacture for export, but this development was thwarted by the manpower dislocation caused by the indigenization programme. Several of the newly established activities experienced manpower problems and several of them failed as a result.

The expanded oil exports allowed the government to reduce its reliance on tariff imposition to generate revenue and solve its balance of payments problems. In this period, the principal purpose of tariffs appeared to be the need to protect domestic industries. Even the emergence of a serious balance of payments disequilibrium in 1976 (which persisted till 1978) did not alter this policy. Rather than impose higher tariff rates, the government opted for quantitative restrictions in the form of import licensing and import bans. However, whatever benefits might have resulted from the lower nominal tariff rates of the period were effectively reversed by the gross over-valuation of the currency. Net effective rates of protection for all activities (except those processing imported raw materials) were negative in the period.[4] Worse still, export-oriented industries were the most adversely affected.

The end of the oil boom around 1980 led to a significant moderation in the economic environment and hence in industrial policy. The basic policy of import substitution was still in place but the extent of use of tariffs and quantitative restrictions was unprecedented. Rather than aiming at industrial growth, the targets were the deepening balance of payments crisis, falling foreign exchange receipts and trade payments problems. The various foreign exchange conservation measures implemented in the period 1982–85 led to several of the industries dependent on imported inputs having to operate considerably below capacity, hence reduced growth and worsening unemployment.

The adoption of the structural adjustment programme (SAP) in 1986 introduced yet another industrial policy regime. The programme represented a fundamental shift in the basic philosophy of economic management at the national level. The SAP was continued in a three-year Economic Consolidation and Expansion Programme (ECEP). Under the new dispensation, export promotion was a major policy focus. And, as a major aim of the new management philosophy was to eliminate, or at least reduce, economic distortions and the bias against tradeable goods, intervention has been reduced and import protection lowered. The reforms include the adoption of a largely market-determined exchange rate and the removal or relaxation of quantitative restrictions on many tradable goods. An exchange rate auction market was established in 1986, a period which also witnessed the abolition of the import licensing requirement. In 1987, a preliminary import tariff and excise taxes review led to the establishment of an interim customs tariff and excise tax systems. These efforts created a substantially more liberal trading environment. Exchange rate over-valuation seems to have been checked, import tariffs are generally lower than the country has experienced since independence and, while quantitative restrictions are still in place, their scope has been considerably narrowed.

It is clear from the foregoing that export promotion, as a policy focus in Nigeria, is a relatively recent phenomenon. Hence, most firms operating in the export market have relatively short export histories.

Export incentives and institutions

Export incentives

Following the explicit adoption of export promotion as the industrialization policy in 1986, a significant number of incentives for exports were introduced and incentives already in existence but not operative were reactivated. All are described in the Export Incentives and Miscellaneous Provision Decree No. 18 of 1986. The relevant incentive structures are as outlined below:

- *Currency retention scheme*: Exporters are allowed to operate special foreign currency domiciliary accounts for export receipts and payments. However, transfers out of the account for whatever purpose are subject to prescribed documentation requirements. The scheme allows for proper monitoring of non-oil export proceeds and easier funding of export-oriented business trips, trade missions, trade fairs, export market research and test marketing. Up to 10 per cent of export proceeds in the case of manufactured goods (5 per cent for primary and semi-processed products) can be readily utilized for such purposes.
- *Export licence waiver*: No export licence is required for the export of manufactured or processed products. Also, exports have been exempted from tax.

- *Export Development Fund (EDF)*: This is a special fund provided by the government to give financial assistance to exporting companies to cover part of their initial expenses for export promotion activities.
- *Export Expansion Grant Fund (EEGF)*: The fund is to provide cash inducements for exporters who have exported a minimum of ₦50 000 worth of semi-manufactured or manufactured products. The incentive element lies in the graduation of the grant according to their volume of export sales.
- *Duty Draw Back, Duty Suspension and Manufacture in Bond Schemes*: The Duty Draw Back Scheme provides for the refund of duties on raw materials including packaging and packing materials. The Duty Suspension Scheme provides exemption from duty on such imports. The Manufacture in Bond Scheme allows imported raw materials to be held in a bonded warehouse for export production.
- *Export Adjustment Scheme Fund*: This serves as a supplementary export subsidy to compensate exporters for:
  (a) high costs of production arising from infrastructural deficiencies;
  (b) purchasing commodities at prices higher than prevailing world market prices but fixed by government;
  (c) other factors beyond the control of the exporter.
- *Pioneer status*: Any manufacturer who exports at least 50 per cent of annual turnover qualifies for pioneer status and accordingly enjoys generous tax holidays and concessions.
- *Tax relief on interest income*: Interest accruing from loans granted by banks for export activities is exempt from tax. With respect to foreign loans, tax exemption on the interest is scaled according to the duration of the loan.
- *Export credit guarantee and insurance scheme*: This helps Nigerian products compete effectively in the international market and insures genuine exporters against some political and other risks including default in payment. Also, under the scheme, exporters can grant their customers some credit facilities.
- *Capital assets depreciation allowances*: This is an additional annual capital allowance of 5 per cent on plant and machinery for manufacturing exporters who export at least 50 per cent of their annual turnover, provided that the product has at least 4 per cent local raw material content or 35 per cent value added.
- *Rediscounting of short-term bills*: This schemes makes provision for exporters of any product to discount their bills of exchange

and promissory notes with their banks in order to increase their liquidity and minimize cash flow problems before the realization of export proceeds from the overseas importer. This facility applies to all export products.

In addition to the incentives discussed above, government abolished export licensing in 1987 to remove some of the administrative bottlenecks. An export processing zone was established in 1991 and an export–import bank began operations in the same year.

The incentives, laudable though they may be, do not seem to be totally effective. The reason appears to be the usual bureaucratic and administrative bottlenecks which have tended to delay the implementation of some, while reducing the extent of usage of others. For example, the Manufacture in Bond Scheme did not take off in 1991 as planned although it had been drawn up two years previously. Similarly, the Duty Draw Back Scheme, though it paid about ₦11 million to about 67 beneficiaries in 1991, is marked by long delays in effecting refunds. The Manufacturers' Association of Nigeria (MAN) has claimed that the scheme has no positive effect on the costing of export products. It appears that the best utilized of the direct incentives is the Export Credit Refinancing and Rediscounting Facility (RRF), under which over ₦2 billion was disbursed in 1991.

Export institutions

Many institutions had been concerned with export activities in the past. However, the most active are currently the Nigerian Export Promotion Council, the Manufacturers' Export Group and the Nigerian Export–Import Bank:

- *The Nigerian Export Promotion Council (NEPC)*: The NEPC was established in 1976 and formally inaugurated in 1977. Its enabling Act was amended in 1979 and later reorganized into the NEPC Decree of 1988. The Decree was aimed at giving the Council both structural and functional responsibilities for spearheading and sustaining a dynamic export drive and implementing various incentive packages contained in the Export Incentives and Miscellaneous Decree No. 18 of 1986. Essentially, the operations of the Council were restructured to reduce bureaucratic red tape. The activities of the Council in promoting Nigerian exports abroad can be summarized as follows:
  (a) It interacts closely with exporters at the level of education and advice. It organizes seminars, conferences and workshops

to create awareness of facilities, support services and procedures in the export field.

(b) It helps to expose exporters to international markets through
exhibitions and surveys of export market potential and the
export markets in communities such as ECOWAS, the EU
and countries such as Kenya, Zambia, Zimbabwe and Uganda.

(c) In conjunction with relevant government agencies such as the
Central Bank (CBN), the Standard Organization of Nigeria
(SON) and the Ministry of Industry, Budget and Planning, it
administers facilities such as the Duty Draw Back Scheme,
the EDF and the EEGF.

(d) It influences policy through recommendations to the government. Such recommendations are usually informed by the
experience and knowledge acquired through interaction with
exporters and international markets.

(e) It presently cooperates with the Raw Materials Research and
Development Council (RMRDC) to see how the manufacturing sector can process primary products such as cocoa and
rubber locally, in order to ensure that they have improved
value added on international markets.

- *The Manufacturers' Export Group (MEG)*: MEG is an arm of
the MAN and operates purely as a pressure group seeking
to influence policy impinging on manufactured exports. Its recommendations (to the government) in this regard usually derive from
the experience of its members. Recently, it issued a position paper
on export-related issues in which it calls for the abolition of the
Export Price Clearance Scheme because it is a disincentive
to export growth. It also recommends restructuring the Duty Draw
Back Scheme so that it can positively influence exporters' costs.
It suggests that, instead of the present practice of refunding
the cost of imported inputs to export manufacturers (which invari-
ably takes an unusually long period), the draw back should be
treated at each year-end as a tax exemption. In its opinion, this
would ensure that exporters push for quick repatriation
of proceeds and many more will be encouraged to export through
the banking system so as to qualify for this rebate. The refund
can then have a positive impact on the costing of the manufactured product, thereby making the product more competitive.

- *The Nigerian Export–Import Bank (NEXIM)*: NEXIM began
operation in 1991. Its objective is to provide export credit guarantees and insurance to exporters. With less than two years
of operation, it has managed to become the most important and

perhaps the most active export institution in the country. As at December 1991 it operates the following schemes and facilities: the RRF, a foreign input facility (FIF), raw materials stocking facility, two reserve facilities and export advisory and education services. Apart from the RRF and FIF, which were carry-overs from the activities of its precursor, the Nigerian Export Credit Guarantee Corporation, the rest were newly introduced in 1991. The Bank appears to have had a successful 1991, as total disbursement under its various facilities were: RRF₦2 billion; FIF₦99 million; Repurchase Facility US$4 million. Total operating profit in 1991 was in the region of ₦133 million. Its funds are principally from its shareholders, the Federal Government and the CBN, as well as multilateral agencies such as the African Development Bank.

TEXTILES

Background

The textiles industry of Nigeria is the third largest in Africa after Egypt and South Africa.[5] The industry, which currently accounts for about 25 per cent of manufacturing value added, has passed through various phases of growth. IS policies induced steady growth in the 1960s, which gave way to rapid growth, averaging 12.5 per cent, in the 1970s when the economy was booming. The recession of the early to mid-1980s took its toll: the cumulative textile production index (1972 = 100) declined from 427.1 in 1982 to 171.1 in 1984. The industry recovered in the late 1980s, achieving an annual growth of about 67 per cent between 1985 and 1991, with synthetic textiles alone accounting for about 80 per cent of the recorded growth.

The industry is the largest employer of labour in the manufacturing sector. It currently accounts for about 25 per cent of total manufacturing employment. Capacity utilization improved between 1986 and 1991. And, with the backward integration programme instituted by many firms in the industry following the strict government directive on the issue in the mid-1980s, the level of domestic sourcing of raw materials was put at about 64 per cent in 1991, a steady improvement from 52 per cent in 1987 and 57 per cent in 1988.

The industry is mainly controlled by large private-sector firms, often with substantial foreign participation. Nigerian law has limited this to 60 per cent of the total equity of textile sector firms but the drive for more capital inflow under the present management philosophy may lead to an upward revision of the ceiling. The major foreign investors within the industry are from Hong Kong, India, the UK, Liechtenstein, the Netherlands, the US, Japan and Columbia.

Current information on installed machinery is not available but, as at 1987, the 37 textile firms in the country were operating 716 000 spindles and 17 541 looms. However the output of the sector has never exceeded 55 per cent of annual domestic consumption, allowing for a thriving trade in imported (mostly smuggled) textiles.

Technological gaps in the industry are illustrated by the fact that 12 mills, representing 61 per cent of the total capacity, spin only cotton. Although nearly 25 per cent of existing mills are integrated mills, modernization of spinning capacity is generally lagging behind technological improvements in the weaving mills. Labour productivity in spinning operations is not high because of low capacity utilization and inadequate provision for on-the-job training.

Low productivity levels limit export possibilities. Nevertheless, the substantially liberated economic environment and the opportunity Nigeria offers to avoid quota restrictions under the Multi Fibre Agreement (MFA) – which is not applicable to Nigeria – have induced some foreign entrepreneurs, mostly from Asian countries, to establish export-oriented plants.

History of firms in the sample

Origin, ownership and structure

The two firms covered by the survey show similarities in ownership structure and, to some extent, achievements but they differ considerably in age, scope of operation and export experience. Aflon Nigeria PLC (ANPLC) was incorporated in 1985 but commenced operation in April 1988. It is a wholly owned subsidiary of Afprint Nigeria PLC, a textile company which in turn is part of the worldwide Kewalram/Chanrai group, which has business interests and social commitments in North America, the UK, West Africa and South and East Asia.

Spintex Mills (Nigeria) Limited (SMNL) was established in 1980 and began commercial operation in June 1982. It is a 100 per cent subsidiary of Sunflag (Nigeria) Limited, a textile company which manufactures knitted fabrics and ready-made garments, with substantial interests in Kenya, Tanzania, Cameroon, India and the UK.

Both ANPLC and SMNL were conceived of as the means of meeting the yarn requirements of their parent companies. SMNL's establishment was influenced by the announced intention of the Nigerian government in 1979 of not only discouraging the importation of yarn but also imposing a blanket ban on it. Both firms have achieved such tremendous expansion that they now export yarn as well as selling on the local market. Both companies have at different times been accorded pioneer status, which entitles them to a 5-year tax holiday under the provisions of the Industrial Development (Income Tax Relief) Decree (1971). Since they were both set up in compliance with the provisions of the Nigeria Enterprises Promotions Decree of 1977 there is a considerable Nigerianization of manpower in both organizations.

Each of the companies is run by a policy board and a professional management team. The ANPLC policy board comprises four members, of whom three are expatriates. Two of the five board members in SMNL are Nigerians. The professional management team of ANPLC consists of the mill manager, the chief engineer, the development manager and the spinning technologist, along with the personnel manager, the accountant and 13 other senior staff in the areas of production, engineering and administration. In the case of SMNL, the management team comprises the managing director, financial director, chief technological executor, export manager, finance controller, two mill managers, personnel manager, chief accountant, chief of shipping, chief of banking and marketing officers.

Performance and development

Since its inception, ANPLC has focused exclusively on the production of cotton yarn, dividing its yarn output simply between finer and coarser counts. Its success story is reflected in the statistics provided in Table 9.6, which reflects astronomic growth in the asset base and modest but respectable growth in sales turnover, operating profit and the number of employees.

Cotton lint remains the only raw material. The company is able to obtain sufficient virgin cotton of the required quality locally to meet 25–35 per cent of its requirement for exports and all of its requirement for domestic sales. The balance of its export requirement comes from imports, on which the company enjoys a Duty Draw Back benefit.

The SMNL appears to be at least a step ahead of ANPLC, having successfully diversified its output. It now produces spun cotton, synthetic yarns, polyester filament yarn and sewing thread for domestic and industrial purposes. The plant for the manufacture of polyester filament yarn was commissioned in 1985 and that for sewing thread in 1988. Because of its diversified output, more types of input are used in the production process. The main types are polifis cotton, polyester chips, polyester fibre, viscose fibre, coning oil and spin finish oil. Apart from cotton, polyester fibre and viscose fibre, which were used in the production process between 1981 and 1986, the others were later additions, used in polyester filament yarn and sewing thread. Of all the raw materials, only polifis cotton is supplied by both the local and import markets. All the other raw materials are imported.

Table 9.7 illustrates the growth of the company, which has achieved even more resounding success than ANPLC as turnover, asset level and employees have all grown tremendously.

Table 9.6 Performance indicators for ANPLC

	1989	1990	1991	1992
Turnover	49.0	63.3	60.9	101.5
Operating profit (₦m)	n.a.	0.8	0.12	2.25
Total assets (₦m)	9.0	6.1	39.3	92.9
Employees	137	139	152	166

Source: Company records

Table 9.7 Performance indicators of SMNL

	1983	1985	1990	1992
Turnover (₦m)	8.7	59.5	349.0	716.0
Total assets (₦m)	16.0	11.0	174.6	304.3
Employees	250	480	909	1 834

Source: Company records

Export history and performance

ANPLC's export activities began in 1991 with export sales of US$1.6 million or ₦16 million. This rose to $4 million or ₦51 million in 1992. Cotton yarn is the company's sole export item. The market channels used by the company are agents which are its associate companies and which bear all risks relating to credit. The target market is the developed countries of Europe and North America, with France, Belgium, Germany, Italy, the UK and the US constituting the major focus.

SMNL entered the export market for the first time in 1987 with cotton yarn and polyester filament yarn. Sewing thread joined the list in 1988. The export sales in 1987 amounted to US$784 464. This rose and fell sharply in succeeding years, with as little as $25 912 in 1988 and as much as $4.3 million in 1992. In the years in which there was a drastic fall in export value, i.e. 1988 and 1989, the company was actually withdrawing from the export market. Company sources explain this move in terms of the relatively lower profitability of export business *vis-à-vis* the domestic market, which was experiencing a chronic shortage of yarn in the period. The export arm of the company was reactivated in 1990 following the massive depreciation of the Naira, which significantly improved the profitability of the export sector. The company also saw the development of its export business as a way of widening the market segment of its products and as a long-term development strategy.

The company employs two market channels for its export business. The first is the use of export agents in connection with export sales to the UK. These agents often assist in distributing to other European countries. The second channel is direct sales to buyers in Cameroon, Italy and Belgium. In this case, the company establishes the link with customers through embassies and chambers of commerce.

External factors affecting export growth

Finance

The problem here is one not of access but rather of affordability. Companies cannot afford high-level exposure in the conventional loan market because of the unusually high lending rates, which have not fallen below 45 per cent for over a year now. Assistance with finance usually takes the form of a soft loan from the parent company and a special export financing scheme such as the African Development Bank's sponsored Export Stimulation Loan (ADB/ESL), which is administered in Nigeria by NEXIM. However, occasional long application processing times at NEXIM often reduce the attractiveness and benefits of loans under such special financing schemes.

Raw materials

Domestic cotton-seed production in the country has continued to be inadequate for domestic demand. The domestic cotton output fell from 82 000 tonnes in 1976/77 to 19 900 metric tons in 1982/83. The present level is an estimated one-tenth of that achieved during the mid-1970s. Given the continuous expansion of the activities of existing firms and the growing list of new entries into the industry (the country now has over 46 large textile firms, as opposed to fewer than 35 in 1980), there is obviously price pressure. This implies increasing costs of production as imports are very expensive under the present exchange rate regime.

ANPLC used to meet a substantial proportion of its local cotton requirement from its sister company, Afcolt Nigeria Limited, which engaged in cotton-seed contract farming. However, the Afcolt experiment was halted some time ago due to accumulated losses. In essence, ANPLC, like SMNL, now procures its cotton from the open market and through importation. SMNL is in a more exposed position, as virtually all of its major production inputs, including over 50 per cent of its cotton requirements, are imported.

Inflation

The country's current inflation is unprecedented in its 33 years of independence. Available statistics put the current price inflation at about 50 per cent. Almost every aspect of the operations of the firms – labour, raw materials, utilities, equipment and rents – is affected, with the consequences eventually expressed in the cost of production.

Infrastructural bottlenecks

The infrastructural amenities in the country are in a sorry state and are grossly unreliable. As a result, both companies have had continuously to make arrangements for treated water, compressed air, standby power generation and storage and warehousing facilities.

All of these divert funds from actual operation and ultimately increase the cost of production.

Bureaucratic and policy obstacles

The primary effect of bureaucratic delays on the export activities of the two companies is to reduce the value and effectiveness of export incentives. Take, for example, the Duty Draw Back Scheme. The aim of the scheme is to reduce the overall cost of production of manufactured exports by providing for a refund of duties on raw materials, including packing materials used in the production process. In reality, it would take a very lucky firm one year after applying to get the refund. Given the volatile nature of the economy under the present management philosophy, the refund when it is eventually received is of considerably lesser value in view of the constantly rising cost of capital and continuously falling exchange rate. This has prompted SMNL to suggest that the Duty Draw Back rates should be revised in line with the change in exchange rates between the time imports are paid for and the time the refund is paid out.

Another disincentive identified by the two firms has to do with the customs officials at the point of shipment. They change the official stamps and recognized signatures used on export documents, which have been internationally approved, without informing the international bodies involved. This often leads to the rejection of a document or a considerable delay.

Technology, marketing, investment, productivity and human resources

Characteristics of demand in the target market and managerial response

Firms operating in the export market for textile products appear to be price takers, the price being determined by demand and supply factors in international markets. In the opinion of SMNL, the demand for its products will always outstrip the supply. This guarantees an increasing or at least constant market share over time. However, the ANPLC revealed that in the last two years its export selling price fell from an average of US$2.80 per kilogram to US$2.58 per kilogram, which suggests that the market could sometimes be over-supplied and the price may need to fall for the market to clear. Furthermore, an over-supplied market enables buyers to compare quality and choose from a wide range of product types. This clearly suggests the need for some elements of marketing.

The two firms have different market penetration strategies. For the ANPLC, this contains:

- credit facilities of 45–60 days.
- discounts of 3–5 per cent.
- door delivery.
- replacement of yarn where there are quality problems.
- prompt settlement of claims.

In contrast, the SMNL practises niche marketing, which entails searching for a small market that is not already penetrated by another firm, where it can operate in a seller's market. Hence it does not give any incentives other than normal quantity discounts to customers. It has no door delivery policy, leaving customers to arrange their own transportation.

Investment strategy and capability

The ANPLC's major investments have been for new plant. Decisions are usually taken on the basis of IRR (internal rate of return) and payback period selection techniques. It has adequate in-house capabilities to carry these out. The sources of finance are soft loans from the parent company, special financing facilities e.g. ADB/ESL, tax exemptions under the Pioneer status provision of Income Tax Relief and, to a lesser extent, bank credit (see pp. 262–3). It has recently been experiencing some difficulties in obtaining foreign exchange from conventional sources because of hoarding and rationing by banks. It has therefore resorted to using its export proceeds. The balance at any time is covered forward. In addition, it is considering changing its sales strategy so that only 50 per cent of export production will be sold forward and the balance will be on a spot basis.

With SMNL, investment decisions transcend new plant acquisition and include lease finance, trade (import) finance, cash management, asset management and portfolio management. Whereas asset management principally relates to the financing of the factory and equipment, portfolio management basically reflects the multinational aspect of the business whereby funds could be transferred internationally to maximize returns. Obviously, such decisions are governed by the economic climate in different countries. Like ANPLC, the SMNL has adequate in-house capability to handle the various investment issues. Its sources of funds are generally similar to ANPLC's.

Technology and productivity

Both ANPLC and SMNL have adopted modern process technology. For cotton yarn production they both use open-end spinning, otherwise known as Autocoro. This technology has several advantages when compared with conventional ring-spinning technology. First, higher production rates are made possible in this case by the use of higher rotor speeds. Second, conversion to yarn from fibre takes place in a single stage instead of the two-stage process in ring-spinning. Third, the size of the finished package is such that it can be used directly by end users without rewinding. Fourth, there is a uniform, unvarying quality. In addition, the spinning machines are fully automated from the placement of empty starter packages to the doffing of fully wound packages. Broken ends are rare and when they do occur they are detected, pieced together and restored to production by an electronically controlled robot which patrols each machine. Finally, production data is logged in a dedicated computer which produces process control reports on demand.

The preparatory capacity in the ANPLC's plant is of the order of 12 tonnes per day. With SMNL it is 16 tonnes, although the company only produces around 11 tonnes per day.

Apart from its open-end spinning process, SMNL also uses a ring-spinning process which, though it is also automated, consists of more processing stages. In addition, it uses a different process technology for the production of polyester filament textured yarn. Most of the technology used comes from Europe, with Germany and Switzerland being the main suppliers of machinery and equipment.

The measure of productivity employed by ANPLC is output per unit of marginal cost of technical production. The productivity of the firm is quite high in terms of both the local and international markets. This is primarily because its plant is fully automated.

Although the use of modern production technology by SMNL has tremendously improved its productivity in the local market, it is yet to achieve a competitive productivity level abroad. The problem lies in the increasing cost of production. In the opinion of the company:

manufacturing product of highest quality will necessitate further increases in the cost of production which may not be absorbed by the local market, which accounts for about 85 per cent of company's total produce. The local economy is not particularly quality conscious, hence there could be a backlash in demand from any attempt to pass quality-induced increases in the cost of production on to customers.

Production linkages and subcontracting

Both the ANPLC and SMNL produce their own supplies and do not subcontract production to other firms or process for other producers. Their interaction with competitors stops at the level of lobbying government on issues perceived to be crucial to the growth of the industry. Usually, such cooperation comes under the umbrella of the textile and manufacturers' group or the spinners' forum of MAN.

Both companies have binding agreements with their local raw material suppliers. In fact ANPLC distributes improved varieties of cotton seedlings to farmers to ensure a supply of appropriate quality raw materials, an arrangement that can be described as pseudo-contract farming.

Both companies have binding agreements with their equipment suppliers because of the specialized nature of the equipment, which means that spare parts can only be obtained from the suppliers.

Human resources and manpower development

The composition of manpower at ANPLC is shown in Table 9.8, which shows a pronounced jump in labour growth between 1990 and 1992, which was the most successful operating period for the company. The human development policy of the company has basically remained unchanged since its inception. It comprises a 4-week induction course for new recruits to middle or upper management, during which the employee learns to work the system. They then enjoy regular further training. General categories of staff are trained on the job, though those studying for professional examinations in their vocation are encouraged with an off-duty 'time allowance' and generous funding in the form of the refund of examination fees and books purchased. At least two technical staff are sent overseas each year for training by the manufacturer of the company's equipment. Recruitment of new employees is usually effected through a standard merit procedure involving advertisements and interviews, with outside consultants assisting.

Workers' remuneration takes the form of salaries and an end-of-year bonus. Salary increment and promotion are often tied to productivity. The general conditions of service in the organization appear reasonable, going by the practice in the industry. Workers get a free lunch, free medical attention and treatment, fairly generous housing and transport allowances and retirement benefits.

The statistics for SMNL presented in Table 9.9 suggest a more consistent growth trend in manpower. The human resources and manpower development policy of the company comprises both local and overseas training. The overseas training is usually reserved for technicians who attend the equipment supplier's training centre once every two or three years. The local training is usually meant for the office, administrative and professional workers, and consists of short and long diploma courses once every two or three years, either in-house or in organized centres such as the Kaduna Polytechnic.

Most senior management staff are from India and are usually recruited there by the company. Senior staff from the local economy are recruited by interview. In most cases, junior workers are recruited through contacts.

Table 9.8 Manpower statistics for ANPLC

	1986	1990	1992
Unskilled labour	3	5	10
Skilled labour/staff	116	116	131
Middle management	13	13	19
Upper management	5	5	6
Total	137	139	166

Source: Company records

Table 9.9 Manpower statistics for SMNL

	1985	1990	1991	1992
Unskilled labour	400	800	1 250	1 400
Skilled labour	30	35	200	350
Management	50	68	84	84
Total	480	903	1 534	1 834

Source: Company records

The remuneration system is similar to that of ANPLC, i.e. usually in the form of a salary and end-of-year-bonus. Salary increments and promotion are often tied to productivity. The general conditions of service match those of ANPLC.

BREWING

Background

The brewing industry is one of the fastest growing branches of Nigerian manufacturing.[6] It contributes about 28 per cent of MVA (Manufactured Value Added) and provides direct employment for over 30 000 persons. The indirect employment associated with the industry is close to 300 000 including the firms producing ancillary services. Beer, which is the most common product, is produced in all states of the country except Bauchi, Borno, Gongola, Niger and Sokoto.[7] There are now 32 breweries producing more than 40 brands of beer. In addition, there are five brands of stout and five brands of malt drinks. In 1987 an estimated 2 billion litres of beer were consumed in the country.

Production has grown rapidly. In the period 1980–82, brewing was the fastest growing branch of the manufacturing sector. The volume of production in 1982 was five times greater than in 1970. Even during 1982–86, when most manufacturing branches experienced severe difficulties and production levels fell significantly, the industry continued to grow slowly. Production fell marginally during 1987 and 1988 due to restrictions on the import of barley malt and problems associated with the use of locally produced substitutes. During this period, capacity utilization fell to an all-time low of about 30 per cent. Increasing success with local substitutes for barley malt has improved the capacity utilization rate to about 64 per cent in 1991.

The search for local substitutes for imported barley malt involved most of the firms in expensive experiments with research and development departments as well as substantial plant conversion expenses. Their efforts were complemented by the independent research endeavour at the Federal Institute of Industrial Research, Oshodi (FIIRO), which, through some of its research report series, demonstrated that lager beer could be produced using sorghum exclusively. Today, most of the more successful firms use maize and sorghum in their beer production process. However, the changeover in input mix has necessitated the use of expensive imported enzymes in the production process.

Description and history of the firm

Origin, ownership and structure

Nigerian Breweries Plc (NBPLC) is the country's pioneer brewery. Incorporated in 1946, it commenced production in 1949. It started as a joint venture between the United African Company (UAC) International, UK and Heineken of Holland. Thus, at inception, it was 100 per cent foreign owned. By the early 1950s, when it began operating fully, some indigenous traders already involved with its products were invited to become shareholders. Under the indigenization policy of the early 1970s the foreign shareholders were forced to sell a significant proportion of their holdings. Today, the company is 60 per cent Nigerian owned and 40 per cent foreign owned. The 60 per cent Nigerian stake is held by company employees and members of the public, while the 40 per cent foreign ownership is split almost equally between CWA Holdings Limited (for Unilever) and Heineken Brouwerijen BV.

The foreign partners now perform the role of technical advisers, with Unilever advising on commercial aspects such as accounting, purchasing, marketing and personnel, while Heineken does the same for technology. Organizationally, the company has four divisions: technical, finance, marketing and personnel, each of which is headed by an executive director.

Performance and development

At its inception in 1949, NBPLC had only Star Lager (Nigeria's first) on the market. Over the years it has broadened its product range. Except for the period 1984–86, when sales volume suffered an annual average decline of about 18 per cent, turnover growth in the company has generally been accompanied by growth in profit and production volume. Thus, when normal growth was restored in 1987, the 51 per cent and 83 per cent increases in turnover and operating profit, respectively, for 1987–88 were accompanied by about 35 per cent volume growth. Similarly, the turnover of about ₦1.7 billion recorded in 1991 was partly the result of 8 per cent growth in sales volume. However, from all indications, product pricing has been the major factor in the impressive growth in operating profits.

Table 9.10 presents indicators of the growth trend in the company. Apart from sales and profit, both net total assets and the numbers of employees have enjoyed respectable growth.

Table 9.10 Performance indicators for NBPLC

	1971	1975	1981	1985	1991
Turnover (₦m)	40.2	75.7	241.1	179.1	1 708.6
Pretax operating profit (₦m)	6.1	12.4	38.5	41.6	422.5
Net assets (₦m)	11.9	29.1	103.6	161.9	1 248.5
Employees	1 720.0	2 243.0	n.a.	3 998.0	4 297.0

Source: Company records

The deteriorating results recorded by the company in 1984–86 reflected the foreign exchange rationing policy of the period, which was necessitated by the severe balance of payments crisis of the post-oil-boom era. The import licence allocation of the company could hardly satisfy one third of its foreign exchange requirements. The government's mandatory backward integration policy in the mid-1980s saw the company establishing a 5 000-hectare farm, estimated to be worth ₦30 million, in Niger State. The farm is highly mechanized and produces mainly maize, rice and sorghum, with soya beans and cow peas as rotational crops. The main crops are used as replacements for barley malt. The changeover in input mix was assisted by the company's ₦2 million R&D facility, which was commissioned in June 1987, and plant conversion costing about ₦100 million.

The company works with highly structured plans, with annual budgets of intentions translated into explicit targets. The decision board sits towards the end of the year to deliberate on the report of each divisional head. Annual budget estimates are made in the middle of year while decisions on annual plans are left till the end of year.

The company has experienced remarkable changes in its technical capability. In 1949 it used to take between 28 and 30 days to produce a bottle of beer but with technological improvement it now takes about two weeks. The change in input content in the late 1980s also involved changes in processing technology.

Different measures of productivity are used for the technical division and other divisions. In the technical section, productivity is measured in terms of the efficiency of plant operation and also in terms of capacity utilization. In other divisions, it is in terms of the accomplishment of assigned responsibility. The company is viewed as a leader in the national industry and in Africa it enjoys a high rating, in terms of both productivity and product quality.

NBPLC concentrates on the production of its beer and related products, leaving ancillary services such as bottles, crown corks, labels, cartons and crates to be supplied by other local manufacturers. In fact, Nigerian law precludes a brewer from producing such ancillary services. Only the companies in the soft drinks industry appear to sponsor firms to produce such services. Backward integration into farming was a special concession granted to the breweries in 1984 following the stringent foreign exchange control measures introduced in that year. It also uses outside transport companies for 60 per cent of total distribution.

The company cooperates with other producers in the industry in lending materials which are urgently required. Under the umbrella of MAN, it cooperates with competitors to discuss issues affecting the industry, e.g. adverse government policy. There is no collusion with competitors in marketing and no cooperation in technical services, probably because most of the local brewers have foreign technical partners.

The prosperity of the company has been preserved by its efficient costing system, which seeks to protect profit margins in a high-inflation setting by adjusting prices in response to changing costs of production. Input costs rose about 1 053 per cent in the period 1982 to June 1992 and selling prices have risen to almost the same extent.

Human resources development

NBPLC's major strength is the quality of its staff, which is of the highest calibre thanks to training and staff development programmes. Both internal and external training occur regularly. Most of the technical training programmes are handled by Heineken, which is known world-wide for its expertise in brewing. The commercial aspect of its training programme is usually handled by its commercial partner, Unilever.

There are two broad categories of employees, management and non-management. Management comprises senior management, middle management and management assistants. Non-management staff is subdivided into senior supervisors, skilled workers and unskilled workers. Technical employees (i.e. engineering and production) comprise about 55 per cent of staff at the management level and 70 per cent at non-management. The changes in the various categories in selected years between 1985 to 1991 are shown in Table 9.11. The company follows standard recruitment processes featuring advertisements, screening and various levels of tests.

Table 9.11 Manpower statistics for NBPLC

Category	1985	1989	1990	1991
Unskilled/semi-skilled	1 944	1 687	1 703	2 013
Skilled	1 306	1 113	1 226	1 257
Foreman/supervisor	388	682	572	552
Senior supervisor	17	87	99	128
Assistant management	157	144	149	156
Management	186	190	193	191
Total	3 998	3 903	3 942	4 297

Critical skills are generally acquired through paper qualifications or on-the-job training. At the management level, a minimum tertiary qualification, e.g. a first degree, is required. After employment, the individual undergoes structured training for about 18 months before being formally recognized as qualified to work the system. For technicians, a minimum of 12 months' training is required. Non-technical graduates undergo a management training programme of 18 months to acquire specific management skills relevant to their vocation. The only exception to this structured programme is for mid-career recruitment, where unexpected gaps in the management structure are bridged with suitably qualified experts from outside the system. This does not apply in the technical division because of its peculiarities: assistance to bridge gaps in the management cadre is always available from the technical partners.

Specific skills training is organized on an in-house basis with suitably qualified trainers in all divisions. Outside resources, both local and international, are often used to supplement the in-house capability. Under the staff development programme, personnel are given opportunities to realize their potential. Their strengths and weaknesses are assessed early in their careers and a career path is suggested which would offer challenging opportunities and rewarding work. Thus, the employee goes on training, locally and internationally, gets specific assignments and is pointed to jobs to grow into in the future. All these factors are articulated into well-laid career and succession plans so that staff members are adequately motivated and identify closely with the business.

NBPLC is a manufacturing concern with many shop floors, so industrial relations are a major plank of management practice in the organization. It has evolved a culture built on understanding between workers and management. Occasional zero-sum relations are usually accommodated.

Remuneration policy is built on a merit-based appraisal system unrelated to age or experience. Working conditions compare well with other manufacturing concerns, locally and globally. Elements of the working conditions include:

- a good safety record.
- fairly generous housing allowances.
- almost free lunch for all levels of management.
- free company medical services.
- free cartons of company products to every category of worker monthly.

The average labour turnover is about 6–7 per cent, which is not regarded as a problem. One minor threat to manpower stability comes from the oil exploration industry, whose members often poach the engineering staff after their rigorous and highly structured in-house training.

Export history and performance

NBPLC entered the export market for the first time in 1986 with about 6 668 small bottles (valued at £24 138) of Star, a mild lager and Gulder, a stronger brew. The number of bottles exported grew to 43 693 (£158 169 or ₦744 710) in 1987 but fell to 22 144 (£80 161 or ₦503 571) in 1988, after which the company withdrew from the market until 1992 when it resumed exports. In 1992 about 156 000 bottles valued at ₦814 115 were sold. During both phases of its export history the target market has been West Africans currently living in the UK and Europeans who have visited or worked in West Africa.

The company's withdrawal from the market in 1988 was occasioned by the ban on the importation of barley malt, which forced the company to look for local substitutes. The initial use of maize and sorghum caused a drastic change in the taste of the products. This problem was solved around 1990 after ₦100 million had been spent on technological change and adaptation, principally the installation of mash filters. In making these changes the company received complementary assistance from its technical advisers in Holland. With the change-over to maize and sorghum, less sugar is used – 5 per cent as opposed to the 15–20 per cent when using barley malt. However, biological catalysts such as enzymes are now required.

The interval between the two export phases saw the emergence of unauthorized, or 'grey', exports. Export strategy now aims at dislodging such grey exports using a price strategy, with the company only seeking to break even in that segment of its operations.

External factors affecting exports

Exchange rates

One major feature of the structural adjustment process which began in 1986 is the emergence of an auction market which determines the exchange rate. The naira has since depreciated continuously. The official rate fell from about ₦0.89/US$ in December 1985 to about ₦25/US$ in April 1993. This has tended to enhance the competitiveness of the company's exports since all aspects of costing and pricing are carried out in the domestic currency. Currently, Star Export is invoiced to the company's export agents at less than US$5 per carton, which appears quite cheap when compared with the average selling price of rival products in the international market.

A side-effect of the present exchange rate management system (perhaps, of the underlying scarcity of foreign exchange) is the rationing and hoarding of foreign exchange by conventional suppliers, i.e. banks. The company sometimes encounters problems with obtaining foreign exchange from such conventional sources of supply.

Raw materials

The shift from barley malt to maize and sorghum has already been described. Both maize and sorghum are supplied locally. The bulk of the company's purchases are on the open market, since the company's farm supplies less than 10 per cent of its requirement. A national grains centre has been established in Jos and this centre ensures that the company's requirements are readily met.

Activities of export agents

The company's export sales strategy has been to use export agents. This strategy failed to yield the desired result during the first phase of its export initiative, in 1986–88. The problem was not with sales but rather with returns, as most of the agents failed to repatriate the foreign sales earnings to the company. An investigation conducted by the company revealed that the fundamental problem was that the agents were selected without any investigation as to their reputation and reliability. Under the present export initiative, new export agents were chosen after adequate screening,. including an interview at the Lagos head office. The company has taken the fraudulent export agents to court and the case is still pending in London.

Tariff levels of African countries

NBPLC has found it impossible to target African markets, especially the neighbouring West African countries, because of their high import tariffs. Most of these countries depend on import duties of up to 90 per cent to generate revenue, which renders imports quite uncompetitive in the local market. The company, in conjunction with other export manufacturers under the umbrella of the Manufacturer Export Group of MAN, has been pressurizing the Nigerian government to use the forum of ECOWAS to address the problem. In the meantime, smugglers are having a field day dealing in the company's products.

Strategies, capabilities and linkages

Production strategies

The production of ancillary materials such as crown corks and bottles is contracted out under conditional contracts which can be terminated if the service is unsatisfactory.

Outside suppliers are relied upon for 90 per cent of the maize and sorghum used. The company used to engage in contract farming but this was stopped around 1990 because the farmers did not fully comply with the arrangement. If the harvest was bad, the farmers would sell on the open market to capture abnormal profits but in a good harvest season they sold their produce and that of other farmers not privy to the agreement (and which they obviously bought at market prices) to the company at the enhanced contract price. The project thus became too expensive to monitor. A plan to distribute the appropriate varieties of sorghum seedlings to farmers in order to encourage continuous supply was never implemented because the pricing strategy was not agreed upon.

In the 1960s and early 1970s, the company used to produce under franchise for labels such as Schweppes. Nowadays all available capacity is utilized for its own production.

Investment strategies

Investments usually take the form of a new product, a new production line or extensions to an existing one. In all cases, the principles of project evaluation are observed. Yardsticks such as the net present value, IRR and accounting rate of return are usually applied to proposed projects. Adequate allowance is made for human factors such as market demand, availability of personnel, government policy, etc. Where the capital requirement is large, the views of the technical partner are often sought. The company has adequate in-house capability in manpower and equipment to handle its project evaluation requirements and has not so far employed outside consultants for such purposes.

Marketing strategies

The export marketing structure (via agents) has already been described. Product occupies a central place in the marketing strategy. This explains the company's withdrawal from the export market following the perceptible change in product quality in the late 1980s.

Price is perhaps the most used marketing instrument. Apart from its relevance in the context of general sales volume, it is currently being used by the company to dislodge those 'grey imports' that took centre stage during the withdrawal from export markets in the late 1980s. Promotion supplements the price and product instruments, mainly with radio and television advertisements and posters.

Innovation strategies

The innovation strategy of the company combines technology search, product development, human resource development and management control processes. Technology search is basically restricted to foreign countries. It is usually carried out on the company's behalf by its technical partners. Under an agreement with the partners, every article published on brewery technology anywhere in the world is sent to the company daily. This prompts the company to carry out a technical review on an almost daily basis, leading to frequent updating of technology.

The place of product development in the innovation strategy of the company is obvious from the development history of the company given on pp. 270–2. However, with respect to the export market, it is not technically new product but rather small bottle versions of existing brands which are exported.

The company's human resource development policy was also described on pp. 272–4. In spite of its extensive, structured and rigorous training programmes, the company does not depend on its staff for any technological breakthrough. Rather, it expects them to be competent to adapt and maintain any relevant technology.

Management control in the organization basically takes the form of formulating corporate plans, deriving annual budgets from plans, translating overall budgets into departmental budgets and setting standards at the departmental level for individual units. There is always one superior officer to check on a worker's performance and to correct errors.

Investment capabilities

Project identification is usually informed by corporate plans and objectives. Assistance in this regard is readily available from technical partners. The organization does not borrow money because it has access to ample funds from its retained earnings. It does sometimes encounter problems with obtaining foreign exchange from banks.

Production capabilities

The beer production process is completely automated. The production technology and machinery are from Europe, particularly the Netherlands. The repair and maintenance of machinery and equipment used to be handled by the technical partners but due to economic circumstances and rising costs the company has set up its own repair and maintenance division. The technical partners only come in when the skill required is beyond the local manpower.

Marketing capabilities

The company maintains its market shares using a combination of price, product quality and promotion, reinforced by an efficient distribution strategy. Market information is usually collected by company salesmen from wholesalers and retailers and analysed by officers in the marketing department.

Product development policies were dictated by the technical partners until after the indigenization policy. One new product, Rex beer, was developed as an experiment with local substitutes for barley malt. Another, Legend Extra Stout, was a response to the activities of a major competitor, Guinness Nigeria Ltd, which introduced a competing beer and a malt drink. Legend Stout was developed to enter the market for stout and so protect profit levels.

For established products, pricing often follows cost trends. But newly launched products are priced at break-even as a deliberate marketing strategy.

The efficiency of the sales force is measured in terms of monthly sales volume compared with monthly targets. The sales force receive more free cartons of company products than their counterparts in other departments.

The factors which have led to success and failure in exporting are:

Success:

- product quality
- price advantage from depreciating exchange rate
- superb technical back-up
- availability of ample financing
- skilful personnel

Failure:

- smuggling of products into foreign markets
- high tariffs of ECOWAS countries
- dishonest licensed export agents
- limited access to foreign exchange

Linkages

The company maintains links with its technical partners as regards its process technology, repair and maintenance and advice on general technical matters. It interacts with factor markets to the extent that it owns a farm and purchases on the open market but it has no binding agreements with suppliers because local supplies of the crops are adequate.

It has no direct links and interactions with consumers except during promotional exhibitions. Its interaction with government policies is limited to cooperation with other brewers under a common umbrella, such as MAN, to lobby government on matters of common concern.

FOOD AND BEVERAGES

Background

The food and beverages industry is one of the most thriving sectors of the economy.[8] It accounts for about 13 per cent of MVA in the country. The country's staple foods are millet, sorghum, yam and cassava, which are produced by small-scale and subsistence farmers. Output of the food sub-sector was heavily affected by severe drought in 1987 and 1988, while the availability of domestic produce since 1987 has been reduced by the high incidence of both official and illegal exports to neighbouring countries in order to take advantage of the beneficial exchange rate resulting from free market reforms which began in 1986.

The beverages sub-sector has produced some of the country's quality products, such as Bournvita, Ovaltine, Milo, Vitalo, Benco, etc. These beverages make intensive use of the country's cocoa-bean production. Intermediate stages of cocoa processing, such as cocoa butter, cake, powder and liquor, have been part of the country's traditional semi-manufactured exports.

Capacity utilization in the industry was as its lowest level, about 34 per cent, in 1988 due to the drought. Nevertheless the ratio of domestic to imported raw materials improved from 52 per cent in 1985 to 65 per cent in 1987. Since 1989, capacity utilization has averaged about 45 per cent, while the local raw material ratio has averaged 62 per cent.

History of firms in the sample

Origin, ownership and structure

Cocoa Industries Limited (CIL) is a manufacturer in the beverages sub-sector. It was incorporated in 1965 but commenced operations in 1967. It was established principally to provide jobs. A secondary reason was to add value to cocoa, which was the country's major foreign exchange earner in the period. It was at first fully owned by the government, but in 1990 40 per cent of the company's total shares were sold under the government's privatization policy. Until the late 1970s a technical partnership agreement existed with Coutinho Carrow Company (CCC) of Germany. CCC installed and ran the plant while Nigerians understudied them. Nigerianization in the late 1970s led to Nigerians taking full control.

Until 1981, CIL was only engaged in the processing of cocoa beans into the main cocoa products, primarily cocoa butter, cake and powder. In 1981, it added an instant cocoa beverage, Vitalo.

The company has a relatively simple structure composed of the board of directors, chairman and chief executive, general manager, assistant general managers, heads of departments including the company secretary, managers, including the chief engineer and chief chemist, officers, supervisors and junior staff. Management by objective is the usual practice but sometimes the principle of democracy is allowed in areas of controversy.

Intra-Fisheries Nigeria Limited (IFN) belongs to the food subsector. It was incorporated in 1974 but commenced operations in 1977 by importing and distributing frozen fish. It set up cold stores with a total capacity of 7 300 metric tonnes in Lagos, Jos and Warri, complemented by a large network of agents and distributors throughout the country.

Over the period 1980–87, the company successfully designed and implemented two diversification processes. In 1980, it started processing smoked fish products, and in 1987 it moved into fish trawling operations. In 1984 the company discontinued the smoked fish due to the exorbitant cost of raw materials, which was occasioned by the licensing of, and subsequent ban on, fish imports. It stopped the processing of dry fish in 1988 for the same reason.

The company equity is 60 per cent Nigerian owned and 40 per cent foreign owned. The policy board has eight members, the chairman (a Nigerian), a managing expatriate director, four other Nigerians and two expatriates based overseas. Like CIL, the company has a simple organizational structure consisting of a board chairman, board of directors, the managing director, operations controller for each of the technical and trawler divisions, and office staff distributed between the technical division, trawler division and operations.

Performance and development

CIL appears to have grown steadily over time. Sales, which remained virtually static between 1980 and 1985, grew by about 25 per cent between 1985 and 1990 and by an unprecedented 182 per cent in 1990–91. Other indicators of the growth trend are shown in Table 9.12. The general picture that emerges from the table is that of modest but by no means consistent growth in vital areas.

Table 9.12 Performance indicators for CIL

	1980	1985	1990	1991
Sales turnover (₦m)	10.8	10.5	13.1	37.0
Net assets (₦m)	14.7	20.1	19.1	28.2
Employees	474	582	445	469

Source: Company records

Until 1981, when production of Vitalo commenced, raw cocoa beans were virtually the only raw material. However, with the addition of Vitalo to its range of products, other inputs were added: skimmed milk powder, sugar, vitamins and minerals, malt extract syrup, lecithin syrup, vanilla and egg powder.

The company has managed to preserve its prosperity by adopting a pricing policy that protects its profit level. Prices are made to reflect cost changes as much as possible. But in the period 1970–84 the Productivity, Prices and Incomes Board (PPIB) allowed only 5 per cent annual increases in selling prices although the cost of production was growing by about 11 per cent. Following the dissolution of the board in the mid-1980s, the prices of the company's products could follow the trend of cost changes. Between 1985 and 1992 prices rose in response to cost increases averaging 20 per cent annually.

This general pricing policy only applies to products focused on the domestic market. The prices of export products are exogenously determined and are usually fixed in contracts. An insurance scheme being designed by NEXIM would compensate exporters for contract losses arising from exchange rate fluctuations.

Slightly ahead of CIL, IFN appears to have witnessed modest but respectable growth. Although Table 9.13 covers only three years, it suggests that sales grew by about 3 per cent between 1980 and 1985 and by 97 per cent between 1985 and 1990. Over the same periods, total assets witnessed tremendous growth, of 416 per cent and 78.7 per cent respectively. However, employee levels experienced 114 per cent growth and then a 47 per cent decline in the corresponding periods.

Like CIL, the company protects its profit level by adopting a policy of replacement costing plus a mark-up. Thus, in 1979–80, when input costs rose by about 47 per cent, selling prices witnessed an average growth of about 50 per cent. Similarly, the 221.4 per cent and 94.4 per cent successive rises in input costs in 1985–90 and

Table 9.13 Performance indicators for IFN

	1980	1985	1990
Turnover (₦m)	19.8	20.4	40.2
Total assets (₦m)	1.3	55.5	99.2
Employees	22	47	25

Source: Company records

1991–92 were more than matched by increases in selling prices of 243.8 per cent and 100 per cent. Export prices are not influenced by the level of domestic inflation.

Human resources and manpower development

The manpower composition of the two companies gives some insight into the relative strength of the companies and their human resources and manpower development policies. Table 9.14 shows the distribution of CIL's employees over categories of status and skills.

Employment at virtually all levels has declined since 1980 but the decline appears less pronounced with the lower and skilled categories. The general decline would appear to reflect the realities of the harsh economic environment in which the company has been operating since the mid-1980s. The abolition of commodity boards in the 1970s, coupled with the adoption of a flexible exchange rate regime around the mid-1980s, has diverted cocoa beans to the export market and created a local scarcity. The effect has been reduced production. Another factor preventing expansion has been the uncertainty hanging over the company since 1990, when the public reacted strongly to the manner and amount of the sale of part of the company

Table 9.14 Manpower statistics of CIL

Category	1970	1980	1985	1990	1991
Unskilled	123	127	204	125	138
Skilled	177	258	273	250	252
Lower	3	56	62	46	51
Middle	10	18	29	14	16
Upper	12	15	14	10	10
Total	325	474	582	445	467

Source: Company records

to some private persons. The ensuing court action has left the company starved of funds.

In spite of the labour rationalization which has apparently occurred, the company's human development policies have experienced only minor changes. On being hired, junior staff are exposed to a one-week induction programme during which they are introduced to the company's self-development programme. Under the programme, they are encouraged to register with an appropriate professional examination body, with the company footing all the costs of training and giving a post-qualification award by way of incentive. Apart from the self-development programme, junior staff undergo several in-house training courses (usually organized along functional lines, i.e. production, marketing/sales, etc.) as well as occasional outside training.

In the case of senior staff, the financial problems of the company have led it to replace all overseas training by local in-house and external training. The in-house training essentially relies on outside consultants. On average, a senior staff member in one of the major functional divisions goes on a training course once in two years.

With respect to recruitment policies and practice, vacant positions are filled as and when necessary. All positions must be approved in the relevant year's budget. Recruitment begins with internal advertisements, followed by a screening process to produce a shortlist. The process is handled internally, by the personnel department in collaboration with other relevant departments. Remuneration is by salary, with incentives such as the end-of-year bonus applied across the board and not tied to productivity. Promotion is often tied to productivity.

By industry standards, the conditions of service in the organization are fair: free lunches, occasional gifts of Vitalo, a free medical facility and fairly generous housing and transport allowances.

The human resources and manpower development of IFN appears less formidable and less structured. The company's manpower composition is shown in Table 9.15.

The major picture emerging from the table is the lack of any consistent trend. Although all levels of employment appear to have witnessed changes, the lower management level seems to have been most affected. This perhaps suggests that this level receives more attention during a rationalization process.

The company does not have any particular manpower development and training programme. Most employees are expected to come

Table 9.15 Manpower statistics of IFN

Category	1977	1985	1990	1992
Unskilled	4	4	3	4
Skilled	3	8	4	10
Lower	4	21	8	10
Middle	2	6	5	6
Upper	3	8	5	5
Total	16	47	25	35

Source: Company records

Note: These figures exclude day workers, whose number varies but never exceeds 10.

with the requisite skills, and training thus takes the form of an induction course to become familiar with the system. Staff members are occasionally sent on local seminars and short-term courses in their individual disciplines.

Most vacant positions at senior management level and above are filled through advertisement, with the interview and testing being handled by the company's senior management, including the managing director. Below the level of senior management, most vacant positions are filled through local contacts (i.e. introductions by known people) and subcontract agreements. Subcontract agreements are the major means of securing most of the semi-skilled and unskilled workers.

The incentive system in the organization takes the form of moderate allowances for housing, meals, transport and education. There are, however, full medical facilities. Labour turnover is small and insignificant. Salary increments are usually tied to productivity but promotion is only occasionally so tied. Workers enjoy a Christmas bonus (usually, two months' salary) which is above average in Nigeria. In addition, due to the high and rising inflation experience of the country in recent times, workers who have more than 10 years' service are allowed to take up to 50 per cent of their expected total entitlement upon retirement for immediate use.

Export history and performance

CIL's export activity began when it commenced operation in 1967, with cocoa butter and cake being exported. These two products, particularly cocoa butter, remain the principal export products, although cocoa powder was given some attention in the 1970s and early 1980s. Brokers provide the main export marketing channel. The target market is the developed countries, especially Europe and the US.

It is difficult to gauge CIL's export performance accurately because data on export sales is only available for a few years. The data shows export sales of about ₦0.6 million in 1985, increasing sharply to about ₦4.4 million in 1986 and further to about ₦6.9 million in 1987 but falling successively to ₦3 million and ₦0.1 million in 1988 and 1989. Sales recovered in the following year to about ₦4.3 million and reached a record of ₦15.1 million in 1991.

IFN's export history is relatively short. It entered the export market only in 1991, with about $0.2 million or ₦1.7 million worth of export goods. The export volume grew to $1.1 million or ₦17 million in 1992. The items exported include processed shrimps, lobsters and sole fillets. The major channels are licensed agents and branches abroad while the target markets are the developed countries of America and Europe. At present the focus is on the US, the Netherlands, France and Switzerland.

The market for the company's exports appears to be large and stable, given competitive pricing, so the company sees no need for aggressive marketing or sales strategies. It contracts out the export arm of its business to an affiliate company – Intercontinental Limited – which organizes shipping, appoints agents and establishes branches abroad for 'on the spot' sales and promotions. So far, the company has no misgivings about this arrangement.

External factors affecting export growth

Finance

Both CIL and IFN have several sources of funding, such as issuing share capital, borrowing and cheap funds from special finance schemes. However, the high and rising interest rate under the free market reforms make borrowing in the conventional loan market unthinkable.

Both companies have access to NEXIM's RRF, which is usually granted at a concessional rate – about 18 per cent compared to the money market's 45 per cent. However, the RRF has a time limit of about 90 days, after which the client is forced onto the open market to seek funds. Clients of NEXIM are now proposing a 180-day duration for RRF so as to avoid the open market. Besides the RRF, IFN utilized an ADB/ESL when buying additional trawlers in 1990/91.

IFN also recently increased its share capital from ₦3 million to ₦10 million.

The financial position of CIL has become particularly precarious following the disagreement between the two shareholders, the holding company for the government and the new private interest. The ensuing court action, which is yet to be settled, has effectively blocked any increase in share capital. The continuously depreciating exchange rate has further increased the cost of borrowing for both firms (though indirectly). Both firms lose considerable funds through the effect of continuous currency depreciation on forward contracts, which are their principal mode of export sales.

Raw materials

IFN does not appear to be facing any problem with obtaining raw material, given its plan to purchase more trawlers in order to procure extra tonnage. But CIL has frequently experienced raw material shortages since the mid-1980s, due to the instability of farm-gate prices as compared to international prices. The vagaries of the weather have not helped. Most local cocoa beans are exported to gain an exchange rate advantage, which creates an artificial shortage of input locally. In reality, between September 1986 and 1989, the domestic price of cocoa beans bore no relationship to international price levels, even allowing for exchange rate depreciation. The unusual overpricing in the domestic market was unofficially attributed to capital flight. Buying at such prices was clearly uneconomical for a local user of the beans. Together with other processors of cocoa beans, the company has now proposed that government should allow imports or ban exports of the beans. In the meantime, CIL deals with this deficiency in three ways:

1 competitive production and farm-gate pricing
2 stockpiling, subject to funds being available
3 strategic price-setting for the international market

Labour market conditions

High and rising inflation causes wages to rise frequently, which flow on to the cost of production. CIL has recently been experiencing an increase in labour turnover, especially in its engineering and production departments, because newly established processing companies see it as a source for technical staff. Apart from the occasional operational effect of the loss of such skilled workers, this has been costing the company money and time in recruiting and training new hands.

Currency depreciation

The present exchange rate regime is very volatile, which makes forward contracts very risky. To counterbalance this, both companies are requesting that the government establish a price insurance scheme similar to that proposed by NEXIM. Such an insurance scheme would compensate exporting companies for losses incurred on forward contracts because of the fluctuating exchange rate. Given its peculiar situation, CIL also suggests a possible return of the Commodity (cocoa) Board which once served to stabilize cocoa prices locally by announcing fixed buying prices at the beginning of each year. CIL also often encounters problems of access to foreign exchange on the official market because of rationing and hoarding by banks. However, it has a foreign currency domiciliary account into which its export receipts are paid and from which authorized payments are made.

Technology, marketing, investment, productivity and human resources

Characteristics of demand in target market and managerial responses

Both CIL and IFN operate in a buyer's market and so are price takers in their export markets. CIL considers that there is an infinite demand for cocoa butter around the world, with no risk of sudden adverse price movements. IFN's market is described as large and stable, with competitive pricing.

Faced with this market condition, neither company uses demand to plan production. They deal primarily on the basis of letters of credit and forward contracts. They both hope to eliminate the disadvantages inherent in these modes of selling, given the continuous depreciation of the local currency, by means of the price insurance scheme which was discussed earlier.

In the area of interaction with customers, CIL relies on the fact that most of its foreign customers, like itself, belong to the International Cocoa Organization (ICO), which vets each member's integrity and credibility. Locally, organizations such as the Cocoa Processors Association of Nigeria (COPAN) and the Cocoa Association of Nigeria (CAN) serve as forums for interaction.

IFN interacts rather differently. Operating through its affiliate company, Intercontinental Limited, its exports are mainly to its agents in the USA, who are responsible for the development of new markets and have done rather well in penetrating the European market. All the company's export products are marketed under the group's brand name, 7 PRIMSTAR.

IFN participates, along with the group, in most European trade fairs, and its products are well known and widely accepted. The company considers that its newly acquired trawlers will be able to process its products to the European market's requirements.

Investment strategy and capability

The basic strategies of the two companies are similar, focusing on profitability calculations using techniques such as net present value, internal rate of return, annual rate of return and the payback approach. Feasibility studies, which are usually handled by their staff, cover issues such as finance, project cost, manpower demand and government policy. In recent years IFN has been focusing exclusively on short-term investment (at most, five years) because of the volatile nature of the economy. It has also been involved in some diversification such as the processing and export of rubber.

CIL's investment continues to be in cocoa processing. The management board usually initiates any new proposal.

Technology and productivity

CIL's production technology is basically European, since that is the source of the equipment. Cocoa cake and powder are often processed to the customer's colour requirements through alkalization. The introduction of nib alkalization (i.e. adding more chemicals to the manufacturing process) has allowed greater colour manipulation. The latest product of the company, Vitalo, is produced by a spray-drying process.

The plant is repaired and maintained locally by the company's technical division. CIL has no formal link with its former technical partners and so does not enjoy any expert advice on technical matters. Some spares have been fabricated locally to reduce the need for imports.

Access to finance, skills, technology and foreign exchange is not a problem but purchasing power is. Open market funds, including foreign exchange, are exorbitantly expensive in the context of the on-going liberalization drive. The company has resorted to leasing factory equipment to solve the problem of obsolescence and worn-out machines but has found the high leasing costs a major strain on its finances.

Productivity in CIL is usually measured in terms of output per unit of labour. It compares favourably with other firms in the food and beverages industry. Its brand of cocoa butter (Oba Brand) is renowned for good quality in the international market, while its beverage (Vitalo) is well received and enjoys a good share of the local market. CIL measures the efficiency of its labour force in terms of productivity per person, compared to set targets. Factory workers' performances are assessed in groups. Incentives are limited to promotion and productivity bonuses.

With IFN, the product technology employed basically centres on sea products such as sole, crab legs, whole lobsters and lobster tails, and shrimps of various sizes and processed in various ways. Until 1988, different process technologies were used for smoked, dried and frozen fish and shrimps. With the end of smoked fish processing in 1984 and dried fish processing in 1988, only the freezing technology remains. The process technology of the company is European and it is reputed to be the industry standard. Virtually all the machinery and equipment involved in the production process is imported from Europe. The plant is, however, repaired and maintained locally, usually by subcontract agreements with Nigerian companies.

The company is a leader in the industry and does not encounter problems in accessing technical skills and technology. It has been experiencing problem of access to finance (due to exorbitant cost) and foreign exchange but has coped with this thanks to the ADB/ESL finance and share issues.

IFN does not use any particular index for productivity measurement. The company concerns itself only with the picture at the end of a budget period (the total output approach). Workers have predetermined tasks which they are expected to accomplish. Output is not directly related to workers' tasks. Productivity incentives are limited to salary increments and occasionally to promotion.

Production linkages and subcontracting

In the days of the cocoa board, the CIL used to have licensed suppliers of cocoa beans, since in most cases the selling price of any particular grade of cocoa beans was fixed and common knowledge. However, since the abolition of the board and the move to a market economy, such agreements are no longer respected by suppliers, who sell to the highest bidder on the open market. Since its inception the CIL has been involved in contract processing. It sometimes contracts its processing to other firms, when it is having problems with insufficient production lines for urgent orders but more often it processes for other producers for a fee. This has been occurring more often recently, to utilize the excess capacity occasioned by the drastic reduction in the scale of its operations as a result of poor funding.

In contrast, IFN sources a great proportion of its raw materials directly through its trawling operations. As a result, it does not have any binding agreement with material suppliers. In addition, it completely processes all its output and no production capacity problems have yet emerged. In fact, with the discontinuation of smoked fish and dried fish in 1984 and 1988 respectively, there appears to be ample space for the expansion of production capacity for existing products. So far, it has not engaged in any form of subcontracting of production.

Innovation strategies

The CIL's innovation strategy takes the form of management control and resource and product development. Management deals with external factors as they affect the company. Performance evaluation is carried out by various levels of management and often leads to new standards or targets. Innovative efforts may be rewarded with promotion, recognition and productivity bonuses. One example of the product development element of innovation is the design and development of Vitalo. The idea behind Vitalo was to find a use for the company's excess cocoa powder. CIL sponsored research to determine consumers' preferences and discovered that the granulated beverage was more popular with consumers than a powdered form, and Vitalo is therefore produced in granulated form.

In contrast to CIL, innovation strategy at IFN combines raw materials' sourcing, product mix and new product development. Following the institution of an 'import-discouraging exchange rate policy' in the country, the company had to look to Nigerian sources for part of its fish requirements. It discovered that a large part of its imports could be sourced locally.

The product mix strategy takes the form of the combination of particular products to satisfy the needs of a particular segment of its export market. With new product development, the company explores its export market to identify niches to penetrate with a new product. For example, crab is plentiful in Nigerian waters: through such a search the company discovered that crab legs and crab meat have good export potential. Rewards for innovative effort are similar to those for productivity, i.e. normally in the form of salary increments, with promotion coming only occasionally.

CONCLUSIONS

This study has documented the management, organization and processing of manufactured exports in five Nigerian firms distributed over the textile, brewing and food and beverages industries. The problems and prospects of manufactured exports have been highlighted and discussed. Most of the firms covered in the study were found to have only short export histories. Similarities among firms are noted in the areas of management practices, cooperation within the individual company's industry and with competitors, investment strategy, pricing policy, innovation strategy and environmental problems. In contrast, significant differences occur in the areas of organizational structure, ownership structure, financing mode, production strategy and capability, marketing strategy, human resources development policy and patterns of linkages.

In general, the major strength of most of the firms appears to lie in strong internal control processes, the use of new production technologies and the careful choice and impressive performance of marketing agents. However, problems appear to exist in the areas of the quality of production, the adequacy of financing, access to foreign exchange and bureaucratic and official control, thus creating a wide scope for official intervention on the part of both the national government and the international community.

APPENDIX: THE INCIDENCE OF LEASING IN NIGERIA[9]

Origin and growth

Leasing as a mode of business finance began in Nigeria in the early 1960s, with the first documented transactions occurring as cross-border leases between Nigerian companies and their UK holding companies. Following the stringent exchange control measures introduced at the onset of the Nigerian civil war in 1966, this relatively low-level leasing business apparently ceased altogether. Activities resumed after the war as the massive post-war reconstruction efforts saw construction companies considering financial options in capital acquisition programmes. Growth in the industry has been particularly strong since the advent of free market reforms in late 1986. At the beginning of this period a few merchant banks such as the International Merchant Bank, Continental Merchant Bank and Nigerian Acceptances Limited, enjoyed market domination. The market has now expanded to accommodate well over 300 lessors. The Equipment Leasing Association of Nigeria (ELAN), which was formed in 1983, today represents about 85 of the most influential leasing companies (as at December 1991), including the financially powerful merchant banks. In 1986, the total assets on lease by ELAN members were worth about ₦100 million. By 1991, total assets leased had risen to ₦895.8 million. This is, however, only about 42 per cent of the total ₦2 billion in outstanding leased assets in the country as at December 1991.

The tremendous growth in the industry in recent times has attracted the attention of the authorities and institutional regulation has begun. One example is the Statement on Accounting Standards (SAS 11) issued by the Nigerian Accounting Standard Board (NASB) in 1991 to guide the reporting format (information disclosure) in the industry.

Products on offer

Both finance and operating leases are offered. Virtually all registered banks and a sizeable proportion of non-bank finance houses offer finance leases. Almost any equipment can be leased under this arrangement, with the lease rentals structured to pay back the cost of equipment fully during the primary period. Operating lease arrangements are not as common and have come to be associated with specialized equipment. Apart from the big-time equipment suppliers such as Leventis, Mandillas and Rank Xerox, a few merchant banks and finance houses operate in this segment of the market. Under this arrangement, the lease rentals are usually not expected to cover the cost of equipment during the primary period.

Market size

The enormous growth between 1986 and 1991 suggests a very large domestic market for leased equipment. Total capital asset financing in the country in 1992 was over ₦30 billion, yet the recorded lease portfolio was only about ₦5 billion (i.e. 17 per cent of the total). Participants in the market find leasing more attractive than conventional loans for a variety of reasons. On the one hand, banks find leasing relatively safer than straight credit advances and have been increasing their exposure in the market. On the other hand, the increasing cost of credit in the deregulated loan market coupled with the effect of the steep currency depreciation on the cost of imported equipment has discouraged many firms from attempting outright asset purchase. It remains difficult to guess the future growth direction in the industry. Recent government provisions have tended to reduce or eliminate altogether the incentives to lessors. For example, as of January 1991, the CBN directed that leasing should count towards banks' aggregate credit volume and almost simultaneously the NASB's SAS 11 ruled that finance leases are not leases and therefore banks as lessors should not claim capital allowances on leased equipment. The capital allowances had previously been a major incentive. However, if the recorded naira value of leased contracts for 1992 (₦5 billion, as compared to ₦2 billion in 1991) is anything to go by, the effects of these developments are yet to manifest themselves in reduced transaction volumes.

Funding arrangements

Funding of leased contracts is basically from own resources. Some banks offer leasing contracts in the form of concessionary financing which involves the use of funds from multilateral agencies such as USAID, EU, ADB, NERFUND (the National Economic Recovery Fund), SME (Small and Medium Enterprises) programme, or World Bank Health Programmes.

Distribution of finance

Of the ELAN member's exposure of about ₦895.8 million in 1991, manufacturing accounted for 52.3 per cent, transport for 27.1 per cent, agriculture for 4.8 per cent, services for 5.1 per cent, government for 0.9 per cent and others (small equipment for the construction, mining, printing and confectionery industries) for 9.8 per cent.

NOTES

1 For further details see, for example, The Sovereignty Budget, Federal Ministry of Information, April 1961.

2 See, for example, Oluremi Ogun, *Nigeria's Trade Policy During and After the Oil Boom: An Appraisal*, University of Ibadan, 1987.

3 For a succinct review of Nigeria's exchange rate practices since independence, see T. Ademola Oyejide and Oluremi Ogun, 'Structural Adjustment and Exchange Rate Policy', in A. Iwayemi (ed.) *Macroeconomic Policy Issues in an Open Developing Economy: A Case Study of Nigeria* (a Ford Foundation Sponsored Book Project, forthcoming).

4 A detailed analysis of industrial incentives in the 1970s can be found in J.W. Robertson, *The Structure of Industrial Incentives in Nigeria, 1979–80*, Research Report of the World Bank, Washington, D.C., 1981.

5 The information in this section is drawn from the UNIDO *Industrial Development Review* series, 1985 and 1988 editions; the CBN, annual reports and statement of accounts (various issues); the Federal Republic of Nigeria, *First National Rolling Plan, 1990–92* (Government Printer, Lagos); and MAN, *Half Yearly Economic Review, January–June 1988*.

6 For references, see *The Brewery Industries: A Major Contributor to Nigeria's Development* (The Beer Sectoral Group of MAN); UNIDO Series (*ibid.*); CBN (*ibid.*).

7 New states have been carved out of these states since 1991. None the less, their policy of no involvement in the production of beer or any alcoholic drink, based on religious belief, applies equally in the newly created states.

8 For further information see UNIDO series (*ibid.*) and CBN (*ibid.*).

9 See ELAN, *Lease Awareness Seminar* January, 1993; Corporate, Corporate Journal on Leasing; 'The New Order' in *Corporate Magazine*, November/December 1991; ELAN, *Annual Report and Accounts 1991*.

10 Kenya

Gerrishon K. Ikiara

INTRODUCTION

Context of the study

This study explores the principal factors underlying the growth and performance of Kenya's manufactured exports. Although Kenya's manufacturing sector has expanded and diversified its production, only a few firms can boast of an impressive export record in the last 25 years. Inability to develop a highly competitive export market continues to pose a formidable challenge to the country's industrial sector, although, since the mid-1970s, the government has introduced a number of export incentives including lower taxation and export compensation. Most firms were originally set up to operate in highly protected domestic and East African regional markets, under an import substitution industrialization (ISI) regime. This made them inward-looking and less interested in export markets.

The sample firms in this study are drawn from the textiles and clothing, food processing, pharmaceutical, metal, cement, paper and packaging, and leather and footwear sub-sectors. The aim was to assess the extent to which technology, government policy, marketing strategies, management, labour productivity, ownership structure and size of firms, and the structure of the domestic market influence the export performance of manufacturing enterprises.

Many of the firms established in Kenya in the colonial era were subsidiaries of foreign companies which saw potential market opportunities in the East African region. The region also had some of the necessary raw materials and cheap labour. Kenya's competitiveness in the regional trade in manufactured goods has been the result of a number of factors. The country had, for instance, a comparative advantage in transportation in the region, a favourable cool climate and a greater number of foreign settlers and businessmen. It also started the industrialization process ahead of many others in the region. British multinational firms dominated the scene during the colonial period but were later joined by other European and American companies. Local industrialists joined the manufacturing scene relatively late.

The Kenyan manufacturing sector

Kenya's manufacturing sector presently contributes about 13 per cent of GDP (Republic of Kenya, 1992).[1] By 1992, manufactured products accounted for 13 per cent of the country's total exports,[2] having fallen from about 16 per cent in 1975. Total industrial output expanded by an annual average of 5 per cent between 1970 and 1990. Most manufactured goods, however, remained uncompetitive outside the Eastern Africa region.

Kenya's manufacturing sector has been rather slow in technological change, unable to attain economies of scale and considerably constrained by foreign exchange shortages. It is, however, quite diversified and includes subsidiaries of such multinational companies as Unilever, Boots, British Oxygen, Brooke Bond and Imperial Chemicals (UK); Pencole, Hoescht, Siemens and BASF (Germany); Bata (Canada); Nestlé and Cementia (Switzerland); Colgate Palmolive and CPC (US); CMB Packaging (France) and the Orient Birhla Group (India). Industrial products manufactured in Kenya include textiles, leather and footwear, plastics, pharmaceuticals, steel products, rubber, electric cables, paper, industrial gases, rubber, ceramics and batteries.

Review of government export policy

Kenya had a regional advantage in the industrialization process in the colonial period due to British industrialists' preference for Kenya when establishing branches in the region. A strong entrepreneurial community, mainly European and Asian, had developed by the end of the 1950s. A good industrial, financial and communication infrastructure was also in place, which became another attraction to foreign investors.

At independence in 1963, the government made deliberate attempts to expand import substitution industries. Ten years (1967–77) in the East African Community (EAC) provided a large market and justification for expanding production capacity. In addition, the government established institutions to provide credit and technical training and allowed partnership with foreign investors. However, the collapse of the EAC market in 1977, and the economic crises in the 1970s and 1980s, left many Kenyan industries with excess capacity.

By the mid-1970s it had become evident that Kenya's manufactured exports to the region were declining and that an ISI regime was no longer adequate, with consumer goods now accounting for only 12 per cent of total imports. In 1974 the government started promoting export-oriented industries. It established an export promotion council and a 10 per cent export compensation scheme for manufactured exports. The rate of compensation was progressively increased in subsequent years until the scheme was abolished in 1993. In 1976 the government set up the Kenyan External Trade Authority (KETA) to strengthen and reorganize export promotion.

In the 1980s the government embarked on a policy of import and price liberalization and a flexible exchange rate system. It established an Investment Promotion Centre to reduce bureaucratic red tape in the processing of new investors' applications. The government also introduced a Manufacturing Under Bond Scheme and established a 'green channel' for exporters to remove unnecessary administrative procedures in exporting final goods and importing raw materials. It begun rationalizing the tariff structures as well, which entailed reducing the number of duty rates and harmonizing classification of items to conform to international standards.

In the 1990s, the government continued to accord exporters high priority and more incentives. In 1993, a 50 per cent foreign exchange retention scheme for exporters was introduced. Corporate tax has also been gradually reduced from 45 per cent in the 1980 to 37.5 per cent in 1992. An Export Processing Zones (EPZ) Authority to promote the development of export processing zones has also been established. In 1990, a privately owned EPZ became operational in Nairobi and the government embarked on development of two more EPZs, one on the Athi River near Nairobi and another in Mombasa. The foreign exchange system was liberalized by allowing an inter-bank foreign exchange market, which enabled importers to purchase foreign exchange from commercial banks at commercial rates.

Kenya is one of the twenty member countries of the Preferential Trade Area (PTA) of Eastern and Southern Africa, which has been trying to promote trade among the member countries at lower tariffs and in local currencies. The PTA Authority has also adopted a planned approach to the development of core industries such as steel, textiles, pharmaceuticals and cement. These are, however, yet to be seriously implemented.

THE TEXTILE AND CLOTHING INDUSTRY

Background

Textiles and clothing account for 12 per cent of total manufacturing value added in Kenya (Coughlin, 1986). The textile and clothing industry expanded steadily between 1960 and 1980 due to increased private sector and government investment and the industry's relative competitiveness in the region. However, it has stagnated in the last decade as a result of inadequate supplies of raw materials, increased imports of second-hand clothing, inadequate modernization of equipment and machinery in government-owned enterprises and a failure to increase exports, especially following the collapse of the East African common market. This inevitably led to low capacity utilization and rising costs.

The textile industry was among the earliest modern manufacturing activities in the country, with the first plant established in the early 1930s by Indian investors. Sunflag was the first integrated textile plant, in 1936, and was later followed by other Indian-owned firms. In the 1960s the government, through joint foreign ventures, further expanded the industry. By 1992 there were 47 medium- and large-scale textile firms in Kenya. There are 15 integrated (spinning, weaving and finishing) textile mills, accounting for 85 per cent of the total installed capacity of 130 million metres of fabric per annum. The industry is expected to expand further with the planned establishment of more mills in the new Export Processing Zones in Nairobi and Mombasa.

The Kenyan textile industry relied heavily on cotton yarn until the 1960s. Thereafter the industry begun shifting away from cotton to synthetic materials following a general world-wide trend. The unreliability and high cost of locally produced low-quality, medium-staple cotton and high duties on imported cotton contributed to this shift. An inefficient processing and marketing structure, partly attributable to the monopoly power of the government-controlled Cotton Lint and Seed Marketing Board, raised cotton prices 60 per cent above world market prices. The quality of this cotton remained poor, partly due to dirty lint and while ginning suffered from poor quality control. The government continued to protect local producers by maintaining high protective tariffs on imported cotton, which further contributed to inefficiency and lack of focus on export markets.

By 1992, synthetic materials accounted for 55 per cent of the total textiles produced in Kenya. This led to the establishment of some nylon and polyester extrusion plants based on imported materials. Wool degreasing and processing facilities were also expanded. Dyes and chemicals are mainly imported, so that the industry had weak linkages with the rest of the economy.

The industry is constrained by the low domestic production of required inputs such as cotton and wool. Foreign exchange constraints have also limited importation of synthetic fibres and other raw materials. As a result, capacity utilization was below 60 per cent in many firms.

It is, however, evident that a number of firms in the textile industry have improved their efficiency, technical competence and managerial capabilities since the 1970s. The private firms appear to be generally better managed than the parastatals. Foreign shareholding and expatriate management teams were instrumental in strengthening technical and marketing management in the industry, especially in 1960s and 1970s. Some of the Kenyan textile firms are owned by business groups which have other international textile operations. Sunflag (Nairobi), for instance, has textile mills in Tanzania, Nigeria and the UK, while Raymond is part of a large international Indian group. Apart from their long experience, these groups brought with them expatriate technical personnel. Such international connections seem to have given some of the firms the advantage of easier access to foreign markets and new technologies.

Kenyan textile firms, especially those owned by the government, suffer from lack of specialization. The minimum economic size of a spinning plant is in the range of 25 000–30 000 spindles but Kenya's average size is about 8 000 spindles per mill. Most mills in Kenya produce small quantities of a large variety of products and so lose any specialization advantage. This has to some extent been dictated by domestic market requirements. Most firms manufacture particular fabrics on order and are therefore forced to accept both large and small orders in order to maintain ties with their traditional customers.

To increase exports, the textile industry requires greater awareness of foreign markets and technological developments as well as intense market research, quick responses to changing conditions, promotion of quality and strict quality control. Most of these conditions have not been aggressively pursued in Kenya.

The sector appears to be split into two groups. One is export-oriented and has adopted new equipment and modern technology to produce relatively high-quality textiles. The other, comprising mainly government-owned firms, uses conventional technology and produces textiles largely for the domestic market.

Histories of the firms in the sample

Origins, ownership and structure

The textile firms covered in this study are Raymond Woollen Mills Ltd, Rift Valley Textile Mills (Rivatex) and Sunflag. The first and third are privately owned while the second is a parastatal enterprise.

Raymond Woollen Mills is located in Eldoret, 300 km from Nairobi. Its head office and sales offices are, however, in Nairobi. The factory was located in Eldoret to take advantage of various tax incentives which were especially important in the 1970s. The firm is a subsidiary of a large textile firm in India. Although its capacity is relatively small, its specialization in high-value synthetic and woollen suiting fabrics, knitwear and garments has given it a high profile in the country, especially because of the high quality of its products. It has the most modern textile plant in the country, equipped with Sulzer spinning machines, 48 shuttleless projectile looms, knitting and finishing machines. As a subsidiary of a competitive Indian multinational textile company, it has better access to superior technology and management. Technology transfer has been mainly through acquisition of new machines and training the workforce.

Rivatex was established in 1976 and is among the few relatively successful parastatal textile firms in the country. The government's 80 per cent shareholding is through the Industrial and Commercial Development Corporation (ICDC). Other shareholders are FIDA (Swiss), IFC (World Bank) and DEG (Germany). Between 1976 and 1980 Rivatex was managed by Siditex, a private managing agent, after which it was turned over to the government. After 1985 Rivatex started to lose its competitiveness due to poor management and failure to revamp its ageing mills.

The firm was established at a time when the country was vigorously pursuing ISI as a key strategy in the development process.

During that time, domestic production of textile products was below demand. The Nytil Mills of Uganda alone was exporting 15 million metres of textile fabrics to Kenya annually. Rivatex increased its production to capture a larger share of the domestic market.

Cloth for kangas is the main product, the 480 000 metres produced monthly in 1990 and 1991 being about 50 per cent of Rivatex's total production. Kanga light suiting and school checks are exported. Other products include kitenge (an African fashion), camouflage for the armed forces, poplin, khaki, drill flannel for children, furnishings and fabrics for skirts.

Sunflag, Kenya's first integrated textile mill, was established in Nairobi in 1936 by an Asian group that had connections with the textile industry in India. It started with one establishment engaged in weaving and garment making. By 1963, Sunflag had three other integrated mills in three establishments employing over seven hundred workers. The local Asian group relied heavily on their Indian connection to modernize their mills and improve their know-how.

Initially Sunflag started with the production of cotton textiles for the local market. In 1960, Sunflag established a large garment plant in Nairobi which produces mainly knitted fabrics, shirts, underwear and blouses. Senior management positions are held by family members, who appeared to have provided the impetus for growth, modernization and the expansion of the mills.

Technology and export history

The Kenyan textile industry has a relatively short export history (World Bank, 1986). Exports are mainly to the neighbouring countries, except for Raymond, which has been able to export some of its products to the European market. Raymond, the most successful exporting firm in the country, gained access to this competitive market through its superior technology. Its Sulzer spinning machines and shuttleless projectile looms considerably reduced costs and improved quality. About 30 per cent of Raymond's products have been exported in the last decade and the company is planning to increase this to 50 per cent.

The main export markets for the company are the PTA region and Europe. Within the PTA region, the company exports to Tanzania, Uganda, Rwanda, Zambia and Sudan. The UK has been the firm's largest export market in Europe and accounted for almost 50 per cent of its total exports in 1989 and 1990. The company has established marketing agents in India and Europe, which has enabled some of its products to reach France, Portugal, India and the UAE. It is also planning to export to the US.

The most important export items for the firm in 1990 and 1991 were blended and woollen tops, which accounted for 36 per cent of total exports, woollen blankets (27 per cent), trousers (17 per cent), fabrics (16 per cent), knitting yarn (4 per cent) and suits.

About 40 per cent of Rivatex's products, mainly kanga, are estimated to go to Tanzania indirectly. Two Mombasa-based Kenyan firms purchase 60 per cent of the total production from the firm and export 75 per cent of it to Tanzania. Direct exports by the firm have been low, around 5 per cent, since mid-1980s. Between 1983 and 1985 the firm established a substantial export market for its kanga fabrics in Oman. This market was, however, lost after 1985 due to the firm's inability to compete with products from the Far East in terms of price. For instance, while Rivatex was selling kangas at US$3.20 per pair, similar products from the Far East were selling at US$1.70 per pair. The firm attributed the lower price of the Far East products to the lower costs of labour and other key inputs there and to support from governments in terms of various concessions.

The total exports of the firm increased in the late 1970s and early 1980s. This has, however, gradually been reversed except for indirect exports to Tanzania. The decline is attributed to the company's inability to improve its price competitiveness, partly due to inflexible labour arrangements, since the firm is not free to reduce the workforce, and partly due to lack of technological improvements or innovations over time. Another factor has been lack of aggressive export promotion. The failure of the firm to exploit the Tanzanian export market directly, leaving it to some of its customers, illustrates its lack of aggressiveness. This attitude is largely attributed to its status as a parastatal enterprise, whose incentives to export are not as strong as those of privately owned firms.

There were signs, however, that the firm had begun to give more attention to the export market after 1989, with Uganda being one of the main targets for export promotion. Uganda's own textile industry has suffered a major decline in the last two decades of political instability and foreign exchange constraints, and it has not been able to modernize its equipment. Although Uganda used to export textile products to Kenya in the 1960s and early 1970s, it is now increasingly importing these products from Kenya.

Rivatex's exports to the rest of the PTA region are insignificant and the company has not made serious efforts to penetrate the regional market. This is partly because they believe that the foreign exchange constraints in these countries would not allow significant trade to take place. A great deal of external trade in the region is tied to donor assistance, where foreign exchange is made available to import products from specified sources. It was also pointed out that local consumers from the regional markets had developed a taste for textiles from developed countries, making it difficult for the firm, like many others in the country, to penetrate the PTA market.

Other factors which had reduced the ability of Rivatex to expand its exports since the mid-1980s include rising local production costs and the depreciation of the Kenya Shilling, which increased production costs and the debt-servicing burden of loans denominated in foreign exchange. Between 1976 and 1992, the Kenya Shilling depreciated by more than 500 per cent against the Deutschmark – one of the currencies in which the loans to Rivatex were denominated. The firm had failed to inject new capital or to modernize its machinery. It had also suffered severe foreign exchange constraints and inadequate domestic supply of local top-level personnel skilled in textile technology, which had forced the firm to rely considerably on expatriate personnel, especially from India. Other constraints were the fact that textile technology is relatively new in the country, the limited training facilities in the industry and the flooding of the Kenyan market with second-hand textile products, often by firms associated with powerful politicians.

The sales department of the firm was also thinly staffed and weak. With only three people, the department was not able to pursue aggressive export promotion. The sales manager, based in Nairobi, was responsible for both domestic and export markets. Export promotion was generally not accorded high priority and was largely undertaken through personal visits by the sales manager.

Raymond, on the other hand, had a better-established and better-designed marketing strategy. It was more adequately staffed, more specialized and more focused. For instance, it had separate managers for domestic and export markets. This, coupled with its use of high-quality polyester-viscose raw materials and the relatively high productivity of workers, enabled it not only to have substantial exports in the region but also to export some of its products to some European countries.

Sunflag was established as an IS firm. In the 1960s it relied largely on second-hand technology from India to produce for the less-competitive, low-income local market. However, as it moved to the East African market and later to the PTA trading bloc in Eastern and Southern Africa it was compelled to upgrade its technology, especially in the processing stage, where semi-electronic machines were introduced in the early 1980s.

External factors affecting growth

Raw material problems

The raw material problems of the textile industry have been due mainly to inadequate foreign exchange allocations from the government, high import duties and the decline of the cotton industry in Kenya. These problems explain the low utilization levels at most textile firms in recent years.

By 1992 the production capacity of Rivatex had declined to an average of 1.2 million metres per month. In the first quarter of 1993 it was only able to achieve 900 000 metres per month, due to severe constraints in obtaining raw materials. The firm had not expanded its capacity since its inception. It is still using machinery originally bought from Germany. Due to mismanagement of the domestic cotton industry and disincentives experienced by farmers, only 40 000 bales were produced annually, although the firm needed about 120 000 bales. The firm relies heavily on imports of long-staple cotton from Egypt and medium staples from Uganda and Tanzania, with the latter accounting for 90 per cent of the imported cotton. There is, however, increasing competition for this cotton from local users in these countries, so that Rivatex and other Kenyan textile manufacturers find it more difficult to obtain their supplies.

Sunflag regarded lack of foreign exchange to purchase chips, dyes and other chemicals as one of the more serious problems affecting the performance of the firm. Although the firm had international suppliers for the necessary raw materials, they were becoming more sceptical of the firm's ability to obtain foreign exchange and were reducing credit facilities. The firm currently uses both cotton and synthetic fibres. Lines using cotton were more profitable in the early years, when the firm relied on local cotton supplies, but cotton utilization had fallen due to shortages.

Technology, productivity and human resources

Technology and design capabilities

Many firms in the Kenyan textile industry still maintain old equipment and use outdated technology in some of their operations. The inability of some of these firms to acquire modern technology is, to a large extent, due to the high cost of the equipment. This problem was more acute for government-owned firms. Having made no changes in the production process for a long time, some of these firms would have to replace their machinery and equipment completely, as well as retraining the workforce. Some of the firms interviewed expected this problem to become even more serious in the future due to the rapid depreciation of the Shilling in the 1990s. Raymond, however, did not suffer from these constraints. It had demonstrated that high-quality, special-finish blended fabrics were possible with new technology and that the productivity of equipment depended on the engineering and other labour skills available to the enterprise.

The relatively small size of the Kenyan market and the collapse of the East African Market in 1977 forced some textile firms, such as Raymond, to look beyond their traditional markets. As a result, the fastest growing export outlets during the 1980s were regional markets, especially in Rwanda, Burundi, Sudan and Zambia. Raymond indicated that its relative success in both domestic and export markets was due to its choice of modern technology. This required the use of experienced textile, mechanical and electronic engineers. The firm attached great importance to technology as a key to its export market.

Over the last 57 years of its existence, Sunflag has continually changed its technology in all production departments. In the weaving section, the firm uses Sulzer projectile looms. But in the early 1960s the firm began experiencing problems in the supply of its main raw material as a result of the establishment of more textile mills in the country. Government-owned mills had some advantages, as they received a larger share of cotton lint from the Cotton Lint and Seed Marketing Board than privately owned ones. In 1964, Sunflag established spinning ginneries for the manufacture of synthetic yarns, which considerably improved its range of knitted fabrics and garments.

The success of Rivatex's kanga exports to Tanzania was attributed to the quality and variety of kangas that the company offered.

Due to the relative specialization of the firm in kanga production, it was able to offer a much wider range of designs than many of its competitors in the region. The firm frequently conducts market research on kanga designs in order to keep abreast of changing customer tastes and sometimes uses consultants to develop new designs in line with changing fashions. Kangas are more than just garments, they have cultural and historical values and are also used as a store of wealth as well as for political and educational campaigns. Their print appeal has gone far and wide and they are now being used as gifts and souvenirs abroad and for many other tourism purposes.

Human resources and skill development

Modern textile equipment requires considerable skill to operate efficiently. The sample firms drew heavily on expatriate technicians as well as their international connections. Over time, a competent and disciplined indigenous workforce had been developed through in-house training, learning on the job and overseas training. On the shop floor, fairly high labour productivity is maintained through close supervision.

The less successful firms require upgrading of equipment, technical skills and marketing expertise. The firms indicated that the use of expatriates was inevitable now and in the future because changes in textile technology will largely continue to come from outside the country.

Raymond, one of the most successful exporters in the industry, has an elaborate training programme. The technical requirements for running the sophisticated equipment are enormous and the firm employed 32 expatriates out of a total of 1 500 employees. These included 30 experienced textile engineers. The production managers indicated that trained labour was an important aspect if the firm was to achieve its production and export targets. Local employees were given rigorous training in the firm's training institute and some were sent to the parent company in India. Training was also vital if the firm was to exercise tight quality control, manufacture some of its spares, develop new fabrics and finishes and keep the mills operating at near-full capacity.

Sunflag, having been established before independence by an Indian parent company, was able to draw and benefit from management controlled and directed from India. Even after independence, this trend continued. Eight top managers, including senior textile technologists, were drawn from India and production and maintenance managers were expatriates. They influenced major management decisions on investment, expansion and pricing, a factor which considerably reduced the powers of local management.

One of the Asian managers justified the need for foreign managers by saying that, in a highly competitive sector such as textiles, it was necessary to have managers who best understood the machines, to avoid wastage, low output, loss of time, frequent breakdowns, mechanical and other difficulties. It was, however, evident that lack of trust in the local management had hindered the development of an 'industrial ethic'. As a result, there seemed to be little commitment, allegiance or loyalty from the workers to the industry. As many as 40 per cent of the firm's workers were hired on a casual basis, introducing considerable instability.

FOOD PROCESSING

Background

Kenya has a large agro-processing industry, reflecting the importance of the agricultural sector in the Kenyan economy. The majority of the pioneering industries during the colonial period were agro-based. A wide spectrum of agro-industries exists today, ranging from processing staple food and fruits, to beverage and tobacco production for both the domestic and foreign markets. Food processing is thus one of the key activities in Kenya's agro-processing industry.

History of firms in the sample

Origins, ownership and structure

Two large firms, one processing pineapple and the other producing a wide range of household products using agricultural raw materials, were studied. Pineapple canning and the production of pineapple juice concentrates is one of the most successful agro-processing industries in Kenya today. It is dominated by one multinational company, Del Monte (Kenya) Ltd, which is owned by the US-based Delmonte Foods International. Almost all of its canned pineapples and juice concentrates are exported.

Del Monte, the only pineapple processing firm in Kenya, started operation in 1965 when it took over from a local company, Kenya

Canners Ltd, which had been in existence since 1948. The company achieved a remarkable growth in export sales between 1970 and 1990 (see Table 10.1).

The second firm studied in the agro-processing sector is East Africa Industries (EAI). EAI was established by the British colonial government in 1943 in Nairobi to achieve a specific wartime objective, i.e. provide food products and other provisions for a large number of soldiers and recruits during the Second World War. The company was consequently expected to reduce imports of non-military requirements and ensure regular supplies. The firm, then under the Kenya Industrial Management Board (KIMBO), manufactured soap and bricks.

Due to the inability of the British government to manage the firm adequately, Unilever joined in partnership with the colonial government in 1956. In 1978 the Kenyan government, through the ICDC, bought 34 per cent of the shares, with Unilever retaining 66 per cent. By the early 1960s, EAI's focus had shifted to the manufacture of household goods for the needs of the indigenous people, many of whom had acquired a taste for a wide range of products. The firm's labour force grew rapidly from 155 in 1965 to over 3 500 workers (including casuals) by 1992 (Table 10.2).

Unilever, with its wide and successful international experience and connections, provided EAI's management training and technology requirements. The Unilever Conglomerate has 529 companies world-wide, from which it draws management and technological expertise. EAI staff are frequently sent for training at Unilever establishments outside Kenya.

Production structure

Del Monte has constructed a large cannery plant backed by workshops, training facilities and a large plantation at Thika, near Nairobi. The factory has a large electronic 'ginaca' machine which processes pineapples efficiently. It has been able to achieve close to 100 per cent usage of the pineapples: the output is 22 per cent solid pineapple, 34 per cent juice concentrates, 21 per cent mill juice sugar and 22 per cent cattle feed. Del Monte produces high-quality pineapple products destined primarily for the European market. The firm's success in the export market can be attributed to processing efficiency, strict quality control on raw materials and final products, a disciplined workforce and a well-designed international marketing network and strategy.

Table 10.1 Production and export trends for Del Monte

	1970	1980	1985	1990
Employment (numbers)	691	4 950	6 000	6 052
Production (000 tonnes)	9.37	30.50	53.32	72.48
Export sales:				
Canned pineapple (000 tonnes)	6.22	24.51	44.47	59.43
Juice concentrate (000 tonnes)	2.70	4.54	6.31	9.60
Labour costs (% of total output)	10.4	9.3	8.5	7.1

Table 10.2 Structure of employment for EAI

Employment	1970	1980	1985	1990	1992
Permanent (numbers)	961	956	1 260	1 260	1 600
Casuals (numbers)	900	1 300	1 630	1 950	1 944

EAI produces four main product ranges; namely body care, edible oils and drinks, detergents and industrial products. The body care products include jellies, body cream, lotion, body sprays and toothpastes. Edible oils include cooking fats, oils and margarines. EAI also produces a range of fruit juices, spices and tomato sauces. The soap and detergent products include beauty soaps, general purpose bar soaps, detergent powder and non-soapy detergents.

External factors affecting export growth

Raw material problems

Del Monte's main raw materials are locally available and include fresh pineapples, sugar and water. The firm relies on its 10 000-acre pineapple plantation at Thika, about 50 km from Nairobi. The pineapple is a perennial plant which yields its first fruit 20 months after planting. Once planted, a pineapple plant can go on producing fruit for several years but the quality and size of the 'ratoons' deteriorate over time. Del Monte harvests only the first ratoon to avoid poor quality. The offcuts obtained during harvesting are then replanted. Because of the scanty rainfall in the area, Del Monte irrigates the crop to stabilize production. The firm relies heavily on imported fertilizers, fumigants, pesticides and hormones to achieve high yields and faster maturation.

Some pineapple production activities are highly mechanized. The heavy investment in farm machinery and the cannery requires an expansion of the pineapple plantation. However, acquisition of more land has become a critical problem in the firm's attempts to expand at its current location, due to rising population density and the attachment of local people to their plots. Further export expansion will thus depend on the company's ability to acquire more land.

EAI, on the other hand, relies heavily on imported inputs. In its early years of operation, the company imported cotton oil seed from Uganda for the manufacture of cooking fats. Other edible oils raw materials were available in East Africa: coconut oils from Tanzania, palm oil from Zaire, groundnuts from Tanzania and tallow and sesame oil in Kenya and Tanzania. However, these are not produced in large quantities and it was uneconomical for EAI to acquire them from these sources. During this period, EAI had a storage capacity of just 800 tonnes. By 1992, the company had expanded tremendously but locally available raw materials were still negligible and it had to rely on imported oils and other raw materials. In recent years, the firm has been intensifying efforts to encourage domestic production of raw materials, especially sunflowers.

Palm oil, the principal input used by EAI, is imported from Malaysia, where Unilever has substantial interests. It is used as a base in the production of most of its products. The firm also uses sunflower seeds, which are grown locally on small-scale farms. An oil crop development project jointly undertaken by EAI and the Kenyan government to supply EAI with oil-bearing seeds stalled when the Kenyan government pulled out, but there have been recent attempts to revive the project.

Exports by EAI were adversely affected in the 1990s by the emergence of competing firms, which appeared to have government support and received first priority in the allocation of foreign exchange to import raw materials. However, with the liberalization of the foreign exchange market in 1993, all firms were expected to operate on a level playing field. But EAI has not won government support for the potentially lucrative oil crops development project because some influential businessmen regarded the project as a threat to their own firms. An attempt by EAI to establish a cattle feeds production line to integrate production activities and improve the efficiency of raw material utilization was also suspended by the government after some heavy equipment had been installed. The production of cattle feeds would have adversely affected firms owned by these influential businessmen.

Export history

EAI is currently one of the most competitive firms in the East African region in the production of household consumables. Its goods, especially edible oils and detergents, are in great demand in the region. The company started exporting in 1978 when the Kenyan government permitted the export of selected items to the Eastern Africa region. One of the first major export items was soap to Uganda. However, due to acute foreign exchange shortages experienced in Kenya around 1987, export quotas were imposed on the firm as the government had insufficient hard currency to allocate to EAI to import the necessary raw materials. The government pegged exports to production levels in an attempt to ensure that the domestic market was satisfied. The quota was progressively increased from 10 per cent (within the PTA region) in 1987 to 30 per cent in 1990.

Neighbouring countries, which constituted a large part of the firm's market, were also constrained by lack of foreign exchange to pay for the goods. However, despite these obstacles, the company remains an important exporter of household consumer goods in the region (Table 10.3).

The firm's exports to PTA countries had increased considerably by 1992. The company has had a competitive edge in the PTA market especially in the export of detergents and body care products. The main PTA export markets continue to be Uganda, Tanzania, Zimbabwe, Zambia, Zaire, Rwanda and Burundi. Limited quantities of some products have been exported to some EU countries.

Unlike EAI, Del Monte's products are mainly for the European market. Less than 5 per cent of total production is marketed locally or in the PTA region. Some of the factors behind Del Monte's success in the export market are its high quality control and ability to fulfil orders on time. Production and export orders are computerized and closely monitored to ensure timely delivery. The firm's distribution system to export destinations is well organized and efficient. It took an average of five days to fulfil orders, which was highly impressive by Kenyan standards.

Table 10.3 Export trend for EAI 1981–91 (000 tonnes)

	1981	*1982*	*1983*	*1984*	*1985*	*1986*	*1987*	*1988*	*1989*	*1990*	*1991*
Export volume	2 350	1 760	3 950	4 000	4 980	6 140	3 800	3 850	3 970	4 210	4 020

Technology and productivity

EAI has more than 30 different products, four refineries and storage tanks in Nairobi and Mombasa. In 1989, EAI completed construction of a large, modern edible-oil refinery. The expansion and improvement consisted of a continuous deodorizing/stripping plant, pre-treatment equipment and an oil blending system. The refinery enabled the company to have a continuous process as opposed to the conventional batch type. The continuous deodorizing/stripping plant accounted for the larger part of the investment. Supply and installation of the plant was done by LURGI, a German company which is one of the world leaders in the supply of such plants. The plant has a capacity to deodorize different types of vegetable oils and utilizes a high-temperature process popularly referred to as physical refining. This type of deodorizing economizes on the use of chemicals and produces a product of consistently high quality. The by-products, mainly distilled fatty acids, are used in the production of high-quality laundry soap. The plant utilizes the latest technology and, in keeping with the high quality requirements, the process control is computerized. The EAI Unilever technological process and operations in Kenya are basically comparable to those in Europe.

Before oil is fed through the deodorizing column, it has to be pre-treated to de-gum and remove colour and any traces of heavy metal ions. The second component of the modernization project performs this function and consists of a revolutionary, Unilever-patented process. EAI was among the first of the Unilever groups to acquire this system. The third component of the equipment modernization consisted of a sophisticated oil blending system which produces many blends of oil. The technology in use permits flexibility in sizes, shape and speed of packaging according to the market requirements. The computerized equipment facilitated quick adjustment to changes in consumer tastes and requirements, which has boosted the firm's competitiveness in both domestic and regional markets.

Apart from expanding capacity, this modern plant utilizes far less energy (steam and electricity) and chemicals per tonne of oil processed. Its installation, as the first plant of its kind in the country, led to faster and more efficient refining and increased capacity, at international quality standards. The technology ensures that wastage of raw materials is kept to a minimum. This was seen as a critical contributing factor in the firm's success in penetrating and maintaining its share of the regional and domestic markets.

Unilever's policy has been to remain as technologically modern as possible. This requires regular training for technical staff. Expatriates from other Unilever operations are contracted by EAI to install equipment, while Kenyan personnel are sometimes sent to other Unilever operations on 2–3 year training programmes.

At Del Monte, all the production processes have kept pace with the technological development world-wide. Emphasis is placed on quality in order to maintain export competitiveness. Quality control was maintained by ensuring fruit freshness. No time is lost between harvesting and processing and attention is given to the optimal ripening and proper sorting of fruit, the correct application of additives and preservatives and air-tight packaging. The firm has progressively improved on these aspects through training, research, supervision of labour, use of improved machines and better husbandry. Quality control begins the moment fresh fruit is delivered at the cannery for processing, which begins within six hours of picking.

Production linkages

Del Monte has developed good backward linkages with some sectors of the economy. Cans, for instance, are produced at an adjacent company (CMB Packaging), while cartons, labels, spare parts and provisions for the cannery and plantation are purchased from various domestic manufacturers. With over 5 000 employees, Del Monte is a major economic force within Thika, one of Kenya's major industrial towns. The economy of the town is closely tied to the performance of the firm.

Much of the vital machinery peculiar to the pineapple industry is made at the firm's own machine fabrication workshop. The innovative workshop produces massive 120-feet-span boom harvesters in addition to manufacturing fumigators tailored to local conditions. Some in-house modifications have also been made to mechanical slicers, crushers and sterilizers/coolers. The in-house equipment, though slightly inferior in engineering efficiency, was said to be more reliable, easily serviceable and more cost-effective. The firm maintains a second workshop for servicing its fleet of 120 vehicles and farm machinery. Among them are two 525-h.p. tractors, the largest pieces of agricultural machinery in Africa. In addition, a sugar recovery plant uses waste pineapple skins to manufacture high-grade refined sugar. The refinery provides 20 per cent of the cannery's sugar needs and has helped the company to integrate its activities.

Transportation is a key element in Del Monte's efficiency. In 1982, a container terminal was installed at the company's cannery plant site. The terminal has a capacity of filling and dispatching over 280 containers a week. Railway sidings at the terminal are in almost constant use and the flat-bed wagons can be hooked into Mombasa-bound locomotives in less than an hour.

EAI also has an integrated production process with good forward and backward linkages. Backward linkages include economic relationships with enterprises engaged in farming, primary processing, paper, plastic, metal and chemical industries. With regard to forward linkages, the company deals with hotels, bakeries and a variety of food manufacturing industries.

Human resources and development skills

Del Monte placed great emphasis on training local employees in all relevant fields, on both the management and technical side of operations. Employees in the agricultural, canned foods processing, management, finance and accounting departments of the firm are all likely to go through the company's training department at least once in their career. The firm uses both in-house and local training institutions to train a pool of workers whom it can rely on in time of need.

The firm also works closely with the Government's Management Training and Advisory Centre, the Directorate of Industrial Training and the Kenya Polytechnic in developing its training programmes. The firm's full-time training manager organizes internal courses, which are supplemented by the on-going local management programmes conducted by reputable local firms. At any one time, about 40 students are enrolled in trade and technical apprenticeship programmes. The company is usually able to retain about 85 per cent of its apprentices, with the rest being absorbed by other industries.

Every year employees are assessed for their training needs in line with their promotional expectations. On average, five members of staff are sent overseas for further training and practical experience within the Del Monte network.

These on-going training programmes have enabled Kenyans to take up senior posts. In the past two years, the number of expatriate employees has dropped from 20 to 9, all of whom held highly technical or senior management positions. This was generally seen by the firm's management as an indication of effective transfer of technology by a multinational corporation.

Between 1980 and 1990, the total labour force increased by 20 per cent, while canned pineapple production increased by 142 per cent (Table 10.1). The largest increase occurred between 1980 and 1985 and was attributed mainly to an increase in labour productivity which permitted expansion without compromising profitability. Labour costs as a proportion of total output declined from 10.4 per cent in 1970 to 7.1 per cent in 1990 (Table 10.1).

THE PHARMACEUTICAL INDUSTRY

Background

Kenya has a well-developed pharmaceutical industry, manufacturing a wide range of products. Where in 1963 there were four main pharmaceutical firms in operation, the number had risen to 23 medium- and large-scale pharmaceutical firms by 1992. The main firms were Wellcome Limited, Beecham of Kenya Limited and Cooper (UK), Dawa Pharmaceutical Limited (Kenya-Yugoslav), Twiga Chemicals and Sterling Health (US), Asia Pharmaceutical EA Ltd and Boots Co. Ltd (India), Mac's Pharmaceuticals, Laboratory and Allied and Ciba-Geigy (Switzerland), Apotex Incorporation, Howse and McGeorge and Phillips (the Netherlands), Harrisons and Crosfield and Bayer Chemicals (Germany) and Cosmos (Kenya). The industry is thus dominated by foreign firms which were established to tap the Kenyan and regional markets. Exports of pharmaceutical products increased rapidly after 1982 due to the greater accessibility of the Eastern and Southern African market. By the late 1980s, exports to neighbouring countries accounted for more than 50 per cent of Kenyan pharmaceutical exports, with Tanzania and Uganda alone taking 40 per cent.

Kenyan pharmaceutical exports faced stiff competition from European traders and manufacturers who had long-established contacts in the regional market. Some of the Kenyan firms, however, have been able to penetrate markets in Eastern Europe, the Middle East and the Far East. The range of products manufactured by Kenyan firms includes capsules, injections, creams, syrups, suspensions, suppositories, antibiotics, analgesics, antiacids, diuretics, glycortoids, haemopoitrics, hormones, hypnotics, sedatives, tranquillizers, caterotonics, vitamins, anti-malarials, anti-amoebics, anti-spasmodics and chemotherapeutics. However, the country still imports large amounts of these drugs. Only about 30 per cent of total annual requirements was produced locally. Capacity utilization varied widely within individual factories for particular products as well as between firms. Foreign firms' capacity utilization was about 80 per cent and 65 per cent for locally owned firms.

Although the industry relies heavily on imported raw materials for its requirements, it has substantial backward linkages. The major domestic raw materials used are sugar, starch, spirits, gum, acacia and crushed capsicum. The industries which produce these raw materials in Kenya include grain and sugar millers, CPC (K) Ltd and the Agro-Chemical and Food Company (ACFC).

History of the sample

Origins, ownership and structure

The study covered three pharmaceutical manufacturing firms: Sterling Health, an American multinational company, and Cosmos and Twiga Chemicals, which are locally incorporated.

Sterling Health is a subsidiary of the US-based Sterling Products International. The firm started business in Kenya in the early 1960s under the name Sterling Winthrop (K) Limited. Kenyans had a minority shareholding in the firm, which had two Kenyans on its board of directors. Part of a large international group with manufacturing activities in over 60 countries throughout the world, Sterling Health (K) has established itself as a market leader and has developed high-quality products to meet popular needs at affordable prices. It has been one of Kenya's leading manufacturers of over-the-counter (OTC) pharmaceuticals and a major supplier of ethical drugs, toiletries, household and industrial products since the early 1960s.

Cosmos Limited, on the other hand, was incorporated in Kenya in 1976 by an Asian family led by Prakash K. Patel, an experienced pharmacist and managing director of an old local pharmaceutical distributor, E.T. Monks & Co. Limited. The firm started manufacturing in 1977 on a small scale and moved cautiously in the establishment of a larger manufacturing facility and building up manpower. It later expanded its shareholding to include other Kenyan Asian entrepreneurs. By 1984, Cosmos had acquired significant experience in the pharmaceutical industry, which enabled it to undertake a major investment project. The project, which involved construction of a pharmaceutical plant, was completed in 1985. The company has a wide range of products.

The third firm, Twiga Chemical Industries Limited (Twiga), started business in Kenya in 1949 under the name EA & CI (EA) Ltd, which was a branch of the African Explosives and Chemical Industries of South Africa. In 1962 the company changed its name to Twiga when its shareholding was acquired by Covenant Industries (UK). Covenant was 50 per cent owned by ICI (UK), with the other half owned by Charter Consolidated. In 1978, Twiga sold 40 per cent of its equity to Kenyan shareholders, among them some of the company's management staff. The company now has two Kenyans on its Board of Directors.

Production and export history

Sterling Health's domination in the production of OTC pharma-ceuticals is a result of the firm's strong research and quality control programme, backed by an aggressive marketing strategy. Sterling's laboratory and production plant is today one of the most modern in the industry. The success of the firm in the export market is attributed mainly to its strict quality control and research. All raw materials are tested thoroughly before entering the production stage. The company manufactures well over 40 products in various categories. It made a major export breakthrough in 1985 when it acquired more modern equipment in its factories, expanded its infrastructure and increased its range of products. It more than doubled exports between 1980 and 1985 (Table 10.4) with the main export items being anti-malarials and detergents. The firm also inten-sified its sales promotion, especially in the electronic media. The firm was able to reduce production costs considerably, which enabled it to sell a wider range of products.

Cosmos, which has a shorter history in the production and export of pharmaceuticals, has also expanded rapidly (Table 10.5). In 1985 Cosmos started production of high-quality drugs in competition with much bigger firms in the Eastern and Southern Africa market. Cosmos' entry to the highly competitive export market was made possible by the installation of an efficient modern pharmaceutical production plant and the use of experienced expatriate and local personnel. The new plant was more efficient, safer and ensured high-standard production procedures. Exports received a further stimulus in the second half of the 1980s through government incentives and the introduction of preferen-tial trade arrangements in the Eastern and Southern African (PTA) market. Cosmos' main export destinations in the PTA market included Uganda, Tanzania, Rwanda, Burundi, Ethiopia, Madagascar and Sudan. The company started production of syringes in 1990 in addition to capsules, tablets and liquid preparations.

Table 10.4 Sales and exports for Sterling Health (KShs million)

	1970	1980	1985	1990
Anti-malarials	9.64 (2.41)	21.93 (5.92)	53.57 (16.07)	69.24 (22.85)
Worm expellants	2.26 (0.61)	4.62 (1.34)	21.59 (6.91)	26.97 (9.44)
Cough preparations	5.23 (1.15)	11.34 (2.72)	14.61 (4.09)	17.65 (5.30)
Paracetamol, painkillers	5.34 (1.55)	10.65 (3.62)	23.85 (9.78)	32.63 (13.05)
Antacids	3.28 (0.95)	5.74 (2.01)	19.57 (8.22)	20.92 (10.04)
Antiseptics, disinfectants	6.34 (1.10)	15.23 (2.87)	16.72 (4.81)	19.48 (6.77)
Detergents, toiletries	14.44 (3.90)	17.76 (6.75)	41.45 (18.24)	50.22 (24.61)
Total sales/ exports	46.54 (11.67)	87.27 (25.23)	191.36 (49.88)	237.11 (92.06)

Note: Figures for exports in parentheses

Twiga is among the oldest pharmaceutical firms in the African market. Until the early 1960s, its activities were mainly confined to importing and distributing animal health products for Cooper McDougall and Robertson in East Africa. As the chemical market expanded, the company ventured into chemical manufacturing, first for the local market, then for the East Africa market and finally, in the mid-1980s, for the PTA market. In 1960 it established an agro-chemicals plant in Nairobi and in 1961 storage facilities for imported mining explosives were constructed in Nairobi, Mombasa, Athi River and Kisumu.

Table 10.5 Production and exports for COSMOS (KShs million)

	1978	1980	1985	1990	1991
Total production	6.41	11.92	24.07	28.85	29.01
Exports	0	0	0.75	6.31	8.22

Twiga's largest line of business has been agro-chemicals, which accounts for 40 per cent of the company's annual turnover. The company makes fungicides, insecticides and herbicides. ICI's own products make up about one third of Twiga's total agro-chemical business, including locally popular products such as Glamaxone herbicides and Actellis insecticides.

Technology, productivity and human resources

Production linkages and subcontracting

Twiga represents a number of other US multinational chemical manufacturers such as Monsanto, Rohn and Haas, and Du Pont in the distribution of some of their products in the region. Monsanto's 'Round-up' herbicide has been one of the best selling products.

Twiga's second largest line of business has been in animal health: it formulates animal health and public health products for another Nairobi-based chemical/pharmaceutical firm, Wellcome Kenya Limited. This business accounts for about 30 per cent of Twiga's total turnover. The main products in this category include Delnav DFF and Armitaz cattle dipping chemicals and aerosol sprays (Doom).

The industrial chemicals division accounts for about 10 per cent of the firm's business. It imports and distributes industrial chemicals such as caustic soda and archon refrigerants from ICI Chemicals and Polymers Group. ICI products account for 40 per cent of Twiga's business in this field. In addition, the company markets soda ash for the Kenya-based Magadi Soda Company and sulphuric acid for the Thika-based Kel Chemicals. The company is also an agent for some international manufacturers of industrial chemicals. Twiga markets ICI explosives and also sells ammonium nitrate for CDF Chinie of France. Ammonium nitrate is then mixed with diesel to form an explosive which is cheaper than dry dynamite. Explosives make up about 7 per cent of the company's total business.

In addition to these lines, Twiga also markets ICI's organic products. The company distributed imported dyestuffs and textile auxiliaries for the textile industry and nitro-cellulose products for the paint industry as well as some pharmaceutical drugs, two thirds of which were manufactured by ICI companies. These are mainly cardiovascular drugs and skin ointments. The rest of the business in pharmaceuticals is basically in anti-nauseants, in which the firm represents Janssen Pharmaceutical of Belgium.

The Kenyan pharmaceutical industry has limited linkages. Most firms have their own laboratories and engineering workshops. The engineering side is, however, relatively underdeveloped, forcing many firms to import most of their spares and equipment. A variety of drug tests have to be done either in-house or by foreign pharmaceutical consultants, imposing enormous costs due to lack of economies of scale. A proposal first made in the 1960s to establish a pharmacy training institute has not been implemented. Some of the firms have had to rely on expatriate pharmaceutical engineers, who are not available locally.

Technology and productivity

Sterling Health operates in an environment of intense competition. However, it has been successful in maintaining a stable share of the local and export markets by producing cost-effective and high-quality drugs. One of the strategies of the firm has been to maintain affordable prices without compromising on product quality, so as to remain competitive in terms of prices and quality.

The firm's laboratory and production units are relatively sophisticated and efficient. Quality control is rigorous, with the firm's management maintaining strict quality control procedures. Several adaptations have been made in bottling and packaging to suit the market conditions and clientele. For example, OTC painkillers are sold in a waterproof and airtight hard casing to ensure the potency of the drug for a longer period. This has also made it difficult for competitors to mimic the drug.

Cosmos had modern equipment from the outset. The management made it a policy to maintain high production efficiency, technical competence and managerial capabilities to match those of more established pharmaceutical firms such as Dawa and Sterling Health. Cosmos appears to have the advantage of having a smaller and more manageable operation which does not suffer from low capacity utilization. It is mainly geared to the production of low-cost drugs.

The relatively new equipment was a clear advantage for Cosmos, as it has enabled the company to establish strong roots and compete successfully with the larger firms. Another advantage was its disciplined and well-trained workforce. The firm is in the process of further expanding its training department, which is perceived as a key to high productivity.

Human resources and skill development

Sterling Health has also developed a well-trained workforce. Its labour force increased from 50 in 1970 to 84 in 1975, after which it rose more rapidly to reach 246 in 1985. By 1992, the firm had over 300 employees, including 12 expatriates and 18 Kenyan professionals.

At Sterling, manufacturing is carried out to high quality control standards. Training is provided either abroad through the parent company or by expatriate consultants. Close supervision is necessary to ensure quality control but some of the managers said that it was sometimes difficult to get the right kind of supervisory talent locally. Sterling Health pays its newly recruited unionizable workers at least 65 per cent above the minimum statutory wage, as a way of providing incentives.

Cosmos increased the number of highly skilled workers, including experienced pharmacists and engineers, from 5 in 1984 to 12 in 1990. Its employees receive training locally and abroad. The firm placed great emphasis on training as one factor in achieving tight quality control on its products, which was seen as critical if the firm's drugs were to meet WHO as well as Kenya Bureau of Standards specifications.

Characteristics of demand in target markets

The directors of Cosmos are well-established pharmacists in the East African region. They described the consumer needs in the region as 'simple and straightforward drug preparations' at prices the poor could afford. Cosmos' management deprecated the marketing by some multinational companies of expensive products which in many instances did not meet the real needs of the regional (PTA) market. The sales manager, a locally trained pharmacist, argued that in most cases expensive drugs do not reach a broad spectrum of people as government hospitals cannot afford them. In most cases, the same amount of money spent on simpler formulations could achieve more dramatic and effective results. Cosmos, however, strives to achieve quality standards and rigorous specifications, knowing that good health care provision is not simply a matter of producing drugs but includes basic understanding of the economic factors which have hindered effective use and distribution of pharmaceuticals.

Twiga has over the years established itself in the PTA market as one of the leading companies in the supply of a wide range of chemicals. The company makes agro-chemicals for export to Rwanda,

Burundi, Ethiopia and Uganda. Exports, which were mainly sold by tender, accounted for about 15–20 per cent of Twiga's business in 1991.

THE METAL INDUSTRY

Background

The main sub-sectors in Kenya's metal industry are steel smelting and hot rolling and the manufacture of wire and wire products, galvanized and cold-rolled steel products and pipes. These sub-sectors are interrelated, as they depend upon each other for the supply of inputs.

The Kenyan metals industry is relatively old, the first firm having been established in 1948. The industry is today dominated by a few Kenyan Asian-owned firms such as Kenya United Steel Company, Steel Africa, Mabati Rolling Mills, Insteel, Kaluworks, Galsheet and Doshi. The two leading Asian families in this industry are the Chandaria and Bhattessa groups, who also have extensive links in India and a number of other African countries.

The base metals industry started by manufacturing mainly nails, then gradually integrated backwards into wire drawing, followed by galvanizing, hot-rolling and remelting, cold-rolling, galvanized sheeting and pipe manufacture. The technology in the metals industry is largely embodied in the equipment and requires considerable skill for maintenance. There has been a conspicuous absence of indigenous Kenyans in the ownership, except for the minority shareholding they have acquired in a few firms recently. The firms rely partly on imported equipment and expatriate technicians but have built up considerable local know-how and skilled manpower.

History of firms covered in the sample

Origins, ownership and structure

The study covered three large-scale firms involved in the manufacture of wire and wire products, steel smelting and hot rolling: Kenya United Steel Ltd (KUSCO), Rolmil (Kenya) Ltd and the Associated Steel Company Limited. KUSCO, the pioneer in the industry, started the first wire products (nail) plant in 1949 and also the first steel rolling and smelting plant in Kenya in 1967.

KUSCO has the biggest mills, controlling about 40 per cent of the domestic market and accounting for about 30 per cent of Kenya's total exports of base metal products. KUSCO's nail plant faces intense rivalry from Nalin Nail Works, another wire products firm. During the 1970s these two firms integrated backward into wire drawing from imported rods. In 1983, Nalin Nail Works set up its Special Steel Mills for wire-rod drawing from billets. KUSCO's steel rolling and smelting plant was set up in an attempt to integrate backwards from nail manufacture, but the company has not been able to utilize this plant fully. Utilization rates in the two plants range between 50 and 60 per cent.

KUSCO has two electric arc furnaces for smelting, one of which has been completely idle since installation due to lack of local scrap and problems in importing scrap. The company has plans to venture into ship breaking to generate scrap locally. It has built expensive billet-making (continuous casting) facilities with the intention of acquiring wire-rod rolling facilities.

Rolmil is a relatively new operation owned by a Kenyan Asian group together with a foreign company (Cloris Co. Limited of Bermuda).

Established in 1966, Wire Products Limited produces mainly semi-processed products, drawn wire and various finished products such as nails, wire mesh, fencing wire, etc. It is one of the five companies owned by a holding company, Industrial Promotion Services (IPS) and the Aga Khan Fund for Economic Development (AKFED). IPS manages four other Kenyan manufacturing companies, i.e. Wakulima Tool Limited, Leather Industries of Kenya, the Plastic and Rubber Company Limited and a textile firm. IPS has a 45 per cent shareholding in Wire Products Limited, the oldest of the four companies. The Industrial Development Bank (IDB) had 30 per cent of the shares with the rest held by AKFED.

Export history

In spite of its recent establishment, Rolmil has made inroads in the export market. While only 12.4 per cent of its total production was exported in 1988, the proportion had risen to 17.1 per cent by 1990. It uses modern technology and does not operate with much excess capacity, unlike the bigger firms in the industry. Rolmil operates in a competitive environment with six other firms which have similar rolling facilities.

Rolmil has integrated its production backwards by developing its own arc furnace for smelting, largely to reduce dependence on other local firms for supplies of inputs. Although the investment in the new arc furnace is likely to create excess capacity, Rolmil justifies it by arguing that dependence on domestic competitors for the supply of its inputs resulted in high costs of production. The firm has captured a significant market in neighbouring countries where it has retained customers by offering them competitive prices and by ensuring that orders are filled on time.

Wire Products Limited exports about 15 per cent of its products directly, while another 25 per cent is exported indirectly by Kenyan middlemen to neighbouring countries. The firm has developed markets in Uganda, Sudan and Somalia where it sold semi-processed wire. It also sells finished products such as nails, welded mesh, fencing wire and reinforcement fabrics to Rwanda and Burundi. Political instability in Uganda, Somalia and Sudan has adversely affected the firm's exports to these countries. The demand for Rolmil's products is, however, generally high and it is at times unable to satisfy the domestic and export demand adequately. While the larger part of the company's products were sold domestically, it has developed a stable export market in the region. The firm's export drive was partly due to export compensation and other export incentives provided by the government. The firm has plans to expand its operations and export to the larger regional markets, especially following more recent export incentives, which now allow exporters to retain 50 per cent of their foreign exchange earnings.

Kenya's metal and engineering industry was initially reliant on the domestic market, where building and construction was rapidly expanding. But the region's relatively under-developed metal industry provided substantial export opportunities for Kenyan metal-working enterprises.

Technology, productivity and human resources

Characteristics of demand in target markets

The success of Rolmil's exports is largely due to the nature of the export market (Uganda, Tanzania and Rwanda). Importers from these countries have not been very discriminating in terms of quality. This has permitted the use of less expensive local steel technologists and engineers, allowing the Kenyan firms to modify their production processes to raise capacity and reduce processing costs. But these were only short-term solutions and some of the firms are realizing that, in the long run, quality will be a decisive factor if their export shares are to be maintained or increased. These firms are already facing a growing challenge from Zimbabwean firms, which are more competitive due to the domestic availability of raw materials.

The Kenyan firms had a comparative transportation advantage in the Eastern Africa region, particularly to Uganda, Rwanda and Burundi. The transportation costs of these landlocked countries inhibited the importation of bulky products from other more distant countries. Their domestic markets are also too small to justify the establishment of steel rolling or wire products mills. These factors have enabled Kenyan firms to retain considerable power in the markets of these countries.

Human resources and skill development

In the last three decades, Kenya has established a large number of technical schools, polytechnic institutions and village polytechnics. These institutions have become a base for supplying the skilled labour required in the metal industry. All three metal industry firms studied had benefited from these institutions.

With an annual turnover of about KSh80 million in 1990, Rolmil had a labour force of about 215 employees. The number of permanent employees has remained more or less the same over the last 10 years. Machine operators are employed with just the basic knowledge acquired in schools and colleges. The firm has a well-established training programme for production staff. Employees are released annually for training in polytechnics and other training institutions. The impact of the training is evaluated by monitoring staff performance. The company also has an active on-the-job training programme and participates in specialized seminars, especially for management staff.

The firm accorded training opportunities to virtually all its senior staff, which had raised the morale of the staff. Factory staff were awarded monthly production bonuses for departments which achieved set targets. Over the past five years, only 12 people had been dismissed and only five had resigned – showing high stability in the workforce. The company's salary level was generally above average for Kenyan industrial employees. The company had generally fair working conditions, which government factory inspectors found satisfactory. Noise and pollution were, however, serious problems, because workers did not seem to use the devices provided to protect themselves.

To cope with unpredictable fluctuations in production, Wire Products Limited has maintained a regular workforce of permanent employees and a relatively large number of casuals, from 50 to 70 at any one time. The biggest handicap of such a high proportion of casuals was inadequate training.

Technology and productivity

The production capacity of Wire Products Limited is 900 metric tonnes of steel products per month. But the actual production is about 500 tonnes per month, a 55 per cent utilization rate. Optimal capacity utilization has been hampered by raw material shortages, due to delays in processing import licences, and breakdowns of production equipment.

Until 1977, when it installed a multi-block wire-drawing machine, the company did not have any wire drawing capacity. It now has three wire-drawing machines. Before 1977, the main input was drawn wire, imported from France, the UK and Germany. Since 1977, the company's main input has been wire rods, imported for the manufacture of construction bars and reinforcement fabrics. For the last 12 years, Zimbabwe has been virtually the only source of wire rods. South Africa, a new entrant, has become an important source because of its more competitive prices and quick delivery of imported materials.

Wire Products uses the cold drawing process, a conventional technology which is being phased out in developed countries. The company obtained second-hand machines at cheap prices. The competitiveness of the firm's products in the export market was based on the inability of neighbouring countries to establish a wire-drawing plant because of the large amount of capital required and their small domestic markets and lack of skilled human resources. This made it difficult for these countries to justify installation of a wire-drawing machine. The firm is, however, aware that this is only a temporary situation and is trying to raise its efficiency and quality in order to retain its share of the regional market. It is also intensifying its marketing efforts in the region and has recently strengthened and reorganized its marketing department for this purpose.

Wire Products mainly exports semi-processed products as dictated by the importing countries' IS policies. Some of the neighbouring countries have already acquired the capacity to produce finished wire products, as the machines used to manufacture end products are generally smaller and cheaper and, therefore, are affordable in some of these countries.

The company also attributed its competitiveness in the export market to the quality of its products. Since inception, the company has maintained a fairly strong quality control department which uses both domestic and international standards. For products destined for the domestic market, the quality control department relied on benchmarks set by the Kenya Bureau of Standards (KBS), while for export consignments customers usually gave their own specifications. The specifications, did not, however, include the chemical composition of the materials, since it had already been determined by the manufacturer of the raw material. The cold drawing process does not change the chemical structure of the material. For products used in big projects employing international specifications, the company relied on higher-quality billets. This market differentiation enabled it to reduce manufacturing costs.

One of the limitations for the company's exports has been a rather conservative marketing strategy pursued in the past. The firm avoided working through established agents or distributors outside the country. It also did not use consulting firms. It relied largely on marketing personnel from the parent holding company, IPS. Due to its dependence on IPS, the company had not fully established a department to market products in the region, but with the present greater focus on export markets it is in the process of creating such a department.

Because of its broad connections in East Africa, IPS handled the publicity for products from its associated companies but the costs were met by the companies themselves. The management staff was also provided by IPS. Due to the considerable level of IPS specialization in marketing in the region, its companies benefited from lower advertising costs and greater knowledge and familiarity with the regional markets.

THE CEMENT INDUSTRY

Background

The cement industry in Kenya consists of two firms: the Bamburi Portland Cement Company (BPCC) and East African Portland Cement Company (EAPC). BPCC, the larger and older of the two, was established in 1954 to produce for local and export markets. EAPC was established four years later in 1958 and produces primarily for the domestic market. Of the two, BPCC has a competitive edge due to its more efficient technological process and more experienced management. It uses a dry process and operates the cheaper coal kilns. EAPC on the other hand had not shifted away from the traditional wet process technology, which is older, inefficient and uses expensive kilns.

History of firms in the sample

Origins, ownership and structure

BPCC and its subsidiaries are incorporated in Kenya. The cement plant is strategically located about 15 km north of the Mombasa harbour, the main exporting outlet. The principal activity of the parent company is the manufacture of clinker and cement derived from coral rock. One of its subsidiaries is engaged in agriculture and the environmental restoration of areas from which coral rock has been excavated. This includes land rehabilitation, fish farming and landscape consultancy. Another subsidiary, though not operational, owned valuable coral land which serves as a reserve of raw materials. This land is expected to provide the major source of limestone for BPCC in the next 20 years.

BPCC started as a joint venture between the Kenyan government and Bamsem Ltd. By 1988, Bamsem held 74 per cent of the shares and the Kenyan government held 16 per cent. The remaining 10 per cent was held by the public through the Nairobi Stock Exchange. In 1990 the foreign investors increased their shareholding. In 1992, the Kenyan government indicated its intention to sell its shareholding in BPCC as part of the privatization programme being undertaken under the structural adjustment programme (SAP). The firm has been operating under a management contract with Cementia A.G. from Switzerland.

EAPC started operations in 1958 and was incorporated in 1963. It has a majority government shareholding (50 per cent). Another 28 per cent was shared between investors in the UK and Switzerland, while local private investors held 22 per cent. The management of the enterprise is, however, wholly local. The plant is located about 30 km east of Nairobi, at Athi River, where it extracts its main raw material. In 1992, EAPC was also listed among the companies to be privatized.

Export history

The cement industry in Kenya is an example of an industry which has substantially lost its export share due to its inability to keep up

Table 10.6 Production and exports of cement for BPCC

	1970	1980	1985	1990	1991
Domestic sales (tonnes)	148 750	111 530	348 330	573 670	648 500
Exports (tonnes)	401 350	638 410	440 000	316 330	451 300
Total production (tonnes)	550 100	749 940	788 330	890 000	1 099 800
Exports as % of total	73.0	85.1	55.8	35.5	41.0

Table 10.7 Basic data for the two cement-industry firms 1990

	BPCC	EAPC
Production process	Dry	Wet
Installed capacity (tonnes per year)	1 050 000	360 000
v. production	827 500	413 000
Markets:		
Local (%)	48	95
Export (%)	52	5
Specific energy consumption:		
(Kcal/kg) clinker	1 130	1 170
(On fuel basis) cement	1 482	1 408
Fuel used	Coal 65 % Fuel oil 35 %	Fuel oil 100%
Cost per unit of output	$48.66	$68.72
Cost structure:		
Raw material costs	Relatively low	Relatively low
Energy costs per tonne of product	$16.48	$23.78
Labour costs	Average	Low
Overall efficiency (operation and maintenance)	Average (needs further improvement)	Poor (needs improvements)
Training programme	Under way	Under way
Development programme	Energy efficiency programme started	Conversion to dry process and to coal use under way

with technological advances in a highly competitive international
market. Cement exports declined in the mid-1980s (see Table 10.6)
due to the near collapse of the international cement market.
Prices fell below levels that could sustain BPCC's cost structure.
In 1985, BPCC's export price was $34 per tonne, which was quite

close to the economic price of about $36 per tonne, landed at Mombasa.

The main inputs used by BPCC are oil, coal, hydro-electric power, fluorspar, iron ore, gypsum and pozzuolana. Production costs increased in the 1980s by an average of 20 per cent per annum, partly due to the persistent depreciation of the Kenyan Shilling. The firm had loans denominated in foreign currencies. This could have been counterbalanced by export sales, but the foreign exchange policies pursued by the government did not facilitate this. The recently introduced retention accounts scheme for exporters is expected to change the firm's position radically for the better. Bamsem's increased shareholding in BPCC brought benefits to the local firm as more capital was injected into the company. Bamsem also drew up an extensive training programme for professionals in the firm. Bamsem initiated further technology improvements using its wide experience in the cement industry in Europe. These positive developments were yielding results by 1991/92. The declining trend in exports was reversed as BPCC once more became competitive in the market.

Between 1980 and 1987 export sales were adversely affected by BPCC's inability to compete internationally, especially when the international prices of cement collapsed. This considerably reduced export volume during the period. BPCC was forced to continue exporting at a loss in order to maintain some of its market share while it awaited improvements in international prices and its own technology. In 1991/92, international prices picked up, domestic prices were decontrolled and technology was upgraded. This boosted exports and improved the firm's profitability.

Technology, productivity and human resources

Technology and productivity

EAPC used a relatively inefficient wet process and relied on the more expensive fuel oil kilns. The company's expansion and conversion to a more efficient process has been constrained by lack of raw materials (limestone and clinker). The firm also suffered from bureaucratic delays in decision-making from the government, its principal shareholder.

Cementia A.G. (Switzerland), which runs BPCC under a management contract, had, on the other hand, quickly taken a number of decisions to ensure that BPCC remain competitive in the export market (Table 10.7). The first was the conversion from fuel oil to coal firing in the early 1980s, the second was the implementation of an energy efficiency programme in 1985. Thirdly, and more significantly, the technological process was improved using an IFC loan and later a Japanese government credit. Lastly, after a protracted tussle with the government over restrictive price controls on cement, BPCC finally benefited from price deregulation in 1992. This enabled it to adjust domestic prices to economic levels to compensate for higher production costs and the depreciating Shilling. These factors played a significant role in BPCC's increasing its export levels from 316 330 tonnes in 1990 to 451 300 tonnes in 1991.

Impact of government policies

The poor performance of BPCC illustrates how inappropriate government policies can run down an otherwise profitable private company to near collapse. Two policies in particular were responsible: the rigid price control on cement sold locally and the failure of the government to remove or at least reduce import duties on coal following the firm's decision to shift to coal firing. Prior to that, BPCC had been using fuel oil, which was costing large amounts of scarce foreign exchange. Coal was cheaper on the world market. For over eight years the government failed to adjust prices to levels that would turn around the firm's performance. As a result, it became difficult for BPCC to secure financial assistance to refurbish the plant. It was alleged that the firm's inability to win the government's favours was because the management was aligned to the wrong political faction. Continuing under-capitalization of the firm placed it in an increasingly poor position. This threatened to wipe out its exports and even made the country a net importer of cement in the late 1980s.

PULP, PAPER AND PACKAGING

Background

Pulp and paper production in Kenya is presently dominated by one firm, Pan African Paper Mills (Panpaper). There are, however, several smaller mills engaged in the production of various kinds of paper and packaging materials. Panpaper accounts for 40 per cent of employment and over 60 per cent of value added in this industry. There are over 20 medium and large enterprises for which Panpaper is the main supplier of raw materials. The industry has linkages with Eastern and Southern African countries, where it provides other industries with packing, printing, wrapping materials and newsprint. The industry is dominated by Indian groups, who have extensive operations in the country and other countries in the region.

History of firms in the sample

Origins, ownership and structure

The firms in the study sample are Panpaper and East African Packaging Industries (EAPI). Panpaper started operation in 1974 as a joint venture between the Kenyan government, the IFC and Orient Paper Mills, part of the Birhla group from India. Its primary objectives were to enable Kenya to reduce paper imports and to earn foreign exchange through exports.

The first plant of EAPI was established in Mombasa in August 1959 with 75 per cent of its shares foreign owned. The second plant was established in Nairobi, in 1963. Each of the plants had increased its workforce to about 300 permanent employees by 1992. EAPI specializes in the production of packaging materials. Among its main products, and main export items, are paper sacks, including those used in packing cement, tea and sugar.

EAPI was one of the pioneers in the region in the manufacture of paper sacks for tea, replacing the wooden chests which had traditionally been used. Following the approval of paper sacks by the World Tea Association, the technology quickly spread. EAPI started manufacturing paper tea sacks in 1980. In 1993 it was the only firm producing this item in the country. Some of the other producers of paper tea sacks are in Sri Lanka, Australia, Zimbabwe and South Africa. Since the quality of paper sacks is generally standardized, a firm's competitiveness in the export market is significantly determined by its ability to keep labour and other costs down.

Export history

As already mentioned, the primary objective of Panpaper was to produce paper domestically to substitute for paper imports and to expand exports. This dual role of saving and earning foreign exchange had only partially been realized. In its early years of operation, Panpaper exported substantial proportions of its output, reaching a peak of 29 per cent in 1978. However, as domestic demand grew, the firm reduced its export share in order to satisfy local requirements. By 1985–86, exports were down to 0.2 per cent of output. However, with expansion in 1990–92, this trend has been reversed and the firm was able to increase its export share to 10 per cent in 1992.

EAPI has been more successful in fulfilling its export objectives. In the 1970s and most of the 1980s, the company exported about 20 per cent of its total output. This proportion declined marginally in the late 1980s because some of the countries which used to import the Kenyan product established their own paper sack plants. In addition, EAPI had experienced some problems in obtaining raw materials. Burundi has been the firm's largest market for tea sacks, followed by Uganda and Tanzania. Its main export markets for cement bags have been Sri Lanka, Brazil, Tanzania, Sudan and Mauritius.

EAPI's success as an exporter was the result of a combination of factors. It was among the first firms to manufacture paper tea sacks. This gave the firm more or less monopolistic power in the region for some time until other countries established their own plants. Moreover, throughout most of it history, the firm has been able to offer competitive prices because of the export compensation scheme. The relatively low labour cost in Kenya was an added advantage. Kenya's labour costs were, for instance, estimated by EAPI's management to be about 20 per cent of those in South Africa. Availability of some of the raw materials locally, especially paper from Panpaper, was another advantage. The firm is among the largest domestic buyers of paper from Panpaper, consuming 900 tonnes of raw materials per month.

The firm has also given sustained attention to export markets. Both the Nairobi and Mombasa branches of EAPI have export departments charged with the responsibility of promoting exports in the region and beyond. Finally, the large domestic demand for paper sacks for tea and cement enabled EAPI to enjoy economies of scale and to supply its products at competitive prices to the export market. The tea industry in East Africa obtained most of its packaging requirements from EAPI. The BPCC and EAPC cement firms continue to be the most important domestic consumers of cement sacks from the firm, which has established a plant in Mombasa to specialize in the production of cement sacks. The rapidly growing horticultural export business has had a significant positive effect on the expansion of domestic demand for paper packaging material.

External factors affecting export growth

Raw material problems

Panpaper uses plantation forests for which it pays royalties to the government, which has a virtual monopoly on the supply of logs since it owns most of the country's forests. The rapid depletion of forests due to increased land use and other competing timber uses has forced Panpaper to launch its own afforestation programmes. The government has also substantially raised royalties, reducing Panpaper's ability to compete against legal imports, which were subject to a 25 per cent tariff. Panpaper has in the last three years established new plants utilizing alternative raw materials such as scrap paper. Duties on imported inputs such as chemicals, higher-priced local logs and depressed paper prices on the world market were external problems identified by the firm's management. The firm had also experienced higher power costs.

Constraints on EAPI's exporting capacity included raw material supply limits from Panpaper and the loss of export markets as some importing countries established their own plants. This was a partic-ular problem for EAPI because the manufacture of paper sacks is essentially a low-technology and low-capital industry. EAPI was also hampered by inefficiency and corruption at the Mombasa Port and under-utilized capacity – 50 per cent in the Mombasa plant and 65 per cent at the Nairobi plant. The seasonal nature of horticultural exports aggravated the under-utilization of capacity during horticul-ture's low seasons. Shipping costs were also high, reducing the competitiveness of the firm's products in Europe and other distant markets.

The recent relaxation of trade links with South Africa eased the problem of raw material supplies to some extent, as the firm was able to receive paper raw materials within 10 days, as compared with 4–5 weeks for materials from Europe. In the last two years the firm has obtained about 40 per cent of its raw materials from South Africa.

Technology, productivity and human resources

Characteristics of demand in target markets

Panpaper produces a wide range of products, including bleached and unbleached papers for packing, printing, wrapping and newsprint, in about 35 grades. This diversity means that it cannot achieve economies of scale. The scale is determined by product diversity and to a considerable extent by the country's varied industrial/consumer needs. Panpaper could not avoid this given the existing structure of the industry. Costs could be reduced if the firm specialized in a smaller range of papers or was able to export more of its output.

Technology and productivity

Over time, Panpaper has established an impressive and well-run operation. Not only has the foreign partner, Orient, effectively transferred some know-how regarding plant maintenance and operation, it has also improved the plant's operating levels. Energy consumption in terms of fuel per ton of paper has been reduced by 25 per cent through equipment modification, better 'housekeeping', and raw material switching. Its technicians have found ways of using new raw materials such as eucalyptus, straw and scrap paper. The company has also modified its processes to use local corn-starch instead of imported TKP (tamarind kernel powder). Its chemical recovery rate of 92 per cent was comparable to that of efficient plants elsewhere. The firm operated a captive caustic soda, chlorine and hydrochloric acid plant, the largest of its kind in East Africa. Its operations, being semi-automated and spread over a broad product range, required more skills than a plant of a similar size in an industrialized country. Its workforce has gradually mastered a significant number of those skills, while its workshop can manufacture various simple spare parts.

EAPI has settled for an intermediate technology and relied on second-hand machines. The firm buys reconditioned machinery which has been discarded by European firms in favour of automated machines. New technology in the manufacture of paper sacks is mainly focused on increased automation and mass production, which are not so crucial for developing countries with small domestic markets. The management of the enterprise argued that reconditioned machines were for the time being adequate and suitable for the Kenyan market.

Human resources and development of skills

Panpaper employs about 2 200 local staff and 235 expatriates. Its rural setting (Webuye), far from major cities, compelled the firm to develop an intensive training programme a year before actual production started, as local skills in paper manufacturing were virtually non-existent. The complexity of the process called for a large number of expatriates. Of the 235 Indian technicians appointed at the start, 30 remained in the firm by the end of 1992. The firm's training school had turned out nearly 3 000 graduates from a variety of technical courses. Several technicians have been sent to India, Europe and North America for advanced training. This intensive effort has yielded results, so that Panpaper has been able to reduce the number of expatriates significantly and keep the plant running at high capacities in addition to expanding capacity and introducing new products. The productivity of workers has increased over time, though it was still below levels in countries such as India.

LEATHER AND FOOTWEAR INDUSTRY

Background

The leather and footwear industry in Kenya was dominated for most of the 1950s and 1960s by a subsidiary of a Canadian multinational, East African Bata Shoe Company, established in 1943. In the 1970s competition from small- and medium-scale producers of leather products and from imported finished products continued to be felt by the larger firms. An increase in the production of synthetic products also posed a considerable challenge to the more expensive leather products.

Leather production receives low protection domestically. Therefore only foreign subsidiaries, or those linked to export markets through subcontracting, were able to compete effectively. The technological threshold is one of the main factors limiting the entry of more firms.

History of firms in the sample

Origins, ownership and structure

Orbitsports was established in 1968 and is fully owned by four members of a Kenyan Asian family. At that time the domestic demand for sports items was rising rapidly, met largely by imports, yet leather was readily available and the skills needed to set up and operate such a firm were not prohibitively expensive. The start-up capital required was also moderate, approximately KSh6 million, excluding the cost of land and buildings. The firm's promoters were already quite familiar with the sports industry, as they used to be key importers of sports equipment. At that time, there was no local firm producing sports equipment.

It is now one of the leading African manufacturers of balls and other sports equipment. Between 1970 and 1990 its total sales increased six-fold, from KSh7 million to 41 million, while total employment rose almost six times from 64 to 352 persons. The total assets of the company in 1992 amounted to KSh42 million, including land and buildings.

Export history

For the first six years, Orbitsports remained the only manufacturer of sports items in the PTA region. Since then, one more firm has been established in Kenya but it does not yet pose serious competition to Orbitsports because of the relatively low quality of its products. A major breakthrough for Orbitsports occurred in 1974 when it entered into a technical cooperation agreement with Adidas, the world's largest supplier of leather balls. The firm paid royalties to Adidas for technical services, including training of the company's workers at Adidas in France, evaluating the quality of raw materials, checking the quality of final products and providing technical advice on the purchase of machinery and equipment.

Investment in new machinery in 1974 doubled the firm's production capacity, to 40 000 balls, from its 1968 level. Further investments in machinery in 1980 and 1985 raised the capacity to 65 000 and then to 110 000 balls.

In 1986, Orbitsports' exports to Africa and Europe amounted to KSh10.5 million, 45 per cent of total sales. By 1990 this had grown to KSh27 million, some 60 per cent of total sales. In the 1990 soccer world cup, Orbitsports supplied almost all of the 300 balls required. Of the total exports of the company in recent years, 70 per cent went to Europe and 30 per cent to Africa. The projection for 1992 was lower, at KSh21 million. The decline was attributed to lack of import licences, which take 4 to 5 months to acquire (problems related to import licences led to the loss of an export order of KSh7 million during the year), import duties on synthetic materials, and the declining competitiveness of the firm due to low labour productivity and inflexible labour arrangements.

Technology, productivity and human resources

Production linkages and subcontracting

Manufacturing balls is highly labour intensive. Due to the high labour costs in developed countries, Adidas found it more profitable to subcontract the manufacture of balls to firms in developing countries. Orbitsports' subcontracting arrangement with Adidas in 1974 was the single most important factor behind its phenomenal success in the export market. Through it, Orbitsports acquired highly sophisticated machines which are still in good working condition, partly due to the company's policy of preventive maintenance. The firm has a full-time engineer whose responsibilities included preventive and breakdown maintenance of the machines, which are overhauled at the end of each year.

The firm's strategy is to market its products aggressively, both in Africa and North America, and to avoid relying too much on subcontracts with Adidas. The firm has already appointed an agent as a first step in this new direction. One of the constraints with regard to North and South America is that Orbitsports cannot export there under the Adidas label because Adidas has another appointed agent there.

To maintain its market share, especially in Africa, the company has adopted the strategy of appointing a large number of distributors to counter competing imports and of giving their agents special terms such as 60 days' credit. The company found credit terms to be the most effective strategy.

Technology and productivity

The company's entry into the export market was attributed to its technical cooperation agreement with Adidas in 1974, which has enabled the company to modernize its technology and pay greater attention to quality control. Between 1976 and 1979, most of the firm's exports went to African countries, with exports to Europe starting in the early 1980s and reaching a peak in 1986, when they surpassed exports to Africa. In 1980, Orbitsports scrapped most of the old machines and replaced them with new ones. This shift followed Adidas' policy of progressively reducing its own production and relying more on subcontracting in various parts of the developing world. By the early 1980s, the quality of the company's products had improved tremendously.

The main competitors in the export market include Pakistan, India, Indonesia, the former Yugoslavia and Hungary. All the main ball manufacturers have technical agreements with Adidas. A number of recent developments have adversely affected Orbitsports' competitiveness in the export market. Some of these are associated with technological changes in the manufacture of balls. Up to 1990, leather was the main raw material. This gave Orbitsports a competitive edge due to the domestic availability of cheap, high-quality leather. The main imports included special chemicals used to coat leather to make the ball water- and scratch-resistant and to stabilize its shape. Up to 1990, the imported content in an Orbitsports football was 33 per cent. Thus, under the circumstances prevailing up to 1990, the firm had the competitive edge over many other Adidas agents.

Since 1990, Adidas has recommended a shift to synthetic, non-woven fabrics in the manufacture of balls. The shift has raised Orbitsports' imported content to 76 per cent, as it has to import its main raw materials. This has immensely reduced the firm's competitiveness against European firms, where the synthetic materials are cheaper than leather. The problem has been aggravated by high import duties on imported synthetic materials. The company has subsequently lost its bids for some export orders to competitors from Asia and Europe.

Another change that affected the competitiveness of Orbitsports in the export market in 1981 was the introduction of a new technology that enabled mechanical punching of holes in leather. This permits stitchers to make more balls per day. Under the previous technology, the holes were manually punched. With the old technology, average productivity per worker was 2.5 balls per day. The average productivity using the new technology is 3.5 to 4 balls per day per worker. Orbitsports is, however, unable to enjoy the full benefits of the new technology because the workers, through their trade union, have strongly resisted revision of a 1968 Collective Bargain Agreement which specified that workers were expected to achieve a target of 2.5 balls per day. The firm has been trying to negotiate a new target of about 3.5 or 4 balls per day in order to match competitors in countries such as Pakistan and India but has thus far had no success. The workers insist that the target should not be raised, arguing that when the company receives large urgent orders it should give the workers more overtime work. Unfortunately overtime work has the effect of raising the labour costs of the firm significantly. When workers are given overtime, many of them are able to achieve much higher productivity, of between 4 and 5 balls per day.

The effect of the existing Collective Agreement between the union and the employer has thus been to raise the labour costs per unit in the firm substantially above those of its main competitors. This, coupled with the shift to synthetic materials in the manufacture of balls, has made the Kenyan firm lose ground to other firms. If the company was able to negotiate higher labour productivity it would be in a position to offer more competitive bids for Adidas subcontracts and to increase its market share in Africa and the rest of the world. According to the information provided by the company, its labour costs were, for instance, more than 40 per cent higher than those of sports equipment manufacturers in India and Pakistan.

Apart from the subcontracting arrangement with Adidas, another factor which explains the company's success in exporting was the priority given to marketing. The overall marketing department was well staffed, with a manager specifically in charge of exports, enabling the firm to focus on the export market more effectively than most manufacturing firms in the country.

In spite of its relative export success, the company is highly cautious in its future plans. It is, for instance, against venturing into high-technology fields because the import content of such ventures would be very high. The management cites the problem of obsolescence as a result of quick technological changes and fears that many Kenyan firms would find it difficult to compete in high-technology fields. The firm intended to continue giving priority to products for which 80–90 per cent of raw materials can be obtained domestically, so reducing its import dependence. Foreign exchange constraints create immense problems in meeting production targets and schedules, due to delays and uncertainties in obtaining import licences.

The loss of the company's export competitiveness to its rivals in Asia and Europe was forcing it to adopt new strategies. One of these is to change its employment policy so that permanent employment and time-rate payment are gradually replaced by more contractual and piece-rate arrangements as a way of raising labour productivity and reducing costs. The firm has also been trying to diversify into the production of other leather products and sporting goods to reduce the risk of continued dependence on ball manufacture in a rapidly changing environment.

SUMMARY

This study has examined the role of technology, government policy, marketing strategies, management, labour productivity, ownership structure and the size and structure of the domestic market as determinants of Kenyan firms' export performance. The enterprise case studies were drawn from the textiles and clothing, food processing, pharmaceuticals, metal, paper and packing materials and leather and footwear industries.

Technological dynamism was found to be one of the most crucial factors determining efficiency and export competitiveness. Most firms that had failed to modernize their industrial processes found themselves unable to increase or maintain their export market shares. Other factors were subcontracting export arrangements, the availability of domestic raw materials and competitive labour costs.

Successful exporting firms in the textile, clothing, leather and shoe industries were those which had either adopted relatively modern technology or been able to establish special niche markets. A textile firm, for instance, which specialized in creative designs for women's cultural garments had been able to establish a stable export market. Another firm's impressive exports were due to a contract with an international firm to supply high-quality balls. The firm's competitiveness also depended on locally available leather and low labour costs. A recent shift to synthetic materials and inflexible labour contracts had adversely affected its competitiveness in the last few years.

In the cement industry, one of the two firms was able to export because it had adopted a more modern and fuel-efficient technological process which reduced costs and produced high-quality cement. Liberalization of prices and imports also helped the firm to increase its profitability and lower costs to international market levels.

The case studies show that private firms with foreign ownership and expatriate management tended to have higher efficiency, technical competence and managerial capabilities. Foreign ownership provided the necessary link to the outside world. This was vital for firms' ability to keep up with changing technological processes. The expatriate management played a key role in the adoption of new technologies, training labour and servicing the new equipment.

Specialization and economies of scale emerged as rather insignificant considerations. Most firms relied on specified varying orders from some traditional customers. This was, for instance, shown in the shoe and ball manufacturing firms and two textile firms. These firms' ability to cope with a range of quality requirements and changing customer needs was important.

The study also shows that those firms that had developed a competent and disciplined indigenous workforce, backed by close supervision, were able to maintain their competitiveness in both local and export markets. Continuous training of the workforce was found to be vital in view of the rapidly changing technologies and increasing quality control requirements. The ability of some pharmaceutical firms to enter the highly competitive export market was due to modern equipment, the adoption of more efficient production processes, the use of experienced expatriate pharmacists, and government incentives.

It was also evident that some Kenyan firms which established production facilities between the 1950s and 1970s have continued to export to neighbouring countries in part because these countries have not been able to establish similar facilities, due either to the small size of their markets or the high costs of installing such facilities. In such cases, the market share of the Kenyan firms in these countries was not necessarily based on modern technology or superior quality but rather because they happened to have some manufacturing capacity which was absent in some neighbouring countries. This was, however, a temporary situation which was rapidly becoming quite rare.

NOTES

1 Manufactured items include those classified under SITC 5–8. They exclude food, beverages and tobacco.
2 This excludes unofficial exports, which account for an estimated 20 per cent.

BIBLIOGRAPHY

Coughlin, Peter, The Gradual Maturation of an Import Substitution Industry: The Textile Industry in Kenya. University of Nairobi, mimeo, 1986.
Republic of Kenya, *Economic Survey, 1992*, Nairobi, Government Printer, 1992.
World Bank, *Productivity, Technology Choice and Project Design: With an Application to the Cotton Textile Sector*, World Bank Report, No. 671–77, Washington D.C., 1986.

11 The Ivory Coast

Oussou Kouassy and Bouabre Bohoun

INTRODUCTION

Context of the study

Ivorian industry was very dynamic until the end of the 1970s. In 1960 there were fewer than one hundred firms with a combined turnover of 13 billion f.CFA.[1] By 1978 this had grown to more than 500 firms with a total turnover of 600 billion. By 1984 the number of firms had again increased, to some 750, with a turnover of 1 250 billion. Average annual industrial growth was 13 per cent until 1973, and 8.5 per cent between 1974 and 1981. Manufacturing value added (MVA) grew by 3.7 per cent between 1975 and 1985. In 1960 the industrial sector represented only 14 per cent of the gross national product: this increased to an average of 23 per cent between 1971 and 1981.

But this growth in Ivorian industry began to reverse at the beginning of the 1980s. The financial and economic crisis the country experienced then hit industrial activity and exposed its structural weaknesses. There was in fact a sharp drop in industrial growth (minus 8 per cent between 1981 and 1983), a collapse in investments and accelerated obsolescence of productive capacity. Annual gross investment decreased by 50 per cent between 1981 and 1987. The crisis also meant slower growth in sales (+18 per cent a year between 1978 and 1984, +14 per cent between 1984 and 1986) and serious degeneration in the financial situation of industrial firms. Between 1981 and 1983 the debt level of industrial firms increased from 1.3 billion to 1.8 billion.

From 1981 onward, the effects of the adjustment measures adopted by the government were added to the difficulties linked to the crisis. MVA fell by 1.6 per cent per year between 1985 and 1990. The main measures affecting industry related to changes in the protection system (removal of non-tariff barriers and the reduction of tariff protection) and efforts to lower taxation and factor prices as well as the introduction of an export subsidy scheme. All these measures were intended to revitalize the industrial sector, so as to correct its weaknesses, increase its competitiveness and promote exports.

In this general context of crisis and major changes, often unfavourable to industrial activities, some firms achieved noteworthy performances on the domestic market and sometimes on export markets. We have studied the reasons for these success stories in the hope of finding measures which would consolidate their present performances and encourage the vitalization of other industrial firms.

This analysis is based on a study of a sample of manufacturing firms selected for their capacity to illustrate these themes.

The methodology used here has two elements:

1 a quantitative approach based on a combination of financial analysis, accounting analysis and incentive and comparative advantage calculations. The necessary accounting and financial data for the quantitative analysis was collected either directly from the firms, or from the Banque des Données Financières' (BDF) of the Ministry of Finance and Planning.
2 a qualitative analysis of the characteristics of some industries and industrial firms. This included a study of their history, human resources management and acquisition and development of technologies, in which information collected during interviews with the main actors was of considerable importance.

Choice of sectors and firms

The choice of firms in the sample is based on the relative importance of the industrial sectors, sub-sectors and the firms themselves in Ivorian industry. The three sectors from which we have selected firms are, according to the Ivorian classification of economic activities:

1 Sector 07: industries preserving and processing food (Capral–Nestlé and Saco).
2 Sector 09: the cooking fats industry (Cosmivoire and Trituraf).
3 Sector 11: the textile industry (Uniwax and Cotivo).

These three industries represent a significant proportion of Ivorian industry, in terms of production, export capacity (especially Sector 07) and the value added they generate. On the basis of the 1985 data, the three industries contribute about 26 per cent of the manufacturing output and 16.1 per cent of total exports. The industries of Sector 07 are the major exporters, with 10.2 per cent of total exports.

Two firms were selected from each of these sectors. Capral and Saco together account for 31.7 per cent of production in their industry but generate just 24.3 per cent of the value added. As for the firms producing cooking fats, they have a very high value added: 18 per cent of the industry's value added against only 16.5 per cent of its total output. The textile firms account for just 1.6 per cent of the value added in textiles.

THE COOKING FATS INDUSTRY

General characteristics of the industry

The fats industry is among the most dynamic industrial sectors and also among the most important sectors in the Ivorian economy. It essentially uses local raw materials (products of Ivorian oil palms) and includes practically all the stages of its transformation, from raw oil to the production of soaps, edible oils, margarine and other derived products.

The industry is dominated by three main actors: Palmindustrie, Blohorn and Cosmivoire. The state-owned Palmindustrie, which has positioned itself upstream of the other firms, is both an agricultural and industrial firm. It even provides managerial support for village plantations and is the main supplier of the three industrial firms of the fats industry. Blohorn, the most important actor in the industry, buys on average 79 per cent of the total production of raw oil and accounts for 85 per cent of the country's edible oil production. Blohorn, which belongs to the Anglo-Dutch group Unilever, has reinforced its dominant position on the edible oil market by taking control of one of its competitors, Trituraf, in 1983/84. Trituraf was formerly state-controlled. Besides edible oils, the firms in this industry produce washing and toilet soaps.

In 1990, the market was structured as shown in Table 11.1 Since Blohorn's takeover of Trituraf, Cosmivoire has found itself in second place. It is now the only competitor of the Blohorn group in the

Table 11.1 Market shares by volume in the soap and oil market 1990 (%)

	Blohorn	Trituraf	Cosmivoire
Edible oils	50–60	32 *	10
Soaps	60	18	15
Purchase of raw oil (120 000 tons)	79	5	15

Note: * Production of cotton oil.

sector. It is a private, entirely Ivorian firm, with 13 per cent state participation.

History of the firms in the sample

Cosmivoire

Cosmivoire was formally created in 1974 under the leadership of an agronomist and refrigeration engineer, who had been managing director of an international petroleum exploitation group. But Comivoire's production activities started effectively three years later.

The firm, whose purpose was the manufacture of washing and toilet soap for the domestic market, was a financial success at its launching in 1977. But it very quickly diversified its production, given changes in its competitive environment. Thus it introduced, with much difficulty, the production of edible oil from 1985/86 and later other derivative products (chiefly margarine).

After a difficult period of adaptation to the oil manufacturing technology on the one hand, and despite very active competition on the domestic market on the other hand, the firm is enjoying good performance and significant expansion. Turnover has risen by 50 per cent in comparison with 1990 and now stands at more than 10 billion f.CFA.

The firm was established with majority Ivorian private funds and since the beginning of the 1980s has had a totally Ivorian shareholding (the 1 per cent of capital owned by French interests having been bought out). However, it should be noted that the firm benefits from support from the Société Financière Internationale (SFI), which is a shareholder in one of Cosmivoire's daughter firms and which opportunely provided a loan of US$2 million in 1987. Given its present performance, Cosmivoire appears to be a successful national firm.

Cosmivoire has an excellent relationship with its Italian supplier of production requirements, which built the equipment necessary for the factory and for the diversification of its production. But these connections remain strictly limited to the sale of goods: Cosmivoire is responsible for the acquisition programmes and for equipment adaptations.

Trituraf

In contrast to Cosmivoire, the Société Ivoirienne de Trituration et de Rafinage (Trituraf) was founded in 1973 with majority state funding. Some 79 per cent of its capital is owned by the state and 15 per cent by the Compagnie Ivorian de Développement des Textiles (CIDT). With starting funds of 650 million f.CFA and a total investment of 1.6 billion, the firm started with a throughput capacity of 70 000 tons per year of cotton seeds, which corresponds to 18 000 tons of oil and 15 000 tons of soap per year. Oil production has always been Trituraf's main activity.

Turnover has grown quickly, from 700 million f.CFA in 1975 (when production began) to 10 billion in 1983, then to 18 billion in 1990. The firm widened its field of activity as early as 1983, when it began to develop soap production from cotton and palm oils. The capital was then increased to 1.3 billion f.CFA. Finance for the extension was easily obtained and construction of a palm oil fractional distillation unit was started. The intention was to exploit the soap production capacity fully and raise edible oil production to 25 000 tons per year.

But Blohorn, which had just passed into the hands of the Anglo-Dutch Unilever, reacted to Trituraf's threat of competition on many fronts by deciding to buy the firm. This was done in August 1983.

The story of this firm is interesting from many points of view. J.C. Rochet, initiator of the Trituraf project, was formerly a director at Blohorn. As a consequence of a disagreement on the evolutionary strategy of Blohorn, Rochet resigned from the board of directors of the group in 1970. With the help of the Ivorian authorities and some private individuals, he founded Trituraf in 1973. The process was greatly facilitated by strong support from the Ivorian State and the CIDT, which saw an opportunity to make something from the 100 000 tons of cotton seeds produced every year in the Ivory Coast and wasted. Moreover, a rapid study of the Ivorian market by Rochet during the preparations for the project revealed the similarities between cotton-seed oil and the palmnut oil produced by cottage industry, much appreciated in the area because it is perfectly suited for frying. On this basis a substantial domestic market was forecast. So Trituraf aimed essentially at the production of oil and soap for the domestic market. The firm also produces oil presses for cotton seed (and, since 1984, soya presses), mainly for export markets.

The takeover of Trituraf by Blohorn in 1983/84 immediately meant specialization between the two firms; Trituraf devoting itself to cotton-seed oil and derivative products.

Performance of the firms

Cosmivoire

Since its creation, Cosmivoire has experienced rapid growth. In fact, from 1.5 billion f.CFA in 1980, production reached 6.9 billion in 1990. At first the firm specialized in the manufacture of perfumed toilet and cleaning soaps but it launched into the manufacture of edible oil beginning in 1986, in response to changes in the market and especially competition on the domestic market.

The industry leader, Blohorn, produces both soaps, edible oil and other products derived from fat, and is as a result in a comfortable competitive position because wholesalers have developed the habit of linking their purchases of oil and soap. This practice, seemingly encouraged by Blohorn since 1984, verges on a system of tied sales. It is to loosen this constraint that Cosmivoire has diversified into the production of oil and other derived products, so becoming a full competitor of Blohorn. This is a good example of product diversification under the pressure of competition.

Looking at Table 11.2, we notice that significant diversification is observable at Cosmivoire from 1988, quickly resulting in the predominance of oil production, which represents more than 60 per cent of 1990 sales. From 1988 on, various derived products were also produced.

Cosmivoire's domestic market share (Table 11.3) increased by a factor of 2.5 between 1985 and 1990 and the importance of exports in its total sales also more than doubled, although the company's share in the total exports of the Ivorian oil industry increased only slightly. There was thus a strengthening of Cosmivoire's market position on both the home and export markets. The firm exports mainly to the local region, with some soap going to European markets. In fact it is hard for Cosmivoire to meet European quality standards for edible oils. Nevertheless, the growth in its market shares indicates

Table 11.2 Sales and products for Cosmivoire (million f.CFA)

	1980	1985	1988	1990
Soaps	1 533.2	2 175.0	2 128.8	2 337.0
Edible oil	–	–	3 906.8	4 370.7
Other	–	–	282.4	152.7
Total	1 533.2	2 175.0	6 918.0	6 860.4

Table 11.3 Market shares for Cosmivoire (%)

	1980	1985	1990
Total sales exported	–	6.2	13.48
Share of domestic market	–	4.8	12.2
Share of export market	18.22	19.13	22.09

Table 11.4 Performance of the factors of production for Cosmivoire

	1980	1985	1990
Production/employee	7.00	9.40	7.60
Productivity of physical assets	1.98	0.85	1.13
Average staff unit cost (f.CFA × 1 000)	–	0.98	0.86

Note: Production/employee = Tax-free value added/Total staff. Productivity of physical assets = Tax-free value added/Net physical capital. Average staff unit cost = Total wages/Total staff.

that the firm has adopted a very active commercial strategy and it seems able to bear competition without great damage.

Productivity per employee (Table 11.4) seems high enough, around 8 on average. It is clearly superior to the average staff unit cost (0.9 on average) and it is very close to the industry average (8.8). The productivity of the physical assets is equally high (1.32) and remains fairly stable. It is also well above the cost of usage of the physical assets, at 0.1.

From Table 11.5, Cosmivoire would appear to be an over-protected firm.[2] This is due to the over-protection of the local market on which it realizes most of its sales. In fact, the negative protection of the export market (nearly –65 per cent) affects the firm only slightly. Cosmivoire also appears to have performed only indifferently, but it succeeded in considerably improving its

Table 11.5 Protection, comparative advantage and financial performance indicators for Cosmivoire (%)

	1985	1990
Protection: ERP		
Domestic market	OP	OP
Export market	-73.7	-55.3
Total activity	OP	173.9
Comparative advantage: DRC	2.12	1.14
Financial profitability: Net result/owners' equity	9.24	13.8
Activity profitability: Net result/total sales	2.58	1.4

Notes: ERP = (DVA/IVA) minus 1 = Effective rate of protection.
DRC = $(L^s * W^s + K^s * r^s)/(IVA * SER)$ = Domestic resources cost.
DVA = Domestic value added.
IVA = International value added.
L^s = Labour stock valued at shadow price.
W^s = Shadow wage rate.
K^s = Capital stock valued at shadow price.
r^s = Shadow price of capital.
SER = Ratio of official exchange rate to shadow exchange rate.
OP = Over-protection.

comparative advantage between 1985 and 1990 (its DRC moves from 2.12 to 1.14), thus remedying its clear handicap of the early 1980s.

These results are easily understandable in terms of the firm's diversification of production. This loosened the constraints of tied sales, enlarged the range of its products and improved its return on equity ratio, which moved from 9.24 per cent in 1985 to 13.8 per cent in 1990. According to the managers of the firm, the improvement in the return on equity played an important part by facilitating the realization of investments and improving its utilization of technical assistance.

Trituraf

Trituraf manufactures three main products: edible oils, soap and presses, of which oil is the most important (see Table 11.6). It is on this product that the firm realized most of its turnover, more than 55 per cent of total sales except in 1984.

The sales of soap, the second product, reached 4.2 billion f.CFA in 1984 (34.7 per cent of total sales). The stagnation of soap sales experienced by Trituraf beyond that date was a general phenomenon. Soap being an everyday product, there is a significant amount of unsophisticated local production and importation (mainly smuggled across the borders). Besides, the fall in people's purchasing power has meant a shift in consumer preferences towards less refined and cheaper soap (from cottage industry and imported).

Trituraf is oriented towards the domestic market (see Table 11.7) but between 19 per cent and 24 per cent of its sales are exported. These exports consist of oil presses going to European markets where presses are no longer produced in significant quantities. Trituraf is thus selling secondary products on these markets, without having a real export marketing strategy.

With sales of 700 million f.CFA, the firm had only 5 per cent of the domestic market when it began its activities in 1975. This share increased to 32 per cent between 1984 and 1988 and to 34 per cent in 1990. The growth in Trituraf's market share, on a domestic market which, especially after 1980, was scarcely growing (with an average annual rate of 1.5 per cent between 1984 and 1990) shows the dynamism of this firm. This success is due to the fitness of its products to the characteristics of the market and a very active marketing policy.

Table 11.8 shows a constant improvement in productivity. Productivity per employee, for example, grew from 5.7 in 1980 to almost 12 in 1990. The high level of productivity and its rapid growth was accompanied by a moderate staff unit cost. Therefore, despite the slight rise in the average staff unit cost in 1985 and 1990, we can say that to a certain extent Trituraf has production factor costs under control.[3]

Table 11.9 shows that Trituraf benefited from moderate protection until 1985 (13 per cent on average). Thereafter its level of protection rose, to become very substantial in 1990 (52 per cent). This corresponds to the general characteristics of protection in the Ivorian economy, with high levels of protection for the domestic market and very low levels of protection, and sometimes negative protection, for export markets. Nevertheless, the weak protection of the 1980s was accompanied by good financial results, which fell in the mid-1980s and recovered again by 1990.

We also notice that the firm was quite efficient in 1980 and 1985, when its DRC was well below 1, but in 1990 the DRC was close to 1. This comparative advantage of Trituraf confirms its efficiency in the use of factors of production, which seems not to be affected by changes in ownership.

Table 11.6 Sales and products for Trituraf (million f.CFA)

	1980	1984	1988	1990
Oil in barrels	3 527.9	5 419.0	7 932.8 (19 842)	9 915.3 (25 028)
Soap	–	4 217.0	2 658.7 (11 842)	3 635.6 (15 014)
Cotton oil presses	1 216.8	1 967.0	2 300.6 (48 948)	2 996.7 (55 373)
Other	22.8	539.0	1 128.2	1 452.4
Total	4 767.5	12 142.0	14 020.3	18 000.0

Note: Figures in parentheses are production volumes in tons.

Table 11.7 Market shares for Trituraf (%)

	1975	1980	1985	1990
Total sales exported	–	23.3	22.8	19.32
Share of domestic market	5.0	–	32.0	34.0
Share of export market	–	18.22	19.13	22.09

Table 11.8 Performance of the factors of production for Trituraf

	1980	1985	1990
Production/employee	5.7	8.7	11.8
Productivity of physical assets	0.8	1.18	1.4
Average staff unit cost (f.CFA × 1 000)	0.9	1.70	2.3

Note: See Table 11.4 for definitions of these ratios.

Strategies and capabilities of the firms

Cosmivoire

Table 11.10 clearly indicates that the firm does not produce under licence. It is the managers of the firm who design the processes and select the machines to be bought. The present plant for both oil and soap production was provided by Italian manufacturers. Cosmivoire's investments (Table 11.11) reached a peak in 1985, the year in which the firm began edible oil production. The firm also pursues a policy of very active management of the machinery inventory and machinery replacement and of the depreciation of fixed assets.

Table 11.9 Protection, comparative advantage and financial performance indicators for Trituraf (%)

	1980	1985	1990
Protection: ERP			
Domestic market	27.00	29.00	124.00
Export market	–25.00	–24.00	–46.00
Total activity	9.00	13.00	52.00
Comparative advantage: DRC	0.58	0.52	0.99
Financial profitability:			
Net result/owners' equity	103.38	50.98	96.50
Activity profitability:			
Net result/total sales	14.10	4.85	6.72

Note: See Table 11.5 for definitions.

Table 11.10 Indicators of the management of technology and human resources for Cosmivoire (million f.CFA)

	1985	1990
Royalties on licences and patents	–	–
Disinvestment	0.1	2.4
Training costs	1.8 (0.05%)	11.7 (2.00%)
Technical assistance fees	6.2 (1.90%)	13.3 (2.30%)

Note: Figures in parentheses show percentage of total wages.

Table 11.11 Investment strategy indicators for Cosmivoire (million f.CFA)

	1980	1985	1990
New investment in physical assets	15.9	382.3	145.7
Total new investment	54.3	437.5	340.7

Table 11.12 Investment strategy indicators for Trituraf (million f.CFA)

	1980	1985	1990
Investment in physical assets	914	599	1 021
Total investment	989	869	1 325

Table 11.13 Indicators of the management of technology and human resources for Trituraf (million f.CFA)

	1980	1985	1990
Royalties on licences and patents	–	–	155.7
Disinvestment	511.4	234.9	30.7
Training costs	4.2	629.7	5.0
Technical assistance fees	115.6	266.7	487.0

Cosmivoire intends to install a computerized control system for certain segments of the production lines soon. These computer tools are intended to ensure the rapid feeding of the oil processors with precise and constant quantities of raw oil. This new system will replace the present manual operation, which is generally less precise and more difficult to control and which often results in losses of raw material in the process. Cosmivoire therefore expects a notable increase in productivity as a consequence of these improvements. The improvements are also intended to increase the technical precision, which is necessary to meet the manufacturing standards required by export markets.

Cosmivoire's technological approach and the implementation of the new technologies require the firm to resort to specialized companies to install machinery and train staff to adjust them. This involves substantial training and technical assistance fees. The notable increase in the training costs in 1990 (2 per cent of the total wages in 1990 versus 0.05 per cent in 1985) shows the firm's desire for independence, although it continues to use expensive foreign technical assistance (from 1.9 per cent of the total wages in 1985, these expenses increased to 2.3 per cent in 1990). Technical assistance was mainly focused on the maintenance of machinery and staff training.

The marked increase in training and technical assistance fees between 1985 and 1990 was due to the diversification into oil production. A French engineer specialized in manufacturing techniques for edible oil was recruited to start the oil factory and to train the production personnel. But the managers of Cosmivoire are conscious of important weaknesses which remain at the level of the production process and labour organization. The principal concerns are the precise definition of employees' tasks, the links between the various segments of the production lines, and the separation of certain functions (especially the technical functions on the one hand and financial and administrative functions on the other).

Cosmivoire's marketing strategy is one of the keys to its success. At the outset, the firm established sales depots at wholesalers and at certain retailers. By doing so it shares the risks inherent to distribution. This system strengthens customer loyalty. The other decisive element in the marketing strategy is the promotion policy. Each product launch is generally preceded by a detailed study and by the identification of simple and perceptible differentiation factors, followed by advertising campaigns backed by the traditional media (newspapers, audiovisuals, billboards, etc.).

In searching for differentiation factors, the focus generally lies on the specific characteristics of the domestic market. The idea is that matching the characteristics of the market is more important than the adoption of the latest technological innovations. In its edible oil production, for instance, the firm is satisfied with a product which is sure to meet the regional quality standards, which may differ from the generally stricter standards in developed countries.

Trituraf

From Table 11.12 (p. 354) we can see that Trituraf invests a great deal, 800 million f.CFA per annum on average over the period of study, with peaks of more than 1.3 billion in 1984 and 1990. The bulk of the investments are acquisitions of physical capital. These investments are essentially self-financed.

The circumstances of the firm's establishment, especially the central role played by the Ivorian State, the CIDT and the initiator, Rochet, determined the venture's access to advanced and suitable technology. Rochet, an engineer and former member of the managerial staff of Blohorn, brought with him his technical experience and international contacts, particularly his links with European suppliers of machinery and materials for the realization of the project. The suppliers were also reassured by the presence of the Ivorian state and CIDT.

The processes and the equipment were progressively put into operation under Rochet's instruction, beginning with the oil production unit in 1976, followed in the early 1980s by the soap factory. The addition of cotton-seed processing was a major innovation in the Ivory Coast, so that the process of setting up production units and processes involved the staff deeply. This quickly resulted in very good local proficiency in running the machinery.

All these elements explain why the firm pays very little in fees and royalties for the use of licences or patents (Table 11.13). There were no royalty costs until after 1985. Outside technical assistance, mainly for major overhauls of production units and the maintenance of the larger plant, is used and is important, especially after 1985. An average of more than 350 million f.CFA of technical assistance fees were paid between 1985 and 1990 but Trituraf is reducing this assistance.

The firm's human resources management is characterized by professional training efforts which are intended to increase the firm's independence. The policy of recruiting skilled Ivorian professionals and employees with at least a general college education has permitted a rapid and sizeable reduction in training costs while building up a qualified and motivated workforce. The technical standard of the staff was so high that after the takeover by Blohorn in 1983 the accent was put on management training, preferably in-house or in Europe. This explains the peaks in the training expenses of 1985 and 1986 (more than 600 million f.CFA).

Given the novelty of its product (cotton-seed oil and derived products) and the presence of two other firms on the market (Blohorn and Cosmivoire), Trituraf decided from the beginning on an active marketing strategy, based on the promotion of its products and the establishment of a diversified distribution network. The size of the distribution network and the externalization of most of its marketing functions explain the high level of brokerage and commissions on sales, which have been regularly increasing since 1980. These costs moved from 11.4 million f.CFA in 1980 to more than 40 million in 1990. Furthermore, the dynamic marketing policy of Trituraf has meant expensive advertising, growing from 41 million f.CFA in 1980 to a little less than 200 million in 1990.

PRESERVED AND PROCESSED FOODS

General characteristics of the industry

Products derived from coffee and cocoa certainly comprise the most important sector of the Ivorian economy. This industry takes care of the local processing of the two main agro-industrial products of the country. Since API was taken over by Saco, and Procaci (today Unicao) was bought by Safica, the sub-sector has been dominated by five main companies. Two of them (Chocodi and Saco) are controlled by the French group Cacao Barry, and one (Capral) by the Swiss group Nestlé. The government has substantial stakes in all the companies in the industry. They are also extremely specialized.

Thus, Chocodi, Saco and Unicao mainly engage in cocoa processing, whereas Capral and the Société Africaine de Torrefaction (SAT) specialize in coffee processing. The majority of the output from the sub-sector is destined for export markets, local consumption being very low (less than 10 per cent on average).

History of the firms in the sample

Capral–Nestlé (Compagnie Africaine de Préparation Alimentair)

Capral–Nestlé was founded in 1962 to undertake the local processing of coffee. It started with an initial investment of about 5 billion f.CFA, an installed capacity of 4 500 tons per year and a total staff of fewer than 100 employees. The state and some private individuals provided some of Capral's capital, which is dominated by Nestlé's 80 per cent holding. Its main product is instant coffee.

In addition to the fiscal advantages provided by the 1959 investment code, a setting-up agreement signed with the government allowed the firm to buy green coffee at local prices, which are sometimes as low as one third or one quarter of world prices. However, in 1984 the government put an end to this arrangement and the fiscal advantages under the investment code expired at the same time.

Capral has been an exporting firm since its creation. Its export rate was already around 80 per cent at the end of the 1970s. The firm has also enjoyed a rapid increase in sales, which have risen from 7 billion f.CFA in 1977 to more than 25 billion today. Its production capacity has also grown very rapidly, reaching more than 9000 tons per year at the end of the 1970s. The company thus has more than 60 per cent of the green coffee processing capacity in the Ivory Coast.

Capral has close relations with its mother firm, especially regarding the international promotion and distribution of its products, technology and training (Nestlé's training centre provides training for Capral's executives). But the firm has total freedom in the management of human resources, the purchase of local materials and supplies and minor adjustments to the machinery.

Saco (La Société Africaine de Cacao)

The company was set up as early as 1962 with government and French private funds (65 per cent of the starting capital belonging to Cacao Barry) of 1.155 billion f.CFA. Saco's essential aim was the local processing of the non-exportable cocoa beans. The maximal exploitation of the installed capacity, 35 500 tons a year, soon required big investments that led to an increase in the capital, which has now reached 1.73 billion f.CFA. Saco also benefited from the advantages of the 1959 investment code and an agreement with the government allowing it to purchase its raw material at local cost prices, according to a special marketing and pricing scheme operated by Caistab, the marketing board in charge of coffee selling.[4]

Saco had a monopoly for about 10 years, after which many state-created companies started trading in the sector. One such was API, set up in 1973 with a production capacity of 35 000 tons per year. Another was Procaci, established in 1974 with a capacity of 30 000 tons per year. Chocodi (1976) had a capacity of only 7 000 tons per year. But in the middle of the 1980s nearly all of these newcomers disappeared. Saco took over API while Safica took over Procaci, which in the meantime had become Unicao. Thus Saco is today both the pioneer and the heir of most of the local cocoa-bean processing activities and the production of various by-products.

Performance of the firms

Capral–Nestlé

Capral's production, as can be seen in Table 11.14, grew quickly till the mid-1980s and then stagnated. The production of instant coffee for instance, which was 7.8 billion f.CFA in 1975, reached more than 24 billion in 1985 and then fell to 22.7 billion in 1990.

The product range was extended in 1981 with the introduction of chocolate drinks and new kinds of instant coffee. The firm also introduced more varied packaging (bulk packs, tins of various sizes and individual sachets). The individual doses of instant coffee and chocolate drinks, in particular, were a great success. These innovations were introduced by Capral itself as a response to the needs of the market.

Table 11.15 shows that Capral is very efficient in both domestic and export markets. Exports are mainly instant coffee destined for Africa, the Middle East and Greece. The company has regularly increased the portion of its products which are exported while strengthening its mastery of the domestic market. Its domestic market share increased from 82 per cent in 1975 to more than 83

Table 11.14 Sales and products for Capral (million f.CFA)

	1975	1980	1985	1990
Instant coffee	7 801.8	10 427.4	24 002.6	22 706.7
Chocolate beverages	–	–	501.4	677.9
Dolca	–	–	–	6.0
Other products	–	108.2	249.2	–
Total	7 801.8	10 535.6	24 753.2	23 390.6

Table 11.15 Market shares for Capral (%)

	1975	1980	1985	1990
Total sales exported	81.85	82.70	83.25	84.72
Share of domestic market	–	81.30	86.70	87.70
Share of export market	95.47	88.01	95.26	91.59

Table 11.16 Performance of the factors of production for Capral

	1980	1985	1990
Productivity/employee	11.20	9.18	20.50
Productivity of physical assets	1.40	1.80	1.45
Average staff unit cost (f.CFA × 1 700)	1.70	0.93	1.63

Note: See Table 11.4 for definitions of these ratios.

Table 11.17 Protection, comparative advantage and financial performance for Capral (%)

	1980	1985	1990
Protection: ERP			
Domestic market	49.00	93.00	60.00
Export market	–58.00	–77.00	–58.00
Total activity	–52.00	–73.00	–52.00
Comparative advantage: DRC	0.26	0.18	0.20
Financial profitability: Net result/ owners' equity	18.95	–4.45	43.50
Activity profitability: Net result/ net sales	4.94	–0.49	6.84

Note: See Table 11.5 for definitions.

per cent, on average, between 1980 and 1990. The involvement of Capral in both the domestic and export markets challenges the conventional views according to which export orientation strategies are opposed to domestic market development.

Productivity per employee (Table 11.16) increased regularly (except in 1985) and reached high levels (11.7 on average) with a peak of 20.5 in 1990. This productivity level is well above the average staff unit cost, which averages 1.4.

Table 11.17 shows that Capral is very much unprotected. In fact, in spite of the high protection of its domestic market, the lack of protection for its exports, which are the larger part of its sales, means that the company faced an average negative protection of about 60 per cent from 1980 to 1990. The relatively important negative protection of its export markets (an anti-export bias) did not prevent the company from recording good performances in export activities. Capral is very efficient, benefiting from a net comparative advantage (with a DRC below 0.3 on average). The company also enjoyed good financial performances, except in 1985 (with a return on equity of about 30 per cent on average).

Saco

Saco's production, as can be seen in Table 11.18, grew rapidly till the middle of the 1980s, and then fell back. When it was set up, Saco manufactured three main products: butter, paste and cocoa presses, and incidentally some cocoa powder. The three main products represented more than 98 per cent of sales. Butter averaged more than 57 per cent of total sales, followed by cocoa paste. In 1980 Saco abandoned cocoa powder production in order to concentrate on its three main products.

From 1985 Saco's operations suffered a decline, particularly noticeable in the export market. This can be explained by the fall in world cocoa prices and the reduction in some advantages it enjoyed as regards the deductions from world prices relating to the quality and size of the processed cocoa beans. These factors, which have to some extent counterbalanced the advantages of Saco relating to the cost of raw materials, must be reflected in the competitiveness of its exports.

The data in Table 11.19 confirms Saco's export orientation. In fact, almost all its output is exported (the figures take into account changes in the stock level). One can note the fluctuation in Saco's markets, including the domestic market, despite its dominant

Table 11.18 Sales and products for Saco

	1975	1980	1985	1990
Cocoa butter	6 093.4	6 868.3	23 574.0	11 420.8
	(8 057)	(5 859)	(10 753)	(14 740)
Cocoa paste	3 111	2 847.2	9 823.9	2 578.8
	(6 965)	(3 595)	(7 808)	(6 538)
Cocoa	1 407.4	921.1	5 112.6	2 114.7
	(8 671)	(3 907)	(13 092)	(17 147)
Miscellaneous				
(cocoa powder)	205.5	414.3	–	–
	(1 580)	(1 364)	–	–
Total	10 817.3	11 050.9	38 510.5	16 114.3

Note: Figure in parentheses show production volume, in tons.

Table 11.19 Market shares for Saco (%)

	1975	1980	1985	1990
Total sales exported	99.20	99.20	99.50	99.40
Share of domestic market	55.00	47.30	47.00	76.00
Share of export market	95.47	88.01	95.26	91.59

Table 11.20 Performance of the factors of production for Saco

	1975	1980	1985	1990
Productivity/employee	5.98	6.34	13.50	5.99
Productivity of physical assets	1.98	2.18	2.33	0.68
Average staff unit cost				
(f.CFA × 17 000)	0.36	0.84	1.80	2.10

Note: See Table 11.4 for definitions of these ratios.

position there. From 55 per cent in 1975, its domestic market share fell in 1980–85 to just 47 per cent, due to the arrival of new companies in the sector, and improved after 1985 to more than 75 per cent. Saco was thus the main beneficiary of the disappearance of companies such as Procaci and API.

Saco's productivity per employee (Table 11.20) is very high, between 5 and 6 on average with a peak of 13.5 in 1985. This performance, among the best in Ivorian industry, is particularly remarkable when compared to the low average staff unit cost of between 0.4 and 2. The productivity of the physical assets, although slightly weaker, remains at acceptable levels (between 0.6 and 2.3). Thus we can say that Saco uses the factors of production efficiently. This is in accordance with the company's focus on controlling production costs and tight management of the plant.

Saco faced negative protection (Table 11.21), of –45 per cent on average between 1980 and 1990, in spite of the relatively high protection of its domestic market (especially in 1980). This is caused by the negative protection of its export market, the core of the firm's sales. But it seems that this constant negative protection is not a decisive factor in Saco's profitability, which fluctuates tremendously. The financial results are determined rather by changes in the structure of the industry. Thus the profitability of the company, which was good until 1975 (the monopoly period) and after 1985 (quasi-monopoly), clearly decreased between 1975 and 1985 (a competitive period).

Whereas the financial difficulties of 1980 were in large measure compensated for by an increase in capital (+50 per cent), the collapse of 1990 (due mainly to the deep crisis affecting the whole cacao industry) has required drastic solutions such as staff reductions and frequent temporary lay-offs. The poor financial results from 1990 are also partly due to the fall in exports, provoked *inter alia* by the lack of support from Caistab although world prices were constantly below local cost prices. Caistab could not face the growing demand for

Table 11.21 Protection, comparative advantage and financial performance indicators for Saco (%)

	1975	*1980*	*1985*	*1990*
Protection: ERP				
Domestic market		OP	15.00	32.00
Export market		–51.00	–50.00	–38.00
Total activity		–51.00	–50.00	–38.00
Comparative advantage: DRC		0.25	0.18	0.34
Financial profitability:				
Net result/owners' equity	20.65	–0.03	33.00	–27.20
Activity profitability:				
Net result/total sales	2.20	–0.01	1.48	–2.90

Note: See Table 11.5 for definitions.

reimbursements and ran into arrears. Such a situation obliged Saco to run into heavy short-term debt.

In spite of a high negative protection and financial vicissitudes, Saco has a DRC under 0.5, showing a comparative advantage in its sector – a proof that it is a high-performing company.

Strategies and capabilities of the firms

Capral–Nestlé

Capral devotes considerable resources to financing investments (Table 11.22). Investment in physical capital, which represented less than 20 per cent of the total in 1975, rose to 70 per cent and 67 per cent in 1985 and 1990 respectively. These peaks in the acquisition of physical capital are linked to the capacity increases of the 1980s.

The company shows here the characteristics of a subsidiary which produces under licence and also devotes significant resources to foreign technical assistance (Table 11.23). In fact Capral, producing instant coffee under a Nestlé licence, pays heavy fees for that. Moreover, the company needs regular technical assistance from the mother firm to carry out these activities, for the selection, installation and maintenance of machinery and the training of executives (training of employees being generally done on the spot). Training to improve the local mastery of the working processes is one of the company's main concerns. Capral's management gives a great deal of attention to the definition of workers' tasks, to workers' skills and their progress in gaining proficiency and the systematic retraining of the whole workforce (employees, supervisory staff and executives). Spending in this area increased from 13 million f.CFA in 1980 to 17 million in 1985 and 21 million in 1990.

Capral has limited possibilities in terms of marketing strategy: its exports (the main part of the firm's sales) are handled by Nestlé-WTC, the trading subsidiary of the Nestlé group. Nestlé-WTC manages the export markets and is in charge of the international promotion of Capral products. It is only the domestic market that is managed by Capral itself. This explains the high commissions paid on sales, more than the advertising expenses. Nevertheless, there has been a steady growth in advertising expenses, while these commissions have not increased. This is a sign of the systematic efforts made by the company to strengthen its position on the domestic market while also striving for strong positions on the export market.

Table 11.22 Investment strategy indicators for Capral (million f.CFA)

	1975	1980	1985	1990
Investment in physical assets	23.7	80.9	242.5	1 394.8
Total investment	242.6	459.8	343.5	2 078.0

Table 11.23 Indicators of the management of technology and human resources for Capral (million f.CFA)

	1980	1985	1990
Royalties on licences and patents	732.4	1 491.5	1 337.8
Disinvestment	1.7	9.5	1.1
Training costs	13.3	17.4	21.2
	(1.20%)	(1%)	(0.09%)
Technical assistance fees	23.4	20.5	36.4
	(200%)	(1.2%)	(1.6%)

Note: Figures in parentheses show percentage of total wages.

Table 11.24 Investment strategy indicators for Saco (million f.CFA)

	1975	1980	1985	1990
Investment in physical assets	68.5	55.7	191.4	107.7
Total investment	93.6	78.8	737.0	382.8

Table 11.25 Indicators of technology and human resources management for Saco (million f.CFA)

	1980	1985	1990
Royalties on licences and patents	0.0	0.0	0.0
Disinvestment	1.6	16.8	31.7
Training costs	1.4	3.4	26.1
	(0.60)	(0.02)	(1.40)
Technical assistance fees	319.9	819.0	683.9
	(140.00)	(51.00)	(40.00)

Note: Figures in parentheses show percentage of total wages.

Saco

Saco has invested regularly since its creation, with total investments peaking at more than 700 million f.CFA (Table 11.24). Until 1985 physical capital was the most important component of total investments (more than 70 per cent in 1985). Since then these investments have become a smaller portion (25 per cent) of the total, showing that investments in trading and marketing activities have become much more important. Saco's investments are generally self-financed.

The processing of the non-exportable grades of cocoa (those with high numbers of black or small beans) required Saco to find an appropriate technology and a method of strictly controlling the production and quality control processes. Since cocoa grinding and pressing techniques are generally standardized, technology management will have to focus mainly on the selection, adaptation, management and maintenance of equipment on the one hand and cost and quality control on the other. Saco uses the basic 'Dutch process', a set of free processes which are not subject to licences and patents and which are widely known all over the world. The selection of machines and the management of the plant are mainly done through Cacao Barry, Saco's mother company, using the group's international network. This technical assistance entails high fees (Table 11.25).

Saco puts much emphasis on cost and quality control. To this end, it has installed a computerized device which provides the firm with day-to-day cost indicators and monthly reviews of the production units. This helps in assessing the technical performance of the various factories and in improving the organization of the working processes. These efforts have, for instance, permitted the Zone 4 unit to increase its throughput from 35 000 tons to 42 000 tons per year. In addition, the technical control helps the company to increase its flexibility, making it easier to meet the various standards and specifications required by some markets. This reinforces its export capacities.

Management of human resources is also seen as a major priority at Saco. Efforts are made to increase the adaptability, discipline and motivation of the workers. Professional training programmes were increased from 1990, in response to the need to reduce the numbers of employees and control costs. The costs of these programmes, which had been around 1.4 million f.CFA, rose to 26 million f.CFA in 1990.

The company exports most of its production. The exports are destined in the first place for Cacao Barry, to supply its production subsidiaries in Europe and the US. Saco also exports to Asia and Australia but even there its operations are organized through Barry's international trading services. This explains the size of the commissions on sales, which were particularly high after 1985. In fact Saco's main customers are factories, so that its possibilities for sales and marketing innovation are very limited.

THE TEXTILES INDUSTRY

General characteristics of the industry

The industry has four large companies: ERG, Utexi, Cotivo and Uniwax. They concentrate on spinning and weaving (ERG, Utexi and Cotivo) and cloth printing (ERG, Utexi and Uniwax). The textiles industry is one of the oldest industrial activities in the country: ERG was founded in 1962 and Uniwax in 1965. It aims at the local processing of the 280 000 tons of raw cotton produced yearly in the Ivory Coast. From this it produces 120 000 tons of fibre per year and 130 000 tons of cotton seed. But only 20 per cent of the cotton fibre receives further processing. This can be explained by the absence of an appropriate development policy for the sector as a whole, the CIDT preferring the export of non-processed cotton fibres.

The industry includes both companies with significant state shareholdings (ERG and Utexi) and private companies which are subsidiaries of multinational groups (Uniwax, a subsidiary of the Anglo-Dutch group Unilever, Cotivo, a subsidiary of the French group Schaeffer and ERG, controlled by the French group DMC). The main final product of the industry is finished cloth. Uniwax specializes in wax prints for the local market, ERG and Utexi meet the local demand for fancy prints. The domestic cloth market has undergone a considerable contraction over the last 10 years: the total consumption of cloth went down from 46 to 30 million metres.[5]

History of the firms in the sample

Uniwax

Created in 1967, Uniwax was at first controlled by Blohorn, which owned 80 per cent of the capital, the other 20 per cent being held by the German group Vlisco. In taking control of Blohorn in 1980, Unilever became a majority shareholder in Uniwax (with 68 per cent of the capital), Vlisco's part diminished slightly (17 per cent) and private Ivorian shareholders entered with just 15 per cent. The installed production capacity was 25 million yards per year but actual production peaked at the beginning of the 1980s at only 15 million yards per year. The company produces only 7.5 million yards today, a production level just above its break-even point, estimated at 7 million yards.

Uniwax has experienced two types of major difficulties. At the end of the 1960s, when the firm was launched, concerns about cost reduction led the management to abandon the last of the three washings which the printed material normally went through as part of the process. The idea was based on the fact that the colours used fade after six manual washings. One fewer wash would reduce total costs while extending the life of the product. This idea proved disastrous because consumers concluded on the contrary that the colours could not resist washing. In spite of the quick correction of the mistake, the negative image of Ivorian wax prints has been a long-term handicap for Uniwax's products in competing with imported wax prints, coming mainly from Holland. This has obliged the company to undertake long and costly advertising campaigns.

Uniwax's other major difficulties relate to the fall in domestic demand, due to the general crisis of the Ivorian economy. This has been exacerbated by a shift in consumer preferences. Some of Uniwax's traditional customers now opt for the top-class 'fancy' prints, of lower quality than wax prints but reasonably good substitutes for Uniwax's products. This situation was further worsened by the unprecedented development of smuggling of imported wax prints via Togo or Gambia and from Nigeria. All these factors have naturally led to enormous losses. Cumulative losses at the end of 1988 were some 2.5 billion f.CFA, that is to say 2.5 times the capital. These losses have been totally covered by reserves and cost reduction efforts. Staff levels have been cut by more than half (from 982 in the middle of the 1980s down to 362 today), and executive positions, apart from those in central and technical management, have been terminated. The company has also had to resort several times to temporary production shut downs (most recently, from 15 November 1990 to 15 March 1991).

This vigorous reorganization has been assisted by significant tax relief measures (decreases in tariffs on imported inputs, removal of taxes on private water pumps and wells, a decrease in taxes on fuel) and more vigorous efforts against smuggling (using counter-measures but also with a reduction in tariffs, making smuggling less attractive).

Cotivo

Cotivo was created in 1974 but started its activities in January 1976. The capital of the company was 3.6 billion f.CFA, shared by the French group Schaeffer (32.5 per cent), the Ivorian government and a state-owned bank, BIDI (27 per cent), other public shareholders (DEG of Germany and the Swiss Sifida) and some other private operators (CFAO, CNF). The management of Cotivo was at the outset put in the hands of Schaeffer. The installed treatment capacity, of 8 500 tons per year of cotton fibre, allows the company to produce 500 tons of raw yarn per year and more than 20 million metres of fabric.

Cotivo was founded by Icodi (Ivoirienne Cotonnière d'Impression), a subsidiary of Schaeffer, to supply it with basic fabric for its 'fancy' printing operations. The firm also supplied other fabric printers in the Ivory Coast (Uniwax and ERG) and in Niger (Soni-textil). At that time, Cotivo's activities were oriented mainly towards the domestic market.

In the early 1980s, there was a shift in the firm's orientation as Icodi stopped its activities and the American group Blue Bell started to produce jeans locally. Blue Bell used Cotivo's fabric, most notably in manufacturing the famous Wrangler Jeans. From that time, the supply of heavy-dyed stretch fabric (denim) to Blue Bell became Cotivo's most important activity after the delivery of unbleached cloth to independent fabric printers. The importance of denim was increased by the establishment of the Challenger company, in the industrial area of Yopougon, to make ready-made denim items. Cotivo thus ceased to have any real contact with the downstream pro-cessing of its cloth, while its weaving capacity increased to 27 million metres (21 million metres of unbleached cloth and 6 million metres of dyed cloth and denim). This capacity has since remained unchanged.

The production of denim for Blue Bell and Challenger forced Cotivo to meet international quality standards and to master denim production technologies. A yarn-dyeing unit and an appropriate weaving system for heavy fabrics were set up, involving significant investments. Some machinery was bought second-hand from Europe and some was new.

The adjustment of the firm to the standards of its new market (jeans) facilitated a shift towards export markets later, when Blue Bell closed down its Ivorian subsidiary in 1985 and when the government introduced an export subsidy scheme in 1986. Cotivo was able to transform itself into an export firm. To tackle the export markets, Cotivo created a European branch in Belgium in charge of exploring and developing the jeans markets in Europe and the US.

Cotivo also bought shares in Utexi in 1987 (8 per cent of the capital) so as to get involved in cloth printing activities and strengthen its position on the domestic market.

We also notice that the shift in the firm's orientation towards exports has resulted in financial costs and some staff adjustment. The firm increased its assets from 1985 to 1990, while regularly reducing its staff except for the managerial staff, whose number increased. These trends are due to the need to adapt to export market conditions, which require additional investments and skilled labour.

Performance of the firms

Uniwax

Uniwax manufactures only one product, wax prints. Its production (Table 11.26) grew regularly until 1985 and then started to fall. Sales, which were 3.5 billion f.CFA in 1975, grew to more than 8.7 billion in 1980 and then to 12.8 billion in 1985. They dropped to 7.5 billion in 1990, a 40 per cent fall. This is another indicator of the difficulties which Uniwax had to face from the middle of the 1980s.

Uniwax's domestic market share (Table 11.27) increased until 1985 but fell sharply between then and 1990 although the firm retained its dominant position. The portion of output going to the export market, which was relatively low until 1985, increased dramatically from 3 per cent to almost 10 per cent over the same period. Facing difficulties on the domestic market (a fall in demand, increased smuggling and shifts in consumer preferences), Uniwax had to turn towards export markets, mainly in the local region.

Table 11.26 Sales and products for Uniwax (million f.CFA)

	1975	1980	1985	1990
Wax prints	3 576.9	8 777.4	12 878.5	7 486.0
Total	3 576.9	8 777.4	12 878.5	7 486.0

Table 11.27 Market shares for Uniwax (%)

	1975	1980	1985	1990
Total sales exported	5.68	6.12	3.20	9.90
Share of domestic market	67.80	66.70	74.50	50.30
Share of export market	17.90	13.40	13.20	–

Table 11.28 Performance of the factors of production for Uniwax

	1975	1980	1985	1990
Productivity/employee	3.26	3.26	4.91	3.28
Productivity of physical assets	2.05	1.74	1.32	0.60
Average staff unit cost (f.CFA × 1 000)	–	0.64	0.91	1.13

Note: See Table 11.4 for definitions of these ratios.

Table 11.29 Protection, comparative advantage and financial performance indicators for Uniwax (%)

	1975	1980	1985	1990
Protection: ERP				
Domestic market	–	139.00	176.00	OP
Export market	–	–30.00	–21.00	–49.00
Total activity	–	110.00	157.00	OP
Comparative advantage: DRC	–	0.91	1.29	1.65
Financial profitability: Net result/owners' equity	24.34	55.40	113.90	–64.00
Activity profitability: Net result/total sales	5.10	6.30	8.80	–8.60

Note: See Table 11.5 for definitions.

Table 11.28 shows that Uniwax enjoys fairly high productivity levels. Its productivity per employee (3.6 on average), is constantly higher than the average staff unit cost (0.9 on average) and well above the industry average (3.04 in 1990). The stability of this indicator is largely due to the simple technology used, the relative age of the plant and the limited possibilities of productivity increases given Uniwax's technical setting. The productivity of physical assets is also relatively high.

Uniwax is an over-protected firm (Table 11.29). Despite the slight negative protection of the export market, the over-protection of the domestic market on which the firm realizes most of its sales confers a very high level of protection. Uniwax, which was very efficient in 1980 (with a DRC of 0.9), became less efficient from 1985 (its DRC rising to 1.65 in 1990). This is in line with traditional views on protection and firm performance. We also note that the good financial performances of the 1980s definitely deteriorated in 1990, with the firm experiencing considerable financial losses.

Cotivo

From the beginning of the 1980s, Cotivo has produced two main products, unbleached cloth and denim. Unbleached cloth is the more important of the two. This product, destined mainly for the domestic market, represented more than 56 per cent of the total sales of the firm until 1987 (see Table 11.30). In 1990, it accounted for only 44 per cent. The fall in sales of unbleached fabric at the end of the 1980s was due to the drop in domestic demand for printed cloth, which is the major use of these fabrics.[6] Total domestic sales of unbleached cloth fell from 11.3 billion f.CFA in 1987 to only 5.7 billion in 1990.

The fall in unbleached cloth sales is also due to international competition, mainly from Asia (China and Pakistan). The fabrics can be imported from Asia via Benin and sell in Abidjan at prices about 25–33 per cent lower than those charged by Cotivo and Utexi. The cloth printers, who face enormous financial difficulties, naturally turn towards those imported fabrics.

Denim, the second product of Cotivo, was originally delivered to Blue Bell and Challenger. Since 1986 it has mainly been exported, especially as administrative difficulties prevent Challenger from getting the fabrics tax-free direct from Cotivo, forcing it to reduce its local purchases of denim. Cotivo therefore exports a large part of its denim production (more than 80 per cent since 1980). But faced with tough international competition on the blue jeans market, again from Asian competitors, Cotivo has had to concentrate on white denim, in which its expertise is greater. This now represents 70 per cent of Cotivo's denim production but unfortunately produces poor profit margins as compared to blue denim and unbleached fabrics.

Cotivo also sells cotton yarn to ERG and bed linen for export, mainly to Italy. The worsening of its position on the domestic market partly explains the firm's engagement in more risky and less profitable activities on export markets.

Cotivo has a dominant position on the domestic market (more than 50 per cent until 1987 and 45 per cent in 1990). It was the only local supplier of denim to Blue Bell (until 1985) and Challenger. Cotivo is also the supplier of Uniwax (the Ivorian wax prints manufacturer) and of other cotton print manufacturers (Utexi and ERG).

Table 11.31 shows the changes in the firm's export performances. Its export rate, for instance, which was only 11 per cent in 1980, was around 50 per cent from 1987. This development is the firm's response to increasing difficulties on the domestic market. The firm has created a market niche in the manufacture of white denim. Cotivo's success with white denim has been eased by the fact that this type of material (heavy-dyed cloth) is no longer produced in Europe, and by the relative disinterest of Asian firms, given the extremely weak profit margins it offers. The success of Cotivo with this product is such that it now represents 70 per cent of its denim production and the firm has a very long waiting list for orders.

Cotivo's productivity per employee (Table 11.32), which is stable between 2.5 and 3, seems rather low but is close to the average for the industry. It is clearly above the average staff unit cost, which unfortunately is increasing every year, moving from 0.57 in 1980 to more than 1 in 1987 and 1990. The productivity of physical assets is also definitely weak. These indicators show that Cotivo is reasonably efficient in the use of the factors of production.

Despite the rise in the protection of the domestic market, Cotivo's total activity has progressively moved from some protection to increasingly marked negative protection. ERP was 38 per cent in 1980 and fell to −4 per cent in 1990 (see Table 11.33). This is due to the increasing exposure of the firm on foreign markets, where it has no protection. In fact, as shown above, Cotivo's exports increased from 11 per cent of total sales in 1980 to an average of 50 per cent in 1987 and 1990.

Table 11.30 Sales and products for Cotivo (million f.CFA)

	1980	1987	1990
Unbleached fabric	4 304.4	5 933.9	3 949.2
	(20 297)	(21 026)	(13 267)
Denim	1 938.4	2 974.7	3 948.3
	(2 638)	(2 857.7)	(4 200)
Others	1 082.2	1 230.4	1 128.5
Total	7 325.0	10 139.0	9 026.0

Note: Figures in parentheses show thousands of metres.

Table 11.31 Market shares for Cotivo

	1980	1987	1990
Total sales exported	11.0	51.0	49.3
Share of domestic market	55.0	52.4	45.6
Share of export market	13.4	13.2	(not known)

Table 11.32 Performance of the factors of production for Cotivo

	1980	1987	1990
Productivity/employee	2.50	3.10	2.30
Productivity of physical assets	0.87	1.01	1.15
Average staff unit cost	0.57	1.09	1.07

Note: See Table 11.4 above for definitions of these ratios.

Table 11.33 Protection, comparative advantage and financial performance indicators for Cotivo (%)

	1980	1987	1990
Protection: ERP			
Domestic market	51.00	97.00	125.00
Export market	−22.00	−19.00	−44.00
Total activity	38.00	16.00	− 4.00
Comparative advantage: DRC	0.84	0.77	1.31
Financial profitability: Net result/owners' equity	9.40	10.20	− 16.00
Activity profitability: Net result/total sales	4.30	3.60	− 6.40

Note: See Table 11.5 for definitions.

This new orientation has obvious consequences for the firm's return on equity ratio, which became negative in 1990 (–16 per cent). In fact, the development of exports as a solution to the difficulties met on the domestic market entailed not only moving out from the umbrella of protection but also emphasizing products with very poor profit margins. The effects are visible in the disproportionate rise in sales volume in relation to sales value between 1987 and 1990. At the same time Cotivo, which had a net comparative advantage until 1987, seems to have lost this advantage between 1987 and 1990. Its DRC moved from 0.7 to 1.31. So the opening to world markets did not mean higher productivity and better financial performances. We noticed management's lack of enthusiasm and perplexity as to the lessons to be drawn from the consequences of their reorientation to export markets.

Strategies and capabilities of the firms

Uniwax

Uniwax undertook major investments in the 1980s (see Table 11.34), despite its having excess capacity. The firm was using only one third of its installed capacity but the needs of the export markets justified new investments, which were self-financed. But apart from 1980, new investments were centred not mainly on physical assets but rather on marketing and trading activities.

Uniwax's cloth printing uses a simple wax-resist technology, with a discontinuous production line including several manual segments. Its inventive possibilities are therefore limited to the design and colours and the choice of the quality of the basic fabrics. The technology is from Vlisco, one of the European partners, which has selected all the machines presently used by the firm. Vlisco also provides Uniwax with the necessary designs and drawings. The firm therefore undertakes very little technical innovation. It does possess a technical workshop which remakes cylinders and the processing and preparation of designs received from Vlisco. Uniwax's lack of technological autonomy explains the high royalties and technical assistance fees paid by the firm, whereas training costs are iow (Table 11.35). Training is mainly limited to maintaining the technical competence of the staff, rather than the acquisition of new technologies. In a sector in which manufacturing processes have undergone rapid progress, Uniwax has to face the realities of international competition with the help of Vlisco, which has permitted it to take over and adapt its technologies and shares especially its designs.

The firm generally produces to meet orders from wholesalers, the chief of which is the trading firm CFCI, a subsidiary of Unilever. The wholesalers trade on their own account, so the distribution of its products does not entail additional charges for Uniwax. Besides, under its contract with Vlisco, Uniwax has to confine itself mainly to the domestic market, where it also faces competition from Vlisco's own products and those of other manufacturers and from 'Fancy' cloth. This limits Uniwax's export possibilities while compelling it to undertake frequent and sustained advertising to hold its place on the domestic market. The six-fold increase in advertising expenses between 1985 and 1990 is linked to the firm's export efforts.

Cotivo

Table 11.36 shows an extraordinary expansion in Cotivo's investments in 1987. Almost 95 per cent of this increase was for the acquisition of physical capital. This corresponds to the reorientation of the firm's activities to export markets, both to counterbalance the difficulties on the domestic market and to take advantage of an export subsidy scheme which the government had just launched.

These investments were for new equipment for spinning, the largest items being the acquisition of open-ended turbines and second-hand looms, including projectile looms. Investments were also made for the preparation of heavy-dyed cloth, mainly for pre-cutting and trimming technologies, as well as in the organization of the activities of the European subsidiary. These investments were mainly self-financed.

But the actual profits accruing from these heavy investments remain doubtful, given the low profit margins of Cotivo's export markets. To these problems, one has to add the non-payment of export subsidies by the government since 1988, as a result of its own financial difficulties. On 31 December 1989, the arrears were some 2.18 billion f.CFA.

Cotivo does not produce under licence, so it does not pay royalties in the normal sense of the term (see Table 11.37). But under an agreement with the German firm Sanfor, its main supplier of the machinery and equipment it required to start operations, Cotivo had to pay from 5 to 8 f.CFA per metre of cloth sold for a period of 10 years, in exchange for an annual inspection of its plant. This agreement expired in 1984. Moreover, a technical assistance

Table 11.34 Investment strategy indicators for Uniwax (million f.CFA)

	1975	1980	1985	1990
Investment in physical assets	27.6	370.2	184.1	355.9
Total investment	31.5	387.2	540.0	710.2

Table 11.35 Indicators of the management of technology and human resources for Uniwax (million f.CFA)

	1975	1980	1985	1990
Royalties on licences and patents		426.0	609.2	278.4
Disinvestment			1.1	1.0
Training costs	8.0	7.0	13.4	17.2
Technical assistance fees		275.4	403.3	168.7

Table 11.36 Investment strategy indicators for Cotivo (million f.CFA)

	1980	1987	1990
Investment in physical assets	47.0	1 238.2	27.3
Total investment	82.0	1 308.0	33.0

Table 11.37 Indicators of the management of technology and human resources for Cotivo (million f.CFA)

	1980	1987	1990
Royalties on licences and patents	1.6	–	–
Disinvestment	5.9	8.3	–
Training costs	–	–	–
Technical assistance fees	215.8	290.8	267.7

agreement links Cotivo to Schaeffer for the refurbishment of its machines and the management of the spares inventory, which is done internationally through the group's purchasing system. The technical assistance also covers help to apply the norms of modern process management and in financial and administrative management. This agreement costs 3 per cent of Cotivo's turnover and accounts for most of the technical assistance fees which appear in Table 11.37.

In the day-to-day organization of its operations, the local executive is definitely autonomous. Production plans and the definition of work assignments, and minor technical adjustments, are carried out by Cotivo's specialist departments.

Cotivo's marketing strategy has traversed the same route as its other activities. Before the advent of Blue Bell, the firm, profiting from guaranteed markets (mainly Icodi and Uniwax), did not invest much in promotion and market search. Later its relations with Blue Bell opened the doors of the American market. Famous brand names in jeans, such as Lee and Wrangler, began to use Cotivo's dyed cloth. The firm felt obliged to respond to those new markets, at first through Blue Bell (until 1986) and through its European subsidiary since 1987.

In fact, from 1987, when Cotivo turned towards export markets, the resources devoted to sales and promotion have grown quite dramatically. Commissions and brokerage on sales, for instance, moved from 1.2 million f.CFA in 1980 to 123 million in 1990, while advertising expenses, which were negligible in 1980, grew to 11 million f.CFA.

CONCLUSIONS

What can be said about firms' performance and export orientation on the basis of this study of six industrial firms in the Ivory Coast? First of all, it is useful to recall that a firm's performance is understood here as its capacity to increase or consolidate its market share in foreign or domestic markets. Over the period of the study, the firms in the sample have achieved respectable performances in terms of sales on various markets and the composition of their product ranges. However, their experiences differed.

Traditional analyses of market performance generally assume that an export strategy will work against domestic market development. This study has not revealed any such an opposition. Capral and Saco, with more than 80 per cent of their sales on export markets and export-oriented strategies, should according to the traditional analysis not be interested in their domestic markets. This is not the case. Capral, for instance, which strives to maintain its export orientation, is nevertheless making significant efforts to improve its share of the domestic market. Likewise Cotivo, which has achieved considerable progress on export markets, nevertheless carries on with its efforts to strengthen its position on the domestic market.

On the other hand, Cosmivoire and Trituraf, although essentially oriented towards the domestic market, have turned to export markets. This was made possible, *inter alia*, by their performance and expansion on the domestic market, whereas Uniwax, with technical potential and the capacity to be competitive on export markets, seems to be a prisoner of its agreement with Vlisco, which confines Uniwax's sales to regional markets.

Only Saco has a true export strategy. Its access to and success on export markets are determined by the international networking of the firm's activities through the trading branch of its mother company, Cacao Barry, and its physical presence on the markets through its European branch.

It is also commonplace to link the performance of firms in developing countries to government policies: the usual argument is that firms in these countries survive only thanks to high protection barriers and incentives, which supposedly generate inefficiency and the waste of resources. Cosmivoire, a medium-sized firm, is an example of a firm enjoying strong protection in its domestic market but still seeking to win ground in export markets against constant pressure from its competitors. In this case, the government policy applies equally to Cosmivoire and its principal competitor on the local market. Hence public policy cannot explain Cosmivoire's dynamism. In fact Cosmivoire's main strength is certainly the boldness of its managers, who are capable of identifying the needs of the market and satisfying them, using simple technologies. Cosmivoire would have performed better if the government had been able to guarantee fair competition within its sector: its main competitor is a subsidiary of a powerful multinational which receives many advantages from the government.

This example proves that government definitively has a role to play in creating the best conditions for competitive markets. In any case, the high protection of Cosmivoire's market has not prevented the firm from improving its DRC. Similarly, government policy in fighting against smuggling by reducing tariffs and taxes on wax prints and reducing production costs has been particularly beneficial for Uniwax's results.

The argument that it is necessary to make intensive use of high technology to build up competitive positions was not confirmed in the case of Cosmivoire and Uniwax, which operate in very competitive sectors. These two firms do not in fact have the necessary resources to acquire the latest technology, unlike their competitors. It is probably the internal organization of the firms and their capacity to identify needs and adjust their products to them that explains their relative success, rather than the capacity to use high technology. As for the firms' linkages, Uniwax's situation is ambivalent: on the one hand it gets support from Vlisco, which helps the firm in acquiring technology and equipment. It also benefits from the trading partnership with CFCI, which helps to sharply reduce its distribution costs. But the constraints under its market-sharing agreement with Vlisco limit its ability to develop an active export strategy. Capral, in contrast, benefits fully from its links with Nestlé, both for labour organization and training and for access to high technologies and the international distribution of its products.

At different levels, Saco with the French group Barry, Trituraf with Unilever via Blohorn, Uniwax with Vlisco and Cotivo with Schaeffer benefit from their parent firms. Cosmivoire is an exception, relying mainly on the experience and motivation of its managers and using its external partnership as a complement to its own efforts. We also note a monopolistic tendency on the part of Blohorn, which, after a vain attempt to eliminate Cosmivoire, succeeded in buying its other competitor, Trituraf.

We should again mention the difficult situation of Saco, a firm which processes cocoa beans and whose evolution is closely linked to the uncertainties of the cocoa market. This raises some particular problems since Saco was established in order to reduce the effects of these uncertainties. The implication is that local processing of raw materials needs to go beyond minimal processing if it is to add value and sophistication to the product, in a true manufacturing activity, and so transcend the raw material markets.

Finally, the shift towards export markets by Ivorian industrial firms (new exporters) has resulted in:

1 heavy investment efforts to bring production technologies up to date to meet international standards.
2 a reorganization and reorientation of sales and marketing strategies, with the need for more appropriate trading networks and more frequent and expensive advertising.
3 a choice of niches and segments on international markets which is often imposed on them and often characterized by instability, with very narrow profit margins. This has sometimes resulted in considerable financial losses.
4 government action, in the form of export incentives (subsidies or other supportive measures), which have proved to be necessary for securing and retaining export markets. On the other hand,

government involvement in the supplying and pricing of raw materials has often generated significant rents, which have been captured by powerful multinationals through their local subsidiaries and which are not necessarily reinvested in local industry. These interventions have often also created various bottlenecks and additional costs for the firms.

These features are an indication of the actions which could be taken to favour an export orientation, which would be of benefit for both the industries concerned and the national economy.

NOTES

1 American billions, of 1 000 million are used throughout. Until the recent devaluation, the African Financial Community (CFA) franc was fixed at 50 f.CFA to one French franc. The current rate is 100 f.CFA to one French franc.
2 The protection indicators (ERP) and comparative advantage indicators are calculated using the methodology set out by Balassa (1989). A detailed analysis and application to the Ivorian industry are offered in Bohoun and Kouassy (1992).
3 The cost figures are in nominal values, without any correction for inflation.
4 The scheme allows Saco to buy cocoa beans at local cost prices including transport and domestic trading costs. When these prices are above world prices, Saco receives the difference back from Caistab.
5 For an analysis of the characteristics of the Ivorian cloth prints market and the nature of its profound crisis in the eighties, see Bohoun *et al.*, (1993).
6 See n. 5.

BIBLIOGRAPHY

Balassa, B., *Comparative Advantage, Trade Policy and Economic Development*, New York, Harvest Wheatsheaf, 1989.
Bohoun B. and Kouassy, O., *La performance des entreprises en Côte d'Ivoire: Analyse des incitations le long des filières agro-industrielles,* Paris, Réseau sur les politiques industrielles en Afrique, CODESRIA/CRDI, 1992.
Bohoun, B., Contamin, B. and Kouassy, O., *Le marché ivoirien du pagne imprimé en Côte d'Ivoire*, Abidjan, ORSTOM/GERIDA, 1993.
Kouadio, Y. *et al.*, *Incitations et coûts en ressources intérieures dans l'industrie agro-alimentaire*, Abidjan, CIRES, 1983.
Marchés Tropicaux, Spécial Côte d'Ivoire, Paris, Marchés Tropicaux et Méditerranéens, 1985, 1990.

Mytelka, L., *Ivorian Industry at the Cross-roads*, Oxford, Carlton University and Université Paris-X, 1989.

Pégatiennan, J., *Stabilization Policy in an Agricultural Dependent Economy*. Unpublished PhD dissertation, Boston University, Boston, Mass., 1988.

Riddell, R., *Manufacturing Sector Development in Zimbabwe and Côte d'Ivoire*, Oxford, Queen Elizabeth House and Overseas Development Institute, 1990.

12 Mauritius

Prof. R. Lamusse

BACKGROUND

Phases of industrialization

The industrialization of Mauritius has gone through three distinct stages: the import substitution (IS) phase which began with the creation of Development Certificate enterprises in 1964; a mixed phase following the passing of the Export Processing Zones (EPZ) Act in 1970, characterized by a combination of IS and export-oriented (EO) strategies; and a third phase in which industrialization strategy and policy became almost exclusively oriented towards exports, during which a number of measures were taken to liberalize trade and prices and reduce exchange control restrictions. Yet a number of features of the earlier IS period remain, especially in the form of high import tariffs on a large number of commodities.

Import substitution

Thirty years ago, Mauritius was in many ways a typical monocrop plantation economy, virtually entirely dependent on sugar, which, with its by-products, accounted for some 98 per cent of total exports. There was, however, one way in which the Mauritian economy differed from many other plantation economies: the sugar industry was predominantly owned and controlled by local interests, rather than by foreign companies. This had led to the emergence of an indigenous business class initially consisting of the planters and their affiliates in commerce, banking, garages and workshops. The development of the sugar industry thus gave rise to a network of local supportive activities and a supply of local entrepreneurial talent. Much of the surplus arising from sugar was at that time exported but the existence of a local plantocracy and of a locally generated surplus were important factors in the later development of manufacturing industries.

The development of manufacturing was originally seen as a means of job creation. During the 1950s, the rate of population increase was some 3 per cent per annum. The problem was how to find employment for the growing labour force. Meade (1961), argued that the sugar industry could not provide any substantial volume of increased employment and that other agriculture was likely to provide employment for only a strictly limited, if appreciable, labour force. Since it was assumed that local savings were a limiting factor, Meade argued that it was necessary to choose labour-intensive industries. Although the point was not made, these would be industries employing low-level technologies.

During the 1960s several measures were taken to encourage industry. Development Certificates (DC) were granted to selected enterprises, entitling them to income tax and other concessions. Industrialization was envisaged in terms of IS, with the certificates going to enterprises which produced for the local market. An existing Agricultural Bank was transformed into the Development Bank of Mauritius, with responsibility, *inter alia*, for helping to finance industry. A complex structure of import duties and quotas helped protect industries in the home market, while the exchange control system made it expensive to export capital and more profitable to employ local savings in local manufacturing.

Export processing zones

These measures had a degree of success, but by the early 1970s the limited scope of import substitution industrialization (ISI) in a country with a population of less than one million and a low *per capita* GDP was increasingly felt. Export industries became the focus of attention. The critical measure was the Export Processing Zones Act (1970). In addition to very favourable tax concessions, the Act permitted firms to import commodities used in the enterprise free of duty.

These measures had the effect of creating two classes of industrial enterprise – 'DC enterprises' and 'EPZ enterprises'. The DC firms remained IS enterprises and branched into exports to only a very slight degree, while the EPZ enterprises were allowed to sell their products on the local market to only a limited extent. It is possible that the failure of DC firms to diversify into export markets reflected their cost structure, which had developed under protection and was thus unable to compete outside Mauritius.

In spite of a levelling-off during the past five years, the EPZ sector has been the most dynamic part of the Mauritian economy. By 1991, manufacturing accounted for 23.3 per cent of the GDP at factor cost. Of this the sugar industry accounted for 2 per cent, EPZ businesses for 12.1 per cent, and other manufacturing for 8.5 per cent. Exports of manufactured goods other than sugar, which were negligible in 1961, amounted to 67 per cent of total exports in 1991 – virtually all from the EPZ.

The success of the EPZ – especially during the 1980s – was due to a variety of factors. Mauritius had a reserve labour force of literate women who were readily trainable for semi-skilled production jobs and whose wage levels were internationally competitive. The island benefited from preferential access to the European market. Various Hong Kong enterprises were seeking new locations in preparation for the take-over by China in 1997 and were attracted by the low wages and political stability of Mauritius. The growing Mauritian business community was seeking new opportunities for profitable investment.

All these factors served to encourage investment in the EPZ and to provide the labour force required. But the EPZ has its weaknesses. Because of low wage levels, and in line with government objectives during the first phase of industrialization, it attracted industries with a high labour/capital ratio. Thus in September 1982, 83.9 per cent of employment in the EPZ was in wearing apparel and a further 5.9 per cent in textile yarns and fabrics. All other industries accounted for only some 10 per cent of total employment. But wages have been rising and there is no longer a reserve labour force. Further expansion based on cheap, literate and plentiful women workers is no longer a viable option. The creation of a single European market raises doubts concerning the conditions of access of Mauritius' products to its traditional markets.

Social changes

Mauritian society has undergone a process of rapid economic and social change and modernization over the last three decades. Previously, Mauritius could be described as a remote, secluded, peripheral, colonial society. Its history of colonization and settlement and the sugar industry produced a society of great variety – a kaleidoscope of races and cultures.

During the last thirty years the island has undergone an accelerated process of development under the pressure of external and internal events. In the first place there was the population explosion and its aftermath. The Mauritian population doubled between 1948 and 1970, leaving Mauritius to cope with a young population, with its challenge to traditional cultures and values, and a rapid increase in the labour force as the younger generations reached working age and entered the labour market. Thirty years ago, families with six or seven children were common; today the typical family has two or three children. Girls stay longer at school, the age of marriage has risen and social attitudes which used to inhibit the employment of some girls have been relaxed.

Secondly, there was the spread of education at the primary and secondary levels. Increasing amounts are being spent by families on education as a means of fulfilling rising aspirations. Education is a fundamental factor and a powerful catalyst in the process of modernization. It improves the quality of labour and enhances its attitudes to social mobility and aspirations. But it may also lead to frustration and maladjustment if the job opportunities do not correspond – as they rarely do in developing societies – to the expectations of school-leavers. In that sense the rapid spread of education in the island in the 1960s and 1970s, while desirable in itself, may have aggravated the imbalances, both quantitative and qualitative, between job opportunities and the aspirations of school leavers.

The third important element in the rapid transformation of Mauritian society was the political and constitutional events which preceded and followed the island's independence in 1968. The strong democratic tradition which developed in Mauritius, and the country's political stability, was very important for the success of the industrialization strategy. More recently, political events, particularly the 1982 general elections and their aftermath, have been instrumental in securing continued popular support for the measures taken by government under the structural adjustment programme (SAP) which in many respects has transformed the local economic environment.

A fourth feature is the mobility and adventurous spirit of Mauritians who, especially after World War II and in the late 1960s, have created a substantial Mauritian 'diaspora'. A large number of Mauritians left the island to work and settle in Europe, South Africa and Australia but they retained ties with their families in Mauritius. As a result, new ideas and attitudes were disseminated within the family network and contributed to the process of change.

Another factor in the process of social change in Mauritius was the opening up of the island itself to the rest of the world. The establishment of frequent air services with Europe, Africa, Asia and Australia and the development of the tourist industry had a profound effect on the attitudes and aspirations of the people. The success of family planning and the consequent drop in the birth rate in turn freed more women from household chores and the care of children for work outside home.

The future of Mauritian industry

In the search for new patterns and new emphases, we must distinguish between the reactions of the local business community and those of investors from abroad. The Hong Kong firm has little to lose from closing down in Mauritius and starting again in another location where wages are lower and trainable workers are available. The locally controlled enterprise has a greater incentive to seek new solutions inside Mauritius.

Industrial development must continue to be predominantly for export. Such industries must therefore be competitive on world markets. They can no longer base their competitive position on cheap labour. They must rather look to increasing labour productivity for continued expansion. One possible means of raising labour productivity is through the use of high technology. This would be a new departure in Mauritius. None of the existing industries employs high technology; the predominant industry – the manufacture of clothing – typically employs low technology. Mauritius lacks the research and development base for high-technology industry. Many enterprises might see the move as a high-risk option. But steps are being taken to strengthen education in science and technology as a preliminary move towards a more science-based industrial structure. The questions to be asked are:

- How realistic is it to see high-technology industry as the dynamic for the next stage of industrial growth?
- What measures could be taken to encourage and assist the development of such industries?
- Are existing firms appropriately structured to move into such industries? If not, how could they be helped or encouraged to do so?
- Are there alternative strategies which would enable Mauritian industry to compete on world markets?

THE FIRMS IN THE SAMPLE

History and structure

Our sample of seven firms includes three import substitution enterprises (ISEs) which produce for the domestic market, with exports accounting for a marginal share of total output. Their entry into export markets has been a fairly recent development. It also includes four export-oriented enterprises (EOEs), which may sell only a small proportion of total production on the local market, under certain specified conditions. The three ISEs are a firm producing chemical fertilizers, with a virtual monopoly of the domestic market, a firm producing edible oil, also with a predominant share of the domestic market (formerly with a monopoly on the domestic supply of edible oil) and a paint manufacturing enterprise. The EOE firms include the leading exporter of knitwear, which is the world's third largest exporter of Woolmark products, a producer of cloth for shirts and trousers, an enterprise producing canned tuna and a small jewellery firm: a fairly wide range of firms, all occupying a vantage position in their respective fields.

The historical background

As expected, the establishment of most of the ISE firms antedated that of the EOE enterprises. The paint manufacturer started to operate in 1964, the edible oil refinery firm in 1968 and the fertilizer firm in 1975. Two of the EOE establishments – the knitwear factory and tuna canning plant – began to operate in 1972 and the other two in 1988 and 1990 respectively.

In the case of the ISE firms, the main reasons for their establishment were the existence of a sizeable domestic market, the availability of land in proximity to the harbour and the incentives given by the government under the DC Scheme. Initially the edible oil and chemical fertilizer firms were granted a monopoly on the local market under certain conditions as to the price, quantity and regularity of supplies. This situation was summed up by the manager of the oil refinery, who said that 'Oil is a political commodity.' Both enterprises operated in a highly regulated environment. It would appear that this close monitoring of operations by the authorities did handicap their performance to some extent. These two ISEs operated on a fairly large scale with substantial equity and the financial participation and backing of large local groups. The third ISE

– the paint manufacturer – began as a small family concern with a mere Rs140 000 in seed capital. At that time all paints were imported from South Africa and Europe by a number of firms. With a booming economy, market conditions were good and the enterprise rapidly increased its share of the local market.

The EOE firms were set up as export enterprises. The knitwear firm was created mainly to take advantage of cheap labour and the privileged access of Mauritius to the then EC market. It was created initially by Hong Kong investors with a minority Mauritian participation. After a few years the Hong Kong shareholders were bought out by Mauritians and since 1977 the company has had an entirely local shareholding. The bulk of the shares is held by a local investment company belonging to a large sugar group.

The tuna canning enterprise was established and operates under a very different set of conditions. It is a joint venture between local and Japanese shareholders. One of the Japanese shareholders owned a fishing fleet and used Mauritius as a transhipment base for its catch of albacore tuna. The establishment of a local tuna canning plant was thus seen as a logical outcome of its other activities in the region. Cheap labour, good shipping facilities and the privileged relationship of Mauritius with the then EC were other considerations.

The manufacture of cloth for shirts and trousers started in 1990. The plant was established by a conglomerate of local and overseas interests and was planned and heralded at the time as a significant move towards high-fashion and high-technology production in clothing manufacture and exports. The firm was equipped with the latest textile machinery available on the European market. However, due to a defective marketing strategy and a narrow and excessively concentrated customer base, sales collapsed and the firm was placed in receivership barely two years after its creation.

The jewellery firm was created by a local group with extensive experience in jewellery and precious metals. This group pioneered export processing in the island with the establishment in 1970 of Microjewels, a firm producing industrial jewellery. It is a joint venture with French partners. The Mauritian side provides the capital, technology and managerial skills and the French partner looks after marketing.

The role of partners

The role of partners varies according to the nature of the product, the scale of operations, the capital structure and the type of market.

In the case of the fertilizer firm, local importers of chemical fertilizer and a foreign (American) company decided to set up a fertilizer factory. The American shareholder provided the technology and the local shareholders – essentially the sugar industry – were the clients. Today it is a public company with entirely local shareholding, in which no individual shareholder holds more than 15 per cent of the shares.

The oil refining firm was created by a foreign promoter in partnership with a local firm. The initial share capital was Rs2.5 million and the firm obtained a loan from the Development Bank of Mauritius. All the former oil importers were invited to subscribe to the capital and were offered a quota and commission on sales. The company is now listed on the Stock Exchange, which has led to a large increase in the number of shareholders. There is now only one overseas shareholder, who owns 4 per cent of the shares.

As mentioned before, the paint company began as a small family concern. It was the creation of one man, its present managing director and chairman. Funds were initially raised within the family. The company is still family-controlled and managed, though with a wider share ownership. It has entered into a joint venture with another large local paint manufacturer, an affiliate of an important local industrial and commercial group. The firm became a public company in 1989.

With regard to the EOE firms, the role of partners would be expected to be different from those of the ISE companies. As already mentioned, the tuna canning company was set up as a joint venture between Japanese and Mauritian interests. The Japanese partners provided the technical assistance and marketing services and the Mauritian side, a prominent and long-established local firm, managed production and the administrative aspects of the enterprise.

The knitwear firm was set up initially as a joint venture by Hong Kong investors with a minority Mauritian participation. All shares are now held by a local investment company, an affiliate of a large sugar group with extensive financial and commercial interests. The Hong Kong investors initially provided the capital and sales outlets while the Mauritian partners looked after the management. Today the firm provides its own financial, marketing and managerial resources. It has recently set up a production unit in the Malagasy Republic, for the production of basic knitwear, while locally it is shifting to the production of more fashionable fancy products.

The cloth manufacturer is a joint venture between the leading Mauritian commercial bank, a large local insurance group, local sugar companies, international financial institutions and the Common-wealth Development Corporation. The French promoter, with a substantial personal stake in the company, is responsible for the firm's production and marketing strategy.

In the case of the jewellery firm, local partners supplied the capital, technology and management while the French partner was responsible for marketing operations.

The size of the enterprises

With regard to size (in terms of employment, turnover and total assets) there are considerable differences among the firms in the sample. On the one hand we have the large ISE enterprises – the fertilizer and edible oil companies – which since their inception have had a virtual monopoly on the domestic market. But the paint manufacturer, in spite of its relatively small size (the workforce is only 151 persons), has now secured 65–70 per cent of the local market.

The EOE establishments also present a very heterogeneous picture according to various measures of size. With 24 production units located all over the island, the knitwear group is by far the leading firm for the production of knitwear. It employs 12 000 people. The tuna canning enterprise also has a sizeable workforce and has substantially increased its production capacity recently with the opening of a new factory in the northern outskirts of the capital. The cloth manufacturer is a medium-sized enterprise with a work-force of around 500. As mentioned before, this firm is in receivership and its future is uncertain.[1] The jewellery firm is a small, specialized unit. Its activities require a great deal of manual dexterity on the part of the operators: the production process is closer to handicraft than to industrial production. The firm employs only 25 people and value added accounts for 56 per cent of total sales. The total assets amount to just Rs2.1 million.

Working conditions

All firms provide amenities such as toilets, canteens and rest rooms for their workers. In spite of complaints about noise and dust at the fertilizer plant and the cloth manufacturer, working conditions are generally reported to be good. Besides the usual amenities, the tuna canning firm also provides bathrooms and bread and tea. Yet their management complains of high labour turnover. Conditions at the knitwear manufacturer are said to be 'excellent and always improving', yet this firm has a relatively high rate of absenteeism.

The organization of production: inputs and outputs

The chemical fertilizer company produces CAN and NPK fertilizers for the local and export markets. The firm is fairly flexible and can manufacture a wide range of granular fertilizers according to market demand. The edible oil firm imports raw oil, from which it produces edible oil to international standards. In the face of a sharp rise in cost, especially labour costs, and regulated prices, there have been significant changes in both process and product technologies. Production is highly automated and the firm now uses continuous rather than batch processing to deodorize and neutralize the oils. This has resulted in higher-quality products, greater flexibility of production operations and substantial savings in labour and energy. But strict price controls have tended to hinder the firm's development.

The chemical fertilizer and oil refining firms both operate round the clock. The fertilizer firm is capital intensive; the automation of production operations has resulted in more production time and higher efficiency.

The paint manufacturer produces a wide range of products – decorative, industrial and marine paints, primers, undercoat, varnishes, thinners, lacquers, fillers and adhesives, printing inks and resins – and continuously seeks to improve the quality of its products. All chemical inputs are imported. The firm has invested substantially in R&D. Owing to labour scarcity and the consequent increase in salaries, the firm has moved to the use of more powerful equipment and less manpower. Although it has a very large share of the domestic market, the paint manufacturer faces strong competition from other domestic producers.

One striking feature of the ISE firms is the fairly extensive range of products manufactured. This demands some flexibility in the technological processes. The EOE enterprises, producing for a wider market and to the specifications of overseas buyers, tend to be more specialized. The tuna canning factory produces canned tuna in oil or brine for export. Inputs consist of frozen fish, cans and oil. The firm also produces pet food and fish meal for the local market. The knitwear manufacturer produces basic and fancy knitwear. Significant changes have been made in process and product technologies – the use of more sophisticated equipment and increasing automation. Some 20 per cent of production is now done on automated machines. There have also been changes in the type and quality of product. Fancy knitwear now accounts for 60 per cent of the firm's total output. The cloth manufacturer produces shirting and trouser cloth from imported yarn, either 100 per cent cotton or blends of polyester and cotton. The firm was conceived as a high-technology venture and was equipped from the start with the latest textile machinery. There has been an improvement in quality standards, with the use of high-quality yarn and with greater quality awareness on the part of the work force due to training and constant monitoring of production and output.

The jewellery producer makes gold chains from imported metal, according to orders and specifications received from its French partners. This is a highly skilled activity which requires much care and precision on the part of the operators. Chains are made by hand with machine assistance.

Exporting history, technology and human resources

Exporting patterns

With regard to the exporting history of firms, we must again differentiate between the two categories of enterprises. For the ISE enterprises, exporting is a marginal activity, while it is the predominant concern of the EOE enterprises. Of the ISE firms, the chemical fertilizer firm is now exporting more: some 6 per cent of its total output goes to regional markets and East Africa. It is currently targeting the East African market. It approaches customers directly and sometimes also employs local agents. With its limited production capacity, the firm has a competitive advantage in those markets which are small, specialized and not likely to interest larger producers and exporters. Its export market is generally low-income customers.

Roughly the same situation applies with regard to the oil refinery and paint manufacturer, who export to nearby markets. The oil firm targets Preferential Trade Area (PTA) markets and countries of the Indian Ocean Commission (neighbouring islands). Its range of products is intended to meet the demand from customers of all income groups. The paint manufacturer exports both low-quality paints and special products at higher prices.

The growth of the EOEs is closely determined by their success at exporting. In the EOE firms the choice of process and product technologies and equipment is influenced by buyers' specifications.

Under these conditions, firms must adapt continuously to market changes, especially those firms operating in the more fashionable, more volatile, higher-value segments.

Their marketing strategy varies according to the type of product. The knitwear manufacturing firm, which is one of the most outstanding successes among the clothing export enterprises, uses both direct approaches to overseas customers and agents. It exports specialized types of products but it also supplies large overseas retail stores servicing medium-level customers. It has built up a network of over 150 overseas clients, with whom it keeps in close touch, through which it is regularly informed about fashion trends. Its sales staff do regular tours of markets. Exports of fancy knitwear, mainly to France, Germany and the UK, account for 60 per cent of its total output. The firm has built a strong reputation for reliability and high-quality fashion products.

In contrast, the cloth manufacturer has an affiliate company to market its output. All marketing operations are controlled by the major partner and shareholder. The customer base is not strong enough and the firm has been hit hard by the recession in the European clothing industry. The European market takes 95 per cent of its output. The decision to concentrate on exports to upper-market customers in Europe was in the circumstances the wrong choice. Furthermore, the government has penalized the firm for misusing administrative channels in order to obtain duty-free access to the then EC. The government has, in fact, refused to endorse the firm's EUR.1 certificate, which would allow this access. As a result the firm's marketing strategy is now being completely altered. It has started recently to diversify its markets and explore middle- and lower-market segments, both locally and overseas. There are many garment manufacturers in the EPZ to whom cloth could be supplied but they have long-term contracts with overseas suppliers who can provide a vast range of fabrics and styles sought by overseas customers. This explains the difficulty faced in trying to market its cloth on the domestic market. Sales collapsed in 1992 and the firm is now in receivership.

The tuna canning firm sells its output in Europe through one of its Japanese partners – Mitsubishi – which employs intermediaries. The establishment of the canning factory in Mauritius was a joint venture by local and Japanese enterprises, each concentrating on a particular aspect of the operation. KGKK (Japan), which operates a fishing fleet based in Mauritius, was one of the initial promoters and is a major shareholder. KGKK is responsible for technical assistance and the supply of fish. Mauritian partners are responsible for the local operations, the capital and management and Mitsubishi markets the product. Increasing competition from other, more efficient suppliers has led to a considerable drop in prices in the European market, where the customers are food distributors and supermarket chains. The by-products of the tuna canning operations – pet food and fish meal – are sold locally.

The jewellery manufacturer operates in a specialized niche. It was established with an eye on the market for high-class jewellery in France. The long experience of the local partner in jewellery and in the management of similar enterprises, coupled with substantial innovative flair, are essential factors. The local firm produces according to the orders and specifications of the French partners.

Development of technological processes

In most cases there have been no major changes in the technological processes employed since the firms were established. No clear link can be seen between the development of process and product technologies and the firms' export performances, although most firms have made some technological changes to adapt to changes in market conditions locally and overseas.

The production processes for chemical fertilizer, refined oil and paint are capital intensive. There has been little change in the case of the fertilizer firm in the technology used since its creation. The oil refinery has moved from batch processing to continuous processing for deodorizing and neutralizing operations. This resulted in products of better quality and savings in energy. They have also introduced consumer retail packs, following the market shift away from buying edible oil in drums.

With growing labour scarcity and the increase in salaries, the paint manufacturer has installed more powerful equipment. New technologies are obtained from visits to overseas suppliers or trade fairs and the firm has invested substantially in R&D to improve quality and to develop new types of products.

In the case of these three ISEs, technological improvements appear to be determined by the nature of the product and by market size. The oil refinery and paint manufacturer have some excess capacity. For the chemical fertilizer manufacturer, demand approximately matches capacity.

The cloth manufacturer was seen from the start as a venture in high technology. Its ill-conceived marketing strategy and a narrow customer base made the firm highly vulnerable to the recession in the European textile industry, and sales collapsed in 1992. This shows strikingly that high technology is not sufficient for success in export markets: adequate marketing strategies and core capabilities are also required.

Human resource development

The types and levels of skills in the firms were fairly comparable. Clerical staff generally have a broad-based education: most of them have passed their 'A' levels. Managerial staff hold a diploma or degree, while production workers have received some form of technical training. The main departments are generally headed by professionals.

Firms have recourse to various forms of training: in-house or on-the-job for factory workers, formal outside training for certain (limited) categories of personnel, overseas courses or tours of factories. Some firms have their own in-house training staff. Recruitment procedures vary between firms. Firms may recruit on the local market or from their existing staff. The paint manufacturer recruits through a local agency or through applications received at the personnel department. The cloth manufacturer recruits in both the local and international markets depending on the level and specifications of the position to be filled. The knitwear firm has sometimes resorted to head hunting to fill key posts. Most new recruits, however, join at the lower rungs of the ladder.

In recent years, some enterprises have used aggressive advertising to attract workers. Poaching of workers, especially skilled personnel, is also common. This contrasts with the situation several years earlier, when most enterprises displayed 'No vacancy' posters outside their premises. Labour relations are smooth and healthy. There have been no work stoppages among the seven firms. The chemical fertilizer firm has encountered some problems with shift workers over weekends, which have disrupted production. The institutional framework inhibits stoppages. Industrial disputes have to go through a series of stages of negotiation and, if this fails, arbitration. The effect is to reduce considerably the risk of disputes degenerating into work stoppages.

In all the firms covered in the study, remunerations are made up of basic wages, fringe benefits, and attendance and productivity bonuses. The remuneration policies of individual firms are often determined by reference to current market wages and practices.

Wages and conditions of employment in Mauritius have long been subject to extensive government regulations. Through the National Remuneration Board, the government fixes the minimum wage for various categories of labour. There are also annual meetings between government, employers and union representatives to decide on compensation for increases in the cost of living.

The tight labour market has had a number of consequences: higher wages, more generous fringe benefits and a better work environment. Actual wages are now much higher than statutory wages. This has forced enterprises to pay more attention to productivity and cost-effectiveness. Some of the weaker, poorly managed firms have not survived the transition.

The tightness of the labour market has been accompanied by a drop in productivity and high absenteeism, perhaps due in part to the sense of security it has generated among workers.

FIRM STRATEGIES

There were a number of bottleneck factors which helped to determine firms' strategies. Access to finance (short-term and long-term) is not a problem for five of the firms: it is very easy for the jewellery firm and satisfactory for the fertilizer and knitwear manufacturers. It is rather difficult for the tuna canning firm and the cloth manufacturer. Access to managerial and technical skills is easy or satisfactory for all firms except the knitwear firm and cloth manufacturer, where it is rather difficult. Likewise access to technology is not a problem (it was rated easy or satisfactory) in all cases except for the knitwear manufacturer, where it is said to be very difficult. Access to foreign exchange does not appear to be a problem anywhere.

We must again differentiate between ISE and EOE enterprises. The type of market and degree of competition differ between import substitution and export-oriented enterprises, and a firm's strategies are influenced by the type of market in which it operates and the competition which it faces.

ISE firms

Investment strategies for the ISEs relate to more mechanization for higher productivity and up-to-date equipment to keep up with international trends, better process control and substantial investment in R&D to improve the quality of the product, and product diversification. All three ISEs give considerable attention to marketing, which is a predominant element of their strategies.

The oil refinery

The production strategy of the oil refinery seems to have been shaped by its former monopoly position and the need to ensure a regular supply of edible oil of the appropriate quality for the local market. Its marketing strategy changed following the liberalization of oil imports in 1988 and the opening of a competing refinery. Their emphasis is on adapting to changing local market conditions, with the introduction of consumer packs in the place of drums, new brands and sizes, and the development of a new public image. The firm also runs consumer promotions and trade offers. Management control processes include 'proper' quality control and the Mauritius Standard Bureau Certification Mark.

Product development also appears on the firm's agenda: the firm keeps abreast of changes in the world edible oil industry. Technology search consists of visits to overseas refineries and membership of leading international societies. Project identification and feasibility studies are done by a team with the help of outside consultants (both local and overseas). Besides developments within the firm itself, such projects have been concerned with the creation of successful subsidiary companies for the production of metal containers and plastics. The management team does the feasibility studies.

Chemical fertilizers

The marketing strategy of the fertilizer firm is to maintain direct contact with overseas clients and to participate in fairs. The firm has recently adopted an 'aggressive marketing policy' in East Africa. On the production side, the firm's strategy emphasizes higher productivity to reduce costs (chemical fertilizers in Mauritius are subject to price control), and technology research and product development. They also employ management control processes.

The Technical manager and technical department team (i.e. the chemical engineer, mechanical engineers, draughtsman and engineering assistant) are responsible for new projects and investments. The technical manager is in overall control of a project from preparation to commissioning. In this regard he liaises with the other heads of departments responsible for production, maintenance, instrumentation and materials handling.

Internal and external linkages were said to be of equal importance, although it was clear from the answers to this question that the various firms defined these linkages in different ways. The picture which emerges is that of a fairly innovative firm, producing to international standards, with virtual control of the local market and aiming at a breakthrough in regional export markets.

Paints

The paint manufacturer, operating in a more competitive market than the other two ISEs, uses a range of marketing strategies such as advertising, public relations, sponsorship of cultural and sporting events and direct contact with buyers. The firm also participates in local and international trade fairs. Recent changes include increases in capacity, better service to customers and keeping a greater variety of products in stock. Project identification and feasibility studies are carried out by the management and financial teams. Such feasibility studies are always carried out before launching a new project or innovation.

Over the years the firm has bought four competing firms which were producing paint for the local market. New products have also been introduced. Since 1985 they have produced inks under licence for Coats SA Ltd, (through a subsidiary company). Activities also include technology search (literature search and visits to suppliers and fairs), expanding its range of products for the local and overseas market, developing internal and external linkages, and human resource development.

With regard to management control processes, standards are set for each type of paint. This was the first paint manufacturer to obtain the MS3 (highest rating) from the Mauritius Standard Bureau.

EOE firms

The industry and market structures within which EOE firms operate are very different from those facing ISE enterprises. EOEs face world-wide competition and sell on open markets. This conditions their strategies.

Tuna canning

The tuna canning firm uses chain production and markets its products through an intermediary. The firm's production capacity has been increased but there has been a considerable drop in world prices for canned tuna. The firm is responding by investing in updated technology. Information about new technology is obtained from suppliers and other foreign firms. The firm's objective is to look for more remunerative markets and possible new products. It has an 'independent approach' regarding internal and external linkages.

Performance is gauged in relation to yield (quantity of canned tuna produced per tonne of fish) and output, while quality is checked regularly to conform to buyers' specifications. Wastage is negligible. Provision is made for feedback and corrective action through inspections, reports and factory and management meetings.

The chief operating officer is responsible for new projects. Feasibility studies are done by the relevant departments: i.e. the trading department does the market studies, the production department the technical studies and so on. Each divisional manager is responsible for the preparation, design and commissioning of projects which relate to his division.

Knitwear

Adaptation is the normal condition of knitwear producers. The knitwear manufacturer in our sample has invested in high technology and R&D, with an increasing proportion of fashionable knitwear in its total output. Owing to rising labour costs, the firm has introduced more efficient and better-performing machines and relocated part of its production of basic knitwear to Madagascar. The firm devotes much attention to the search for new and improved technologies. Technological improvements are the responsibility of the directors and heads of departments together with the technical team. The head of a department identifies a new project with the help of his subordinates. Responsibility for project preparation and design lies with the head of department under which the project falls, while feasibility studies are carried out at the appropriate level. It is the selling price of the article which 'decides' the feasibility of the project.

Both the chain approach and the polyvalent team approach to the organization of production are used. The firm's marketing is by direct contact with buyers, with production capacity rather than sales opportunities seen as the limiting factor.

The firm is paying more attention to strengthening external linkages. It has an active training policy (comprising both in-house and outside training) and an R&D department which is very active.

Cloth manufacturing

The firm's investment strategies relate to product diversification and R&D. The firm uses the chain approach with specialization in production, although its aim is to introduce the polyvalent team approach. In its marketing strategy, the firm uses direct contacts with prospective buyers, participation in local and international fairs and publicity. The firm's marketing strategy is being completely revised following the collapse in sales described above. The aim is to increase the customer base both locally and abroad.

The firm is continually required to come up with imitations and adaptations because it is expected to offer new customers what they have been buying elsewhere. At the same time the firm must adapt to fashion trends. The firm is not actively searching for new technologies but keeps itself informed through overseas business contacts.

Product development is largely a matter of changes in design. The CAD and technical management departments are fully trained and equipped to conceive and develop new designs and qualities. Changes in designs and the development of new products are done in close collaboration with the marketing commercial division following customer demands and fashion trends. Projects are identified by a team of two or three persons with overseas experience in the relevant field.

The firm is devoting more attention to internal linkages: its aim is to establish excellent communications and team spirit throughout the entire plant. External linkages take the form of contacts with all the textile-related companies in Mauritius. However, we must bear in mind that this firm faces severe financial difficulties following the collapse of its sales on the export markets, and is currently in receivership. According to our latest information, it may have ceased to operate altogether.

Jewellery

The jewellery firm produces jewellery to specifications received from its French partners. The emphasis is on fine craftsmanship, rather than volume of output. The firm has invested in high technology and uses the polyvalent team approach whenever it is possible.

As mentioned before, the jewellery firm is a small, specialized unit in which the general manager directly supervises various stages of operation. The local firm contributes capital, its experience in jewellery and high-precision operations (watch repairs) and experience in the management of similar ventures. All other aspects, including marketing, are looked after by the French partners. There is little real innovation. Change is limited to imitations and adaptations and technology search is primarily carried out by the French partners.

Project identification is done by a team, while a single person is responsible for feasibility studies, project preparation and commissioning. New products are tested with the firm's 'test workers'. The firm provides both in-house and external formal training.

LINKAGE CAPABILITIES

Consultant services

All the firms in the sample, with one exception, occasionally use consultants' services, mostly to meet their training needs. This is particularly important for the knitwear enterprise, which wishes to improve internal communications and to create a sense of duty and responsibility among its workers. Consultants' services are also used by the cloth enterprise for marketing. These services are crucial for the survival of the firm, since it has failed to export the bulk of its production, as it had originally planned. The firm is now engaged in an active search for markets both overseas and locally. Marketing consultants are also used by the edible oil enterprise, partly because it has lost its monopoly over the local market and has to face local competitors as well as increasing imports.

Licensing and management agreements

Only one firm in the sample, the jewellery firm, has a licensing agreement, with its French partners. In fact all its production comes under this agreement. The firm also has a management agreement with the same partners. The paint manufacturing enterprise is producing inks under a licensing agreement too. However, this accounts for a negligible fraction of its total output.

Management agreements with foreign partners seem to be directly related to the level of foreign participation in shareholding. This is evident in the case of the jewellery firm and the cloth manufacturer. However, the cloth firm discontinued its costly management agreement recently because of the firm's financial problems.

Joint ventures

The paint manufacturing enterprise set up a joint venture with another local company which was already in the same line of business. The purpose was to obtain a major share of the local market.

Joint ventures are important for EOEs because these facilitate, for the local partners, access to technology, material inputs and markets. Ultimately, joint ventures increase the competitiveness of EOEs. Thus the jewellery firm, which has to compete with well-established jewellers in France, could not have started operating had it not been a joint venture. Similarly, the knitwear enterprise, although very successful internationally, has set up business in Madagascar, where labour costs are lower. Such investments will increase the firm's production capacity and make it more competitive in international markets.

Technical services

With the introduction of new technologies, new firms would be expected to rely heavily on providers of technical services, unless the firms have their own technical personnel. Only two firms in our sample have so far made use of outside technical services. The edible oil enterprise requires these for the servicing and maintenance of its computers. The knitwear enterprise also has an agreement for the maintenance of its computers, which are partly used for design and production.

Linkages with input suppliers and financial institutions

Most EOEs and ISEs maintain links with their suppliers of equipment to keep up with new types of equipment coming on the market and to evaluate their usefulness. These links are also maintained to ensure that after-sales service and maintenance are provided.

As for links with financial institutions, these refer mainly to links with commercial banks which are used for normal banking transactions. In addition, the services of insurance companies are also required for the insurance of the assets of the firms.

RESPONSE TO EXTERNAL FACTORS

Labour shortages

Given the labour shortage which industrialists have been facing in recent years in Mauritius, firms would be expected to shift to more capital-intensive production whenever this is profitable. This is confirmed by two firms in our sample, the paint manufacturer and the knitwear manufacturer. It is also interesting to note that these firms report that they have recently been recruiting skilled rather than unskilled labour, indicating that higher capital intensity may require higher skill intensity also.

Interaction with product market conditions

EOEs in the sample keep up with aggregate demand trends overseas and with changing conditions in their export markets. Business newspapers, specialized reports and contacts with customers provide them with the necessary information. In fact regular links with customers are maintained through personal visits, phone calls and written correspondence. The ISEs also maintain regular links with their local customers through personal visits.

Not all firms maintain links with similar firms or competitors. Four firms in our sample do this indirectly through employer or producer associations. The main objective is to exchange information on their respective industries.

Government policies and regulations

The firms in the sample had little to report in this section of the questionnaire. There has been no reaction to changes in the exchange rates of the major currencies used for trade transactions, although hedging is now possible for exporters as the central bank allows them to engage in forward exchange transactions. Similarly, there has been little reaction to the recent reduction in interest rates (an average of 3 percentage points): only one export enterprise, the knitwear manufacturer, reported that it had increased its borrowings to buy more machinery, as it wishes to increase its capital intensity, given the tight labour market conditions.

NEW TECHNOLOGIES AND EXPORTS

To clarify certain points, we have probed deeper into the relation between the export experience of the enterprises in the sample and their level of technology. It appears that the firms generally use modern technology and invest in new and more efficient equipment in order to increase production capacity, improve product quality and cut costs. At the oil refinery, recent purchases of equipment comprise a continuous refining plant (1988) and bottle blowing and filling equipment (1992). The firm now has on order a bleaching and filtration plant. The fertilizer firm has installed a modern nitric acid plant and an NPK plant. Its latest piece of equipment is a high-efficiency nitric acid absorption column acquired from Rhone Poulenc under a licence agreement. The knitwear firm has this year installed new equipment for knitting and dyeing. Its aim is to keep in step with technological improvements elsewhere in order to introduce more advanced production methods to fulfil export orders and cut costs. The firm endeavours to maintain its position on export markets through productivity increases with the use of modern technology. It also achieves cost reductions through better control of raw material, reduction of wastage and just-in-time stock procurement. The paint manufacturer also uses up-to-date technology. The last piece of equipment was acquired in 1992, with the aim of increasing production capacity. The firm uses up-to-date production methods to cut costs and remain competitive. It has secured a foothold in export markets owing to its reputation for quality and competitive prices.

In short, it appears that these enterprises are generally innovative and keep up with technological improvements. Better organization of production and the use of modern equipment for greater efficiency, quality improvement and cost reduction are the main aspects of their competitive strategies. These enterprises purchase their equipment directly from machinery suppliers who generally send their own technicians for the installation of the equipment. Routine servicing and maintenance are performed by the firms' own staff or are contracted out to local workshops.

The next question concerned the extent to which the firms acquired new skills and improved their organization as a result of their export experience. The oil refinery acquired new skills through regular contracts with leaders in the edible oil industry and professional institutions. It claims to have gained considerable experience in achieving customer satisfaction since it introduced a market-oriented strategy two years ago, after a 23-year monopoly of the local market and a production-oriented strategy. The fertilizer firm states that its export experience has been very beneficial in improving its marketing skills. It now has considerable experience and plans to start a free port trading company. The paint manufacturer has introduced new types of products to suit the requirements of export markets. For the knitwear firm, production is directly related to international market requirements and this has necessitated continuous improvements in skills, standards and organization.

How far have the firm's past industrialization histories helped in building skills for subsequent exporting? This question concerned only those ISE firms that have recently begun to export. According to the fertilizer firm, past industrialization experience helped a good deal but 'export is a game which [the firm] had to learn the hard way through extensive marketing missions'. The oil firm for its part attributes its recent performance on export markets to its new market-oriented strategy and its emphasis on consumer satisfaction. In the case of the paint manufacturer, local production enabled the firm to set up a research and development laboratory staffed with good technicians. As a result the firm can now supply 'tailor-made' products for the export market.

Generally it appears that the recent entry of ISE enterprises to export markets builds on experience gained over the years in producing for the local market. To that extent the export market may be seen as an outgrowth of the domestic market. Exporting forms part of a rational strategy for those firms' future expansion and development.

NOTE

1 The final draft for this contribution was submitted in March 1993. There may well have been changes with respect to this and other companies in this rapidly evolving sector.

BIBLIOGRAPHY

Meade, J.E., *Report to the Government of Mauritius: The Economic and Social Structure of Mauritius*, Port Louis, Government of Mauritius, 1961.

Appendix
Survey questions

This questionnaire is prepared to guide the thinking, coverage and assessment/evaluation by the researcher. It should provide a guide of what to identify, assess and make judgement about.

A. Firm history

A1. Basic information

A1.1 Name of firm
A1.2 Year of establishment
A1.3 How and why it was established; conditions under which it was established

A2. Ownership structure

A2.1 Ownership structure and how it has been changing over time
A2.2 Role of various partners and how it has been changing over time

A3. Size of establishment over time (1970, 1980, 1985, 1990)

A3.1 Size of the firm in terms of employment
A3.2 Sales
A3.3 Total assets

A4. Production

A4.1 Main products and activities and major changes over time
A4.2 Main inputs and changes over time

A5. Strategies followed in terms of

A5.1   Intentions
A5.2   Means of implementation
A5.3   How the relative strengths of various departments have been changing to reflect these strategies

A6. History of exporting and changes over time (1970, 1980, 1985, 1990)

A6.1   Items exported
A6.2   Market channels and destination
A6.3   Type of target markets
A6.4   Marketing strategies followed

A7. Technological processes (Identify and describe the process and make your assessment)

A7.1   Changes in process technologies introduced and adopted, and adaptations over time
A7.2   Changes in product technology (types and quality of products) introduced and adopted, and improvements made over time

A8. Productivity and quality changes over time (selected years e.g. 1970, 1980 and 1990)

A8.1   Cost per unit of main product
A8.2   Inputs per unit of main product
A8.3   Changes in quality
A8.4   Indicate any other available measures of productivity (e.g. output per unit of labour, domestic resource cost, total factor productivity)
A8.5   How does productivity compare with that of other local firms in the industry? How does it compare with that of firms in other countries?

A9. Human resource development and changes over time (1970, 1980, 1985, 1990) (Describe the status, changes and make own assessment)

A9.1   Types and quality of skills (levels of education, departments and activities in which they are engaged)
A9.2   How various critical skills have been acquired
A9.3   Forms of training employed (e.g. in-house training, training in other local institutions, training in other countries)

A9.4   Recruitment policies followed

A9.5   Assess extent and significance of labour turnover

A10. Identify and assess linkages with other industries and institutions and changes over time

A10.1 Subcontracting

A10.2 Demand conditions

A10.3 Types of markets served

A10.4 Relevant structure of industry and markets in which the firm has been operating

A10.5 Suppliers (inputs of equipment) and any changing relationships

A10.6 Providers of technical services

A10.7 Policies and regulations which have impinged on the firm's activities and decisions

B. Firm strategies (Identify and describe the various strategies followed)

B1. Investment strategies

B2. Production strategies

B3. Marketing strategies

B4. Innovation strategies

B4.1 Imitations

B4.2 Adaptations

B4.3 Technology search (locally and foreign)

B4.4 Product development

B4.5 Internal and external linkages

B4.6 Human resource development

B4.7 Management control processes (setting standards, measurement of performance, how decisions on corrective action and feedback are made)

C. Core capabilities (Identify and assess the status and changing conditions of the core capabilities)

C1. Investment capabilities

C1.1 Project identification

C1.2 Feasibility study (market study, technical study, management study, financial study)

C1.3 Project preparation, design, setting up and commissioning

C1.4 Mobilization and management of resources (short-term and long-term finance, managerial and technical skills, technology, foreign exchange)

C1.5 Human resource development:
1.5.1 Types and levels of skills
1.5.2 Recruitment policies
1.5.3 Approaches to upgrading of skills
1.5.4 Labour relations
1.5.5 Remuneration policies and practice
1.5.6 Quality of working conditions

C2. Production capabilities

C2.1 Production management (planning, scheduling, work procedures and execution of orders)

C2.2 Production engineering (raw material control, material use standards, standard production times, quality control)

C2.3 Repair and maintenance

C2.4 Access to critical resources (finance, skills, technology, foreign exchange)

C3. Organizational capabilities

C3.1 General management capabilities (sharing responsibilities, long-term direction, definition and clarity of policies and procedures, and whether these are adhered to and reviewed for effectiveness, measurement and analysis of performance, information flow and its utilization in decision-making, awareness of external factors, other linkages impinging on the firm)

C3.2 Management of technology

C3.3 Division of labour

C3.4 Mobilization of resources and capabilities to cope with new situations

C4. Marketing capabilities

C4.1 Ability to maintain market shares

C4.2 Collection and analysis of market information

C4.3 Product development policies

C4.4 Pricing

C4.5 Distribution

C4.6 Efficiency of the sales force and incentives

C5. Innovation capabilities

C5.1 Search for new ways and routines in respect of investment, production, marketing and organization

C5.2 Research and development activities

C5.3 Technology sourcing and adaptations

C5.4 Market research (study of market trends, potential markets and possibilities of introducing new products)

C5.5 Introduction of new technologies in production, marketing and administration and other firm activities

C6. Identify and describe factors which have accounted for success/failure in exporting; indicate how these factors have changed over time

C7. How is the firm dealing with deficiencies in capabilities in various areas which deemed important for the success of the firm? In what way can government and other institutions help?

D. Linkages and interactions with the socio-economic environment (Identify and describe the various linkages and make your own assessment of the relationship and changes over time)

D1. Consulting firms

D2. Licensing agreements and management agreements

D3. Joint ventures

D4. Providers of technical services

D5. Factor market conditions

D5.1 Labour market

D5.2 Capital market

D5.3 Land

D6. Product market conditions

D6.1 Aggregate demand trends

D6.2 Export demand conditions

D6.3 Structure of demand

D6.4 Links and relations with customers

D6.5 Interaction with local and foreign competition

D7. Interaction with government policies and regulations (identify and assess)

D7.1 Macroeconomic policies (e.g. exchange rates, interest rates, import liberalization)

D7.2 Sectoral policies

D7.3 Regulations (supportive or obstructive)

D8. Linkages with various input suppliers

D8.1 Relations with equipment suppliers

D8.2 Relations with input suppliers

D8.3 Relations with service providers

D8.4 Interactions with financial institutions (local and foreign)

Index

Page references in *italic* refer to tables.
Where similar topics refer to different countries in one sub-heading, this has usually been indicated by using the initial letter of the country after the reference (e.g. exports (N) ... for Nigeria)